Readings in Comparative Public Administration

READINGS IN COMPARATIVE PUBLIC ADMINISTRATION

Edited by
Nimrod Raphaeli
The Hebrew University in Jerusalem

ALLYN AND BACON, INC. BOSTON

Library of Congress Catalog Card Number: 67-13540

Printed in the United States of America

for Ellen

Preface

It is difficult to define precisely what a book of readings in an embryonic field ought to include so that it is neither unmanageable nor unrepresentative. In the final analysis it is the editor's understanding and biases regarding his subject matter that determine the articles presented. It is upon the assumption that the purposes of comparative public administration are twofold—to compare and contrast, in analytical and conceptual frameworks, varying administrative systems; and, more recently, to enrich and enlarge the literature and knowledge about development administration—that this book is predicated. Three types of articles are presented: those dealing with individual bureaucratic systems or "culture areas," which Professor Fred W. Riggs labels "idiographic"; those dealing with development administration; and, most important, those dealing with conceptual, analytical and ecological aspects of the field.

The absence of all but passing references to public administration in the United States is intentional. Since most, if not all, textbooks on public administration in this country reflect American experience, it is assumed that students have already gained some acquaintance with it.

The extensive bibliography provided at the end of the volume will, it is hoped, be useful for further study and research.

Three of the contributors to this book—James R. Brady, V. A. Pai Panandiker and I—worked under Professor Ferrel Heady of the University of Michigan. I am confident that they feel, as I do, a deep sense of appreciation for his gentle and stimulating leadership and his never-diminishing personal kindness.

My thanks are extended to all those who gave their kind permission to reprint most of the material included in this volume.

Finally, I wish to thank John J. DeRemigis and Clayton E. Mottaz, of Allyn and Bacon, for their patience and encouragement, and Mrs. Susan D. Prindle for her many editorial improvements.

Nimrod Raphaeli

Ann Arbor, Michigan

Contents

Readings in Comparative Public Administration

SECTION 1

Introduction to Comparative Public Administration

Comparative Public Administration: An Overview

NIMROD RAPHAELI
The University of Michigan

UNLIKE COMPARATIVE POLITICS, whose pedigree can be traced back to Aristotle, comparative public administration is a newcomer to the community of academic instruction and research. Woven into the executive branch of government, and traditionally overlooked in comparing the legislative, the executive, and the judiciary, public administration itself had no identity until the early part of this century. Between the two world wars comparative public administration was a sub-unit of comparative government courses, primarily concerned with legalistic aspects of public administration in European countries and, to lesser extent, with colonial administration. But the emergence of new nations and the increased involvement of the United States in world affairs since the Second World War has stimulated a drive, largely in this country, for a more thorough understanding of the emerging nations' political, economic, social and administrative institutions. This drive has generated a wide range of diversified research activities both on and off university campuses.

Systematic research and teaching methods in comparative public administration were first conceived at a Conference on

Comparative Administration held at Princeton in September 1952, under the auspices of the Public Administration Clearing House. A subcommittee under Professor Walter Sharp was formed to develop "criteria of relevance," and the parent Committee on Public Administration of the American Political Science Association assigned to the following "terms of reference":

1. to *review and assess* the existing state of knowledge of the field of foreign and comparative public administration;
2. to identify *major research needs* and priorities;
3. to suggest ways and means of stimulating *new types of studies,* emphasizing the comparative aspects of national administrative systems; and
4. to prepare a *general research guide* or design for such studies, including one or more specific proposals for pilot projects based upon field work in foreign countries.[1]

The subcommittee published its report a year later, in September 1953, outlining research priorities and suggesting a method for the study of comparative administration. Among the working papers appearing with the report was an "Outline of a Suggested Method of Study of Comparative Administration" prepared by Wallace Sayre and Herbert Kaufman. The outline was based on two assumptions: that "the ordering of relationships in hierarchical patterns is assumed to be common to all societies"; and that data about these patterns could be obtained through a set of questions.[2] These questions largely reflected Western experience—as Alfred Diamant aptly put it, they "reflected the innocence of earlier efforts in comparative administration."[3]

Although the outline was shelved for lack of funds, scholarly interest in the subject has mounted ever since. From this "tentative beginning" as Waldo describes it, comparative public

[1] Committee on Public Administration, Subcommittee on Comparative Public Administration, "Final Report" (September 1953), reprinted in *The Sayre-Kaufman Outline, A Research Design for a Pilot Study in Comparative Administration,* CAG Occasional Papers (January 1966), p. 2.

[2] *Ibid.,* p. 7a.

[3] Alfred Diamant, *Bureaucracy in Developmental Movement Regimes: A Bureaucratic Model for Developing Societies.* CAG Occasional Papers (October 1964), p. 83.

administration has, in less than a decade, developed into a "contemporary 'movement' of considerable size, complexity and intensity."[4] The extent of its growth can be easily inferred from the diversity of the literature published in the last decade. A few works which might be considered signposts are William J. Siffin (ed.), *Toward the Comparative Study of Public Administration;*[5] James D. Thompson (ed.), *Comparative Studies in Administration;*[6] Brian Chapman, *The Profession of Government;*[7] Ferrel Heady and Sybil L. Stokes (eds.), *Papers in Comparative Public Administration;*[8] Joseph LaPalombara (ed.), *Bureaucracy and Political Development;*[9] and Fred W. Riggs, *Administration in Developing Countries: The Theory of Prismatic Society.*[10] To this must be added the "output" of the summer seminars held since 1963 under the auspices of the Comparative Administration Group (CAG) of the American Society for Public Administration.

Siffin's volume, which included a theoretical model and six case studies, was actually responsible for popularizing comparative public administration in the academic community. It was also instrumental in identifying the concern of comparative administration with developing countries. Of the six case studies, only one represents a developed country (France), while the other five are concerned with developing countries (Turkey, Egypt, Bolivia, the Philippines, and Thailand). The major shortcoming of the book, shared by similar works, was that the model and the case studies were not related conceptually. Nevertheless the volume, which represented a field "very much in its infancy," was a very useful beginning, although it needed to be "supplemented tenfold" before generalizations could be made.

4 Dwight Waldo, *Comparative Public Administration: Prologue, Problems, and Promise.* Papers in Comparative Public Administration, Special Series: No. 2 (Chicago: American Society for Public Administration, 1964), p. 6.

5 (Bloomington, Indiana: Department of Government, Indiana University, 1957).

6 (Pittsburgh: University of Pittsburgh Press, 1959).

7 (London: George Allen & Unwin Ltd., 1959).

8 (Ann Arbor, Michigan: The University of Michigan, Institute of Public Administration, 1962).

9 (Princeton, New Jersey: Princeton University Press, 1963).

10 (Boston: Houghton Mifflin Company, 1964).

II

Comparative public administration, like any discipline comparative in nature, must face two elementary questions—a question of purpose, and a question of methodology. First, why do we need to compare; and, second, how do we go about doing it?

We compare to learn the distinctive characteristics of a particular administrative system or cluster of systems; to find out what makes certain administrative features work well in one country or era while they fail dismally in another; to identify the factors—cultural, political, and social—that are involved in success or failure; to explain the differences in behavior of bureaucrats and bureaucracies in different countries and cultures; and, finally, to discern what changes, if any, ought to be introduced and how they can be introduced, to improve the performance of a bureaucracy. Above all, we compare to arrive at a conceptual knowledge rather than a knowledge of details. As Robert Dahl insisted two decades ago, "as long as the study of public administration is not comparative, claims for a 'science of public administration' sound rather hollow."[11]

How we compare is an infinitely more complex question to answer, largly because of the variety of methods that are available. However, Shils offers a concise statement as to what constitutes a comparative method:

> An inquiry may be considered comparative if it proceeds by the use of an analytical scheme through which different societies *may be systematically compared* so that, by the use of a single set of categories, their identities and uniqueness may be discovered and explained. The analysis is comparative if the explanation draws on variables and the values of variables that are applicable to the description and analysis of societies widely different in time and place from that under immediate consideration. An inquiry into a particular society will be considered comparative if its descriptions and explanations assert, imply, or permit the systematic

[11] Robert E. Dahl, "The Science of Public Administration: Three Problems," *Public Administration Review,* Vol. 7, No. 1 (1947), p. 8.

juxtaposition of that society or of some sections of it with other societies or their corresponding sectors.[12]

III

In reviewing the recent literature in comparative public administration, including the CAG "Occasional Papers," it is possible to distinguish two principal "motivational concerns,"[13] one dealing with theory (Riggs refers to it as "nomothetic"),[14] and the other with development administration. These concerns are not, of course, mutually exclusive. An increasing number of "theories" and "models" are concerned with development, just as works in development administration are concerned with "theory." The distinction is analytically necessary, however, if comparative public administration is to develop what Kaufman called "criteria of relevance" and "criteria of adequacy" for "theoretical" and "applied" studies.[15]

The relationship between theory and practice has always been difficult to define. The theory may be so abstract that it has no practical application, or so concrete that it provides little or no insight into specific relations. Scholars dealing with develop-

[12] Edward Shils, "On Comparative Study of New States," in Clifford Geertz (ed.), *Old Societies and New States* (New York: The Free Press of Glencoe, 1963), pp. 17–18.

[13] Ferrel Heady suggests five such "motivational concerns." These are: "(1) the search for theory, (2) the urge for practical application of knowledge to the problems of developing countries, (3) the incidental contribution to comparative politics generally, (4) the recent interest of scholars trained in the continental administrative law tradition, and (5) the intensified analysis on a comparative basis of perennial problems of public administration." See: "Comparative Public Administration: Concerns and Priorities," in Heady and Stokes, *op. cit.*, pp. 2–3.

[14] The nomothetic approach, according to Riggs, "seeks generalizations, 'laws,' hypotheses that assert regularities of behavior, [and] correlation between variables." Fred W. Riggs, "Trends in the Comparative Study of Public Administration," *International Review of Administrative Sciences,* Vol. 28, No. 1 (1962), pp. 9–15.

[15] Herbert Kaufman, "Conceptual Framework for the Study of Comparative Administration" (Report), reprinted in The Sayre-Kaufman Outline, *op. cit.*, p. 26.

ment, in particular, feel the defects in the theory-practice relationship, and are constantly hindered and frustrated by them.

In addition to the two concerns mentioned, there is a third, Riggs's "idiographic" approach, a traditional concern with the study of bureaucracy of an individual country or "culture area."[16] Because students of comparative public administration need some acquaintance with individual bureaucratic systems before they can understand the more complex comparative method, this volume includes a section of studies of individual bureaucratic systems. The significance of the book is the readings themselves, which are not intended to represent any single orientation, and it should only be necessary to point out that most works which appear in Section 2 and a few works in Section 3 are idiographic.

A fuller discussion of the areas of theory building and development administration may be useful.

IV

The study of comparative public administration is greatly concerned with theoretical frameworks. The ultimate task of theory in this area is to clarify the differences and similarities found among bureaucratic systems and to demonstrate meaningful relationships. To achieve these tasks, various theories and models have been constructed.

Although in the ensuing discussion the terms *model* and *theory* are treated as synonyms, as they are by Simon and Newell,[17] and Waldo,[18] other authors have made distinctions between them. Leys, for example, distinguishes "between a *theory* of the behavior of some set of phenomena, and the logical

[16] Riggs, "Trends in the Comparative Study of Public Administration," *op. cit.*

[17] Herbert A. Simon and Allen Newell, "Models: Their Uses and Limitations," in Leonard D. White (ed.), *The State of the Social Sciences* (Chicago: Chicago University Press, 1956), p. 66.

[18] Professor Waldo uses "model" interchangeably with "schema" and "theory," "meaning in all cases a conceptual framework to organize and manipulate data." *Comparative Public Administration, op. cit.*, p. 36 n.

model of which theory is an interpretation, and which gives it explanatory force." He then asserts that "a logically sound model is not guarantee of good theory; but a model which is logically defective cannot furnish a theory at all, or at least not the theory we need."[19] Put differently,

> A model is an explicit statement of the structure which a scientist expects to find in any mass of data. The structuring of expectations is implied in any theoretical formulation. The construction of a model additionally requires that the structure be made explicit with reference to concrete "sets" of data which it is intended to organize. Modeling thus becomes a method of genuinely integrating theory (a structure of expectations) and research (a mass of data) by means of explicit postulates and hypotheses.[20]

In models symbols are substituted for reality and detail is sacrificed to elegance and explication. No matter how "complete" and "sophisticated" a model may be, the real world is always different. The importance of a model is that it provides a conceptual frame from which to view a complex reality. A model can never embody the whole reality, just as a manikin cannot embody the human form. Since a model is a formal structure, it cannot be "right" or "wrong." The only criteria of judgment are the model's applicability, usefulness, and communicability.[21]

In the study of bureaucratic systems, bureaucracy as a concept can be classified according to various criteria. The "ideal" model of bureaucracy, constructed by Max Weber, has been the single most influential item in the literature of public administration and, subsequently, of comparative public admin-

[19] Colin Leys, "Models, Theories, and Theory of Political Parties," *Political Studies*, Vol. 7, No. 2 (1959), p. 129.

[20] Ernest R. Hilgard and Daniel Lerner, "The Person: Subject and Object of Science and Policy," in Daniel Lerner and Harold D. Lasswell, *The Policy Sciences* (Stanford, California: Stanford University Press, 1951), pp. 28–9.

[21] Lynton K. Caldwell, "Conjectures on Comparative Public Administration," in Roscoe C. Martin (ed.), *Public Administration and Democracy* (Syracuse, New York: Syracuse University Press, 1965) pp. 234–5, lists three problems of concept and methods inherent in comparative studies: (1) comparability, (2) commensurability and (3) relevance.

istration.[22] Weber's classification is made on the basis of three types of authority: traditional, charismatic and legal-rational. Each type is given an appropriate type of administrative staff, although it is the bureaucratic type whose base of authority is legal-rational that has attracted the most attention.[23] Diamant has provided very useful appendices to his article "The Bureaucratic Model: Max Weber Rejected, Rediscovered, Reformed,"[24] which contrast legal-rational and traditional authority and their administrative staffs. In the "purest type" of legal-rational authority, the administrative staff are subject to authority in their official capacities, organized hierarchically, and remunerated in money. Each office has defined functions and is filled by free selection. Bureaucracy is a career system wherein the office is the primary occupation of the incumbent, appointments are governed by technical qualifications, and promotion is determined by seniority and/or achievement.[25]

This "ideal type" of bureaucratic staff has been criticized on a number of grounds. Friedrich asserts that there is nothing "ideal" about bureaucracy, and that the term "ideal type" is "unfortunate."[26] Diamant's article, and Heady's article in this volume, review some of the derivations of Weber's ideal type,

[22] For an introduction to the literature on bureaucracy see Robert K. Merton *et al.* (eds.), *Reader in Bureaucracy* (Glencoe, Illinois: The Free Press, 1952); and Max Weber, *The Theory of Social and Economic Organization,* edited with an introduction by Talcott Parsons (A Free Press Paperback, 1964) esp. pp. 329–341.

[23] See, for example, Peter M. Blau, *Bureaucracy in Modern Society* (New York: Random House, 1956), ch. 2; Reinhard Bendix, *Max Weber: An Intellectual Portrait* (Garden City, New York: Doubleday & Company, Inc., 1962), pp. 423–430; Robert V. Presthus, "Weberian vs. Welfare Bureaucracy in Traditional Society," *Administrative Science Quarterly,* Vol. 6, No. 1 (1961), pp. 1–24, and "The Bureaucratic Model," in *The Organizational Society* (New York: Alfred A. Knopf, 1962); George B. Pepper, "A Re-examination of the Ideal Type Concept," *American Catholic Social Review,* Vol. 24, No. 4 (1963), pp. 185–201; William Delany, "The Development and Decline of Patrimonial and Bureaucratic Administrations," *Administrative Science Quarterly,* Vol. 7, No. 4 (1963), pp. 458–501; and special issues on Max Weber of *American Sociological Review,* Vol. 30, No. 1 (1965), and *International Social Science Journal,* Vol. 17, No. 1 (1965).

[24] In Heady and Stokes, *op. cit.,* pp. 88–89.

[25] *Ibid.,* p. 88; and Weber, *op. cit.,* pp. 329–336.

[26] Carl J. Friedrich, "Some Observations on Weber's Analysis of Bureaucracy," in Merton, *op. cit.,* p. 28.

and the principal criticisms levelled against it. A more recent argument, advanced by Litwak, is that Weber's model "is most efficient when the organization deals primarily with uniform events and with occupations stressing traditional areas of knowledge rather than social skill."[27] In other words, Weber's model may be adequate for an ongoing government bureaucracy, but cannot deal with problems arising from development and nation building.

Weber's model has been followed by a number of other typologies; for example, Fritz Morstein Marx's four types of bureaucracy—guardian, caste, patronage and merit—which combine historical and behavioral traits.[28] Litwak suggests three models of bureaucracy: (a) Weber's model, (b) a human relations model, and (c) a professional model.[29] Brecht distinguishes between four kinds of bureaucracy on the basis of their power.[30] Recently, Banks and Textor suggested a typology of modern, semi-modern, transitional and traditional bureaucracies.[31]

Of considerable relevance both to the bureaucratic model and to methodology is S. N. Eisenstadt's *The Political Systems of Empires*.[32] This ambitious work analyzes thirty-two political systems—twenty-seven protobureaucratic empires and five prebureaucratic states. Eisenstadt sets out to explain the social and political structure of the major historical empires—the Chinese Empires, the Sassanid Empire, the Roman and Byzantine Empires—and the European states in the Age of Absolutism. He analyzes the causes of their development, survival, and disintegration. Variables such as bureaucratic machines, the elite groups and the media for social control are compared to illuminate the similarities and differences in the evolutions of the political systems. Eisenstadt is concerned primarily with two questions.

27 Eugene Litwak, "Models of Bureaucracy Which Permit Conflict," *The American Journal of Sociology*, Vol. 67, No. 2 (1961), p. 177.

28 *The Administrative State: An Introduction to Bureaucracy* (Chicago: University of Chicago Press, 1957).

29 Litwak, *op. cit.*, p. 182.

30 "How Bureaucracies Develop and Function," in this volume.

31 For a fuller description of the typology see Forward's paper in this volume.

32 (New York: The Free Press of Glencoe, 1963).

First, what factors permit the institutionalization of a political system? And second, once the political system is established, what conditions are necessary for its maintenance? Eisenstadt's central hypothesis is that in order for political development to take place, two conditions must be met: the political sphere must be differentiated from the social institutions—that is, autonomous political goals must develop—and "free floating resources" controlled by the elite must be created. Recently Eisenstadt has further hypothesized that the bureaucracies of contemporary developing nations show "crucial similarities" to those of the empires, particularly with regard to the following political orientations:

a. maintenance of service orientations to both the rulers and the major strata (which, in the societies in early stages of modernization, is usually greater emphasis on the services to the rulers) ;

b. development into a passive tool of the ruler with little internal autonomy or performance of services to the different strata of the population;

c. displacement of service goals to the various strata and to the polity in favor of goals of self-aggrandizement, usurpation of power exclusively in the bureaucracy's own favor and/or in favor of a group with which it becomes closely identified.[33]

V

The bureaucratic model is not the only model useful to comparative public administration. There are several others whose uses and limitations are worthy of review here.

Fred Riggs has distinguished between an inductive model or "image" and a deductive model or "ideal type." Inductive models "tend, essentially, to be built by impressionistically associating a set of variables derived from experience, by inductive reasoning, however incongruous some elements in the picture may be." In deductive models, on the other hand, "all variables are shown to be logically related to each other, regardless of how

[33] S. N. Eisenstadt, *Continuity of Modernization and Development Administration: Preliminary Statement of the Problem.* CAG Occasional Papers (January 1965) , pp. 24–5.

far the result may appear to depart from observed situations."[34]

One of the earliest inductive models for comparative public administration was constructed by Riggs himself in his seminal work, "Agraria and Industria."[35] The model seeks to provide "a system of hypothetical categories for the classification and analysis of realities, including patterns of political and administrative transition."[36] It utilizes a broad range of categories covering the essential characteristics of a society to examine the administrative system in the context of the social system as a whole. The assumption underlying this approach is that every society comprises a vast network of interrelated parts, any one of which can only be understood in relation to the others and to the whole. As Riggs states it, "our basic assumption is that administrative behavior is not erratic and 'uncaused,' but constitutes an integral, interacting part of the total society and government of which it forms a part."[37] He establishes two "ideal types" of society—agricultural and industrial—each of which contains a hypothetical system of public administration which "may provide a basis for analysis of empirical administrative systems."[38]

Riggs's model remains heavily indebted to the structural-functional approach for its scope, approach and bias. The continuum which stretches between the *Agraria* and the *Industria* models is not so much an historical dimension as a "functional-theoretical" one.[39] It depicts the interdependence of administra-

[34] Fred W. Riggs, "Models in the Comparative Study of Public Administration," in *Models and Priorities in the Comparative Study of Public Administration.* Papers in Comparative Public Administration, Special Series: No. 1 (Chicago: American Society for Public Administration, 1963), p. 6.

[35] Fred W. Riggs, "Agraria and Industria—Toward a Typology of Public Administration," in Siffin, *op. cit.,* pp. 23–116.

[36] Siffin, *op. cit.,* p. 9.

[37] Riggs, "Agraria and Industria," *op. cit.,* p. 23.

[38] *Ibid.,* p. 28.

[39] Scholars in the natural and social sciences, as in the humanities, usually adopted either of two relatively distinct analytic approaches to their respective subject matters. These approaches are normally labelled "structural" and "functional." Structuralists usually seek to describe phenomenal forms (social systems) and the relational processes (behavioral systems) concomitant with those forms. Functionalists seek to explain (or predict) the significant functional relationships that specific forms and processes bear or will bear to each other.

tive systems and the societies in which they operate at two distinct points of "equilibrium." Possible lines of development between these two points are postulated but never dealt with. The two poles must be considered in much the same way as Weber's "ideal types," their value lying in their abstractness, not in their historical reality. As Almond argues, the modern "industrian" system "never exists by itself, but always has an 'agrarian' system inside it."[40] Moreover, the conceptualization in the Agraria-Industria model is so abstract that, while it catches the gross distinctions between different societies, the smaller distinctions within societies and between social systems with similar structures escape notice altogether. Concepts such as particularism, ascription, universalism and achievement are so general that they subsume a great many facets of behavior which could better be investigated and understood if differentiated conceptually. In his "Sala" model, which appears in this volume, Riggs avoids this pitfall of "cosmic dimensions." He implicitly accepts Presthus' plea "to bite off smaller chunks of reality and to research these intensively, using as their guide 'middle range' theory which attempts to abstract from the whole social context some limited but, hopefully, meaningful segments for analysis."[41] In the "Sala" model Riggs's variables—heterogeneity,

[40] Gabriel A. Almond. "Introduction: A Functional Approach to Comparative Politics," in Gabriel A. Almond and James S. Coleman (eds.), *The Politics of the Developing Areas* (Princeton, New Jersey: Princeton University Press, 1960), p. 23. Riggs himself tried, in a later work, to correct this impression by stating that industria and agraria models are not strictly deductive but, rather, are "images" which could be located between the fused and the refracted models. See his "Models in the Comparative Study of Public Administration," *op. cit.*, p. 43 n. The concepts of fused and refracted models are explained in his article in this volume.

[41] Speaking of the need for theory in comparative public administration, Presthus points out that:

> Such theory need not be of cosmic dimensions. Social science has turned away from vast theoretical systems of Pareto and Marx because conceptualization at such levels has not provided basis for empirical research.

See Robert V. Presthus, "Behavior and Bureaucracy in Many Cultures," *Public Administration Review*, Vol. 19, No. 1 (1959), p. 26. Morroe Berger's work on Egyptian bureaucracy, which appears in this volume, probably represents a middle range theory *par excellence*. See also: Guy H. Fox and Charles A. Joiner, "Perceptions of the Vietnamese Public Administration System," *Administrative Science Quarterly*, Vol. 8, No. 4 (1964), pp. 443–481.

formalism, overlapping and nepotism—are not only more manageable but are empirically verifiable and, hence, more useful.

A recent empirical study which utilizes "middle range" theory is Eldersveld's "The Dimensions and Relevance of Bureaucratic Contact with the Public in India,"[42] which was conducted in Delhi State. Eldersveld is concerned primarily with five "theoretical propositions for the developing social and political system in India:"

> *1.* If citizens are to be properly involved in the system and in the achievement of system goals, administrative contacts with the public to be relevant, must be extensive, continuous, and *penetrate* to those sectors of the population most 'traditional,' most probably alienated, and most vital for the success of developmental goals.
>
> *2.* If citizens are to be properly involved in the developing India of today, these administrative contacts if relevant should lead to greater *information* and knowledge, instrumental and substantive, about governmental programs, policies, plans and goals.
>
> *3.* If citizens are to be properly involved, these administrative contacts, if relevant, should result in greater citizen *belief* in, and support of, governmental actions and programs. One should not expect, however, that there will be unanimous consensus over goals or means, but rather a consensus by the large majority that programs exist which are worthwhile, and feasible.
>
> *4.* If citizens are to be properly involved, these administrative contacts, if relevant, should inspire *confidence* on the part of the public in the integrity, efficiency, and 'bureaucratic style' of officials, leading to a feeling that officials care about the citizenry, treat them fairly and, thus, in sum, that the individual citizen counts in the system and that his actions are considered meaningful for the system.
>
> *5.* If citizens are to be properly involved, these administrative contacts, if relevant, should tap the realistic aspirations of the common man, appeal to these aspirations, whether strictly utlitarian or idealistic, and motivate the individual to *action* and achievement, which is significant for the citizen as well as for the system.[43]

The objects of analysis are five: penetration, information, belief, confidence and action. Eldersveld's primary objective was

[42] Published as "Bureaucratic Contact with the Public in India," *The Indian Journal of Public Administration,* Vol. II, No. 2 (1965), pp. 216–235.

[43] *Ibid.,* pp. 218–9.

to find out whether bureaucratic contacts with the "common man" in India are functional and relevant to social and economic change in that country.[44]

VI

The models and conceptual schemes in comparative politics have been especially relevant to the development of comparative public administration. "Conceptually," it was asserted recently, "the boundary between the political system and the administrative system is the boundary between an analytically defined macro-system and analytically defined micro-system."[45] Alfred Diamant, in his article in this volume, reviews in detail the development of the various models, theories and approaches in comparative politics and their relevance to comparative administration.[46] However, a few comments are in order here.

Political science and public administration share a concern with *individual* political and/or administrative systems, their structures and their modes of operation. So comparative politics and comparative public administration share a concern with theory, conceptualization and methodology. Waldo finds "much in common in outlook and aspirations" between comparative politics and comparative public administration "movements," because both "have taken the entire world as their scientific universe, [and] both have been engaged in an heroic attempt to

[44] It is beyond the scope of this introduction to go into Eldersveld's illuminating findings. The purpose is to draw the attention of the reader to this study's methods of survey research and their application to comparative studies. On the potentialities and limitations of survey research methods, see Donald C. Pelz, "Survey Research in Public Administration," *The Indian Journal of Public Administration,* Vol. 10, No. 4 (1964), pp. 608–624. The reader's attention is also drawn to "A Proposal for a Statistical Approach to Comparative Administration: The Measurement of National Bureaucracies," by Blanche Davis Blank (CAG Occasional Papers, July 1965). Patterned after *Cross-Polity Survey* by Banks and Textor, the study provides items which are considered suitable for quantification.

[45] Robert T. Holt, *Comparative Politics and Comparative Administration.* CAG Occasional Papers (February 1966), p. 6.

[46] In a forthcoming paper, "Political Development: Approaches to Theory and Strategy," Diamant broadens the scope of his review.

find or create theoretical constructs adequate for the tasks of world-wide comparison." Finally, both share two principal objectives: " (1) to discover, define and differentiate the 'stuff' (politics or administration) to be compared, wherever in the world it may be; and (2) to develop criteria of differentiation that are useful in ordering and analyzing the 'stuff' once it has been identified."[47] To accomplish the latter objective, scholars in comparative politics and comparative administration have increasingly resorted to constructive taxonomies, occasionally supported by what is referred to today as the "data movement."

The number of these classifications is already unwieldy, yet it continues to grow.[48] Diamant lists a great many of them in his article, and to enlarge upon them here would be superfluous. Their significance is that their existence is evidence of the lack of objective criteria of differentiation in this field. For example, Ghana under Nkrumah has been referred to as a "Mobilization System" by David Apter; a "Dominant Mass Party System" by Milton Esman; and a "Totalitarian Oligarchy" by Edward Shils —to list but a few. Would post-Nkrumah's Ghana be then called "Modernizing Autocracy," "Authoritarian Military Reformers," or "Modernizing Oligarchy"—to use different classifications by the same authors?

One is reminded of the proverbial camel struggling through the eye of a needle. As narrated by a British psychologist:

> In trying to predict the success of the hazardous enterprise we should wish to know the height and width of the camel, and the height and width of needle; given these unidimensional measurements we could predict with reasonable accuracy. But suppose we were told merely the "bigness" of the camel, that is to say, its height multiplied by its width, and the "bigness" of the eye of the needle, calculated in a similar manner. This "bigness" is multi-dimensional measurement, and gives very little information. The eye of the needle might be "bigger" than the camel, and yet the camel might get stuck. It might have ample height to spare but be too broad in the beam.[49]

47 Waldo, *op. cit.,* p. 11.

48 A good number of these schemes appear in Diamant's article in this volume.

49 H. H. Eysenck, *Uses and Abuses of Psychology* (Baltimore, Maryland: Penguin Books, 1962), p. 24.

Since most taxonomies are in this sense "multidimensional," they fail to provide reliable "criteria of differentiation." Those in comparative public administration would be unable, for example, to measure accurately the *degree* of centralization in various administrative systems. It seems likely, therefore, that such works as those of Lipset,[50] Deutch,[51] Banks and Textor,[52] and Almond and Verba,[53] which are among the products of the "data movement" and are more unidimensional, may in the long run lay the foundation for more sophisticated and rigorous standards for analyzing political institutions.

VII

It is evident that a substantial foundation of model- and theory-building has been formed, both in comparative administration and in related fields, upon which more sophisticated schemes can be constructed. As social scientists began increasingly to draw upon mathematics and statistics, model-building grew in popularity and refinement. Although sociometry and econometry,[54] for example, improved both theory formation and application, they likewise showed that social and economic factors are not invariably reducible to static quantities. The difficulty is that most of these factors depend on human action, which cannot always be made to fit mathematical formulas. It is imperative, therefore, to avoid a procrustean model which arbitrarily forces data to fit. LaPalombara warned against models that are "stultifying" either for policy makers or for their

50 Seymour Martin Lipset, "Some Social Requisites of Democracy: Economic Development and Political Legitimacy," *The American Political Science Review,* Vol. 53, No. 1 (1959), pp. 69–105.

51 Karl W. Deutch, "Social Mobilization and Political Development," *The American Political Science Review,* Vol. 55, No. 3 (1961), pp. 463–515.

52 Banks and Textor, *op. cit.*

53 Gabriel A. Almond and Sidney Verba, *The Civic Culture: Political Attitudes and Democracy in Five Nations* (Princeton, New Jersey: Princeton University Press, 1963).

54 Although the emergence of something like *bureaumetry* is not yet imminent it is hardly far-fetched.

operation-oriented agencies.[55] Indeed, as Caldwell somewhat caustically observed, model-building "costs little," contrasted with the effects and resources needed for field work.[56]

VIII

Two primary concerns in comparative administration have been identified: theory-building and development administration. In recent years there has been increasing concern with developing nations, particularly with the problems of their administrative systems. CAG seminars have been almost exclusively devoted to three identifiable "clusters of problems": (1) the political dimensions of development and administration; (2) the process of development planning; and (3) the administrative systems of developing countries.[57]

A number of factors seem to account for this focus. First was the intangible, almost romantic attraction developing nations have had for many Westerners. With little information available outside of anthropological studies, these countries have presented virgin territory for research. Second was the availability of funds to support travel and field research in all branches of the social sciences. Third was the need of aid-giving agencies to know more about the countries which they assist. The failure of the earlier efforts of technical assistance agencies to transplant Western administrative institutions and practices to developing countries—often the same countries which sought Western scientific innovations—showed administrators, as Siffin suggested, the need "for something more than a homespun approach to public administration."[58] And fourth, and most important, was the need

[55] Joseph LaPalombara, *Alternative Strategies for Developing Administrative Capabilities in Emerging Nations.* CAG Occasional Papers (November 1965), p. 1.

[56] Caldwell, *op. cit.*, p. 236. LaPalombara, *Ibid.*, p. 59:

> We are very long on theory and still poverty stricken as far as research findings are concerned. . . .

[57] Milton J. Esman, *The CAG and the Study of Public Administration: A Mid-Term Appraisal.* CAG Occasional Papers (January 1966), p. 8.

[58] Siffin, *op. cit.*, p. 6.

to abandon existing political and philosophical norms as the emergence of new countries brought problems which political science, in its historic Western orientation, was not equipped to handle.

In the throes of change, comparative administration became a convenient incubator for a number of embryonic subjects which did not fit into classical political science or Western public administration—subjects dealing with modernization and nation-building, and with various administrative structures, functions and behaviors commonly identified as "development administration." The most concise definition of development administration is offered by Weidner. The term, he says, "refers to the processes of guiding an organization toward the achievement of progressive political, economic, and social objectives that are authoritatively determined in one manner or another."[59] Development administration has widened its scope beyond the traditional functions of public administration. In most, if not all new nations, one of the functions of the state bureaucracy is to bring arbitrary economic power under public scrutiny to improve the lives of the underprivileged majority. The new states are determined to maintain control of enterprises in the category described by Lenin as "Commanding Heights." The government's authority reaches its highest point whenever planning techniques or measures to speed up industrialization are introduced. As such socio-economic activities increase, it is only natural for the bureaucratic machinery to enlarge itself. Therefore, a rapid program of planning and an expansion of bureaucracy often take place simultaneously.

But in order for public administration in developing countries to accomplish its tasks, it must itself undergo fundamental reforms. The relationship between economic development and ad-

[59] Edward W. Weidner, "Development Administration: A New Focus for Research," in Heady and Stokes, *op. cit.*, p. 98. One cannot help noticing, however, the inadequacy of the concept for a precise expression of the structural deficiencies of public administration in developing countries. In this sense, the French concept of *sous-administration* (literally, under-administration) seems more adequate. See, for example, M. J. L. Quermonne, "Les Sous-Administration et les Politiques d'équipement administratif," *Revue française de Science Politique,* Vol. 9, No. 3 (1959), pp. 629–667; F. Gazier, "Les problèmes spécifiques de l'administration publique en pays sous-développé," *Civilisations,* Vol. 11, No. 2 (1961), pp. 144–158.

ministrative reforms has not, therefore, followed a path para
to the one existing in the developed (mainly Western) countr
For while in the developed countries economic growth prece
bureaucratic reforms, in the emerging countries, administrat
reform is being enacted while economic development is stil
gleam on the horizon.

IX

In many respects development administration would
into Professor Leavitt's classification of managerial, as disti
from non-managerial, jobs. "We can partially differentiate m
agerial from other jobs," he noted some years ago, "by empha
ing the *change*[60] quality of managerial problems as against t
relatively static quality of tasks at lower levels. The manag
deals largely with unknowns. He is a solver of *unprogramm*
problems."[61] In a recent article Thompson followed simi
lines, suggesting that development administration implies org
izational ability to innovate; and that for an organization to
innovative certain "general requirements" and "structural
quirements" must be met. But here is the rub: among t
general requirements are "uncommitted money, time, skills, a
good will," and included in the structural requirements a
"structural looseness," free communications, and decentraliz
"assignment and resource decisions."[62] A bureaucracy meeti
these requirements would, by definition, be already develope

A somewhat different approach is taken by Alfred Diama
in his bureaucratic model, which he constructs for those syste
he terms "Development Movement Regimes."[63] Diamant
model is fashioned after Weber's "ideal type," but, he emph
sizes, it differs from Weber's in three ways. (1) It is not "a pu

60 Italics in the original.

61 Harold J. Leavitt, *The Managerial Psychology* (Chicago: Universit
of Chicago Press, 1958), p. 236.

62 Victor A. Thompson, "Bureaucracy and Innovation," *Administrati
Science Quarterly*, Vol. 9, No. 1 (1965), pp. 1–20.

63 Diamant, "Bureaucracy in Development Movement Regimes:
Bureaucratic Model for Developing Societies," *op. cit.*

ideal-typical," for it contains several types of administrative staffs and authority systems. (2) Although it assumes a correlation between the "nature and form of legitimacy system" and the "organization and functioning of the bureaucracy," it does not propose, as Weber did, an "inescapable one-to-one relationship between type of legitimate authority and type of administrative staff." (3) It does not attempt "to employ the *substance* of any of the three Weberian bureaucratic types—traditional, charismatic, legal-rational—for the analysis of any single, or cluster of, bureaucracies in transitional political systems."[64] Diamant's model also differs from Weber's in that it is prescriptive and therefore both inductive and deductive. The model categorizes the characteristics of bureaucracy in the "development movement regimes" into three major clusters: functional, behavioral and structural. Eight functional, four behavioral and six structural characteristics are suggested, and the behavioral and structural characteristics are correlated with functional ones.[65]

The model is intended to maximize the effectiveness of a modernizing polity, but there are difficulties in application. Although, as Diamant has argued, the model is not ideal-typical, it is nonetheless idealized. While it provides a highly constructive approach toward creating the kind of bureaucracy most suitable for undertaking the tasks of modernization, it is nevertheless imbued with value assumptions. And of course the crucial element remains the willingness of those who would be most affected by the model to heed it—a variable which is beyond the control of any advisory plan.

X

The study of development administration has focused increasingly on the ecological dimensions of development and of administration in particular. A fundamental difference between early and recent studies of comparative administration is that the former assumed cultural dimensions to be constant and conse-

64 *Ibid.*, p. 47.

65 *Ibid.*, pp. 73–82.

quently disregarded the effects of culture upon administration. The ecological approach, on the other hand, asserts that administrative behavior is not random—it is an outgrowth of the interaction of cultural traits and values and the administration—in short, that the administrative culture is an extension of the greater social culture.

The need for ecological studies of administration was seen almost two decades ago by Robert Dahl. For studies of administration to be comparative, he said:

> *1.* Generalizations derived from the operation of public administration in the environment of one nation-state cannot [simply] be universalized and applied to public administration in a different environment. A principle *may* be applicable in a different framework. But its applicability can be determined only after a study of that particular framework.
>
> *2.* There can be no truly universal generalizations about public administration without a profound study of varying national and social characteristics impinging on public administration, to determine what aspects of public administration, if any, are truly independent of the national and social setting. Are there discoverable principles of *universal* validity, or are all principles valid only in terms of a special environment?
>
> *3.* It follows that the study of public administration inevitably must become a much more broadly based discipline, resting not on a narrowly defined knowledge of techniques and processes, but rather extending to the varying historical, sociological, economic, and other conditioning factors that give public administration its peculiar stamp in every country.[66]

The emphasis upon ecological studies, where culture constitutes a very significant variable, derives from the field of human ecology, whose thesis is that human behavior is largely shaped, if not determined, by the physical universe. But in a recent paper, Riggs rejects the "deterministic implications" of ecology for human beings and institutions—the view of political and administrative behavior "as nothing more than the outcome of a particular configuration of interacting pressures. . . ." He argues persuasively for a non-deterministic view of ecology, asserting that "ecological theories [should] specify the influence of a sub-

[66] Dahl, *op. cit.*, p. 11. Also John Merriman Gaus, *Reflections on Public Administration* (University: University of Alabama Press, 1947), Ch. 1.

ject upon its environment as well as the impact of environment upon the subject," and that, "until the two reciprocally related sets of transactions are examined, an ecological pattern has not been established."[67]

Studies of the mutual influence of administrative systems and their environments are still in the embryo stage. They are difficult by their very nature, since they require an understanding not only of public administration but of the wider aspects of political, economic, sociological, and physical processes as well. Nevertheless, one cannot really comprehend public administration in certain countries in the Middle East, for example, without understanding Islamic heritage, social culture, and even the geophysical conditions of the area. There are a large number of questions that can only be profitably studied ecologically: for instance, the relationship between the extended family system and nepotism; the effect of cultural or religious fatalism on decision making; the effect of an agrarian economy on the degree of centralization of a given administrative system; the relationship between socialization and legitimation of authority; and even the impact of climate on administrative efficiency. Certainly there is untapped potential in ecological studies which renders the area worthy of further exploration.

XI

This introduction, as well as the readings which follow, is intended to provide a general overview of comparative public administration, its major trends and emphases. It seems appropriate to draw some inferences from the discussion for the reader to consider in approaching the selections.

As is apparent, comparative public administration is a study of public administration on a comparative basis. But what can be properly compared is far from obvious, in view of the almost infinite number of legitimate variables. Regardless of its pragmatic concerns with the bureaucratic systems of individual

[67] Fred W. Riggs, *The Ecology of Development.* CAG Occasional Papers (September 1964), p. 5.

countries or with development administration, the ultimate concern of the discipline has been and will continue to be theory and methodology. It seems that we have reached the "take-off" stage in the methodological area, although our conceptual equipment is not uniformly dependable and our instruments need greater refinement. To achieve a refined and sophisticated methodology—in other words, to reach a scientific method of analysis—the following conditions must be met:

First, a Focus on Relationships. While description and measurement are basic techniques in a scientific method, their importance lies in the precise statement of relationships among phenomena under given conditions. For this reason ecological studies in comparative public administration may transcend what Forward calls the "intuitive and *a priori* assumptions concerning the relationships of bureaucracy to other societal systems." They can also provide a sharper distinction between what legitimately falls within the administrative realm and what falls within the ecological realm—a distinction of utmost importance for such projects as technical assistance programs in public administration.

Second, the Use of Abstract Concepts. Scientific method involves deliberate attempts to simplify the understanding of relationships through abstract concepts which permit generalizations. The scientific method requires that concepts limited to particular geographical areas or times be replaced. In the comparative studies of public administration such broad concepts as particularism, ascription, universalism, and achievement could be better investigated and understood if reduced to their basic components, that is, if differentiated conceptually.

Third, the Development of Operational Definitions. If concepts are to make any meaningful contribution to our understanding of administration, they must be bridged to "raw experience." Science requires that concepts be defined by a series of operations which permit the sensory perception and identification of the phenomena concerned. Such operational definitions make possible repetition of observations in many places and at many times.

In sum, what we need is a set of related and interdependent definitions, abstract concepts and hypotheses, which can be tested and identified by observation, experience and research. It is only then that the objective of the authors of *Comparative Studies in Administration*[68] to establish a valid theory "which will encompass all types of administration and be adaptive to all cultural or historical contexts," will be accomplished.

As to the future of the field, it does not seem that limiting or enlarging its scope would, as Lynton Caldwell has suggested, confront comparative administration with a dilemma. It is Caldwell's contention that if comparative administration should continue to focus on problems of development, it would "in fact cease to be comparative public administration," and would have "transformed itself into a development administration effort in which use of comparative methods would be secondary to a substantive objective—to understand the development process."[69] On the other hand, he contends, should the movement broaden its scope it would run the risk of losing the thrust which has propelled it since CAG began its activities.

If comparative administration is a method of analysis it is hardly important whether its substantive objective is developmental or not. Moreover, there is no reason why the result of broadening its scope should not be enrichment rather than emasculation of its effort. The field is at an embryonic stage, and what is to grow out of it is yet to be determined.

One of the foremost students of comparative politics recently observed that "In comparative studies, general theory remains more separate and distinct from the practice of research than is healthy for a satisfactory job of analysis. Imagination leaps ahead of the sober limits of operations."[70] Certainly imagi-

[68] Thompson *et al., infra,* p. 60.

[69] Caldwell, *op. cit.,* p. 240.

[70] David E. Apter, *The Politics of Modernization* (Chicago: University of Chicago Press, 1965), p. 422.

nation is the basis of innovation, but in our search for theories and models we must not overlook the crucial questions of relevance and utility. As we proceed in our endeavors we must seek in our method "a point somewhere between the grasshoppers and the drones."[71]

The Relevance of Comparative Politics to the Study of Comparative Administration

ALFRED DIAMANT[1]
Haverford College

STUDENTS OF COMPARATIVE public administration can find in comparative politics a considerable body of substantive materials directly related to their own concerns, as well as increasingly sophisticated and self-conscious efforts at methodological clarification. This division between methodological and substantive contributions is to some extent arbitrary and artificial. Students of comparative politics, by focusing on certain data or problems, are led to a particular method for handling these data. Thus they contribute not only a substantive body of information but, in some cases, also a distinct methodology.[2] On the other hand, those concerned only with questions of method nevertheless approach this problem from a certain body of empirical data,

---

71 *Ibid.*, p. 423.

Reprinted from *Administrative Science Quarterly,* Vol. V (June 1960), pp. 87–112, by permission of the publisher and the author. [Abridged.]

1 The author would like to thank his colleague at Gainesville, Alfred Clubock, for helping him clarify his ideas and shape his conclusions. The responsibility for the present form of these ideas and conclusions is, of course, his own.

2 A good example of this is Brian Chapman, *The Profession of Government: The Public Service in Europe* (New York, 1959).

and thereby can give us insight into some political systems.[3] Too often, unfortunately, substantive studies are marred by the lack of ordered presentation of data, while methodological efforts seem to be totally unrelated to the problems of empirical research.

Although one might easily despair at bringing about a union of theory, comparative method, and empirical research in political science, one must nevertheless assume that there is an indissoluble connection between them and that what Durkheim said about sociology applies to politics as well: "Comparative sociology is not a separate branch of sociology; it is sociology itself, to the extent that it is more than merely descriptive, and hopes to account for facts as well."[4] If comparison is essential, no matter what our concept of the study of politics—whether descriptive, theoretical, or predictive[5]—the question is: what is it we hope to do by making comparisons? Macridis has put it succinctly thus: "To give us an explanatory frame of reference in terms of which we can account for differences and uniformities . . . is the central problem of comparative analysis."[6] This value-free approach to comparative studies is the dominant one: we want to get at the facts—which we cannot do unless we have some method for ordering them—and beyond that, we would like to make some progress toward pinpointing causality, though there is no general agreement in political science that we either

[3] David Apter, A Comparative Method for the Study of Politics, *American Journal of Sociology*, 9 (November 1958), 221–237, which grew out of research on West African political systems.

[4] *Les Règles de la méthode sociologique* (Paris, 1947) , p. 137; quoted by F. X. Sutton, "Social Theory and Comparative Politics" (unpublished paper prepared for a conference under the auspices of the Committee on Comparative Politics of the Social Science Research Council, Princeton, N.J., June 1955) , p. i.

[5] Gunnar Heckscher, *The Study of Comparative Government and Politics* (London, 1957) , p. 15. This is the report of a round-table conference on teaching and research in comparative government held by the International Political Science Association in Florence, April 1954. The book, though based on the reports at Florence, is essentially Heckscher's synthesis.

[6] Roy Macridis, "Interest Groups and the Political System in Comparative Analysis" (paper prepared for a meeting of the Southern Political Science Association, November 1959) , p. 9. Professor Macridis gave permission to quote from his draft.

can or ought even to attempt to get at this particularly vexing problem. . . .

This concern with the connection between theory and practice has produced, in the field of comparative politics, a considerable body of writing on what is wrong with the discipline and how one ought to proceed with research to produce meaningful results. What is the condition of comparative studies in politics today? What is the nature of comparative techniques? Are these techniques and methods appropriate for the study of administration? These are the questions this paper will try to answer.

History, politics, and administration

The problems and difficulties of comparative studies of politics are not peculiar to that discipline alone:

> Questions concerning the validity of results, the need for hypothesizing, the establishment of a general theory, etc., obviously relate no more to comparative government than to other aspects of political science. In most cases they are common to all social sciences or even to the whole field of humanistic study.[7]

In fact, the issues of comparability in politics merge with the broad philosophical questions concerning the nature of evidence, assumptions about causality, and the like. In particular, questions about evidence (the result of empirical investigations) and the validity of criteria of comparison are at the heart of the current difficulties with comparative studies of politics. It might be useful to see, therefore, not only how a closely related discipline such as history approaches the problem of evidence but also how research in administration can gain in scope by perceptive use of the tools and concepts of the historian.

Growing up originally within the bosom of history, political science in recent decades has completely disowned its parent and has sought for explanation in almost all other quarters than in history. The study of public administration, in particular, has taken a firm nonhistoric stance and has only recently come to

[7] Heckscher, *op. cit.*, p. 17.

realize that "history"—social, cultural, economic, political—has a tendency to play tricks with POSDCORB and the scalar principle when applied in Costa Rica and Thailand. This rediscovery of the historical matrix as a dimension of social sytems justifies this look at the historian's approach to the problem of evidence. . . .

The immediate question is: what is the relevance of this historical framework for the problem of studying and understanding a political system or an administrative agency? The answer is that any model of politics must be a dynamic one, that will account not only for the interaction of political forces at a given moment, but also for their evolution over longer periods of time.[8] This historical dimension of social research has recently been emphasized by Lipset. He noted that both Radcliffe-Brown and Weber had repeatedly emphasized that there is no conflict between the "historical explanation" of a social system and the one which "is obtained by showing . . . that it is a special exemplification of laws of social psychology and social functioning. The two kinds of explanation do not conflict but supplement one another."[9] A striking application of this historicultural dimension to the theoretical as well as practical problems of administration has appeared in Sutton's report on his technical assistance experience in Thailand. In this report he stated bluntly:

> The solution of present-day problems in Thailand must be undertaken against the backdrop of two . . . historical facts. . . . In searching for the basic orientation of the Thai bureaucrat in modern times, one must turn to the ancient traditions of Indian thought which condition his responses to the modern challenge. . . .[10]

To this list of recent voices calling for a renewed emphasis on the historic dimension in the comparative study of adminis-

[8] Dankwart A. Rustow, New Horizons for Comparative Politics, *World Politics*, 9 (1957), 546–547.

[9] Seymour Lipset, Some Social Requisites of Democracy: Economic Development and Political Legitimacy, *American Political Science Review*, 53 (1959), 85, n. 32.

[10] Joseph L. Sutton, "Culture and Technical Assistance" (Paper delivered to the 1959 meeting of the American Political Science Association, Washington, D.C., September 1959), p. 2.

tration should be added that of S. N. Eisenstadt.[11] His examination of historic bureaucratic systems has already produced valuable insights into two problems which, though perhaps no longer relevant to the modern Western world, remain crucial for the bureaucratic systems of transitional societies in Asia and Africa. The problems analyzed by Eisenstadt of legitimation and the political struggle within bureaucratic systems seem to be basic issues facing Thailand, Ghana, Pakistan, the Philippines, and the like, judging from the reports about these countries by Riggs, Pye, Apter, Braibanti, and others. . . .[12]

MODELS AND COMPARATIVE METHODS

[The] search for a "conceptual framework,"[13] which has dominated the current literature of comparative politics, stems from the desire to transcend the limitation imposed by a narrow, parochial, noncomparative, static, descriptive, and monographic method.[14] Students in comparative administration whose horizons were pushed back by the needs of the United States and the United Nations in overseas operations, and whose work was hampered by the same limitations as those of comparative poli-

[11] Political Struggles in Bureaucratic Societies, *World Politics,* 9 (October 1956), 15–36; and Internal Contradictions in Bureaucratic Polities, *Comparative Studies in Society and History,* 1 (1958), 58–75.

[12] See for example Fred Riggs, "A Paradoxical Model and Financial Administration" (Bloomington, Ind., 1959; mimeo.); Lucian W. Pye, "Armies in the Process of Political Modernization" (Cambridge, Mass., 1959; mimeo.); Ralph Braibanti, The Civil Service of Pakistan, *South Atlantic Quarterly,* 58 (Spring 1959), 258–304; and David E. Apter and Robert A. Lystad, "Bureaucracy, Party, and Constitutional Democracy: An Examination of Political Role Systems in Ghana," in *Transition in Africa: Studies in Political Adaptation* by Gwendolyn M. Carter and William O. Brown, eds. (Boston University African Research and Studies Program, African Research Studies No. 1; Boston, 1958), pp. 16–43.

[13] Those at the Florence round table stated unequivocally: "A minimum requirement for comparison is that it should be based at least on a 'conceptual framework,' that is, a number of conscious and consciously interrelated concepts which are applied to the cases brought into comparison" (Heckscher, *op. cit.,* p. 69).

[14] Roy Macridis, *The Study of Comparative Government* (Doubleday Short Studies in Political Science, No. 21; Garden City, 1955), ch. i.

tics, began to look for help (especially for studies cutting across several cultures) to this methodological literature in comparative politics. Here methodological frameworks, conceptual models, configurative schemes, institutional and/or functional approaches confronted them in a bewildering array. It seemed that any one of these might be a feasible way of doing field research and ordering the data collected. Why was it, that with so many different methods proposed for research, very little research was actually being done on the basis of these very models, schemes, and frameworks?

The principal reason for this gap between conceptualization and research is that the proposed schemes are often constructed on such a gross or macroscopic level that it is impossible to move from them to the level of actual empirical research. These models are elegant, logically self-consistent, but of little help to the researcher in the field. If, by chance, resources are provided to do the research, the findings might very well fit the prescribed model, but there is controversy over whether violence has been done to the "reality" of the social systems under investigation.[15]

In this welter of models, frameworks, schemes, and so on, two broad categories can be discerned. There are, first of all, what can be called the "general system" models, which set up a conceptual scheme for something called a political system or a society to apply to one or several societies. The second category, to be termed a "political culture" scheme starts from the proposition that societies and political systems are so diverse that one must first classify them before one can establish methods for comparison. After examining these two major categories some attention will be given to a number of other studies which have some relevance for comparative administration, although they are not as self-consciously methodological as the "general system" and the "political culture" literature. . . .

"General system" models

The "general system" method, operating at the most macroscopic level of generalization ought to be based on a general

[15] See for instance Daniel Lerner, *The Passing of Traditional Society: Modernizing the Middle East* (Glencoe, 1958).

theory of politics, though most of the writers in this group avoid this particular problem. David Easton, following up his work in *The Political System*[16] recognizes the need for such a general theory, but denies that there is a royal road to it. Rather, he suggests that several approaches are possible and indicates that "system theory, with its sensitivity to the input-output exchange between a system and its setting offers a fruitful approach."[17]

Defining politics as making and executing authoritative decisions for a society, Easton proposes that political life be separated, for purposes of analysis, from the rest of social activity and that it be seen as a system which takes in inputs in the form of demands and support and produces outputs in the form of policies and decisions. In any political system scarcity prevails with regard to most things people want; therefore not all demands can possibly be met. We must determine first how demands arise and assume their particular character in society, and then how these demands are transformed into issues or inputs. However, in order to keep going a political system also needs inputs in the form of support. The main reason for focusing attention on support as a crucial input is the need to find out how systems manage to maintain a steady flow of inputs without which the system would not absorb sufficient energy from its members to be able to convert demands into decisions and policies, i.e. outputs.

This input-output model of Easton's is probably the most generalized of the "general system" experimental models produced in recent years. However, others operate on levels only slightly less abstract, and of these, four will be presented: two by Macridis, one by Apter, and the one suggested by the Evanston Seminar.

After reviewing a number of alternative approaches to the problem of comparative method, including the problem approach, a "checklist of politics," and area studies, the Evanston Seminar[18] suggested as their preferred solution a "conceptual

16 New York, 1953.

17 Easton, An Approach to the Analysis of Political Systems, *World Politics,* 9 (1957), 400.

18 Research in Comparative Politics: Report of the Inter-University Summer Seminar on Comparative Politics, Social Science Research Council, *American Political Science Review,* 47 (1953), 641–657.

scheme" which they claimed would aid in classifying data for empirical research and for hypothesizing. Although the members of the Evanston Seminar insisted that conceptualization was needed at all levels of abstraction, from the modest single-problem one to the global level, the model produced by the Seminar was clearly of the "general system" type and open to the same criticisms as all the other models in that category.

The Evanston seminar started with the assertion that politics is a universally discoverable function, which provides society with decisions having the force and status of legitimacy, that is to say, politics enforces decisions against deviationists and sees to it that they are obeyed. Machinery also exists that enjoys the monopoly of legitimate authority, whose exercise is justified by the legitimacy myth. The political process is, therefore, a struggle between power aspiration and policy aspiration groups for legitimacy status. The outcome of this struggle is determined by the effective power structure, and the end condition, legitimacy, reflects the value system of the society. The tasks involved in analyzing this political system are four: First, the legitimacy myth must be analyzed and related to the general myth structure of society. Second, one must inquire into the political aspirations, political processes, and effective power factors of the political system. Next, the complexity and ultimacy of the decision-making system must be studied. Finally, a theory of change must be elaborated which will account for the tensions between formal and informal processes.

In his first attempt in 1955[19] Macridis constructed a general model, which had four categories of analysis: decision making, power, ideology, and institutions. Under the first category he asked such questions as: who makes the decisions, how are decision makers selected, what are the steps in the deliberative process, and what are the contents of decision? Under the second heading he defined power in terms of authority and identified the instruments of power. Under the third category he inquired after the sources of dominant political ideologies, and under the fourth and final heading he developed criteria for the classification of political institutions.

19 See note 14.

Macridis' more recent attempt at model building is more sophisticated than his earlier one, but still does not seem to meet the two tests of utility Macridis himself set up for model building: Does it help the student find out what he wants to find out? And, can the question be so formulated as to give an answer in empirical terms, giving the broadest possible meaning to the term "empirical"?

In this more recent model, Macridis defines a political system as "a system of action in which individuals and groups act for the realization of certain objectives that at one and the same time reflect both interest and desire to translate it into authoritative decisions that are binding upon the body politic."[20] We note in this definition both elements of Parsons' sociology, articulated most prominently in comparative politics methodology by Gabriel Almond, and the "authoritative decision-making" definition of the political system of Easton. A political system according to Macridis involves three descriptive categories: a structure of authority and purposes, a social and interest configuration, and a deliberative and decision-making structure which includes political parties and governmental authorities. It seems that both of Macridis' models fail to meet their author's own tests of utility.

Apter, whose work Macridis acknowledged in his more recent model, distinguishes three dimensions for comparative research: social stratification, political groups, and government.[21] In the analysis of the social stratification system several questions must be asked: how are roles defined; what are the institutionalized criteria of stratification—economic, political, religious, and so on; and what are the recruitment patterns into the major groups of the system? Government is defined as referring to a concrete group; it is the most generalized membership unit possessing defined responsibility for the maintenance of the system of which it is a part and which has a practical monopoly of coercive powers. Whatever empirical form a government will take it has certain structural requisites (authoritative decision making, accountability and consent, coercion and punishment,

20 Macridis, "Interest Groups and the Political System in Comparative Analysis," p. 16.

21 Apter, *op. cit.*, p. 232.

resource determination and allocation, and political recruitment and role assignment) as well as a certain format (dictatorial, oligarchical, indirectly or directly representative). Finally, Apter deals with political groups and the structure of their membership and leadership, which he considers to be the chief agents for modifying the stratification system.

TABLE I

SUGGESTED SCHEMES FOR COMPARATIVE ANALYSIS*

EVANSTON SEMINAR	MACRIDIS I	APTER	MACRIDIS II
Legitimacy myth	Ideology		
Power	Power	Social stratification	Authority and purpose
Decision making	Decision making	Government	Deliberation and decision making
Theory of change			
	Institutions		
		Political groups	Interest configuration

* The models on which this chart is based are identified in footnotes 18 (Evanston Seminar), 14 (Macridis I), 3 (Apter), and 6 (Macridis II). On the whole, an attempt has been made to place comparable dimensions on the same horizontal line.

Although social stratification, groups, and government seem to be discrete categories for analysis, Apter must continually adjust for two factors: (1) the setting in which each system operates, and (2) the manner in which the three dimensions continually impinge on each other and seemingly change continuously under analysis. "The impulses thus deriving from types of political group leadership strongly affect the way in which both government format and social stratification will be manifested in society." And again: "Such leadership reflects ideological positions which range in their degree of commitment to the social stratification system."[22]

[22] *Ibid.*, pp. 221, 227.

The distinction between Apter and many of the other recent model builders is his rediscovery of government as the central element of his system. Government is viewed as a maximizer, "sending out streams of satisfactions"; it plays a "crucial and strategic role . . . in a going social system." Although Apter makes a passing acknowledgement to Easton and his input-output scheme, the strongest influence on Apter is to be sought in Parsons' sociology which he acknowledged in his earlier work, *The Goldcoast in Transition*. . . .[23]

"Political culture" models

The "general system" models discussed above have a common failing—their remoteness from empirical research. They need, as Sutton has pointed out,[24] to be combined with a classification of societies and political systems, if they are to be made operational for comparative administration. A number of these classifications have been developed, of which the best is Almond's "political culture" scheme.[25]

Almond begins his classification of political systems with a series of definitions: a "role" is that organized sector of an actor's orientation that constitutes his participation in the interactive process, and a "system" is an ensemble or a "structure" of roles. Finally, Almond defines "political" with Weber as the legitimate monopoly of physical coercion over a given territory or population. A "political system" is, therefore, "the patterned interaction of roles affecting decisions backed up by the threat of physical compulsion."

However, every political system is imbedded in a particular pattern of orientation to political action, in what Almond calls a "political culture." In some instances several political systems share a common political culture (as in the United States and Great Britain), while in others a single country may contain several political cultures, each of which extends beyond the boundaries of that one country (as in Central Europe).

23 Princeton, 1955.

24 F. X. Sutton, *op. cit.*, p. 8.

25 Comparative Political Systems, *Journal of Politics,* 18 (1956), 391–409.

Almond outlines four political cultures into which the political systems operating the world today can be divided: (1) the Anglo-American (including several of the Commonwealth countries); (2) the Continental European (excluding Scandinavia and the Low Countries, whose political culture is midway between the Anglo-American and the Continental European); (3) the preindustrial and partially industrial (outside Europe and North America); and (4) the totalitarian. . . .

Although a number of attempts have been made to develop political culture models and to design research strategies embodying this concept, they will probably not provide tools for research that will be as useful as those designed by Almond;[26] for actual research needs, they tend to establish a dichotomy between a Western and a non-Western political culture and to assume that all the world's political systems can be subsumed under these categories. The evidence already available clearly contradicts these rigid categories.

The case for the existence of a non-Western political culture has been well stated by Rustow:

> The specialist in non-Western politics . . . will at times be perplexed by many profound differences in the political patterns he encounters. . . . But a broader view reveals that the impact of the West and of modern industrial civilization has resulted in similarities both in the cultural and the socio-economic setting and in the political process itself.[27]

Rustow himself, Pye, and a group of political scientists suggesting a research strategy for non-Western politics have contributed significantly to the drawing of the outline of a non-Western political system.[28] The cultural and socioeconomic setting of

[26] In a preliminary report on his research on Italian bureaucracy Joseph LaPalombara acknowledges his indebtedness to and emphasizes the utility of Almond's "political culture" scheme, The Utility and Limitations of Interest Group Theory in Non-American Field Situations, *Journal of Politics* 22 (1960), 36–37. See also Gabriel Almond and James S. Coleman, eds., *The Politics of Developing Areas* (Princeton, 1960).

[27] Rustow, *op. cit.*, p. 537.

[28] Rustow, *op. cit.;* Lucian W. Pye, The Non-Western Political Process, *Journal of Politics,* 20 (1958), 468–486; and George McT. Kahin, Guy J. Parker, and Lucian W. Pye, Comparative Politics of Non-Western Countries, *American Political Science Review,* 49 (1955), 1024–1027.

these non-Western systems is characterized by a concern with the problems of economic development and the closely related problem of administrative inexperience, which tends to hamper and retard the rate of growth considered essential by the new nations. This desire to develop economically is, in turn, part of a larger complex of attitudes which can be summed up by the term "insecure nationalism." This feeling of insecurity is heightened by the present hazards of the international scene caused by the cold war. Finally, there is a strong cultural ambivalence in many of these non-Western societies: hatred as well as admiration of the West, eager emulation and indignant rejection of Western ways.

The political process which has developed in this setting may be characterized thus: the political sphere is not sharply differentiated from the remainder of the society. As a result there are few explicitly organized interest groups with functionally specific roles, political actors have less clearly defined and functionally specific roles, and there is a high degree of substitutability of roles. There is further a lack of consensus about legitimate forms and purposes of political action. As a result parties and aspiring elites take on a *Weltanschauung* character, easily turning into revolutionary movements, and resorting to revolutionary action because they do not trust the other participants in the political process to honor the ostensible rules of the game. This failure of consensus gives rise to charismatic leaders and helps strengthen the affective or expressive aspect of politics at the expense of the problem-solving or public policy aspect of politics. Third, many of the emerging non-Western polities are culturally, racially, linguistically and otherwise heterogeneous. Usually, a number of autonomous communities exist within the political boundaries of the new state, and a poor communications network intensifies their separateness. Finally, in these rapidly developing communities there is a high rate of recruitment of new elements into politics. The political leadership often is very young, and there are sharp generational differences between them and the older leadership who fought the struggle for independence from colonial rule and is more deeply attached to Western traditions.

It is very illuminating to compare this model of the non-Western political process with a research strategy proposal for western European politics. First of all, there is an existing body of research results which drew strong criticism from the research strategy group: "The legal-historical-philosophical approach . . . is not by itself adequate to discover how serious these cleavages and alienations are, for by admission the basic problems of civic loyalty and political cohesion lie in large part outside the formal governmental framework."[29] It would seem that consensus, which the non-Western analysts considered a most important concern, had received little attention.

The research needs in western European government and politics identified by the group making the report were as follows: studies of legal institutions and processes about which nothing is known at all today, studies of the actual functioning of governmental institutions, and studies into nonlegal institutions and processes.

While the emphasis in the non-Western world is on social organisms and patterns of action, in the West nonlegal institutions are listed last as a type of research needed. This discrepancy is further emphasized by the research approaches recommended for western European politics: historical studies, institutional studies, process studies of public policy decisions, attitude studies, and community studies. Again we note the emphasis on formal governmental institutions and processes in western European political research.

Some additional tools

Before undertaking a general evaluation of the methodological approaches analyzed in the preceding pages, other tools for comparative studies developed in recent years deserve some attention. One of these was fashioned by the team of social scientists who participated in the RADIR (Revolution and the Development of International Relations) project at Stanford

[29] Gabriel A. Almond, Taylor Cole, and Roy Macridis, A Suggested Research Strategy in Western European Government and Politics, *American Political Science Review,* 49 (1955), 1043.

University. Two of the RADIR monographs proposed methods for a comparative study of elites and of symbols.[30] In one, RADIR set out to collect data on elites under four headings: origins (social, political, economic, and so forth); skills (symbol, violence, or bargaining specialists); accountability (to whom *do* the elites listen); and perspectives (how do elites view the world and what might be their code of action based on this world view?). On the basis of this evidence RADIR then proposed several hypotheses about elites and elite behavior. In essence, this is a "general system" approach, but by focusing more narrowly on elites, rather than on entire social systems, it should be useful in the study of administrative elites. Unfortunately, subsequent publications under the RADIR project did not meet the high expectations aroused by the earlier policy papers, and the entire project seems to have been discontinued.

Keeping in mind Sutton's admonition that Thai bureaucrats could be understood only against the background of Buddhism, one might take a look at the RADIR proposal to develop a comparative study of symbols. In the introductory volume of the symbol studies series Lasswell, Lerner, and Pool viewed myth as a means of creating solidarity and proposed to ask: what circumstances lead to the rejection of a myth and its replacement by another myth, and how can myth be transmitted successfully? They conclude that myths will be abandoned if adherents experience deprivation under it and that a new myth will be presented and be accepted. Again, by focusing on a specific phenomenon, like myths, it might be possible to develop an understanding of similarities and differences in myth structures and thereby further the comparative studies of political systems or administrative structures or functions.

One of the methods proposed by RADIR for the comparative study of the symbols which make up a myth is latent structure

30 Harold D. Lasswell, Daniel Lerner, and C. Easton Rothwell, *The Comparative Study of Elites: An Introduction and Bibliography* (Hoover Institute Studies, Series B: Elites, No. 1; Stanford, 1952); and Harold D. Lasswell, Daniel Lerner, and Ithiel de Sola Pool, *The Comparative Study of Symbols: An Introduction* (Hoover Institute Studies, Series C: Symbols, No. 1; Stanford, 1952).

analysis, which is described as "a method for solving the problem of inference from manifest (observed) data to latent structures (nonobserved continua)."[31] The usefulness of this technique for comparative study has been illustrated recently by Lerner in the study of the transition process in the Middle East, in which the countries of this region were ranked "traditional" to "transitional" to "modern" based on findings collected through survey research and subjected to latent structure analysis.[32] This is a tool which might easily be used for comparative study of bureaucratic systems of different countries and cultures, or even for comparing different elements within the same bureaucratic system. . . .

Finally, attention should be called to some efforts at comparative studies using reference group analysis.[33] Sociologists and social psychologists have realized that for a fuller understanding of much of social behavior, one requires a knowledge of the process through which men relate themselves to groups toward whose values they refer their own behavior, and with whom they compare themselves in judging their own situation. This method was used extensively in the studies of the American soldier in the Second World War,[34] but it has also been used to study actions of groups in a number of national communities.[35] Again, one can make no extravagant claims for reference group analysis as a tool in comparative studies, but this tool will certainly be directly applicable to concrete research problems in administration. . . .

31 Lasswell *et al., Comparative Study of Symbols,* p. 75.

32 Lerner, *op. cit.,* reproduces the questionnaire which was administered in the field (Appendix A, pp. 415–433), and provides a methodological statement concerning the use of latent structure analysis (Appendix C, pp. 438–446).

33 Seymour Martin Lipset and Martin Trow, "Reference Group Theory and Trade Union Wage Policy," in *Common Frontiers of the Social Sciences* by Mirra Komarovsky, ed. (Glencoe, 1957), p. 394.

34 Samuel A. Stouffer *et al, The American Soldier* (2 vols.; Princeton, 1949).

35 See for example the study of differential strike rates in the United States, Canada, Sweden, and Great Britain, in Arthur M. Ross and Donald Irwin, Strike Experience in Five Countries, 1927–1947: An Interpretation, *Industrial and Labor Relations Review,* 4 (1951), 323–343, reported in Lipset and Trow, *op. cit.,* p. 401.

Comparative politics and comparative administration

It should be immediately apparent that there is a much closer connection between theory and practice in the "political culture" schemes and some of the other techniques which have been examined in the preceding section than in the "general system" approach. But even here the researcher in comparative administration might insist that he has not been furnished with any tools which will aid him directly. If this analysis seems to be harsh on the theorists, this has not been caused by a personal bias in favor of empirical research and against "general system" theorizing. Nevertheless, it seems that in recent years the model builders either have had no concern with the implementation of their models for research in the field or have constructed models which helped them directly in working with particular political systems but were of little help to other researchers dealing with other societies or political systems. On the other hand, the builders of narrow-gauge models usually dealt with only a single country or political culture. Neither method seemed to produce either data, analyses, or concepts that enriched the general methodological arsenal of comparative study.

There are essentially three criticisms which can be directed against the "general system" models: (1) Their connection with empirical research is very remote, and it is often very difficult to establish this connection at all. (2) Although the "general system" models ought to be based on a general theory of politics, we do not have such a theory at the present time. Apter, for example, establishes three dimensions in his model but finds that it is almost impossible to keep the three separate, even for analytical purposes. It would seem the difficulties he encounters stem directly from the lack of a general theory of politics without which the relationship between these three dimensions (stratification, groups, and government) cannot be defined and dealt with satisfactorily. (3) One of the chief drawbacks of the general system model is the one identified by Francis X. Sutton: the impossibility of approaching all societies with a single conceptualization about social systems. Following Sutton, one wonders whether a model developed for the comparative study of primitive African political systems, as was Apter's, will prove appropriate for western Europe.

But the "general system" models are not totally lacking in utility for research. Their chief attraction is this: given the rapid movement towards industrialization and modernization in many parts of the world, it is conceivable that in the future the political systems of Western and non-Western societies will have more in common than they had in the past. In the future a single model of a society may yield more useful and more nearly valid results in social research than it does at present.

The "general system" model most relevant for comparative administration is Easton's input-output scheme. It helps us to be aware of the dual character of the administration as both producer and consumer, as most directly concerned with sending out streams of satisfaction, and also with collecting inputs, both for its own use and for processing them into outputs needed by society to keep the system going. The European area specialist in particular has a tendency to take for granted the "neutral" role of the bureaucracy. It would seem that his having to analyze a European administrative system on the basis of an input-output model would force him to point out aspects of bureaucracy usually neglected in the analysis of European public administration.

Leaving aside Easton's input-output proposal, the schematic presentation of the major dimensions of the other four "general system" models presented shows that they all center around a very small number of very general categories. A developmental analysis indicates further that power and decision making (social stratification and government, respectively, in Apter), are dimensions present in all four models, including Macridis' second model, where "authority and purposes" combine ideology and power of his earlier model. The last two models, however, have eliminated specific references to ideology and have instead added "groups" as a dimension of their comparative schemes, acknowledging the growing impact of interest-group analysis in comparative politics. Even Macridis, who denies that there exists a group theory of politics, nevertheless makes interest-group configuration one of the major elements of his most recent model. The arrival of interest groups on the comparative politics scene has a twofold importance for comparative administration. First, it calls attention to the formal and informal roles of interest groups in the administrative process, and, secondly, it facilitates treating the bureaucracy or administration itself as an interest group, participating with other groups in the decision-making process, or recognizing it as a major element of the stratification system.[36]

This schematic presentation also serves to underline the very general character of the "general system" models. "Power," "decision making," "social stratification" are categories which can do little beyond providing a basic orientation for research. The differences between cultures, or within the same culture between national societies, will, in practice, be very great. The comparative researcher, relying only on these conceptual tools but unfamiliar with the specific cultures or national societies (or tribal systems, as in Africa), will simply not know where to find the determinants of administrative behavior or the administrative process.

The student in comparative administration should not be permitted, however, to bypass this "general system" model literature. In addition to some of the specific advantages indicated above, it will help him become more sensitive to some of the fundamentally similar traits of all social systems and social forces.

One of the principal drawbacks of the "political culture" approach, apart from the previously mentioned tendencies to use oversimplified categories like "Western" and "non-Western," is that these classificatory schemes are essentially static and make no allowance for social or other forms of change. For example, there is considerable evidence that in some of the continental European political systems, the modernized, industrialized segment is becoming the predominant element, pushing the preindustrial and older middle-class components into the background. As a result a profound change in the form and content of politics is in

[36] Macridis, "Interest Groups and the Political System in Comparative Analysis," sec. II, pp. 6–15. LaPalombara is even more outspoken: ". . . a general interest group theory does not exist, and . . . it is necessary to examine comparatively some middle-range propositions about interest groups in order to ascertain if the interest-group focus has any utility at all for the construction of a general theory of politics" (*op. cit.*, p. 30).

progress in these countries. As the old cleavages disappear, and it has been suggested that they have begun to disappear in France, the bureaucracy, once one of the participants in the conflict between major camps or "spiritual families," will become less a contender in, and object of, political conflict and more a neutral instrument serving a higher-consensus society. Finally, the more detailed the classification of political cultures and the more nearly it fits many existing societies, the less the scheme will serve as a vehicle for generalization based on evidence from a wide variety of sources. Once all bureaucracies have been analyzed in a manner that highlights their unique qualities, the chance for comparisons along some major dimensions will probably have been lost.

The advantages of the "political culture" schemes, however, outweigh their shortcomings: they meet the need for a classification of societies; they are much easier to make operational, though not all the difficulties of this process have been solved; and by defining some of the basic units of the political system and then relating them to the broader political culture, they enable the researcher to investigate the varieties of "roles" and show how these vary from one political culture to another. In this way the researcher remains continually aware of the specific social matrix in which these political institutions and processes operate, and it is this awareness that is lacking in the "general system" schemes and that is responsible for their seeming so abstract to the researcher.

Lipset suggests that it is possible to define certain aspects of a social system in theoretical terms and compare them with similar aspects in other social systems. However, one must always realize that

> complex characteristics of a total system have multivariate causation, and also multivariate consequence, insofar as the characteristics have some degree of autonomy within the system. Bureaucracy and urbanization, as well as democracy, have many causes and consequences. . . . Thus, in a multivariate system, the focus may be upon any element, and its conditions and consequences may be stated without the implication that we have arrived at a complete theory.[37]

[37] Lipset, "Some Social Requisites of Democracy," *op. cit.*, p. 105.

For example, Sutton's analysis of the Thai bureaucracy showed that there was no single factor "causing" the attitudes of Thai bureaucrats.[38]

In his attempt to construct a comparative model for the study of politics, Apter put his finger squarely on the central problem when he insisted that he was not concerned with the basic properties of a system qua system but with the treatment of empirical systems in general through the comparative observation of empirical systems in particular. In short, he found that handling comparative data at the macroscopic level was a difficult task.[39] On the other hand, the more restricted the model becomes, the more difficult it is to make generally valid observations from it. Furthermore, we can set up narrow-gauge problems only if we already have a well-developed knowledge about several of the political systems under scrutiny—in short, if we already know what we are trying to find out. Is there no way out of this dilemma at the present time?

The author thinks there is. Today the researcher in comparative administration and comparative politics will find a variety of tools which will serve him well if he uses them properly. "General system" models will help clarify certain fundamental traits of social systems but will not yield specific operational concepts for the comparative study of personnel systems and fiscal management. "Political culture" schemes, if their classification is intelligently constructed and based on accurate and reasonably up-to-date information, can be made directly applicable to comparative studies in politics and administration. They should prove especially valuable in formulating inquiries into the problem of bureaucratic responsibility and control. Some of the possible uses for the other tools, mentioned here all too briefly, have already been indicated. There can no longer be any excuse for adding to our already bulging store of unusable and useless data by disregarding the array of methodological aids for research available to us today.

38 Sutton, *op. cit., passim.*

39 *Op. cit.*, p. 222, n. 4.

The Variety of Models

DWIGHT WALDO
University of California at Berkeley

THE QUESTIONS THAT I want to raise in this discussion are these: What models—or *analogies* or *idioms*—have been used in the study of administration, especially *public* administration? What are the typical *products, uses,* and *limitations* of the various analogies and idioms? To what extent are various models interchangeable or uniquely insightful? Are there useful models yet undiscovered? Note that I say I want to *raise* these questions; I do not claim to lay them at rest.

I begin with a reference to a fable and a book in philosophy. The fable is the old, familiar one of the six blind men of Indostan. You will recall that these six men not only touched various parts of the elephant, but interpreted what they touched in terms of previous concepts, so that the "elephant" became assimilated to quite different things: a wall, a spear, a snake, a tree, a fan and a rope. To put the same idea in the words of an artist friend, "The eye is blind to what the mind does not see." In this case, the hand was blind to what the mind did not see.

The book in philosophy to which I refer is *World Hypotheses; A Study in Evidence,* by my colleague Stephen Pepper. The thesis of the book is that all conceptions of nature or reality or the universe that have been spawned by philosophers since the beginning of time are reducible to a few basic "models." All philosophic systems that are "intellectually respectable," for which there is reasonable evidence, can be classified under one or

Reprinted from Dwight Waldo, *Perspectives on Administration* (University, Alabama: University of Alabama Press, 1956), pp. 26–49, by permission.

more of four headings, namely: Formism, Mechanism, Contextualism, and Organicism.

These are "hypotheses" about the nature of things, as the title of the book indicates, but they are hypotheses with roots, so to speak—not fashioned from nothing or found in dreams, but arising out of concrete experience.

In a chapter on "Root Metaphors," Pepper develops what he calls a root metaphor theory and method. Philosophies or world hypotheses are generated analogically, he holds. "The method in principle seems to be this: A man desiring to understand the world looks about for a clue to its comprehension. He pitches upon some area of common sense fact and tries to see if he cannot understand other areas in terms of this one. This original area becomes then his basic analogy or root metaphor."

World Hypotheses is a technical treatise in philosophy, and it is not germane to explore it further. I have referred to it only because in a very rough way it is my own model for what I want to do. I want to see what "root metaphors" have been used in exploring and explaining the phenomena of administration. My presumption or thesis is that most, or at least much, learning is by analogy; that we proceed from known to unknown, and conceptualize the unknown in terms of the known. Certainly there are limitations to this presumption if it is pushed too far. But it could be buttressed by much data from psychology; perceptions made meaningful by conceptions, particulars falling within *Gestalten,* and so forth.

As I proceed I am going to cast my net wide. Probably I shall be wrong in some of my facts or implications. I can only hope that the results in terms of perspectives or insights will outweight the sins committed. Also, the "models" I profess to see are not all on the same level of generality. Some of them apply to all of administration, some only to parts of administration, some view one type of administration in the mirror of another, some apply to the *study* and others to the *practice* of administration. This is a rough "first time over." Refinement can come—if the approach has any merit—later.

It is logically or historically fit to begin with *law as a model,* with public administration viewed as, or through, a legal system. Thus viewed, administration appears primarily as a complex of legal norms or framework of rights and obligations, and when one "studies administration" what he focuses upon is an official definition of proper relationships between persons or bodies within the system proper, and between persons and bodies within the system and those outside. The "law proper" and court systems are the concrete images in such a person's mind when he approaches administration.

This is an old and familiar perspective or model. It is the perspective that predominates in modern Western Europe—with, of course, differing national emphasis. It is a perspective that extends beyond modern Western Europe, to ancient Rome and modern Japan, for example.

It is a perspective familiar also in the United States, in many ways and to many people. But anyone who is familiar with the discipline of public administration knows that the literature of the discipline is unsympathetic to the legal perspective. Public administration as a discipline begins, one might say, by and with a repudiation of the legal perspective. The preface of the first textbook—White's first edition—states: "The book . . . assumes that the study of administration should start from the base of management rather than the foundations of law, and is therefore more absorbed in the affairs of the American Management Association than in the decisions of courts."

This was our Declaration of Independence. But the *War* of Independence is yet to be won. Perhaps it never will be and perhaps even it never should be. Administration in a constitutioned. On the current American scene, lawyers and public inevitably carried on in the context of "oughts" officially sanctioned. On the current American scene, lawyers and public administrationists offer competing perspectives and skills. They compete as individuals and professional groups for status and rewards, in a way I always think of as comparable to the Seventeenth Century struggle in England between common-law lawyers and prerogative-law lawyers. A recent bitter exchange in the *American Political Science Review,* which many of you would have noted, was another engagement in the continuing struggle.

This is not the place to explore all that is involved in the lawyer-public administrationist controversy, but I will say parenthetically that I wish there were more attention given to the matter. I have the impression that the issues are very important, that partisanship on both sides is understandable but unfortunate. Of course I feel that lawyers can learn a great deal from public administration. But I wonder if public administration is not now mature and strong enough to pay more attention to legal aspects of administration.

Probably the most pervasive and important model in American administrative study in the Twentieth Century is the *machine model*. This cannot be conclusively demonstrated; in developing the case much evidence of a merely circumstantial nature must be accepted. But altogether the case is impressive.

There is first of all the fact that in the literature of administration there is considerable mechanical metaphor. This is particularly true of the early literature. Chapter Three of White's first edition was entitled, "The Administrative Machine," and Willoughby's 1927 textbook has a section labeled, "The Administrative Branch as a Single Piece of Administrative Mechanism." Back of these textbooks stands the Scientific Management movement, and the literature of this movement was sometimes heavy with mechanical metaphor. See, for example, the works of Harrington Emerson.

Back of the Scientific Management movement, in turn, was a cultural orientation toward the machine. A good case can be made that the characteristic "root metaphor" of the modern period is the machine. I refer to the popularization of the Cartesian-Newtonian conception of the universe as a machine. Following this thought forward one would recognize that the machine model itself changes with time, especially with Twentieth Century developments in physics. These new developments are reflected in some recent writings, particularly those of Herbert Simon. But the older notions of the universe-as-a-clockworks, or the universe-of-billiard-ball-atoms, form important substrata for much thought.

At a different level, one can say of modern man that he is culturally deeply affected by day-to-day living in intimate association with actual machinery. And Americans are probably most deeply affected in this manner. It presumably will not escape the notice of the historians of the future that the Scientific Management movement in the United States arose at the same time as the "arrival" of the internal combustion engine and the extensive mechanization of daily living. My point is that the importance of the machine model is by no means measured solely in the amount of machine metaphor. What is assumed may be more important than what is made explicit.

The case can be argued at length. I should hold, for example, that the concept of *efficiency,* which is at or near the center of administrative study, is a product of the machine. Achieving efficiency in administration is conceived analogously to achieving efficiency in machine performance. There must be good design—organization charts equal blueprints—parts must be adjusted properly one to another; friction must be reduced; power loss prevented, and so forth.

There is much less use of *organic analogy* than of mechanical. But we can still find many examples of its use. Mary Parker Follett, for example, made use of organic language and analogies rather often. Remember also the development by John Gaus in a previous lecture in this series of the idea of the ecology of organization; an attempt to see organizations in relation to their environment is certainly evident among current trends. Look also at the introductory section of Kenneth Boulding's *The Organizational Revolution,* where there is use of ecological analogy in attempting to account for the lush growth of organization during recent decades.

One of the most frequent themes in the early literature of the public administration movement was that *business administration provides a desirable model for public administration.* In fact, the slogan "More business in government" reached far beyond the public administration movement. As is generally recognized at this point, not only were business tools and techniques imported into government administration; business ethics and philosophy had an impact.

Quotations illustrating the business impact could be multiplied. Two will suffice. One is from Woodrow Wilson's famous 1887 essay; "The field of administration is a field of business." The other is from William Redfield's *With Congress and Cabinet,* and was quoted approvingly in White's first edition: "Do you ask just what government departments are? I reply that in general they are great business establishments running factories, buying goods, distributing products, employing workmen of many kinds, engaged in building, navigating, traveling, research, publication, farming, instruction, and in almost every kind of production activity."

It is interesting to note that Redfield includes research, farming and instruction among "business" activities. This well illustrates the theme that ours is a "business civilization." Because we are so immersed in it, it takes an effort of imagination to appreciate the pervasiveness and significance of the business ethos; but unless you do this you will not understand the rise of administrative study in the United States. Incidentally, however, the influence between business and government administration is not all one way. Someone could do us a significant service by tracing out the impact of public administration on business administration. To what extent, for example, is the growing concept of the public responsibilities of big business a result of diffusion from public administration?

Of course, during the past generation the application of the business model to public administration has greatly declined. This can be attributed to many things—primarily to the loss of prestige suffered by business during the Great Depression and to the opportunities offered public administrationists by the New Deal. But the business model is still used, and in some quarters is still popular—despite much writing in denial of its desirability or its applicability. It should be noted again, too, in order to make the story complete even in rough outline, that the business model itself has undergone great change. From business practices and ideology of the 1880's to those of the 1950's is a far cry indeed; compare the spirit of Taylor's *Scientific Management* with that of a recent issue of *Fortune*. Perhaps one should guess—thinking of Elton Mayo and the Harvard Business School—not that the business model is less influential, but that the model has changed.

A final thought under this heading: It seems to me that those engaged in the study of comparative administration, and especially those engaged in technical assistance, might find the significance of the business model in America to be very great in exploring differences and compatibilities. Even in other Western countries one thinks of as having had a significant or even typical capitalist development, there is nothing closely comparable to the many business influences and developments of the past hundred, and particularly the past fifty, years.

In business administration, one type of administration served as the model for another. I turn briefly now to *military administration* as a model; in this case one type of "public" administration serves as the model for another. What I want to call attention to is the fascination with military administration of the early leaders of the public administration movement, and what, altogether, is an impressive amount of carry-over in terminology and concepts.

The German Army, before and during World War I, was regarded as one of the administrative wonders of the world, and Charles A. Beard and others testified to its interest to early students. "Staff and line" terminology is military in origin, and staff concepts owe much specifically to the German General Staff. Nor is the military influence limited to the pre-World War I period. Go back and examine Mooney and Riley's influential *Onward Industry!* Or for that matter, note the frequent references to the military in Gulick and Urwick's *Papers on the Science of Administration.*

In a different vein, Max Weber's famous conceptualization of bureaucracy owes a great deal to the military model. It is probably not an accident that Weber was thoroughly familiar at first hand with the Prussian military; the Prussian army probably came nearer to fitting the ideal-typical criteria for bureaucratic organization than any other actual organization. And of course it should be remembered that, historically speaking, civil and military bureaucracies grew up as adjuncts one of the other in modern states. There is food for thought in the idea that perhaps more than we know our administrative theories and mores are military in origin; or, put in another spirit, that out of the sweat and blood of forgotten multitudes of soldiers has been distilled for us priceless knowledge about co-operative enterprise.

Religious organizations, especially the Catholic Church, have provided some students with a perspective from which to view administration. Mooney and Riley, for example, gave religious administration considerable attention; and in *The Functions of the Executive* Barnard finds in the perdurance of the

Catholic Church the supreme example of administrative efficiency. Incidentally, serious historical and scientific study of the administration of the Church remains to be done, to my knowledge. It is one of the things that everyone talks about but nobody does.

Incidentally also, I can't forbear referring to Earl Latham's provocative essay on "Hierarchy and Hieratics." In this case theology is taken as the model—in a satirical vein—and administrative theory is viewed as a species of theology, rather than as science.

Some writers have viewed administration and administrative study from the *perspective of ideology,* either in the specifically Marxian or in the more general sense. J. Donald Kingsley's *Representative Bureaucracy* is a highly provocative study, from a framework at least loosely Marxian, of the neutrality of the British Civil Service. Here the theme is developed that this civil service is "neutral" only because of and with respect to its middle-class milieu. If you will forgive me the reference, my own *The Administrative State* is an attempt to view the literature of the public administration movement against the backdrop of a larger intellectual history. Attention is called also to a different approach: to the attacks of both Elton Mayo and Chester Barnard upon what they regard as pernicious ideologies obstructing a scientific approach to the study, or a constructive approach to the practice, of administration.

Another perspective is provided by *politics.* I refer here to the evaporation of the old distinction between "politics" and "administration," and the conscious or unconscious adoption in administrative study of conceptual tools in use in other areas of political science. The plural "tools" is used because there are various ways in which "politics" can be conceived, and to think of the phenomena of administration to *be* politics, or as *interfused* with politics, is really to suggest various perspectives.

The focus can be placed upon the activities of recognized political figures—mayors, legislators, governors, and so forth—as they affect administration; and in doing so, common-sense concepts and familiar descriptive methods may be used. Or there may be analysis of pressure group tactics in influencing administration, or of some aspect of "office politics." Or there may be very elaborate use of the terminology and tools of recent behavioral science. In this latter case "politics" is likely to be rewritten as "power."

The "politicizing" of administration could be documented at great length, but I cite only two examples. One is the Inter-University Case Program, which has published a large number of cases in which the political or power aspects are prominent. The other is the writings of Paul Appleby, which not only portray politics-in-administration, and analyze the political process in administration, but present a philosophy of the politics of administration in a democratic society.

Other writers have viewed administration through the *spectacles of economics.* I have reference here to the analogies, more or less conscious and explicit, between economic systems and administrative systems. A concrete administrative system may be viewed as a sort of miniature economy; and in such expressions as "the economy of incentives," both the concepts and the terminology of economic science make their appearance.

Use of the perspective of economics has been carefully argued and must be accorded very respectful attention. It is the central theme, I should say, of Chester Barnard's *The Functions of the Executive;* and Herbert Simon's *Administrative Behavior* not only acknowledges indebtedness to Barnard but explicitly proposes the use of additional concepts from economics in conceptualizing administrative processes. More recently the economist Kenneth Boulding, in *The Organizational Revolution,* has argued that the conceptual apparatus of economics be imported wholesale into organizational analysis.

Some view administration through the lens of *society.* To them an administrative system is a social system, a complex of social-psychological phenomena. In general, there are two varieties of this perspective, two channels of influence. One arises from and is identified with the Western Electric experiments at Hawthorne in the late twenties and early thirties, and with the name and writings of Elton Mayo and his associates, particularly at the Harvard Business School. The revelation that there are important social aspects of administration should perhaps be capitalized—REVELATION—so impressive and influential were the Hawthorne findings in some quarters.

The other source of the social perspective has been sociologists and social psychologists. There were, to be sure, competent people identified with these disciplines connected with the Hawthorne experiments. But what I mean to make clear is that there are various students—Reinhard Bendix, Philip Selznick, and Robert Merton, for example—who have used and contributed to a "social" perspective without being associated in any way with the Hawthorne experiments. In fact, what we are dealing with under the broad heading of social perspective is a wide-ranging variety of models; nearly all the concepts and tools of sociology, social psychology and cultural anthropology become relevant to administrative study if the premise is accepted that an administrative system is a social system.

At the risk of over-simplification and misunderstanding, I want to say a word about the relationship of the social perspective to the mechanical and the organic. I suggest that in a sense it stands between the two. The historical significance of the Hawthorne Revelation was that it made apparent to many whose approach to administration was strongly mechanical, in the spirit of the Scientific Management movement, that there are important social and—loosely—organic aspects of administrative phenomena. A merit of the social perspective is that it recognizes the non-rational, spontaneous, and adaptive aspects of collective human behavior without committing the "organismic fallacy" or retreating to a Burkean position that *only* the "natural" is possible or legitimate. In short, administrative phenomena have some qualities better understood by an organic rather than a mechanical perspective, but both need to be qualified.

Art provides another model or perspective. I refer to the considerable amount of argument to the effect that the practice of administration is properly conceived as an artistic performance, not as a matter of executing scientific formulae. An analogy that has been used—though I cannot identify its source—is between an administrator and the conductor of an orchestra: each takes many people of diverse talents and functions, and by artistic skill creates something that is greater than a sum of the parts. Somewhat the same thought was conveyed by the cover of the old *Public Administration Review,* published at Syracuse: a picture of an administrator sitting at his desk, and, in a semi-circle upon his desk, batteries of telephones with lines running to a variety of enterprises, symbolized in little vignettes around the edge of the cover.

Ordway Tead is prominent among those who have called upon the art analogy, as, indeed, the title *The Art of Administration* suggests. To quote a sentence: "Administration is, in short, a fine art because it summons an imposing body of special talents on behalf of a collaborative creation which is integral to the conduct of civilized living today."

Opposed to art as a model is, of course, *science as a model.* For every one who has argued that artistic creation is the meaningful analogy, a dozen have argued in our profesional literature that the administrative study or practice is or ought to be a science. Thus Woodrow Wilson, Charles Beard, W. F. Willoughby, Luther Gulick, Herbert Simon, and many others. The general idea is of course a familiar one and need not be labored. I will only note that the matter becomes very complicated when pursued, for notions of science have changed, as a perusal of writers from Wilson to Simon will demonstrate. Perhaps *mathematics* as a perspective or model should be mentioned in this connection, for Simon has experimented in stating organizational theory in symbolic or mathematical form, and if I judge some of the social science currents correctly we shall be seeing more of this type of endeavor.

Ethics is still another perspective. A few writers have emphasized the element of moral choice, as against calculation of efficient means, in administrative decision-making; or the important role of the administrative process as a whole in the moral life of the community. Wayne A. R. Leys' *Ethics for Policy Decisions* is prominent among the first type, and Paul Appleby's *Morality and Administration* is prominent among the second.

Now, as I said at the beginning, I realize that all of what I have been calling models or perspectives are not at the same level of generality, importance, and so forth. The fourteen I have enumerated are patently heterogeneous and widely varying in the importance of their roles in administrative study. The list could be extended at some length, and a few more of the possibilities can be indicated.

In some recent cases the model seems to be a *communica-*

tions system. Communications is currently a subject of growing interest, a center of inter-disciplinary work, and this wave of interest and growing knowledge is reflected in various ways in administrative study. There is an important element of the communications approach in Barnard, in Simon, and in Boulding. It can be applied in various ways and at different levels; for example, with the focus upon mechanical aids to communication, upon semantic problems in communication, or upon the psychic mechanisms involved. In a thesis now being written by one of my students, organizations are viewed as structures to minimize or stabilize anxiety—in the broad psychological meaning of anxiety—with the communications system of organizations transmitting signals by which anxieties are regulated or adjusted.

The *brain* or *"creative mind"* can serve as a model. I refer here, for example, to Graham Wallas' distinction between "will" and "thought" organizations and his approach to the civil service as a problem in getting it to act as a thought organization—to get "new ideas" or do "creative thinking." Mary Parker Follett also comes to mind in this connection, because of her Quakerish sense of "creation" through collaborative effort. And there are also Norton Long's recent essays on how the getting and sifting of new ideas can be "built into" administration.

It seems to me that if we are serious about abandoning the politics-administration distinction—if we are serious about policy being "made" in administration—this line of inquiry needs to be taken very seriously. I would, incidentally, distinguish this conception of "creative mind" from that of "goal seeking" or "problem solving." That is to say, it is rather common to conceptualize the administrative apparatus as a sort of calculating machine which solves problems that are fed into it, but this is essentially the politics-administration idea. The point is that some have also thought of the administrative apparatus as *devising* and *setting* problems.

Finally, *system* might be said to be the model in some cases. Many of the models that have been cited are systems; thus machines, organisms and economies are systems. So in a sense this is a cross-classification or master model into which many models fit. But attention is called to a trend in social science to turn attention to the *idea* of system, or the *system-as-such*. There has developed a body of doctrine called systems theory, or general systems theory, centered around the postulate that there are universal aspects of systems, wherever they are found—for example, in a machine, an organism, an economy, or an organization. The leading concepts of systems theory find expression in such terms as homeostasis, input-output system, boundary-maintaining system, feed-back mechanisms, and so forth.

One who has been sensitized to systems theory can find a great deal of it in our literature—there are important elements of it in Barnard and Simon—and it is on the increase. But it is so far almost entirely covert; that is, some of the essential ideas are there in the idiom of some model named above, but the idea of system theory "in general" is not expounded. One exception occurs to me. This is in Boulding's *The Organizational Revolution*. Here the general theory and its putative applicability to organizations are made overt.

So much for my catalog of models. Now for a few observations and conclusions.

It is obvious that very often one model or idiom can be translated into another with approximate exactness. This was just indicated in the discussion of systems theory writers. If one is concerned with the idea that organizations or administrative systems tend toward an equilibrium, or at least have "equilibrating mechanisms" in normal course, this idea can be developed and expressed in the language either of the machine or of the organism. Or it can be developed and expressed in the language of economics, since so much of economic theory views economic phenomena as equilibrating systems. Or it can be developed in the more or less special language of systems theory, using terms such as receptor, transmitter, and effector.

In cases in which there is interchangeability of model, three criteria would appear relevant to the model selected. One pertains to the student and his experience and motives. Obviously, motivation is important, and if past interests and activities can provide incentive and meaning in studying administration, there is much to be said for choosing the model to suit the student. Another criterion in choosing the model is precision, or the exact adaptability to the task. If systems theory provides more precise tools *which are useful* it would be folly not to use them, though other theory provides similar tools. A third criterion is communicability. Not only the experience and motives of the researcher, writer or teacher must be considered, but the experience and motives of those to whom administrative knowledge is to be communicated. Models have pedagogical as well as heuristic functions.

Although there is a considerable area of interchangeability among models, there is also a considerable, and probably larger, area of non-interchangeability. In many cases, certainly, the choice of model is decisive; that is to say, determinative of the type of questions asked and the answers found. This is indicated, for example, in the historic and continuing conflict between the "legal" and the "management" approaches to administration. Perhaps a fruitful approach to resolving this conflict, or making it more bearable and beneficial, would be to search for models which do not pose the sharp alternatives of traditional ones. One which might possibly serve this purpose has not been mentioned, although it has been appearing rather frequently in social science literature: *the medical model.* Not a few social scientists think of their proper role as analogous to that of the medical scientist or physician—or psychiatrist; to wit, the producing and maintaining of "normal" or "mature" individuals in a "healthy" society. This is a perspective congenial to American jurisprudence in the Twentieth Century, and one that public administrationists might find agreeable. I do not want to be understood as arguing for this development, however, as I personally believe that the medical model presents very thorny ethical and philosophical problems.

Other examples of conflicts between models can be cited. For example, if one approaches public administration with a determination to reshape it in the image of business, he is hardly likely to be concerned with structuring it to perform the function of "creative mind." Or perhaps in this case it would depend upon which business model were chosen. But clearly, if one thinks of the administrator as creative in the same sense that an artist at an easel is creative, then he is unlikely to present to us as the fruit of his interest a set of mathematical formulae.

To illustrate how choice of models sets questions and thus dictates answers, let me indicate what may be an important limitation of the machine model. If one thinks in machine terms, he quite naturally thinks a problem posed is the increase of efficiency by the reduction of friction. The idea that friction in the form of conflict may be *good*—that is to say, serve desirable social purposes—is eliminated by definition, so to speak. But this is a respectable notion. I refer, for example, to Peter Drucker, Clark Kerr, and others, who have held that the proper function of a labor union is to oppose management, not to agree with it—that social ends are served by friction that in the opinion of most people is socially wasteful, if not directly harmful. Mary Parker Follett has advanced the notion of "constructive conflict," but she has been almost alone among American writers on administration in this respect. Her reliance upon the biological instead of the mechanical model is probably significant in accounting for her atypical position.

My own point of view is that since administration is so large a subject, and still in many ways so dark, we should open upon it all the windows we can find; that all models and idioms have their virtues—and their vices; that as we proceed we exercise as much intelligence and good will as we can command in determining what any particular model can or cannot do for us.

Comparisons of Phenomena

JAMES D. THOMPSON, PETER B. HAMMOND, ROBERT W. HAWKES, BUFORD H. JUNKER, and ARTHUR TUDEN
University of Pittsburgh

THE STUDY OF comparable phenomena—similar yet somehow different—is indispensable in the search for variables, their range of variation, and the consequences of those variations.

Reprinted from James D. Thompson (ed.), *Comparative Studies in Administration* (Pittsburgh: University of Pittsburgh Press, 1959), pp. 8–14, by permission.

The dominant schools of administration have established curricula and research programs on the assumption that each field of administration rests on unique elements, on constants and variables which are not merely different in degree from one field to another but are different in kind. The challenge to this position has come from those who assert that administration, in whatever context, is basically the same phenomenon. They have advanced a series of abstract models or theories of administration, management, organization, decision-making and communication. The comparative approach seems to be the most promising way of settling this issue. If in fact there are important similarities in the several types of administration, comparisons should reveal them. Yet to the extent that the more abstract formulations may conceal important variations, comparison should act as a correcting factor.

This raises the important question of what is to be compared. For reasons which are more accidental than logical, "comparative public administration" has been synonymous with cross-cultural or cross-national studies of administration, and "comparative business administration" has referred to business outside of the United States, or to the foreign operations of American firms. While the cultural dimension undoubtedly is essential to our understanding of administration, as our earlier discussion of environments makes clear, the comparative study of administration cannot be limited to cultural comparison alone.

The three functions of administration indicated earlier[1]—having to do with organizational structure, organizational purposes, and organizational exchanges with the environment—are appropriate subjects for comparison. Each of these is subject to variation or difference and thus is amenable to comparative research and conceptualization. If organizations differ in structure, we must seek to understand why this occurs and how it affects the contexts of administration. If organizations differ in purposes, we must examine the effects of purposes on other aspects of administration. If organizations operate in different kinds of environments, we must learn how environments impinge on and shape organizations, administrative functions, and administrative processes.

[1] See p. 7 of original. [N.R.]

Another urgent task at this stage in the development of administrative science lies at the conceptual level. Present conceptions of the relevant variables allow only crude bases for differentiation. If organizational exchange with the environment is an important aspect of administration, we can compare this in differing contexts only to the extent that we can conceive of differences among environments and differences of exchange relationships. But as yet there is no adequate "typology of environments," no authoritative catalog of exchange relationships which would permit us to classify with complete confidence two instances as similar or different. If organizational structure is an important aspect of administration, we need concepts which will allow the sorting out and classifying of specific cases. Here we have several varieties of concepts, but none which we can embrace with assurance. And finally, we lack a conceptual framework for dealing with organizational goals or purposes.

These problems will require a great deal of effort before they are solved. It is significant, however, that the mere statement of administration in comparative terms focuses attention on these weaknesses of our present conceptual equipment.

Comparison of theories

The comparison of phenomena provides only a partial solution to our problems. The comparison of *alternative theories* or models in reflection against the same phenomena or pattern can mark the turning points in the development of administrative science.

Opportunities to make the crucial observations which differentiate weaker from more powerful theories do not occur frequently, but we must be alert to them when they do. Such opportunities will become more frequent as our theories become more general, hence more abstract. The less abstract theories seldom overlap each other, so they do not offer competing predictions about what will occur in the same kind of situations.

The two aspects of comparison go hand-in-hand. Studies of comparable phenomena can lead to greater generalization by way of abstraction, and this in turn makes possible the comparison of competing theories.

THE IMPORTANCE OF PROCESS. Administration was defined by what it *does,* by the functions it appears to perform or the requirements it seems to satisfy. Such a definition points to the importance of *identifying patterns* of administrative action and of *discovering their association* with the functions of administration.

The comparative approach is indispensable for uncovering the states or outcomes which are associated with particular patterns of administrative action. Administrative science cannot, however, rest with the discovery of association or correlation. Ultimately, we believe, the study of administrative processes—of *how* particular patterns bring about particular functional consequences—will be essential, and vice versa.

Administration is a dynamic phenomenon, and it is imperative that the strategy employed for investigating it gives assurance of focusing on dynamics rather than statics. Reliance on correlation or association—useful in providing clues—does not provide that assurance, as experience has demonstrated repeatedly in the social sciences.

There is, for example, the trap of spurious correlation, whereby two events appear to be associated but in fact have no connection or are connected only by being associated with still a third event. There is the danger of projecting into correlation an element of inevitability, and thereby assuming a linear, evolutionary development rather than a dynamic development. There is the ever-present possibility of overlooking two-way interaction of variables, or "feed-back loops," and thus obtaining a most distorted set of half-truths about administration. There is the danger, which has plagued many of the social sciences in their recent history, of "single-factor" analysis, which assumes that a particular consequence results from one variable when in fact a complex pattern of variables is responsible for that consequence.

A focus on administrative processes seems to offer the best assurance against the temptation to be content with association, and reduces our reliance on the particular genius of the investigator. In the definitional context already advanced, those *pat-*

terned sequences of behavior which bring about, maintain, or curtail organizational structure would constitute an administrative process. Likewise, those *sets of behavior* related to establishing, maintaining, or dropping organizational purposes constitute an administrative process. The *patterned sequences of behavior* which provide or deny modes of interaction with relevant environments would also constitute an administrative process. In each case, the crucial question is *how* one pattern of behavior leads to another pattern of behavior, and so on through a chain until a functional requirement is satisfied.

If the history of other sciences has a lesson for us, it warns that sequences of activity should be conceived neither as random nor as inevitably determined. Organizations and those who administer them are not free agents, nor are they automatons who respond automatically to forces in a field. Within the limits established by reality, alternatives, choice points, or "breaching" points are presented to organizations.

We have only vague notions about the frequency and the nature of these choice points, but until they are understood together with the behavior which results in the selection of one course rather than another, a serious gap in our understanding of administration will remain. What sequences of activity lead to the establishment or modification of organizational structure in one form rather than another? What patterns of behavior bring about the adoption or rejection of organizational purposes? What activity patterns bring about the identification of relevant parts of the environment and lead to the selection of alternative systems of interaction with that environment?

The growing diversity of conceptual schemes for investigating such processes reveals that *process* can be treated on several levels of abstraction, which can be viewed as the now classic rungs on the abstraction ladder. We have implied *three* administrative processes, one for each of the postulated functions of administration. It makes sense, we believe, to speak in more general terms of *the* administrative process, and to conceive of it as a general model which takes on more specific characteristics depending on the administrative function involved.

Whatever the number and nature of such conceptions which ultimately prove useful, the development of process models can lead to hypotheses about administration that go beyond taxonomy and allow for the development of prediction.

RELATIONS WITH OTHER FIELDS. No dynamic discipline has rigid, unchanging boundaries or definitions of its field. The approach to administration taken above is no more than an approximation which, through further research, will be modified and expanded repeatedly through the thoughtful activities of a great many people. Clearly, however, administrative science overlaps several established disciplines, and its gradual development will grow not only out of the efforts of those who consider themselves students of administration but also out of work by those squarely in the established disciplines. Administration has many facets, each of which has been of concern to at least one of the several disciplines.

The present content of administrative science consists largely of concepts, data, relationships, and hypotheses first developed in psychology, sociology, anthropology, economics, political science or such emerging fields as cybernetics and game theory. Progress has been slow; the development of new understandings out of combinations of older knowledge is a formidable task, and much remains to be done. The contents of neighboring fields often have relevance for administration which has never been brought into view. The perspective of administrative science needs to be trained upon such contents—either by specialists in that discipline or by administrative scientists sufficiently close to the discipline to translate it accurately—first to discover such items and translate them into administrative frameworks, and second to interpret their meanings in new contexts.

Ultimately the results of such searching of a multiplicity of disciplines, together with newly emerging data and conclusions from other research, must be integrated into larger systems of understanding which we call administrative theories. Progress toward new knowledge always is slow; it is especially difficult where the necessary synthesis is of parts whose meanings often are concealed by diverse terminologies, and have been tailored to fit a variety of discrete conceptual schemes. Just who will do the necessary translating, interpreting and integration, and what forms these will take, is problematic. But in light of the approach to administration taken in this paper, a few notes on the possible contributions of other fields may be in order.

If administered organizations are subsystems of larger systems, they must be examined in light of their interdependence with the larger systems. We must look to cultural anthropology and sociology for their understandings of the dynamics of complex societies. Economics can contribute insight into the role of the firm and similar units in the larger economic system. Political science, history, and law can illuminate important aspects of the interaction between organizations and their roles in larger governmental and judicial systems.

If administered organizations are designed to persist over significant periods of time, history should have much to reveal about the rise and decline of such organizations in relation to the larger context. If specialized delimited purposes are characteristic of administered organizations, contributions should be expected from a number of fields of study. History, for example, might illuminate the adaptive aspects of administered organizations which revise their purposes as the larger system changes. Students of business and government relations have contributions to make, as do students of civil-military relations or union-management relations.

Complex organizations are made up of smaller units or groups and consequently the study of groups both in the field and in the social psychologist's laboratory can provide valuable information about organizational dynamics. Again, because administrators in organizational contexts are part of a larger analytic category of individuals in a social context, social psychology will have much to contribute toward an understanding of the ways in which administrative processes vary with the nature of administrators.

The newer fields of study, such as game theory, cybernetics, information theory, and general systems theory, likewise have much to contribute. Not only have these tended to be multidisciplinary, but they also appear to have broken out of traditional disciplines precisely because those who developed them attached fundamental significance to the study of processes. These new fields can be reasonably described as *process disciplines,* and as they develop and refine models of process phenomena, administrative science will have additional, essential resources upon which to draw.

It appears inevitable that for some time to come, we will have much more to learn from other fields than to contribute to them. Hopefully, however, administrative science will have creative roles in the array of disciplines. As a multi-disciplinary field, it must seek syntheses, and synthesize results in new understanding. As an hypothesis-testing field, administrative science must seek new knowledge about social behavior in a particular large context, and this knowledge should have significance for the established disciplines.

SUMMARY. The objective has been set as a valid theory which will encompass all types of administration and be adaptive to all cultural or historical contexts. A strategy for moving toward that objective has been outlined. The strategy involves focusing on complex organization as the unit of analysis, but to see the organization both in a larger context, in interaction with its environment, and in terms of its parts. The strategy also requires identification of organizational requirements and, thus, of administrative functions. It calls for comparative studies which will point up the effects of variations in important variable dimensions, and calls for an ultimate analysis of administrative processes as explaining how observed relationships among phenomena are brought about. Finally, we have asserted that progress toward the objective requires the contributions of many disciplines and the synthesis of these into new understandings of administration.

Section 2

The "Idiographic" Approach

Civil Service in Ancient Times: The Story of Its Evolution

The Hon. J. H. Hofmeyr

I have given as my subject "The Evolution of the Civil Service in Ancient Times." It would be possible in dealing with that subject to make one's range exceedingly wide. There were civilizations with carefully ordered systems of administration not merely hundreds, but thousands of years before even the city-states of Greece and Rome came into being. With that civilization I do not intend to deal. For considerable though our knowledge is to-day of the administrative systems of ancient Egypt and Babylonia, even of the Hittites, yet that knowledge, based as it is almost entirely on archæological material, has many disconcerting gaps. Moreover, and this is a more important consideration, those states have contributed very little to the growth of our modern political ideals. While we can no longer commence the study of the development of civilization or of art and culture with Greece, as our not very remote ancestors did, but must go back to Egypt and Mesopotamia and Crete and Asia Minor to get a proper understanding of that development, we can still, without any very

An address delivered to the Pretoria Regional Group of the Institute of Public Administration. Reprinted from *Public Administration* (Journal of the Royal Institute of Public Administration), Vol. 5, No. 1 (January, 1927), pp. 76–93, by permission.

great loss, neglect those early civilizations in the study of political institutions. It is to the city-states of the Greeks and the Romans, and no further, that we go back for these notions of personal freedom, political fair-play, and the expression of the popular will which the modern state at least tries to make effective. It was there that those ideas were given birth. We are still in the line of an unbroken tradition. And so what I am setting out to do is to show how in the ancient city-state men found the means to carry on the administration of their own affairs, and how as there was evolved out of that city-state a great world-empire, there was in due course forged an instrument of administration which may appropriately be described as a Civil Service. I think it will surprise us to learn how long it took to forge that instrument, how well on the whole men got on without it, and how for a considerable period interests of great magnitude and extent were directed with only a very rudimentary system of administration. Perhaps it may prove to be a sobering thought to us administrative officers of to-day.

Let me be more specific. I shall attempt first to show you how in those early communities of the Greeks and Romans, where the ideas of liberty and self-government first took shape, the work of administrating the affairs of the state was carried on, and I shall speak more especially of Athens as typical of that class of community. Then I shall go on to describe how, when the city-state of Rome gradually grew until it became a great empire, it by a slow process of evolution solved the problem of providing for the efficient administration of the vast interests which were entrusted to it. And then perhaps I may be able to suggest to you how this efficient system of administration, this truly Imperial Civil Service, became too strong for the state which created it, and how it was by its stifling local initiative and killing political freedom, the bureaucracy made a big contribution towards the destruction of the Roman Empire. And possibly that may suggest to us that an efficient Civil Service, though a good servant, may be a very bad master. May I say just one word by way of introduction? This is a subject in regard to which the available information has increased tremendously in comparatively modern times. I go out of my way to emphasize that because most people to-day think that classical studies, unlike scientific studies, are stationary, that the classic makes no advance in knowledge, that he buries himself in age-old times, and chews over and over again the food which those who have gone before have only too completely digested. The truth is, of course, that there are branches of classical study which are as scientific and which admit of as rapid extension in our knowledge as any science. My subject . . . partakes of that character, that is so because the ancient writers were not interested in the details of administration and therefore the age-old times have little to tell us on that topic. The classical historians were interested in the vices of the Roman Court, the villainies of the Emperor, and the sufferings of the aristocracy, but of the much more important question of how the affairs of the people were administered they have little to say. And I suppose, if the truth be told, we are still the same to-day. Most people find many more absorbing subjects than that of our own Civil Service. They are interested in it only when they feel that the cost of maintaining it has become too great a strain on the tax-payer. But to return, it is because of the reticence of our ancient authorities on this subject that we have had to attempt to extend our knowledge of ancient systems of administration by exploring other sources of information. We have found such sources more especially in the study of the inscriptions of all kinds which have been unearthed in all parts of the ancient world, and are still being unearthed year after year, forming a steadily increasing body of knowledge and information. Of these inscriptions the most valuable for our present purpose have been those engraved on tombstones, where it was customary to give a full record of the deceased's career. It may be that the student of two thousand years hence will yet find himself lamenting his inability to supplement the scanty reference to the Civil Service in our African literature by digging up and deciphering tombstones in the Pretoria cemetery. If only out of consideration for the historian of the future, we might well follow the example of our Roman predecessors and record on the tombs of our Civil Servants how long they served as third-grade clerks, when they became senior clerks, and whether they ever attained the giddy heights of headship of a department.

It was, as I have already suggested, in the early Greek communities that the idea of self-government first took shape so that the way was prepared for the development of a Civil Service as the instrument through which the popular will might function. Now, that idea of self-government found its expression in what is known as the city-state; it will therefore be worth our while to consider just what the city-state was and how it came into being. Let us deal with the second suggestion first. Like many another historical question, it can only be answered by reference to material conditions. First one must mention the conformation of Greece. Greece is one of the three South European peninsulas, but it differs from the rest in that while Spain is a solid square and Italy a solid wedge, Greece is a confused mass of capes, bays, and islands. Apart from the countless islands and the deep gulfs which give the sea access into the heart of the peninsula, the most striking feature of its geography is its mountainous character—the ratio of mountain to plain is 20 to 1. . . .

We think ordinarily of a mountainous country as one of ridges and of valleys, which run more or less parallel, and broaden out as the streams grow larger. But in Greece the land falls not in valleys, but wild plains or levels. The mountains tend to form almost rectangular enclosures, from which the outlet for the water is often by some underground passage. The cultivable land is therefore for the most part divided up into little isolated squares of territory, which are often made extremely fertile by the soil brought down from the mountains. Now, I think that you will readily infer that a country like this, . . . falls naturally into a number of independent units, and that control by a centralized authority is a task of some magnitude. In ancient times when inter-communication was difficult, it was all but impossible. Even in these days of the railway and telegraph it is by no means easy.

The other factor that I want to mention is the climate. Greece has a summer which, like our own, is long and sunny. Unlike what our own should be it is rainless. Its winter is cold while it lasts, but brief. It is therefore naturally a land in which men lived an outdoor life. In Northern Europe, and even here in South Africa—for our ways of life are still in the main North European—the dominating feature of urban life is steady, monotonous activity going on indoors, often in a cramped and sedentary position. But in Greece most occupations, both of business and of pleasure, took place out of doors. The Greek man used his house simply for sleeping and for eating. For the rest he lived on the street and in the market place. If it rained, well, no matter, the city built colonnades round the market place and there he could preserve his activities. The geographer Strabo tells us an illuminating story of a town which got into debt, and had to mortgage and eventually to forfeit its colonnades. But then it rained, and every one was miserable. The citizens were excluded from the colonnades, they could not stand out in the rain, and as for taking their friends to their houses, well, that simply was not done. And so at last the creditors took pity, and withdrew the interdict. The life of the Greek, then, was essentially a life of fellowship—a club life on a large scale—and the tendencies in that direction were powerfully fostered by the fact that the economic system was founded on a basis of slavery, which meant that, since much of the manual work was done by slaves, the amount of leisure enjoyed by the free citizen was greatly increased.

Now, one inevitable result of this was the stimulation of a narrow local patriotism and of an intense interest in the affairs of the local community. To have the centre of Government anywhere save in its midst was to remove all the life from society, for to the Greek with his developed club life politics were the very breath of his being. The Greeks were great talkers—you know how St. Paul found the Athenians always eager to talk of any new thing—and the thing of which they talked most readily was their city. And so the Greek was not a family man, but a political being, as Aristotle called him, and that political being found his true expression in a small community with sovereign independence in its external relations, and as far as its internal affairs were concerned, with a system of Government and administration which aimed at identifying as closely as possible the citizen with the state. That form of community was the city-state, a state in the form of a single city with a rural area round it, but a state in which the inhabitant had no political rights except as a citizen of the city. The size of the city-state might vary. The largest of the Greek city-states, that of Athens, extended over a territory of 1,200 square miles. From the constitutional point of view Rome was still a city-state when it had grown so as to comprise most of the lands round the Mediterranean Sea. But whether a man lived 30 miles from Athens or 1,000 miles from Rome, it was only as a citizen of the town of Athens or of Rome that he could exercise those privileges. A city-state might then be described as a municipality with jurisdiction over a much larger territorial area than the modern municipality, and with the sovereign powers of an independent state.

What, then, were the special features of this type of state from the point of view of the subject that we are considering? I shall take as typical the city-state of Athens of some 23 centuries ago with its 12,000 square miles of territory and its population of some 200,000 free men and women and 200,000 slaves. The first thing to challenge our attention is the fact that this not inconsiderable community with a highly developed civilization, the ruler at one time of a fairly extensive oversea empire, was able to carry on its own administration with hardly anything of a permanent civil service. The only permanent officials were those who performed duties of an insignificant character—heralds, servants, messengers, clerks of the lower grade, and the like. And of these the majority, and probably a very large majority, were slaves, the property of the state and not free Athenian citizens. If we ask how Athens contrived to carry on practically without Civil Service, the answer must be that she was able to do so because she realized the ideal of democracy much more thoroughly than do our modern democratic states. A well-developed Civil Service and a thorough-going democracy do not always go too well together. The democratic state must always be on the watch against the possibility of the Civil Service, which it created as the instrument for giving effect to its wishes, becoming the means of thwarting those wishes. I express no opinion on the more or less cynical comment which will doubtless be made that it is often a good thing that those wishes should be thwarted.

I have said that Athens—and other Greek States too—realized the democratic ideal much more fully than do our modern democratic states. The noblest exponent of Athenian democracy aptly summed up its essential feature in the words, "We call our constitution a democracy, because its working is in the hand not of the few, but of the many." With us it may be that the sovereign power is in the hands of the many, who exercise it when they go to the ballot box, but the working of the constitution does not lie with them. At Athens the man in the street not merely exercised his sovereign powers more frequently than is the case with us, but he also took a very much larger part in the actual working of the constitution than is possible to-day. For every now and then his turn would come to carry out some of the functions which to-day are performed by members of the Permanent Civil Service. "Democracy," it has been well said, "is meaningless unless it involves the serious and steady co-operation of large numbers of citizens in the actual work of the government." It was there that the Greek democracies succeeded and that our democracies, considered as democracies, fail.

For the outstanding thing about such civic life was the identification by the citizen of himself with the State, and coupled with this fact and to a large extent its cause, the remarkable extent to which the average citizen participated in the affairs of the State, and did directly apply the principle of self-government. We in these days describe ourselves as self-governing democratic communities, towns and provinces and nations, and yet to the average citizen the government is something quite distinct from himself. It is the Town Council or the Provincial Council or Parliament, in each case a body outside of himself. Once a year, or once every three years, or once every five years, he may (or may not) help to choose that government. But in the interval the government is to him an alien body set over him, functioning through a no less alien Civil Service issuing its commands, "Thou shalt" and "Thou shalt not," directing him to pay a toll tax or a licence fee, forbidding him to shoot game during the greater part of the year, interfering with matters of all kinds, small and great, in his daily life. For most of us the government of city or province or nation is represented by the policeman and the tax-collector. It is a means of repressing the individuality of the citizen. To the Greek all this would have seemed merely ridiculous. For at Athens there was no government as distinct from the people. The Athenian felt he was the government as much as any one else or the government was just the whole body of the people. Government existed in Greece not for repressing, but for expressing the personality of the individual. And so it was that the Greeks were not painfully taught, as we need to be taught, to value local independence. They grew up unable to conceive of anything else. And all this brought with it, of course, a spirit of devotion to the service of the State, such as we seek in vain to-day. We find it, it is true, in the time of a great national emergency. But in the Greek city-state it was no less evident in time of peace than in time of war—so much so that the greatest of Greek statesmen could speak with no more than pardonable exaggeration of his fellow-citizens, as "not only in the hour of danger, but in the work and leisure of every day, setting their state before wife and family, bringing dispositions that are lovely in private life into the service and conduct of the community, spending their bodies as mere external tools in the State's service, and counting their minds as most truly their own when employed on its behalf."

How, we may next ask, was this spirit created? It was produced by the identification of the citizen with the actual government and administration of the State in all its phases. In the constitution of the Greek city-state there were three elements. There was the sovereign legislative body which consisted not, as ours does, of representatives of the people, but of the people itself, or at least of all who cared to attend its meetings. It met four times a month, discussed all major matters of policy, and at its meetings any one citizen had exactly the same privileges as the other. It was supreme not only in theory, but in practice. Then there was the executive body, not as with us a select cabinet . . . , but a council of five hundred. It was elected by lot, functioned for one year, and no citizen could hold office more than twice. It was intended that it should consist of the average unambitious person, and that every one should have the chance of holding office at least once a lifetime. And finally, there were the administrative officers, who carried on the detailed work of the administration. They were not permanent civil servants. That would have been in conflict with the theory that every citizen should at some time during his life have the right to bear the burden of assisting in the performance of some part of the public business. The officials were therefore appointed from year to year. One or two high financial officers held office for four years, the rest for one year only. The military officers and the chief financial officials were elected by popular vote, and were eligible for re-election. The vast bulk of the officials, however, some of them occupying posts of considerable importance, were appointed by lot, and could not hold the same office twice. The only real safeguard against incompetence, as it was also a safeguard against bureaucratic control, was that for the most part the officials were associated in committees, and the important decisions were taken, not by individuals, but by boards. Subject to this safeguard, and also to some very rigid precautions against corruption and dishonesty, it was held to be safe to trust the average man, and to allow the public work to be done by a succession of amateur civil servants. The Greeks would have justified it by saying that the quick wits of the average Athenian were worth more than experience of routine and all the mystery of red tape officialdom.

I have referred to the advantages of this system from the point of view of promoting the identification of the citizen with the state. But, of course, from the point of view of efficiency it is open to obvious criticisms. On the whole it worked much better than the civil servant to-day would believe to have been possible—yet it did disclose from time to time the weaknesses to which it was liable. And it was, it seems almost unnecessary to point out, only possible at all in a small state. A large part of the interest of the study of the history of Rome is derived from watching how Rome, which started as a city-state with a constitution based on similar principles to those which I have been describing, eventually outgrew that constitution as it became a world-empire, struggled vainly to govern its empire with its old municipal constitution—an attempt necessarily as ineffectual as would be the attempt to govern the British Empire with the municipal constitution of Pretoria—and was at length forced to evolve a new constitution and new administrative machinery, creating in the process a civil service similar to what we understand by the term to-day. The constitution of the Roman Republic was, as I have already indicated, that of a city-state. In Italy, as in Greece, the city-state flourished. And the underlying principles of its constitution, when after centuries of struggle it attained a measure of fixity and stability, were those of Athenian democracy. In theory and in essence it was the same, but the innate conservatism of the Romans, and their disposition to worship discipline, tempered the excesses of the Athenian constitution and profoundly modified it in the actual working. At Rome, as in Athens, the Assembly of all the citizens was sovereign, but there were many checks on the exercise of its sovereignty and especially when the growth of Rome made it an unwieldy body, the power actually exercised by it grew less and less. At Rome, as at Athens, there was a large executive body called the Senate, but its members held office, not for a year at a time, but in effect *ad vitam aut culpam,* and its membership was practically confined to those who had held the highest posts in the Civil Service, so that it was much less a democratic body than was the council at Athens. And at Rome, as at Athens, most of the administrative work was carried on, not by professional Civil Servants, but by untrained amateurs, holding office for the most part for a year at a time, grouped in committees so as to prevent the growth of individual power, and forbidden in most cases to hold the same office more than once. But at Rome these officials were always chosen by election and not by lot, and they came as a matter of practice, though not of constitutional theory, to be elected almost exclusively from a privileged class of families, marked out by wealth and ancestral distinction. Moreover, the number of such officers at Rome was smaller than at Athens, and there was no payment for services rendered to the state. The consequence was that, though the main principles underlying public administration were the same as at Athens, the identification of the citizen with the state which resulted therefrom at Athens was not secured at Rome.

At Rome, then, as at Athens, there was in republican times no permanent Civil Service worthy of the name. There were of course non-elective officers, probably for the most part slaves, who performed the minor administrative tasks, but the machinery of government would seem to us totally inadequate even for the town of Rome, and it was in the third century B.C., quite apart from any consideration of the provision necessary for administering the Empire which Rome was then already beginning to acquire. The elective officers had to carry on as best they could. It would seem that they helped themselves out by utilizing for work of the state the services of their own slaves and dependants, and they were relieved to some extent by the performance by the

Senate of administrative functions, especially in matters where that element of permanence and continuity was required which could not be provided by officials who changed annually. But even if we consider that to-day we are over-administered, Rome, considered even as a Municipality, must be regarded as having been very much under-administered.

In due course, however, the Municipality came to rule a great empire. By 270 B.C. Rome was the mistress of all Italy south of the Po valley, 200 years later she was the ruler of practically all the lands around the Mediterranean Sea. And the amazing thing is that at the end of that period the administrative system of Rome was still in principle practically unchanged. She was no nearer having a real Civil Service than she had been 200 years before. To account for this three points must, I think, be emphasized. In the first place, the Romans were, as I have already said, a tenaciously conservative people. With them the power of tradition was stronger than it has been with any people in history. As things had been, so they were content they should remain. A new departure in constitutional or administrative procedure was not lightly embarked upon. They preferred to stretch a traditional system to the very breaking point. The second point is that the administrative problem of this new Roman imperial state was the inverse of the corresponding problem in a new modern state. Take the case of the Transvaal. With us central Government came first, and right from the start it had to deal with a wide area inhabited by a scattered population. Local government was left to develop later. And the real solution of the administrative problem of the Transvaal, being as it is a matter of creating satisfactory instruments of local government, not only urban, but rural, is still in the future. But the lands which Rome conquered, at least in the first part of its imperial history, were already settled communities before she became their ruler. They were organized for the most part on the city-state basis. So that if Rome was willing to make use of the existing machinery, there was no need for her to build up a new administrative machinery of her own. And that brings me to the third point. Rome's expansion was not dictated by a deliberate policy of Imperialism—her Empire grew up largely at haphazard —Rome became an imperial power almost in spite of herself, and for that reason failed to face up the problem of developing a satisfactory system of imperial administration. Of course, what I have said is not quite in accord with the common view of the growth of the Roman Empire. The ordinary conception of the Roman Empire is still, I suppose, that of some vast machine which existed to make the world Roman, and which was inspired by the spirit of Jingo Imperialism at its worst. Yet when we come to look into facts, we find that, save for a few persons and a few short periods, Imperialistic expansion was not the watchword of the Roman people, and that no Empire has grown up with less of a deliberate policy on the part of the conquering nation than that of Rome. Lord Bryce, in one of his "Studies in History and Jurisprudence," pointed out that it took the Romans three times as long to build their Empire as it took the British in India. He found the explanation in the greater difficulty of their task; it should be sought rather in their greater unwillingness to undertake the responsibilities of Empire. And it was of a piece with this attitude of mind that when Rome conquered a people she did not seek to impose a cast-iron administrative system upon them, or to send a horde of officials to administer their affairs; she left them as far as possible to govern themselves in their own way. And so when Rome conquered Italy, she did not set out to regulate the concerns of the Italian communities. Her policy was rather to enter into a series of offensive-defensive alliances with them, alliances which were for the most part on terms of nominal equality, except for the fact that Rome was to have the control of foreign policy. The Italians were known as socii—allies, not subjects. It is significant that there is no word in the Latin language corresponding to our word "subject." Though the Italians might be dependent allies, they were still in the first place allies. Such a system could, of course, be administered without throwing too great a strain on the governmental machinery of Rome, or necessitating expansion or reconstruction of it to any considerable extent. And when Rome made conquests outside Italy, she proceeded on the same lines. Distance, however, made it necessary to appoint provincial governors. But Rome met this need by a simple extension of her existing machinery. The higher officials, after their years of office in Rome, went out to spend a year in one or other of the provinces. They took their staffs with them. At first, at least, there were very few officials in the provinces. The provincial communities were left to manage their own affairs, as did the Italians. The function of the Governor was little more than of one of general supervision. Here again, then, there was no growth of Civil Service. There was not even created at Rome anything in the way of a colonial office to keep in touch and control the provincial governors.

Characteristic of the administrative principles of the Roman Republic was the way in which it dealt with the problem of collecting taxes. Rome had come to be a large Empire with large responsibilities and large revenues. The alliances of the provincial communities with Rome were less favourable than those of the Italians, for they had to pay tribute, in the form of tithes or fixed money payments. There also fell to be collected customs dues and the like, succession duties, an Auction Sales Tax . . . and other imposts. Now taxes, as we know only too well, cannot be collected without large staffs, and the administrative principles of the Roman Republic did not accord with the creation of large staffs. The problem was therefore solved in another way. Private companies were formed to collect the various taxes, and the state entered into contracts with the highest bidders. The company undertook to collect a certain tax, and to pay into the state treasury the amount specified in the contract. Anything which it might collect over and above that amount it kept as its profit. The short fall, if any, it had to make good. It is a system which has an attractiveness all its own for any one who is engaged in the framing of a budget. The publicans of whom we read so much in the New Testament, usually in conjuction with sinners, were simply the officials of these tax-farming companies. They were viewed, I need hardly remind you, with even greater dislike than that with which the public regard those officials who have to assess us for the income-tax or poll-tax to-day. Such, then, was the obviously inadequate administrative system of the Roman Republic. It broke down inevitably under pressure of the growth of the state—the wonder is that it lasted as long as it did. Of that Roman conservatism alone can provide the explanation. The process of decay of the Roman Republican constitution was a slow one; the causes of that decay were many, but not least among them was the collapse of the administrative system. That, as much as anything, made a change in the direction of a real Imperial constitution imperative. The administrative breakdown was evident both in Rome itself and in the provinces. Rome had become to be a very considerable town, exercising all the magnetic attraction of a capital city. And a large city had problems all its own, problems quite beyond the scope of such administrative machinery as the old Roman Republic had available. Much of the disorder and confusion which prevailed at Rome during the last century of the Republic was due to this administrative breakdown, and would have been prevented, or at least minimised, had there been an efficient Civil Service. And in the provinces the position was at least as bad. Gradually the conception of the provinces as estates of the Roman people, awaiting exploitation, had come to prevail. By the provincial governor, holding office for a short time, without salary, and subject to no real control from Rome, the period of his administration came to be regarded as providing a golden opportunity to make a fortune at the cost of the provincials. The absence of any Civil Service in the provinces meant that there was no organization interested in their good government, and no check on the rapacity of the governors. The provinces were shamefully maladministered, and the failure of the Senate at Rome to prevent this misgovernment by members of its own order cried out to high heaven for a change of system. The provinces were being ruined, and ultimately they could not but drag Rome down with them in their ruin. There was no salvation for the Empire, save in the supremacy of a strong man at Rome, and the development of an efficient and carefully-controlled Civil Service. That solution of the problem Julius Cæsar first attempted to provide. His success was incomplete and short-lived. He went too fast and too far for Roman conservatism, and he paid the price. The Ides of March showed that, if there was to be a breach with tradition at Rome, it must be slow and gradual. That was the lesson which was learnt by Augustus, the grand-nephew of Cæsar, who after a long struggle found himself in the position in which Cæsar had been. Augustus was the real founder of the Roman Empire, just because he learnt this lesson, and because he succeeded in making the Romans believe that he was not really founding anything at all. For that reason the development of the Roman

Imperial constitution was perforce a gradual process, and the growth of the Roman Civil Service which was linked up with it was no less gradual.

Augustus might well have said, in the words that were first used not long after his death, that he came not to destroy but to fulfill. He did not set about the destruction of the Roman Republican constitution—his aim was rather to amplify it and adapt it to new conditions—but he knew full well that this work of adaptation was but the first step in a long process which could end only in the conversion of Rome into an Imperial despotism. But while he lived, and for long after, the forms of the Republic survived. There was still an Assembly, still a Senate, still officials, who in his time continued to be elected by the people, but after his death came to be chosen by the Senate. But inside of this Republican constitution he found a place for himself. Building very skilfully on republican precedents, he managed to concentrate in his own person a large number of prerogatives, all of which had been held in the past by different individuals, but which when held together by a single person, placed that person in a position of supremacy. In theory Augustus was merely the most important citizen of Rome—in fact, he was its ruler. Policy, however, and respect for tradition induced him to maintain republican forms, and especially to emphasize the importance and dignity of the Senate. And so there came to stand out two great authorities in the state—the Emperor, for so Augustus was in fact, though not in theory or in name, and the Senate. The constitution, as modified by Augustus, has aptly been called a diarchy, which means the rule of two concurrent authorities. And this diarchic principle was logically worked. Both Senate and Emperor constituted supreme law-courts. Both Senate and Emperor had powers of legislation. The Senate governed some provinces, the Emperor others; the Senate controlled one state treasury, the Emperor another. And one might mention many other points of the same kind. The Augustan constitution, then, was a diarchy in theory, and on the administrative side at least, it was a diarchy in fact. But it was a diarchy which tended inevitably to become a monarchy, and that Augustus quite obviously contemplated.

I have emphasized the constitutional aspect of the work of

Augustus, because it was these constitutional changes that gave him the opportunity of setting about the solution of the problem of administration. We have seen that as far as possible he maintained republican institutions. He could therefore do little to change the existing administrative machinery, but by virtue of the diarchy he had created a new sphere of administration for himself, and though even there he showed great respect for Republican institutions, he had within that sphere a free enough hand in building up a new system of his own. And since that sphere grew considerably in his own time, and was, he knew full well, destined to keep on growing until it comprehended the sphere which he left to the Senate, he was satisfied that ultimately his system would prevail, and that thus the administrative problem would be completely solved. Moreover, while he left the Senate freedom within its own sphere, he expected, again with good reason, that it would improve its own administrative machinery, partly because of the influence which the Emperor had with the Senate, and which could, if wisely exercised, achieve much, and partly by the force of the better administrative methods within this sphere of the Emperor's activities.

And so Augustus set about the task of creating a real Civil Service. There was a mass of public work waiting to be done, either old duties hitherto neglected, or new duties now first realized or extended by the growth of the Empire. The need of a new executive was indeed great, and to that problem Augustus applied himself. His innate caution and conservatism prevented him from carrying out his work to a logical conclusion, but he at least laid the foundations on which it was possible for his successors to build. Let me enumerate some of the principles which underlay his work, principles which he, first of the Romans, adumbrated, and which provided the basis of further advance. First of all, he was, as one might expect, forced to abandon the ideal of an unpaid service. That had led in the first place to the limitation of the choice of officials to the privileged classes, and in the second place to the exploitation of the provinces by unsalaried governors. The principle of pay was therefore introduced. Next the custom of limiting the tenure of office to one year was dropped. Officials were now to be appointed for longer periods, and the prospect of taking up the Civil Service as a profession was opened out. Along with these two principles went that of "the career open to talents." Office was no longer confined to the privileged classes. The first steps were taken in a process, which ended up in a state of affairs where it was possible for a man to start at the bottom and rise to the top. Next the principle of the state carrying out its administrative duties through its own officials was accepted. The system of farming out the taxes was checked. Augustus made a commencement with the establishment of state departments for the collection of the taxes, and pending such time as the state should be ready to take over the whole of this work, he provided for the rigid control of the operations of the tax-farming companies. Finally, it must be mentioned that Augustus initiated machinery for the adequate control of his officials, especially those in the provinces. He, and his successors after him, took a keen interest in the welfare of the provinces, their administration was carefully supervised, and as a result the Roman world entered on a period of unprecedented prosperity.

It was characteristic of the conservatism of Augustus that, in one important respect, he maintained, one might almost say, he went back to, the Republican tradition. It was a keynote of his policy that the local communities should have the largest possible measure of administrative freedom. The city-states were encouraged to look after their own affairs, and in the newer provinces, to which the city-state system had not penetrated before the Roman conquest, it was deliberately encouraged. It was typical of this policy that the towns retained a large measure of freedom even in such matters as coinage, and distinctive systems of weights and measures. The Roman Empire, therefore, continued to be for long a federation of municipalities. That contributed greatly to the contentment of the various subject peoples, and also to their economic welfare and to that of the empire itself.

The administrative system of the Roman Empire was therefore characterized by what we should regard as an extreme measure of devolution. One result was a simplification of the administrative problem with which Augustus was faced. The task of recruiting an Imperial Civil Service assumed much smaller proportions than it would otherwise have done. Yet, such had been the neglect in Republican times, it was quite big enough. It will, perhaps, be not without interest to note what were the elements out of which Augustus proceeded to build this, the first great Civil Service of history. The first of these elements was the Equites. Originally the Equites were a section—the cavalry—of the Roman army, the qualification for service being based on wealth. Later they lost all military importance, but remained a distinct class or order in the state, distinct on the one hand from the privileged senatorial order, as being outside of the charmed circle of the nobility, and distinct on the other from the populace by virtue of their wealth. They were a kind of upper middle class, and it was from their ranks that most of the Roman capitalists came. It was they too who made up the companies which collected the taxes on a contract basis. In the last century of the Republic they aspired to political power, and the struggles between them and the Senate were a contributing cause of the downfall of the old constitution. When Augustus became master of the Roman world one of his problems was that of the Equites. He had to check their tax-farming activities, and in his political scheme of things, he could find no room for them. By a characteristic stroke of policy he at once solved this problem, and attached them to his own person as a counter-weight to the Senate, by laying it down that most of the more important offices in the Emperor's sphere of administration should be reserved for Equites. This course had the added advantage, that he secured the benefit of their business training and constructive ability in the important duties which he had undertaken. The other element was a very different one. One of the results of Rome's imperial wealth was the tremendous growth of slavery. In the last century of the Republic the richer nobleman had households of slaves, often running into three figures. Now, many of these slaves came from the civilized East, and were men of culture and education. Some of them were skilled artisans, others undertook what we would regard as professional work, such as medicine or teaching, while others again were well-trained secretaries and clerks. I have already suggested that in Republican times the elective officials of state used their slaves in carrying out their state functions. Augustus extended this custom very considerably.

After all, he posed as being just like any other Roman senator; his house was not an official palace, but merely a large nobleman's residence, and so in carrying out the duties which the state entrusted to him, he made use, as any other nobleman might, of his slaves. If good service warranted such a reward, the slave might in time be given his liberty, and perhaps continue to serve his former proprietor on a salaried basis, and so by degrees the private servants of the Emperor came to be in a very real sense the servants of the state. Thus it was that the largest elements in the building up of the first real Civil Service came from the ranks of the slaves. Let us not, however, judge the Roman slave by what we know of slavery in the 18th and 19th centuries. Many of these Roman slaves were men of ability and distinction, so much so that some of those who started as slaves ultimately occupied positions of influence and authority, second only to that of the Emperor himself.

Augustus had many problems to solve—only in a few cases did he follow out his solution, and left it to his successors to work out. The problem of the Civil Service was one of these. In two respects in particular he left much work to be done by those who came after him. In the first place, there remained the task of welding together the disparate elements of Equites and slaves. And secondly, there was the problem of grading the service. But not all of Augustus's successors were able men, and some of them had many preoccupations. It was not until a century and a quarter after his death—in the time of Hadrian—that the task can really be said to have been completed. The principles of Augustus had by then been fully worked out, and the Roman Empire at last had a satisfactory organ of administration. The generation after Hadrian was probably the best period in the history of the Imperial Civil Service, just as it was in the phrase of Gibbon, "the period in the history of the world during which the condition of the human race was most happy and prosperous." But the creation of an efficient Civil Service is something which may have a Nemesis peculiarly its own. The process of growth is not easily checked, the servant of the state may become its master, and the rule of the bureaucracy may be worse than that of the despot, if ony because there is no natural term to its existence. It was not very long after Hadrian that evidence of the dangers of bureaucracy began to appear. We have seen that much of the prosperity of the Empire had been due to the large measure of liberty left to the local communities. The Empire had started as a confederation of municipalities. The towns for the most part made admirable use of the liberties and the peace they enjoyed, and there was great development on every side. But as was inevitable, these liberties were in some cases abused, and the central government had to step in. Having done so, it did not content itself with setting things right, and then withdrawing to act merely in an advisory capacity. The opportunity of creating a new Civil Service department was too tempting to be thrown away—it has not lost its attractiveness even in our own days—and the regimentation of the local communities proceeded apace. The result was a crushing of initiative and the decline of prosperity. That was, however, merely a foretaste of what was to happen in a wider sphere. In time the stifling and oppressive atmosphere of an all-powerful bureaucracy came to spread not merely over local government but throughout the administration of the state. It is of interest to note how that came about. The third century of our era was one of great disturbance and difficulty in the Roman Empire. There were fightings without and fears within, invasion and pestilence and economic confusion, and a long period of civil warfare between a succession of aspirants to restore and revivify the apparently disintegrating Empire. It was Diocletian who, though not a Roman, not even an Italian, is perhaps more typical than any one of Roman thoroughness and efficiency. With the abstract cold-blooded logic of the mathematician, he proceeded to reorganize every department of the Empire's work. One can almost see him setting about this task with compasses and measuring line. To him the system was everything, the human factor nothing. He was not the first or the last man to set out to put the universe right by framing a mould of cast-iron rigidity, into which everything had to fit, but he, unlike the rest, was the master of the legions of the world, and his theories therefore were given practical expression.

And an important part of his work was the reorganization of the Civil Service in accordance with the rigid canons of a logical efficiency. He developed its functions tremendously. The state was to regulate the life of the citizen at many more points than had hitherto been customary, and for this a very much larger Civil Service was necessary. Not only was it larger, it was also more powerful. In the person of Diocletian, the Roman Emperor stood out at last as a declared autocrat, and the Civil Service was the instrument of his autocracy. Moreover, in the organization of the Service he showed his passion for thoroughgoing consistency. He divided and sub-divided, graded and classified, and indeed organized, the public departments as official hierarchies on military lines. Gibbon has summed up the work of Diocletian in two sentences: "He divided the Empire, the province, and every branch of the civil as well as military administration. He multiplied the wheels of the machine of government, and rendered its operations less rapid, but more secure." Diocletian undoubtedly achieved his immediate objects. He checked the administrative anarchy which had threatened under his predecessors to destroy the Empire, he secured efficiency, and he probably gave the world better government than it had for long enjoyed. But in the end the bureaucratic system, which he devised to prevent anarchy and save the Empire, was a potent factor in its destruction. His Civil Service was intended to be the instrument of an autocratic ruler. Under a weak Emperor—and among the successors of Diocletian there were many such—the instrument inevitably took the place of the ruler, and there is probably no form of tyranny which is further reaching than is that of an all-powerful bureaucracy. It is a fact that the most tyrannical of Roman Emperors ruled a contented world.

The successes of a Nero and a Caligula reached little further than the aristocracy of the town of Rome. But the whole of the Roman world was oppressed by the burden of the fourth-century bureaucracy. In the final stages of the process of crushing civil liberty in the Roman Empire the chief agent was not the Emperor but the Civil Service. Another result of the work of Diocletian was the disappearance of initiative in the Service as a result of its hierarchic organization. The Civil Service machine does little to encourage initiative at the best of times. Diocletian might almost be regarded as having set himself deliberately to discourage it. That was because of his fear of the advancement of able and ambitious men, for it was just such men who by their conflicts had almost brought the Empire to its ruin during the preceding period. And last, and perhaps most significant of all, is the fact that, in improving the organization of the state, he tremendously increased the expenditure. Now, budgets can in such circumstances only be made to balance by the imposition of taxation—a fact which many people seem to be singularly unwilling to grasp in the sphere of Provincial finance—and Diocletian was forced to resort to new methods of filling the coffers of the state. Under his successors the tendency to extend the functions of the state and increase its size continued to prevail, and with it of course the growth of taxation kept pace. Ultimately the fiscal system of the Roman Empire came to be one of the most burdensome and oppressive in financial history—and it was not made any less burdensome by the procedure followed out by the government in the collection of the taxes. The taxes were assessed most unscientifically, and were made much more oppressive by the exactions of the omnipotent bureaucracy. The result was the hampering of industry and agriculture, and in the end the destruction of the foundations of the economic welfare of the Empire. Ultimately the increase of taxation, which was a result of growth of the Civil Service, was one of the most effective causes of the fall of the Roman Empire.

And so Rome, which began by being under-administered, ended up by being grievously over-administered, and owed its destruction very largely to that fact. Of the two states the latter was undoubtedly the worse.

On that note I shall close though I shall refrain from pointing any moral. That I shall leave to you. But perhaps what I have been saying may remind you of the old tag that there is nothing new under the sun. The problems of Civil Service administration that come up to-day are not presenting themselves for the first time in human history. Many of the notes that I have struck may have seemed almost modern in their familiarity. One might be pardoned for thinking that we have been caught up in a cycle which is retraversing its ancient course. History, we are told, repeats itself. And yet I have still enough of the optimism, which is natural to an academic atmosphere, to believe that the study of history and the application of its lessons may sometimes be not without avail in preventing that repetition.

The Venality of Provincial Office in China and in Comparative Perspective

ROBERT M. MARSH
Cornell University

I

Advancement in the provincial bureaucracy of nineteenth-century China depened slightly more on the purchase of substantive posts (*chuan shih-kuan*), particularly posts of the highest ranks purchasable, than on any other single factor yet analyzed. This finding is based on a sample of 1,047 officials, drawn from six different directories of provincial officials (*T'ung-kuan lu*); Shantung, 1778 and 1859; Hupei, 1831; Honan, 1837; Anhwei, 1871; and Hupei, 1879. Among these officials neither seniority nor family background, nor recruitment path nor age at receiving the *chin-shih,* was quite as decisive as purchase in facilitating ascent in the nine-rank hierarchy.[1]

The author gratefully acknowledges financial support of this research from the Rackham School of Graduate Studies, University of Michigan, and from the American Council of Learned Societies. Reprinted from *Comparative Studies in Society and History,* Vol. 4, No. 4 (July, 1962), pp. 454–466, by permission of the publisher and the author.

1 For a more complete analysis, see Robert M. Marsh, "Formal Organization and Promotion in a Pre-Industrial Society," *American Sociological Review,* V, 26 (August, 1961) and *The Mandarins: The Circulation of Elites in China, 1600–1900* (New York, 1961). It should be noted that none of these factors, including purchase, was *strongly* correlated with advancement. Even a multiple correlation of eight factors with advancement leaves about half of the total variation in advancement unexplained.

Beneficial from the point of view of personal advancement, the purchase system *qua* system unleashed a host of administrative and other evils, and therefore can be studied also as a form of corruption. During the late Ch'ing period many of the normal features of the bureaucracy—examinations, triennial merit assessments, punishments, introductions and recommendations, laws of avoidance, etc.—were thrown into disregard as a result of the purchase system. A few examples of the consequences of the sale of office will suffice.

Once in office, purchase officials resorted to the "squeeze" and became money-grabbers in order to realize a profit on their investment. The profit realized from a low post could be used to purchase a higher post. The officials who conducted the purchase system engaged in numerous malpractices. Between 1816 and 1830 over 4,000 sham *chien-sheng* certificates were issued.[2] Provincial governors were lax in checking on the merits and demerits of purchase officials.[3] Many men borrowed from money-lenders in order to purchase ranks and posts. Government revenues could thereby be monopolized and manipulated by money-lending shops.[4] Purchase officials were said to have unstable and superficial temperaments and other undesirable traits.[5]

It behooves us to analyze the dynamics of the purchase system more thoroughly, both from the standpoint of career advancement and from the standpoint of corruption. I shall attempt to do this, first, by critically examining the *concept* of corruption; second, by outlining the structure of the purchase system and its trends; third, by showing which kinds of officials in the above *T'ung-kuan lu* sample did or did not resort to purchase; and fourth, by explaining the Ch'ing purchase system in terms of comparative public finance.

[2] Hsü Ta-ling, *Ch'ing-tai chüan-na chih-tu* (The System of Purchasing Offices by Contributions During the Ch'ing Period) (*Harvard-Yenching Institute Monograph Series,* No. 22) (Peking, 1950), p. 146, hereafter cited as Hsü, *CTCNCT.*

[3] *Ibid.,* p. 144.

[4] *Ibid.,* p. 142.

[5] *Ibid.,* pp. 132–134; A. W. Hummel, ed., *Eminent Chinese of the Ch'ing Period, 1644–1912,* 2 vols. (Washington, D.C., 1943), I, 547.

II. The concept of corruption[6]

Absolutist ethical and normative definitions have come to dominate the study of corruption. The medieval Schoolmen traced corruption to man's "insatiable greed," and from the Enlightenment and the nineteenth-century democratic State we have inherited the definition of corruption as "the misuse of public funds by an official in order to illegally enhance his income." The scholastic view is inadequate because it ignores the influence of varying *institutional* conditions on corruption. The post-Enlightenment definition is time-bound and contains a value-judgment. The traditional official is better seen in terms of the values of his own society and time, in which his role resembled that of the *businessman* in important respects. In Ch'ing China the official was somewhat like a businessman in that (1) he received little formal salary and (2) he had to bear a part of the expense of his office himself. He was more likely to act as a businessman than to view himself in post-Enlightenment terms, i.e., as a servant of the whole community, an executor of the general welfare whose income was strictly limited to the objective contribution of his services to the public.

Qua businessman, compelled to maximize his profits, the official sought not perfect free competition; instead, he sought by every means to become a *monopolist.* As a monopolistic seller, he sought to sell (his services, authority, etc.) at the point of the buyer's (his constituency's) highest indifference curve. It is this process, by which the businessman-official became a monopolist in order to maximize his gain, which post-Enlightenment values have labelled as "corruption." But when these values are put aside, it becomes clear that the amount of an official's income

---

[6] My discussion of the concept of corruption is heavily indebted to Jacob van Klaveren, "Die historische Erscheinung der Korruption, in ihrem Zusammenhang mit der Staats- and Gesellschaftsstruktur betrachtet," *Vierteljahrsschrift für Sozial- und Wirtschaftsgeschichte,* Bd. 44 (Dec. 1957), pp. 289–324. This monographic-length article was continued in Bds. 45, 46 and 47 of the same journal.

depended not upon an ethical evaluation of his contribution to the general welfare, but upon the market situation and upon his skill at discerning the point on the public's demand curve at which he could realize maximum gain. Finally, it must be remembered that in most historical situations, officialdom did not enjoy pure monopoly. Rather, a situation of duopoly or oligopoly existed, in which officials competed with landlords, merchants and other local leaders for available goods and services. In short, the initiative to corruption could come from some segments of the "public," as well as from officials themselves. The extortion practiced by officials had its counterpart in the bribery *of* officials by powerful landlords and the like.

III. The structure of the purchase system and its trends

The sale of office or rank was resorted to at various times in Chinese history as a source of emergency government revenues. These revenues were intended for relief in times of famine or other natural disasters, for public works, such as river construction and repair projects, for opening up and colonizing new frontier lands, for general administrative expenses, and for military expenses and the payment of foreign indemnities. It is well known that these financial needs were exceptionally pressing in nineteenth-century China and that this led to the sale of office on an unprecedented scale.[7]

At its fullest development, the Ch'ing purchase system included not only the purchase of brevet rank (*Chüan hsu hsien*), degrees in the recruitment system (*ch'u-shen*),[8] and substantive post (*shih-kuan*), but also enabled officials to cancel out

[7] See Feng Kuei-fen, *Chiao-pin-lu K'ang-i* (Protests from Chiao-pin-lu), "Pien-chüan-li i," 1885 ed., ch. 1/17b-19b; T' and Hsiang-lung, "A Statistical Study of the Chüan-chien System in the Tao-kuang Period," in *She-hui k'o-hsüeh tsa-chih,* II, December, 1931; Hsü, *CTCNCT*.

[8] Especially the *chien-sheng* degree (li chien-sheng), but also *kung-sheng,* and at times, even *sheng-yuan* and *chü-jen,* were sold. Hsü, *CTCNCT,* 84–88.

their demerits (in connection with the *chuan chia-chi*) [9] and made it possible to purchase posthumous titles for one's ancestors (*chuan feng-tien*).

I am here concerned with only two of these types of purchase: with the purchase of the *chien-sheng* degree, because this was the most common form of purchase,[10] and with the purchase of substantive posts, because this was the most important in the advancement of officials and also because it brought the most harm to the administration.[11] Of all the substantive posts sold, those in the lowest or "unclassed" rank (*wei ju-liu*) were the most in demand because they cost the least. But one could purchase posts as high as the fifth rank in the capital or the fourth rank in the provinces, and as high as the third rank in the military bureaucracy.[12]

Of my total sample of 1,047 officials, 53 per cent were recruited through passing examinations (*kung-sheng, chü-jen, chin-shih*), 27 per cent as *chien-sheng* purchasers (*chüan-shu, pao-chüan, chüan-na*), six per cent as licentiates for academy study (*sheng-yuan*);[13] four per cent rose from the ranks of clerks (*li, kung-shih, pi-t'ieh-shih*), two per cent through the *yin*-privilege (nomination by relatives holding a high office) or the School for

[9] For example, in late Ch'ien-lung times (late eighteenth century), it cost a first-rank official 900 taels to cancel out a punishment, a second-rank official 820 taels, a third-rank official 740 taels, etc. During Hsien-feng, 1851–1861, it became cheaper to do this. Hsü, *CTCNCT,* 88–89.

[10] The purchase of the *chien-sheng* made one a Collegian in the Imperial Academy (*Kuo Tzu Chien*) and enabled one to compete for the higher degrees without having passed the lower ones, and also made one eligible for official appointment. The majority of *chien-sheng* did not actually remove to Peking to study in the Imperial Academy. Hsü, *CTCNCT,* 84–86 and W. A. P. Martin, *A Cycle of Cathay,* 2nd ed. (London, 1897), p. 329.

[11] The reform proposals of Ting Jih-ch'ang, Chang Chih-tung, Chang Chien and Feng Kuei-fen were all concerned with the harmful effects of the purchase of substantive posts. I shall return to this matter at the end of this paper.

[12] Hsü, *CTCNCT,* 80–82.

[13] Legally, *sheng-yuan* could become officials only through purchase (with minor exceptions). But I decided to omit the six per cent who were recruited as *sheng-yuan,* rather than assume that they had suppressed the fact of their purchase. The analysis is limited to those for whom there is positive evidence of purchase.

Bannermen (*kuan hsüeh-sheng*) and eight per cent through other, miscellaneous means.[14]

After their initial recruitment to the bureaucracy, 38 per cent of the total sample were listed as having resorted at least once to the purchase of substantive posts; the other 62 per cent had no record of this type of purchase during their careers.[15] Some of the 62 per cent listed as non-purchase officials might have actually resorted to purchase but suppressed the fact from the Directory (*T'ung-kuan lu*). Also, since 23 per cent of the sample were under forty years old, purchase might have occurred later in their careers.

TRENDS OVER TIME. Some well-known changes in recruitment and advancement can be seen if we examine trends over time in the sample.

First, recruitment through the *yin*-privilege had all but disappeared in the sample after the mid-nineteenth-century. Second, examination-path officials, so large a segment of officialdom during Ming and early Ch'ing times, began to be replaced by *chien-sheng* purchase recruits as the nineteenth century wore on. Third, recruitment on the basis of military merit and "bandit" suppression became more common during and after the Taiping Rebellion than before it. Fourth, while the purchase of substantive posts became more common over time, the inroads of this kind of purchase became significant only at the level of lower-rank posts. There was no increase over time in the purchase of fourth-, fifth- and sixth-rank posts, but the percentage of officials who had purchased seventh- or lower-rank posts increased from only 18 per cent of the 1831 officials to 35 per cent of those in 1871 and 42 per cent of the 1879 officials. We know from an independent source[16] that by 1902, about 70 per cent of all

[14] *I-hsü* on the basis of military merit (*chün-kung*) or "bandit" suppression (*chiao-fei ch'u-li*); "Filial, Scrupulous, Square and Upright" (*Hsiao-lien-fang-cheng*).

[15] Purchasers were called *kuan-sheng, chüan-sheng* or *chüan-yuan.* To go to Peking to submit the required amount of silver for purchase was called *shang-tui.* The receipt of purchase was called *chih-chao.*

[16] *Kuang-hsü erh-shih-pa nien Chih-shu Hou-pu tao fu t'ung t'ung chou hsien ko kuan chien-ming lü-li ts'e.*

TABLE I

PERCENTAGE OF PROVINCIAL OFFICIALS, BY METHOD OF RECRUITMENT PURCHASE OF POST, AND BY TIME PERIOD, 1778–1879

METHOD OF RECRUITMENT	DATE OF T'UNG KUAN LU 1778	1831	1837	1859	1871	1879
Chin-shih; chü-jen; kung-sheng	92%	67%	66%	48%	35%	20%
Chien-sheng	—	17%	19%	31%	41%	48%
Sheng-yuan	3%	5%	5%	4%	10%	10%
Yin-sheng; Kuan-hsüeh-sheng	—	5%	3%	1%	—	8%
*All other methods**	5%	7%	7%	16%	14%	14%
Total	100%	100%	100%	100%	100%	100%
N	39	109	294	288	147	92
NUMBER AND RANK OF POSTS PURCHASED						
Plural; Rank 4–6	—	9%	5%	3%	9%	3%
Single; Rank 4–6	—	9%	8%	7%	6%	9%
Plural; Rank 7 or lower	—	6%	4%	7%	7%	1%
Single; Rank 7 or lower	—	12%	15%	24%	28%	41%
Never Purchased	100%	64%	68%	59%	50%	46%
Total	100%	100%	100%	100%	100%	100%
N	39	109	294	288	147	92

* "All other methods" incl. "up from the ranks," "filial," etc.

minor officials had resorted to purchase. We also know that it became progressively cheaper to purchase posts during the nineteenth century.[17]

[17] Hsü, *CTCNCT,* tables following p. 111.

Of the men who began their career by purchasing the *chien-sheng,* 86 per cent subsequently also purchased substantive posts. On the other hand, 83 per cent of the examination-path recruits have no record of later purchase of posts. In this sense, purchase was a *way of life* for some officials, just as the complete avoidance of purchase was a way of life for other officials. We turn now to the question, what kind of men followed these disparate ways of life?

IV. Purchasers and non-purchasers

The ratio of non-purchase officials to those who purchased the *chien-sheng* and/or substantive posts varied considerably according to the province officials came from. In general, men from the remoter and less prosperous provinces (Yunnan, Fukien and Kwangsi) were more likely to be non-purchasers than were men from provinces closer to the capital and wealthier (Kiangsu, Chekiang, Chihli and Honan).

The relation between family background and purchase is a complex one. Men from local elite families (degree-holders but not in office) were more likely than men from Banner, official and commoner families to enter through the examination system and to avoid purchase altogether. Of the men from elite families, 77 per cent were examination-recruits; only 12 per cent were *chien-sheng* purchasers and only 22 per cent purchased substantive posts. Men from commoner families were more likely than others to purchase the *chien-sheng;* men from non-Banner official families were more likely than others to purchase substantive posts and more likely than all but commoners' sons to purchase the *chien-sheng.* Bannermen were the least likely to become officials through the examination system, but were not as likely to resort to purchase as were the sons of official and of commoner families.

My findings can be summarized by adding the percentage of men from each type of family background who purchased the *chien-sheng* to the percentage who purchased substantive posts (see Table II). The total score gives a summary measure of the extent to which men resorted to these two kinds of purchase. In descending order of likelihood of purchasing, we have:

TYPE OF FAMILY BACKGROUND	PURCHASE SCORE
Non-Banner Officials	83
Commoners	78
Bannermen	57
Local Elite	34

Purchase as a way of life, then, was much more characteristic of men from non-Banner official families and commoner families than of men from degree-holding, local elite families. Bannermen resorted to purchase less than non-Banner officials' sons and commoners' sons, but more than men from local elite families.

Not only were men from official families the most likely to resort to purchase, but among these men, the *stronger* the official

TABLE II

THE RELATION BETWEEN FAMILY BACKGROUND AND PURCHASE*

STATUS OF FATHER, GRANDFATHER AND GREAT-GRANDFATHER LEGAL STATUS	% OF SONS RECRUITED THRU: EXAM SYSTEM	CHIEN-SHENG	% OF SONS PURCHASING SUBSTANTIVE POSTS
1. *Bannermen*[a]	26%	24%	33%
2. *Non-Banner Officials*	48%	35%	48%
3. *Local Elite*[b]	77%	12%	22%
4. *Commoners*	47%	38%	40%

* Columns one and two (exam system and *chien-sheng*, respectively) should be viewed as one table, column three (purchasing substantive posts) as a separate table. Columns one and two show how men from a given type of family background (e.g., Bannerman) were *recruited* to the bureaucracy; column three shows what percentage of the *same* men resorted to purchase after initial recruitment. Columns one and two in each row across do not total 100% because the percentages of men recruited through *other* means (e.g., up from the ranks of clerks) have been deliberately omitted from this table. (See Marsh, "Formal Organization . . .", *op. cit.*) The difference between each percentage in column three and 100% is the percentage of men from that type of family background who did *not* resort to the purchase of substantive posts.

[a] Bannermen include Manchu, Mongol and Han Chinese families.

[b] Local elite refers to families with degree-holders but no officials.

tradition in their families, the *more likely* they were to resort to purchase.[18]

What are the implications of these findings? From the point of view of the distribution of wealth in Ch'ing society these findings seem quite understandable. If the sons of officials were the heaviest purchasers, it was probably because they were, on the average, the wealthiest stratum in the society. As for commoners, while purchase was beyond the means of most of them, enough of them were wealthy to account for my findings.[19] Bannermen were members of a privileged stratum, and had many advantages even if they did not resort to purchase.[20] Finally, men from local literati families may have avoided purchase for lack of money, or because their ideological beliefs strongly prejudiced them against the purchase system.[21]

One other provocative finding should be stated. The surest route to high office was never through the purchase of low-rank posts (those in the seventh-rank or below). Men who purchased only these low posts did not outdistance examination-path and non-purchase officials. Only those who purchased the more expensive posts in the fourth-, fifth- and sixth-ranks (the "higher purchasers") could expect to reach high-rank posts (ranks one through four) more often than did non-purchasers. But even this

[18] The purchase score (computed as above) varied from a high of 87 for men with a "very strong" official tradition in their families to a low of 44 for those with only a "minor" official tradition in their families. "Very strong" here means that a man's father, grandfather, and great-grandfather had all been officials, or that the father and one of the other two ancestors had been officials. "Minor" here means that only the grandfather *or* the great-grandfather had been an official, not the father. See E. A. Kracke, "Family vs. Merit in the Civil Service Examinations under the Empire," *Harvard Journal of Asiatic Studies*, 10 (1947), pp. 103–123.

[19] This follows from the fact that only a small percentage of officials were from commoner families and that their number constituted only an infinitesimal fraction of all commoners in China.

[20] Manchus could enter the bureaucracy through the School for Bannermen (as *kuan hsüeh-sheng*), could receive military commissions as sub-lieutenant (*Hsiao-ch'i hsiao*) and did not have to compete with Chinese in the examination system. It was said that clerks (*pi-t'ieh shih*), of whom most were Manchus, could become rich within ten years. Hsü, *CTCNCT*, 169.

[21] We noted earlier that only 17 per cent of the examination-path recruits purchased substantive posts. This percentage may have increased at the end of the nineteenth century (see Chang Chung-li, *The Chinese Gentry*, Seattle, 1955, 140), but it is clear that most examination recruits felt considerable antipathy toward purchase officials.

advantage was not always enjoyed by the higher purchasers. Theirs was a surer route to high office in 1831, 1837 and 1859 than in 1871 and 1879. In 1871 and 1879 *non*-purchasers were more likely than even the higher purchasers to reach posts in the top four ranks. In 1871 and 1879 the only thing the higher purchasers accomplished was to rise from low- to middle-rank posts more often than did non-purchases.

In Table I it was shown that an ever-increasing proportion of officials resorted to the purchase of low-rank posts as the nineteenth century wore on. But, if the findings in Table II are representative, they suggest that the impact of purchase *upon promotion and advancement* did not follow this same ever-

TABLE III

THE RELATION BETWEEN PURCHASE AND RANK REACHED BY TIME PERIOD, 1831–1879

	PURCHASE OF SUBSTANTIVE POSTS:		
HIGHEST RANK REACHED BY TIME PERIOD	NONE	RANK 7–9	RANK 4–6
1. *Hupeh 1831, Honan 1837, Shantung, 1859*			
Rank 1–4	12%	2%	30%
Rank 5–6	11%	11%	64%
Rank 7–9	77%	87%	6%*
	100%	100%	100%
Number	(430)	(159)	(85)
2. *Anhwei 1871, Hupeh 1879*			
Rank 1–4	33%	6%	15%
Rank 5–6	20%	17%	76%
Rank 7–9	47%	77%	9%*
	100%	100%	100%
Number	(116)	(90)	(34)

* Evidently, the small group of officials who had purchased rank 4–6 posts but were currently serving in *lower* (rank 7–9) posts had been demoted in rank subsequent to their purchase. Such demotions were, of course, not uncommon. If purchase officials were as "corrupt" as they are generally believed to be, then the striking fact is, perhaps, the relatively *small* percentages (6 per cent and 9 per cent) of these purchasers who had been punished by demotion in rank.

increasing trend. Rather, Table III shows that the impact of purchase on the attainment of high-rank posts was *reduced* during the T'ung-chih period (1871 and 1879 data) in contrast to the Tao-kuang and Hsien-feng periods (data for 1831, 1837 and 1859). Though the *tendency* to purchase increased, the *efficacy* of purchase (as opposed to non-purchase) in attaining high office received at least a temporary setback during the administrative reforms of the T'ung-chih Restoration.[22]

To state that purchase officials failed to monopolize high office and that *most* purchasers did not rise higher in the bureaucracy than non-purchasers is not to minimize the evils of the purchase system. Much of the financial corruption and maladministration said to result from the purchase system may be attributed to the myriad low-rank purchase officials.[23] But this raises the question, if the sale of office was so harmful, why was it allowed to continue until the end of the dynasty, despite attempts to abolish it?[24] This question, which most students of the purchase system in China have not raised, may be answered with reference to the insufficient flexibility in the structure of public finance in China.

V. Public finance in comparative perspective

Thus far, we have analyzed the purchase system only in terms of *personnel administration*. Our analysis would be incomplete if we failed to recognize that an important explanation for the persistence of the purchase system lies in the realm of public finance. The sale of office was, after all, a means of tapping sources of emergency government revenues. This was true not only in China but in many other premodern states: the later Roman, the Byzantine and Ottoman empires, the Papal

22 See Mary C. Wright, *The Last Stand of Chinese Conservatism* (Stanford, 1957), Chap. 5 *et passim.*

23 For a discussion of the evils of the purchase system, see Hsü, *CTCNCT,* 106, 132–34, 142–46; Hsu Tao-ling Chung-kuo fa-chih shih lun-lüeh (Outline Essay on the History of Chinese Law) (Taipei, 1953), 131–132; Chang, *op. cit.,* p. 140.

24 See Hsü, *CTCNCT,* 153–166. The purchase of substantive posts was stopped in 1902, revived in 1904, and prohibited again in 1906. All other aspects of the purchase system continued until the end of the dynasty. Hsü, *CTCNCT,* 71.

States, the Mughal empire and many Hindu states of India, and in seventeenth-century Western Europe. The appropriation of officers' commissions by regulated purchase continued in the British army until well into the nineteenth century, and offices were also sold in the colonies of North and South America.[25]

What was there about Ch'ing public finance—in contrast to that of modern governments such as the United States—which made the purchase system a necessary source of revenue in the first place? There are only four possible sources of revenue in any government: taxation, increasing the money supply relative to the rate of physical production (i.e., inflation), domestic loans and foreign loans.[26] It must have been inflexibilities in one or more of these sources of revenue which gave rise to the purchase system and enabled it to persist.

Consider first taxation, the major source of revenue in any government. There were certainly inflexibilities in Ch'ing taxation: the rate of the land tax had been fixed "in perpetuity" starting in the first half of the eighteenth century. Large revenue sources were permanently committed to provincial governments for their use. Taxation was regressive (rather than progressive, as in modern governments), uneconomically collected and inadequately controlled after collection. It was unpopular and gave rise to much evasion. But taxation was not the *major* source of inflexibility, for the Ch'ing did expand tax revenues through the salt tax, the *likin*, and, especially, the Maritime Customs.[27]

Second, the Ch'ing did resort to inflationary measures.[28]

[25] Max Weber, *The Theory of Social and Economic Organization* (Glencoe, Ill., 1947), 350; K. W. Swart, *Sale of Offices in the Seventeenth Century* (The Hague, 1940), 117 *et passim;* Ernest Barker, *The Development of Public Services in Western Europe, 1660–1930* (N.Y., 1944); Elinor G. Barber, *The Bourgeoisie in Eighteenth-Century France* (Princeton, 1955), 106–120.

[26] Kenyon Poole, *Public Finance and Economic Welfare* (New York, 1956).

[27] By 1887 the revenue from the Maritime Customs had become nearly 50 per cent of the total Ch'ing revenue. But despite its success it was insufficient to meet the heavy emergency needs of the dynasty. Ch'en Chih-jang, *The State Economic Policies of the Ch'ing Dynasty, 1840–1905* (University of London, Ph. D. thesis, 1956), 178–179, Table 24.

[28] Some 40 per cent of the military expenses in the Taiping Rebellion were covered by the issue of paper money. These inflationary measures allowed temporary military financing, but in the long run further weakened the Ch'ing financial structure. Ch'en, *op. cit.,* 88–89.

Therefore, this too was not the major source of fiscal inflexibility. The major source of inflexibility lay rather in the government's avoidance of the practice of issuing domestic loans, the third source of public revenue. The modern conception of *public debts* was lacking; the idea of the throne as a borrower and payer of interest on its loans was traditionally abhorrent. But even if the throne had favored domestic borrowing, public willingness to invest was limited by the low level of voluntary savings and by the fact that the wealthy minority preferred either to invest in land or to hoard. In addition, there was no adequate technical market organization for the efficient handling of loans. The limited range of activities of the domestic banks and other institutional investors also prevented the government from borrowing, even if it had wanted to.

Opposed to the issuance of interest-bearing loans, the Ch'ing had no alternative *domestically* but to request "contributions" from the Liang-huai salt merchants and the Canton Hong merchants.[29] But these "contributions" were linked up with the purchase of office, and the drawbacks of the purchase system tended to counterbalance its advantages.

Unable in the long run to significantly increase revenues through domestic borrowing, the Ch'ing was finally driven to foreign loans. At first, an individual official or a provincial government borrowed from foreign business firms, but by 1895 loans were handled by groups of European bankers, dealing only with the central government. It is unfortunate, of course, that the inflexibilities of domestic borrowing were not overcome before the government found it necessary to resort so heavily to foreign borrowing. Foreign debt forces a country to "transfer valuable goods and services abroad to meet the interest charges on the external debt and possibly to amortize some of its principal."[30] Had the Ch'ing borrowed domestically, the interest paid on the debt would have been paid by Chinese to Chinese: there would have been no direct loss of goods and services. It is

[29] Between 1738 and 1804 the Liang-huai salt merchants alone contributed 37.4 million taels, and the Canton Hong merchants almost four million taels between 1773 and 1832. In 1894, more than ten million taels were contributed from various sources. Ch'en, *op. cit.,* 168–169, Table 25.

[30] Paul A. Samuelson, *Economics* (New York, 1958) , 350.

for these reasons that "the gross burden of foreign borrowing is higher than that of domestic borrowing."[31]

This was recognized by men like Li Ching-pang and Sun Chiao-hsiung during the Kuang-hsü period (1875–1907). They proposed that the government issue interest-bearing domestic loans, on the model of the Western nations, as a substitute for the purchase system and for foreign borrowing.[32] Of the numerous proposals stating alternatives to the purchase system, many were impractical; some were enforced only temporarily. Only in 1905 was a domestic bond issue tried out by Li Hung-chang in Chihli[33] The new workable and beneficial proposals—mining, issuing bank notes, establishing modern banks and developing commerce—were under the control of foreign merchants.

Swart concludes his comparative study of the sale of office with this comment: as long as the sale of office occurs in an undeveloped form, it is merely the product of still primitive forms of administration. But when it is exploited widely by absolute, irresponsible governments *because of fiscal motives,* it is characteristic of politically declining societies, such as the Byzantine Empire, the Caliphate of the tenth century, the *anciens regimes* in France and Spain, and nineteenth-century China.

31 Paul A. van Philips, *Public Finance and Less Developed Economy* (The Hague, 1957), 107.

32 Li Ching-pang wrote: "China traditionally has no precedent for government borrowing. There is no harm in gradually initiating government borrowing, first from commercial sources. Ask officials in the Dependencies and Tribute States and Tax Grain Administration, and Grain Intendants to subscribe a certain amount [of loans] and give them bonds in return, with a definite maturity. Clearly designate certain public revenue as guarantee. Also, *chou* and district officials should persuade salt merchants, the local elite, the rich, the exchange banks and the pawnshop merchants to loan the government money. Annually recognize certain interest as a regular expenditure of local government, and punctually pay it in order to strengthen the government's credit; then government borrowing can be effected. Once this is done, although the purchase of substantive posts be forever stopped, how can one worry about a shortage of government revenues?" *Ch'ou-k'uan t'ing-chüan san-i* (Three Discourses on Financing without Purchase) in *Huang-ch'ao ching-shih wen san-pien,* 1898 ed., li-cheng erh 23/la, quoted in Hsü, *CTCNCT,* 164. Sun Shiao-hsiung wrote: "Western nations all have government borrowing. Why should China not also try? Borrowing foreign money is most depleting, and less desirable than domestic borrowing." (*Ibid.,* 23/2b), quoted in Hsü, *CTCNCT,* 164.

33 C. J. Stanley, "Chinese Finance from 1853 to 1908," *Papers on China,* III (1949), 13.

"Systematic sale of offices deprived the government of an efficient and reliable body of officials, strengthened the oligarchic tendencies, created a discontented elite and disrupted the financial system."[34] A further similarity is that in many traditional societies, the sale of office only really came to an end after the outbreak of revolution—a revolution which in effect transformed the State from a traditional into a modern entity.[35]

General Problems of the French Civil Service

JERZY S. LANGROD
University of Paris

THE CIVIL SERVANT embodies the State. In this sense, France is what the Germans call a *Beamtenstaat.* Its salient feature is the existence of a definite professional group engaged in active service to the State which monopolizes the right to execute the will of the sovereign and assumes the entire moral and legal responsibility for the public welfare.[1] Public Administration is the Civil Service itself: an organized group of officers whose human characteristics always prevail over any engineered structure. Public Administration must be considered as a phenomenon of human organization which is to be studied by the Social Sciences and cannot be explained by rules of management or by juridical formulae alone. Thus we can understand more clearly the need for "rewriting the formal equations in order to take

34 Swart, *op. cit.,* 123.

35 *Ibid.,* p. 126.

* Reprinted from *Some Current Problems of Administration in France Today.* (San Juan, Puerto Rico: University of Puerto Rico School of Public Administration, 1961), pp. 23–40, by permission of the publisher. [Abridged.]

1 See Fritz Fleiner, *Beamtenstaat und Volkstaat,* Festgabe fur Otto Mayer (Berlin: 1916), 2nd edition, 1925.

into account the human factor."[2] We are now aware of the powerful influence of social and individual psychological forces on the management of human affairs (*maniement des hommes*). We recognize human relations, sociological aspects of collective behavior, the role of informal organization, and the ineffectiveness of purely formal bureaucratic reasoning. We are coming more and more to realize that a purely juridical approach to administrative problems from a merely legal viewpoint which is indifferent to the human factor, is as inadequate as a purely technical approach from the mechanistic "Science of organization" viewpoint. (Those who adopt the latter become so fascinated by the streamlined image of the rational man that they consider him only as an element of productivity and, by imprisoning him in technicalities and quantifications, they neglect his personality) . . . .

While there are other forms of the *Beamtenstaat* in Western Europe, for example in Germany and Austria, they are significantly different from the French. It was the French civil servant who provided the core of the unification of France in the 17th Century, and whose devotion to the common interest, whose competence and *esprit de corps* now form the foundation of the strengthening and modernizing of France. His sense of continuity and his steadfastness lend permanence to changing regimes and blend the traditionalism of the past with modern dynamism.

In the 16th Century, the ancient Administration of royal officers, whose positions were often hereditary, patrimonial, and merely honorary, was replaced by a group of *commissaires* who were appointed by the king, were responsible to him, and could be dismissed.

An administrative hierarchy with ministers at the top emerged, and—in spite of some efforts to establish a committee system (or *polysynodie*) of collective responsibility—a monocratic, "impersonal" Civil Service was established. At least twice, France provided the administrative patterns for other continental countries: once in the 15th century when Maximilian I of Germany (also Duke of Burgundy until the Treaty of Arras in 1479) set up an administrative system in Austria (from whence it

[2] H. Ford, "Challenge of Human Engineering," *Advanced Management*, XI (June, 1946), p. 48 ff.

spread to Bavaria and elsewhere) according to French practice and structure, and again in the 19th Century when the pattern of Napoleonic Administration was carried all over continental Europe. Thus, throughout Europe we find an analogous "administrative geometry," that is a symmetrical scheme of vertical (hierarchic) and horizontal (specialized) administrative interconnection, as well as an impersonal or objective orientation of civil servants toward the public good, and integration of administrative rules into the system of public law. Thus genuinely administrative activity became possible and a *régime égalitaire* replaced the ancient mosaic of inequalities and privileges.

The Civil Service gradually became a profession or a lifetime vocation, a way of life, a kind of "secular clergy" (in the words of Fleiner), and a living technical apparatus. A tradition of Public Service gained strength and specializations unknown in medieval times developed to correspond to the complexities of an ever larger and broader scope of activities. A separate code of rules governing civil servants became an important part of the new administrative law which emerged during the early years of the 19th Century. Contrary to developments in Britain, the concept of labor by contract exempted the Civil Service relationship. The same reasoning which dictated the creation of a special set of administrative laws to govern the activity of Public Administration, compelled the unequivocal recognition that the relation of the civil servant to the State is something special, unlike the relation of labor to private enterprise. The Civil Service was seen to be so intimately linked to the public good, that it could not be treated on the same level as private employment. This recognition became the basis of special statutes governing State officials. These statutes aimed at securing a regular and continuous public service and a chain of command within the hierarchy, as well as guaranteeing the subjective rights and the justifiable economic interests of the administrative personnel. Thus in France, as generally on the European continent, the Civil Service is in a special legal condition. Regulated by public law, it is characterized by the "impersonal" nature of its public work, by political neutrality and general impartiality, and by the material dependence of all civil servants on the State (which assures their continuation in offices and gives them economic security and various other legal rights).

The French civil servant (*le fonctionnaire*), finds himself, therefore, from the moment he is formally appointed to his office by a standard procedure and not by a private labor agreement, in a special legal and social condition (*situation statutaire, réglementaire*), which is unilaterally, legally regulated and, in principle, uniform for all officers of the same rank and category. Before 1946, this regulation was largely implicit in the judicial decisions of the Council of State. But in 1946, the law of October 19 brought together in a general code all principles formerly set forth by administrative judges.[3] In 1952, another law was passed to regulate the positions of civil servants in all local self-governing communities. In this way the legislator confirmed the special legal status of civil servants, a status which tends to unify the whole corps of administrative officers. Nevertheless this legal definition of status concerns only officers of the ministerial and the prefectoral staffs, it does not apply to persons in the military services, to magistrates in the court system, nor to "private" employees of public enterprises. Thus "regular" government service including field offices (but excepting teachers, members of the Council of State or of the *Cour des Comptes,* university professors, etc.) is uniform. Although those special categories are subject to certain legal exemptions, the same broad principles involving, for example, restrictions of the private activities of civil servants, conditions of service, and certain universal rights, duties, and responsibilities govern all.

Let us state briefly the characteristics of this new legal framework and indicate its social, psychological, and economic implications.

ONE, all civil servants of the State Administration (excluding employees of government business enterprises and of special industrial or commercial public agencies) are integrated into a general system and unified by law.[4] Completely equal treatment

[3] As regards the new statute of Civil Service in France of February 4, 1959, see *Appendix,* p. 124 ff.

[4] In the last thirty years their number has more than doubled. The Civil Services have grown from 489,000 in 1914 to 980,000 in 1946, and 1.095,000 in 1950. In 1956 (after a slight decrease) their number increased again to 1.073,000. This statistic does not include 245,000 professional soldiers, but it does take into account 283,000 teachers and professors of State schools (at all levels) and 207,000 postal employees.

is guaranteed by the law's prohibition against all discrimination, as, for example, discrimination against women. The same general principles apply equally to all: a consequence of democratization. . . .

Two, the higher echelon of civil servants who formerly constituted one classification (*cadre supérieur*) are now, since 1946, divided into two formal classifications.

The first classification concerns "civil administrators" (*administrateurs civils*) and corresponds to the British *administrative class.* This group consists of all the higher clerks who are selected through the National School of Public Administration in Paris (*Ecole nationale d'Administration*).[5] These clerks are graded differently according to their particular assignments and duties. They are divided into five ranks. Promotion to a higher rank is granted according to merit and convenience rather than seniority, at least in principle. Only under exceptional circumstances will someone be appointed as a civil administrator who did not go through the National School, and in such a case the individual must have served at least ten years at a lower rank. Such extraordinary appointments are limited by law to 10% of the required number.[6]

The second new classification is that of "executive secretaries" (*secrétaries d'Administration*) which corresponds to the British *executive class.* This grade includes all those who hold the higher non-clerical jobs, such as accounting, translating, etc. Members of this classification are recruited from secondary school graduates through competitive examinations.[7] They are differentiated according to the ministry they serve and divided into four ranks. Promotion is strictly by merit, although, within each rank, seniority determines one's degree or position in the echelon. An extraordinary appointment as *secrétaire d'Administration* (i.e., without the competitive examination) is possible after

[5] This category (cf. Chapter I) includes all those who hold administrative posts in the ministries and their field offices as determined by law. They are recruited exclusively through this school.

[6] Decree No. 45–2414 of October 18, 1945; The Provisional Government of the French Republic, *Réforme de la Fonction publique* (Paris: Imprimerie nationale, 1945), p. 83.

[7] Ordinance No. 45–2283 of October 9, 1946, the Provisional Government of the French Republic, *ibid.*, p. 55.

twelve years of service. Such appointments are legally limited to 10%.

This new system of classification in no way contradicts the basic principle of legal unification and equalization of the Civil Service as a whole. It represents merely an adaptation of the internal structure of the Civil Service to the different types of administrative work. Thus the civil administrators must adapt their functions to the overall policies of government; they must provide directives for the executive; they must prepare programs of legislation, and coordinate public services. The executive secretaries, on the other hand, are technicians within the various agencies who carry out, from day to day, the specialized technical functions required of them. The new division, therefore, does not create a kind of caste-system, but represents an adjustment (similar to that in the British Civil Service) to the requirements of different purposes. It reforms the classification system and adapts the initially unified selection procedure to diverse requirements.

THREE, as we have already seen, the aim of the new law is to lessen the, formerly absolute, dependence on seniority for promotion, and instead to strengthen the emphasis on individual merit and on unique requirements and qualifications.

FOUR, the new recruitment procedure is no longer based on coopting top-ranking civil servants, as it was prior to 1946, but has been made to conform to the development of democratic policies. Today, even low-ranking civil servants can enter the *grands corps de l'Etat,* the central (ministerial) Administration, and other higher services, if they can pass the competitive entrance examination and the course of study of the *Ecole nationale d'Administration.* Young university graduates may also compete. This change of procedure has enormous psychological and legal significance: it guarantees a high cultural level for all an unbiased selection, a standardized preliminary training, the candidates' awareness of the *sens de l'Etat* (conception of the State) professional attitudes, and a high level of morality without an *esprit de caste* or clannishness. The intermingling of people with diverse backgrounds during a common course of study also creates a feeling of comradeship throughout the higher ranks of the service which survives for life and affects day-to-day practices.

Moreover, a training program in private business management for third-year Senior students of the *Ecole nationale d'Administration* help to reduce antagonism between Public Administration and private enterprise. Thus, in France,—contrary to American procedure—examinations and evaluations, during the school years, are geared, as they are in Britain, to a system of a general liberal education. In the United States, the Civil Service candidate who has practical experience in a special job is favored. This emphasis on specialization is categorically rejected in France. Those who aspire to the higher ranks will gain personal experience in administering at the *Ecole nationale d'Administration* during two long periods of field training (involving both implementing and planning policies). The training is supervised, but requires taking genuine administrative responsibilities. The entrance requirements and individual admissions to the School are kept above any suspicion of patronage, political influence, or favoritism. For example, the final examination as well as the competitive entrance examinations are supervised, not by the staff of the school, but by outside professors or administrators invited for this purpose.

Five, the law of 1946 unequivocally recognizes the right of civil servants to organize a union, a right which had been fought for and denied for many years. The associations formed since 1946 are not mere "company unions" (*amicales*) as they had been since 1855, but independent organizations similar to the socialist-inspired trade unions of privately employed wage earners. As trade-unionism, or syndicalism, became in 1945 legal for civil servants, this trade-union movement came to the active defense of the social and economic rights of their profession. The members of the Civil Service are now organized to bargain, and, if necessary, fight collectively for their rights. This victory of trade unionism—a storming of the formerly impregnable fortress of the old Roman-inspired *imperium*—brings the members of the administrative personnel closer to the fighting proletariat no matter how much the public administrators embody the state. . . .

Six, the law of 1946 not merely recognized trade unions for civil servants, but integrates them into the general structure of personnel administration. Thus the *Conseil supérieur de la Fonc-*

tion publique—the chief consultative and quasi-judicial body in all Civil Service matters—which consists of twenty-four members appointed by the Council of ministers, includes twelve who are nominated by and represent the trade unions. The council is divided into two parts: an administrative and a trade union section. The groups may deliberate either apart or together. . . . Thus we see that the State, regardless of all criticism does invite the participation of the civil servants themselves in their own management. For the last ten years, this participation has been successful, and therefore it has been extended to servants only contractually related to the State. Civil servants are, thus, no longer subordinated as in the old Napoleonic pyramid. Political and social forces have weakened the hierarchical structure and interposed themselves in the chain of command from the chiefs of Public Administration to the lower ranks of civil servants.

This machinery of special labor relations committees and personnel boards is organized on all levels of the Civil Service. While a similar system of joint negotiation boards or arbitration councils operates in Great Britain, its trade union character seems far more pronounced in France. The French pattern gives the rank and file of the Civil Service explicit, or formal, representation in the organisms responsible for the organization and functioning of the Civil Service.[8] The responsibilities of these French organisms are far broader than those of the British Whitley Councils. For example, they may suggest reforms for the sake of greater economy or efficiency. They are also smaller than their British counterparts and are able, therefore, to be more efficient. . . .

SEVEN, the French civil servant is, like every other French citizen, completely free to hold any personal political opinion or any religious belief he wishes. Although he is an administrator, he is also a citizen. He is, of course, restricted by his obligation to be loyal to the State and its government, even if he does not agree with a given principle or policy But his political neutrality and objectivity need not go beyond his official duties. He remains entirely free in his private life, and this freedom is protected by law. . . .

It is consistently reaffirmed by the judicial decisions of the

[8] Carter, 2nd edition, *op. cit.*, p. 362.

Council State.[9] Consequently, a civil servant has the right to run for political office (unless this is incompatible with his duties) and may take a leave of absence for this purpose. . . .[10]

EIGHT, even if the rights of the civil servant to his liberties as a citizen outside of the Civil Service are guaranteed by law, his rights within the Service must also be protected, since there is always danger of arbitrary action within the framework of a tightly knit hierarchical organization. Rules of procedure concerning all disciplinary action provide this protection. Every civil servant is given the opportunity by semi-judicial methods to defend himself against any political attacks which might endanger his career. . . . [T]he civil servant may claim compensation or indemnity for any wrong he may have suffered (*Contentieux de l'indemnité*). Thus the rights of the civil servant are protected and responsibility in matters of discipline is enforced.

NINE, all civil servants may be released from their ordinary duties or separated by commendment from their original administrative branch (*cadre d'origine*) without losing any rights of promotion and retirement they have acquired previously. Such a release is based on the request of the person concerned, and may be for as short a time as six months or for five years or longer. A civil servant may be released to work in another branch of Public Administration, for a public corporation, for an international organization, or to teach abroad, to undertake a special mission, etc. Thus personnel at the higher levels may be interchanged and the right man can be used in the right place unconfined by formal and technical restrictions.

TEN, the Law of 1946 determines the monthly salary of civil servants as well as the various kinds of supplementary pay, such as pay for dependents, residence allowances, etc. The law of 1946, tried to establish a salary scale starting at 20% above the national legal minimum wage. . . .[11] Salaries in France are very far from

9 See, for example, the famous case involving the admission of Communists to the *Ecole nationale d'Administration.* Decision of May 28, 1954, of the *Assemblée plénière;* see the analysis of this *"affaire de l'Ecole nationale"* by C. J. Hamson, *Executive Discretion and Judicial Control* (London: 1954).

10 It is important to bear in mind, in this connection, that all public school teachers and all professors in State universities are civil servants.

11 The national minimum wage is determined every two years and reflects the current subsistence level.

being as high as those, for comparative positions, in the United States or in Great Britain. French civil servants must live according to lower middle class standards. To some extent, the future of this Civil Service depends on solving this economic problem. The solution is the hoped-for result of current research and of continued changes during the present period of transition.

Why, one might ask, are there still so many young men willing to enter the Civil Service, in spite of its economic drawbacks?[12] The answer lies in the traditional desire of the French for stability and security; that is, for a steady job in a predictable life-time career with the hope of retirement and a pension at a given age; for complete legal protection and guaranteed social, political, and economic rights; for the sense of political participation in the actions of the State; and for a permanent feeling of belonging to a well-ordered social whole. Moreover, in spite of all other social and economic changes, the Civil Service has maintained its prestige, and thereby continues to attract young people.

The famous French *grands commis* particularly—the top-ranking civil servants who have remained for centuries the backbone of the administrative organism—symbolize a great tradition and deserve the respect they receive. Although political regimes have changed, the *grands commis* performed the same significant public functions, and—as Mirabeau (1789) put it—their devotion to public service almost represented a "second religion."[13] They all had special executive ability, as a result of far-sighted vision, or imagination, in dealing with administrative problems, much experience, education, and devotion to the public welfare. The presence of these qualities has traditionally upheld the high standards of the permanently established branches of French Public Administration. In the contemporary State, the directors

[12] As Roger Grégoire (Former *Directeur de la Fonction publique* in France) states in his monograph on this theme: "*malgré les vicissitudes de la Fonction publique, les candidats continuent d'affluer . . . , l'avenir reste ouvert,*" *op. cit.*, p. 346.

[13] Study, for example, the careers of the Marquis de Vauban (1633–1707) and Anne-Robert Turgot (1727–1781) before the Revolution; Claude Beugnot (1761–1835) and Pierre-Louis Roederer (1754–1835) under Napoleon I; Bugeaud d'Isly (1784–1849) under Louis XVIII and Charles X; Eugéne Baron Hausmann. *Perfet de la Seine* (1809–1891) under Napoleon III; or those of Joseph Gallieni (1846–1916) and Louis Lyautey (1854–1934) both *Maréchaux de France* under the Third Republic; and many others.

of the various ministries as well as the members of the three *grands corps de l'Etat*—the Council of State, the *Cour des Comptes* and the *Inspection des Finances,* all of whom are graduates of the National School of Public Administration—carry on this secular tradition of service. The directors of ministries manifest experience, practical skill and efficiency, stability and perseverance, judiciousness and a consistently administrative (rather than political or narrowly technical) point of view. This is the case, in spite of the fact that, unlike British practices, more and more technicians, such as engineers or physicians, direct specialized technical departments.[14] Nevertheless, administrators *per se*—many of them women—continue to exert their influence. The members of the mentioned three major bodies (*grands comps de l'Etat*) hold a variety of administrative posts and are specialists without being lost in technical details, or technicians of the broad outlook (i.e., generalists). They represent humanistic learning, a flexible or indogmatic philosophical outlook, a theoretical understanding coupled with practical good sense. In characteristically French fashion, the truly creative spirit among the younger generation shows perhaps itself among the public officials, rather than among the private businessmen. For this reason, a young man who joins one of these bodies of administrators wins great recognition: he is highly esteemed by the general public, he becomes experienced in managing key administrative posts, and consequently he is offered many important and well-paid positions in government and privately owned businesses. Unfortunately, a gifted and ambitious young man may enter the higher ranks of Public Service for precisely this reason: to step later into a lucrative and socially rewarding position with private enterprise. Nevertheless, while he is a member of the Civil Service, he influences the actions of the ministry in which he serves as well as of the legislation—via committees of Parliament—and the policies of other administrative departments. The continual rotation of persons leads to the valuable exchange of skills and ideas which is an important aspect of the French Civil Service.

Thus a structural and functional equilibrium is maintained throughout all branches of government service. The direc-

[14] Most of these are graduates of the *Ecole Politechnique* of Paris.

tors of ministries and the chiefs of their subordinate bureaus are permanent civil servants who combine a broad theoretical outlook with practical experience through their training in the National School of Public Administration while the ministers and their direct staff (*cabinet*), who advises him and like himself represents political trends, come and go. Since administration and politics are thus kept parallel, the administrative chiefs in the ministries can generally afford to remain politically neutral. Since the ministers themselves and their "political" staff change frequently, the administrative chiefs retain a good deal of power: even if some ministers remain in the government for a long time, they shift from one department to another and thus seldom have the opportunity to learn very much about the operation of any one ministry. The administrative chiefs, therefore, are the ones who engage in long-term planning and concentrate on the non-political mission of their departments. On the contrary, the short-lived *cabinet ministériel,* advisor or representative of the minister who is responsible to parliament (comparable to the Secretary General of each British ministry), reflects the politics of the moment and provides a link between the minister himself, or Parliament, and the permanent Civil Service. Thus purely political influences are kept in their proper channel and the services of the ministry can be freely performed.[15]

This dualistic administrative organization, which is difficult for the foreign observer to understand, provides the synthesis of opposing qualities which makes for the equilibrium mentioned above. Thus the temporary and the permanent, the political and the administrative, the imaginative and the traditional, the fluctuating and the stable elements of governing are harmonized.

In summary, we can see that the French Civil Service has ceased to be what it was—in the eighteenth century—for de Tocqueville: "the aristocracy of the new society." It is socially transformed—unionized, democratized, and economically weakened. It is still in transition, looking for new forms of expression. Yet it remains an intellectual and active elite, progressive in its social vision and ideas of management. As Herbert

[15] The *Cabinet ministériel* frequently consists of technical experts temporarily on leave from some other government agency. Statistics indicate that a high and constantly increasing percentage belong to the *grands corps de l'Etat.*

Luethy states: "It can be said, paradoxically enough, that in France politics and the State machine function in two watertight compartments. For generations France has been searching for a workable system of government without finding it; and the observer who looks only at the political façade, the government, and the parties asks in bewilderment how a country can possibly manage to survive in such a condition, let alone preserve an international status. *Is not the answer that it is because the Administration works so well,* or rather, whether it works well or not, that it works with such consummate smoothness that the only field left to politicians is that of ideology? . . . This Administration has impressed its characteristics upon the whole structure of the country . . ."[16]

Thus the French Civil Service, recently reorganized, demonstrates an extraordinary adaptability and a willingness to change with the times and the broad pattern of social evolution, while it remains faithful to its traditional goals of public service.

16 Luethy, *op. cit.*, p. 18.

The British Civil Service: Its Present Methods of Recruitment and Promotion and Their Implications for New States

HILTON M. POWER
Foreign Policy Association, San Francisco

INTRODUCTION

In any study of comparative problems of public administration the widespread influence and reputation of the British Civil Service and the former Indian Civil Service is germane to many

Reprinted from *New Zealand Journal of Public Administration,* Vol. 27, No. 1 (September, 1964), pp. 9–22, by permission. [Abridged.]

of the new nations in Africa and Asia which were either former colonies or dependencies of Britain, or have adopted the British system in whole, or in part, as a model for their own civil service. In so far as other nations may choose to adopt, adapt or continue to use the British Civil Service as a model, it is desirable to have some understanding of the origins, the structure and the changes which have been and are being made in the British Civil Service as well as their implications for the new nations.

Though it would be difficult in the compass of this report to enumerate particular instances, there is a general tendency for models to be adopted without sufficient modification for local conditions and, also, to be understood in their theoretical purity rather than their actual application. This naturally leads to a gap between theory and practice which can often be confusing as well as harmful.

For these reasons this paper will examine the following major aspects of the British Civil Service in the light of present-day conditions:

1. Competitive entry into the civil service.
2. The division of the civil service into functional classes.
3. Modes of promotion as between classes.
4. The criticism of this system in terms of present-day needs.

Historical development of the British civil service

The British Civil Service arose out of the failure of the Crown to establish an efficient central administration and the increasing demands of Parliament to exercise some control over the expenditure of money it voted for the servants of the Crown. English society in the eighteenth century was exemplified by corruption, privilege and inefficiency. In so far as administration existed it was exercised through a system of patronage with offices granted or sold by the aristocracy, much in the same fashion as they conducted their large landed estates. Though many government or administrative services were efficient, there was an overwhelming tendency to provide places for the friends, relatives or retainers of the privileged landed aristocracy and frequently the appointee was far from qualified either mentally or physically to occupy what was often a sinecure.

By the mid-nineteenth century a number of great names in English public life had raised their voices in support of reform. Burke was one of the first to propose a "Plan for Better Security of the Independence of Parliament and the Economical Reformation of the Civil and Other Establishments." He was followed by Lord Macaulay who was able to establish an Indian Civil Service, the two Mills, Bentham and other Utilitarians including Chadwick. This agitation for a civil service which would meet the needs of nineteenth century Britain led to the Trevelyan-Northcote Report of 1854 which laid down the principles for a Permanent Civil Service. . . .

Lord Macaulay in 1853 had brought down his recommendations to the East India Company for staffing its Indian Civil Service. The central contribution Macaulay made to the recruitment of probationers was the suggestion that all should be selected by open competitive examinations after university training. It has been said that the rule of merit demonstrated by free competitive examinations deserves to rank as one of the great administrative inventions of the past century.

Macaulay's ideas were partially adapted by the British Civil Service Commission in May 1855 when an Order in Council prescribed a system of pass examinations as a basis of recruitment. These examinations would be administered by the Civil Service Commission after consultation with the departments concerned. This method was not an outstanding success. However, the Trevelyan-Northcote Report which embodied Macaulay's scheme went further and over a period of years the major ideas were,adopted. The Report is referred to often and its recommendations are still considered as an indispensable part of a good civil service. Unlike present-day ideas of what a Report should be, this was exceedingly brief and managed to make its case in some 25 quarto sheets.

Its recommendations were:

1. Competitive examinations under a central control for the service as a whole to replace partonage by the heads of departments.

2. There should be a division of the service between those concerned with intellectual work and the more mechanical side of administration.
3. The principle of unification was implied in the recommendation for a single system of recruitment for the service; in the suggestion for inter-departmental promotion and transfers based generally upon merit.
4. Promotion by merit was to be instigated through regular reports on officers, the selection of a short list of names when a post had to be filled and the recommendation that a reasoned statement should accompany the choice of the person for the post from the short list.

Although not all these recommendations were implemented at once, this briefly is the basis upon which the reputation of the British Civil Service rests. Before examining these several recommendations, the manner in which they have been implemented and the gradual modifications which have been wrought over time, the role of the Civil Service Commission and the Treasury should be briefly described.

The civil service and the treasury—guardians of virtue

The Commission came into being as a result of the Trevelyan-Northcote Report by Order in Council, 21 May 1855. It was made up of three Commissioners and its task was to conduct tests for "the Young Men who may from Time to Time be proposed to be appointed to junior Situations in any of Her Majesty's Civil Establishments." This ensured that there was a common channel of entry for all posts on the "establishment" and the control was later strengthened when the Commissioners, again by Order in Council, 4 June 1870, were given extended powers to control the entry of not just the administrative group, but other groups with less exalted roles to play in the civil service.

Though the Commission was responsible for the manner in which recruits were admitted, the head of the Treasury in 1867 had conferred upon himself, or by usage acquired, the title of "Head of the Civil Service." Today there are six commissioners appointed by Order in Council which, though it adds dignity to their office, does not provide any formal guarantee of independence or security of tenure. The commissioners rank as a separate department, but their budget must have formal Treasury approval, and the commissioners and their staff are career civil servants subject to the same conditions as those they certify for employment. The Commission is organised upon hierarchical lines with the First Commissioner in effect as the chief administrator and the others with special responsibilities such as examination, scientific adviser and engineering adviser. . . .

The Treasury plays an important part in the management of the civil service because it exercises the Crown's prerogative in all matters relating to its servants. This power is clearly and broadly stated in an Order in Council—"The Treasury has power to make regulations for controlling the conduct of Her Majesty's Civil Establishments, and providing for the classification, remuneration and other conditions of service of all persons employed therein, whether permanently or temporarily."

Day-to-day control over the myriad of details governing the pay conditions and size of the civil service is carried out by the Establishment Division of the Treasury. This division works with the departments of government, each of which has an establishment section (similar to our idea of a personnel section) responsible for the recommendations in regard to promotion, training, pay and classification of the department's staff. . . .

Recommendations of the Trevelyan-Northcote Report

Competitive examinations were thought of in relation only to the administrative class which was the relatively small group of officers who would be working closely with Ministers in charge of departments, and would be called upon to proffer advice and counsel based upon a thorough knowledge and background of the administrative history of the department. For this relatively small group of civil servants, two considerations applied in deciding upon the appropriate qualification. An excellent general education was an obvious prerequisite, and for this it was considered the best products of Oxford or Cambridge should be the target group. Besides the belief that a genuine ability to write good Latin, or excel in mathematics, provided the possessor with the basic qualities of mind needed to deal with the thorniest questions of administration, there was also the necessity for the civil servant to be of a similar social background as the political heads of departments with whom he would have to work. For these reasons, it was felt a good honours student from the two major universities would meet the requirements.

The division of the service between those concerned with intellectual work and the more mechanical side of administration, was an obvious necessity prompted by the nature of the task and the means to accomplish it then available. A major qualification at that time was a good hand and an ability to copy neatly, rather than any innate powers of expression or composition. Until the early twentieth century when the typewriter came into vogue, a large part of the civil service was employed upon the simple repetitive tasks of copying letters and papers required for a relatively small staff of administrators.

In any case, this is how the original distinction was made between the First Division, composed of university graduates, the Second Division recruited from boys with a tested knowledge of reading, writing and arithmetic, and the relatively large group of copying clerks who probably needed only to have a good hand. These divisions were later reorganised as the work of the government expanded; the copyists were replaced by female typists, the role of management of sections and divisions was entrusted to the executive class, formerly the Second Division, and the First Division became the *élite* administrative class.

As a result of a further growth and expansion of government starting with the First World War, a new group of specialists had to be added who were recruited not on the basis of a competitive examination, but because they already had achieved specialist qualifications in medicine, law, science and a host of other technical and sub-technical fields of knowledge.

In the third recommendation lie the seeds of the changes which circumstances and pressures after the First World War forced upon the civil service, as it constantly attempted to adjust to its increased responsibilities whilst not departing from the spirit of the idea of recruitment by examination. A single system of recruitment has been maintained but promotion by merit has blurred the sharp outlines of each of the classes of the civil service. Also, the principle has been maintained of a unified service which permits an officer to move from one department to another, if he so desires.

The basic idea of promotion by merit has never been questioned and when supported by regular reporting on the performance of each officer, as well as the necessity for those deciding upon promotions to justify their choice in writing, it has meant that though favouritism[1] is bound to be practised, it is not so flagrant as to sap the morale of those most affected.

At this point it is worth examining the British Civil Service in more detail to see whether, for example, it is in fact as neatly arranged into several classes of workers, each carefully selected to play his, or her, role in the determination and execution of policy and led by a *corps d'élite* of 'ubiquitous amateurs who know next to nothing about almost everything.'[2]

Recruitment and promotion

Selection is by open competition involving written and oral tests, the latter declining in scope and importance as one moves down the pyramid. To join the administrative class straight from a university will require two interviews as well as a stiff formal examination. Should the candidate feel he is short on academic merit but has certain personality and leadership qualities commonly in demand for an officer in the administrative class, he may choose the much discussed 'Stoke D'Abernon' method which involves elaborate tests of personal qualities where the candidate is observed in action with other candidates performing simulated, administrative battle exercises.

1 Admiral Lord Fisher is supposed to have said as the First Sea Lord, 'favouritism is the secret of successful administration'.

2 Frank Dunnill, *The Civil Service*. London: George Allen and Unwin Ltd., 1956, p. 11.

A person just out of grammar school at about 18 years of age wishing to enter the executive class will have one interview as well as a comprehensive examination.

A person who wishes to become a clerical officer and who comes straight from an undistinguished academic career in a grammar or secondary modern school at 16 to 18 years of age has only to pass an examination and is spared an interview.

All this suggests a rather rigid hierarchical system which places each in his appointed position according to ability and opportunity and allows little interpenetration between the bifurcated segments of the pyramid. This may well have been the intention of the Trevelyan-Northcote report at the time it was published.

In 100 years changes in the political philosophy of society, as well as the impact of two world wars, have transformed the neatly conceived system into a more heterogeneous group in which background, experience and education are belied by the traditional appearance and behaviour of a member of the administrative class.

This is well illustrated by the following table which shows the several grades of the administrative class and the numbers which entered it by examination or by promotion from another lower class.

CHART I[3]

CENTRAL STAFF RECORDS, 1 JULY 1953

	ENTERED BY EXAMINATION	ENTERED BY PROMOTION	TOTAL
Permanent Secretaries	26	8	34
Deputy Secretaries	47	21	68
Under-Secretaries	132	85	217
Assistant Secretaries	339	364	703
Principals	558	723	1,281
	1,102	1,201	2,303

3 W. J. M. McKenzie, *Political Quarterly*, Vol. 27 (1956), pp. 136–137.

Or if one examines the executive class, Professor W. J. M. McKenzie's calculations show the following position in relation to the composition of this group in 1954 expressed in percentages.

CHART II[4]

EXECUTIVE CLASS

Entrance by competitive examination at 18 years of age	18.6%
Entrance by special competitive examination	7.9%
Limited competition	12.4%
Filled by promotion from clerical grades	61.1%

It is now evident that because of the strains imposed by the expansion of government services the educational system could not produce suitably qualified entrants at the ages of 16, 18 and 22 years of age to fill the available positions. This is further borne out by some interesting facts relating to the appointment of administrative principals in 1950 and 1954. During this period it was customary to permit 20 per cent of the positions available to be filled by those in the executive class through a competitive examination. This particular form of promotion is available only to a very few officers who have the educational background for entry to the administrative class, but for one reason or another, first entered the executive class instead. In many cases this would be due to failure to qualify in the first instance for entry to the higher class, or because after a period of war service they were too old to compete in the entrance examination. In addition to this method of promotion, i.e., by examination, after some years of service in a lower class, individuals may also be promoted on a departmental recommendation based upon service and performance. There is one other mode of post entry promotion which applies mainly to specialists who may be transferred from a specialist classification to one which requires a predominance of administrative abilities.

Thus you have the principal's grade in the administrative class made up for the periods 1950 and 1954 as follows:

[4] *Ibid.*, p. 137.

CHART III[5]

	1950	1954
	%	%
1. Entry by open competition (directly from university)	44	52.6
2. Entry as a result of examination after service in a lower class	14	14.1
3. By promotion from the executive class	36	25.6
4. From other classes by transfer	6	7.7

As a footnote to this particular trend, in the year 1955 only 31 university graduates were accepted as a result of the open and competitive examination, although there were 50 places available.

AN EVALUATION

The British Civil Service has changed, though not in spirit, from the ideas contained in the Trevelyan-Northcote Report. It continues to be based upon the competitive examination as a means of entry, although this has been modified to permit upward movement from class to class by promotion based upon merit. There is still a unified service based upon the belief that though special knowledge of a particular department is needed and can be acquired, it should not be prized above wider experience in a succession of different tasks.

There is a tendency for the British Civil Service to be given considerable unqualified praise by foreign observers and, apart from the Crichel Downs incident, one might say there have not been any extravagant exposures of basic weaknesses. Yet these do exist and some of the more prominent ones will be examined here. The weaknesses and deficiencies that have attracted most attention in the post-war period are directly related to the additional burdens placed upon the central government and its servants to administer a greatly expanded range of welfare

[5] *Ibid.*, p. 135.

services. The welfare state serves more citizens more often, with a wider range of services, and this brings the civil service into constant contact with the governed and more certainly exposes whatever vulnerable points it may have. The new responsibilities of the civil service are such that the theory in regard to initiating and carrying out policies has been moved further down into the solid midriff of the service pyramid. Ministers are supposed to determine policy and through the administrative class hand down the necessary directives to cover all contingencies. In practice, it has been found a great many questions of policy 'bubble-up from below' and may be decided by members of the executive class or very junior administrative officers. This interlocking of managerial and policy activities is well illustrated by the Crichel Downs case. From this development, in so far as it can be substantiated, the focus of attention is shifting from the administrative to the executive class, especially in regard to selection, training and promotion as its functions have broadened and become far more important than in the past.

The administrative class plays a key part in the definition and execution of policy. The following statement by Sir Warren Fisher to the Tomlin Commission[6] clearly defines the duties of a senior civil servant.

> Determination of policy is the function of ministers, and once a policy is determined it is the unquestioned and unquestionable business of the civil servant to strive to carry out that policy with precisely the same energy and precisely the same good will whether he agrees with it or not. That is axiomatic and will never be in dispute. At the same time it is the traditional duty of civil servants, while decisions are being formulated, to make available to their political chiefs all the information and experience at their disposal, and to do this without fear or favour, irrespective of whether the advice thus tendered may accord or not with the minister's initial view. The presentation to the minister of relevant facts, the ascertainment and marshalling of which may often call into play the whole organisation of a department, demands of the civil servant the greatest care. The presentation of inferences from the facts equally demands from him all the wisdom and all the detachment he can command.

[6] Report of the Royal (Tomlin) Commission on the Civil Service, Evidence p. 1268 (CMD 3909, 1931), from H. R. G. Greaves, *The Civil Service in the Changing State*. London: George G. Harrap and Co. Ltd., 1947, pp. 48–49.

> The preservation of integrity, fearlessness, and independence of thought and utterance in their private communion with ministers of the experienced officials selected to fill the top posts in the service is an essential principle in enlightened government; as—whether or not ministers accept the advice thus frankly placed at their disposal, and acceptance or rejection of such advice is exclusively a matter for their judgment—it enables them to be assured that their decisions are reached only after the relevant facts and the various considerations have, so far as the machinery of government can secure, been definitely brought before their minds. . . .
>
> . . . I should like to record my complete disagreement with any suggestion that the type required and suitable for the service is the man who 'plays for safety.' There is no business in the world which needs higher qualities of mind and character than the British civil service; and this need is certainly not likely to decrease as the scope of government activity expands.

This very small group of officers has traditionally been recruited by competitive examination straight from universities at about 22 years of age. The procedure tends to select a preponderance of young men with liberal arts degrees, and because of the traditions of higher education in Great Britain, very few with training in the natural sciences, the social sciences and certainly without any formal training in public administration. Lord Bridges, formerly Head of the Treasury, justifies the recruitment of the generalist from the university on the following grounds:

1. Such training cultivates a capacity to analyse complicated situations.
2. It develops the ability to set out results clearly and accurately.
3. It also develops an inner determination for truth rather than a solution.[7]

The argument has been advanced and generally accepted that this method of recruitment still favours the socially privileged, and thus the higher ranks of the civil service tend to be the preserve of one class, and so not necessarily reflecting the mores of the society. Oxford and Cambridge provide the largest proportion of recruits and though attendance at these two universities is not restricted to the wealthy, there are certain social and educa-

[7] Lord Bridges, *Political Quarterly,* Vol. 25 (1954), p. 323.

tional barriers for the student of working class parents to surmount before admission.

The arguments for and against this situation are not our concern except in so far as the absolute dominance of the competitive examination by students from the more privileged sector of society, is slowly being reduced. In 1953 there were 52 successful candidates for admission to the administrative class, 26 from Oxford and 15 from Cambridge, with 11 candidates from the provincial or red-brick universities. Seventeen of the candidates had been to public schools and 35 to grammar schools. However, 12 students came from the working class homes and seven of these had attended either Oxford or Cambridge. This does illustrate the fact that with all its rigidities, the British system of education by providing student scholarships permits the exceptional student who can stay the course to penetrate the hallowed establishment. The Angry Young Men around whom most of the articulate opposition to a privileged and stagnant society has coalesced are still able to demonstrate the relatively higher cost of education to lower income groups and thus the need for an even more liberal approach to financing education for all.[8]

As was seen above the purity of the social composition of the higher civil service has been 'contaminated' by promotions to the administrative grades in periods of civil service expansion; also by the Treasury's acceptance of the need to reserve a proportion of vacancies for officers in lower grades who can qualify by special examination; and the undoubted impact of wider educational opportunities which have lessened the advantages of social influence or privilege.[9]

Another factor which has influenced the composition and performance of the administrative class in recent years has been the growing number of specialists who have been promoted to the administrative class. This change is probably valuable in so far as it has diluted the tradition of generalists occupying the key administrative positions in an age of specialisation.

During the Second World War and since, the Treasury has made use of specialists, mainly economists, for temporary ap-

[8] John Vazey, *The Social Costs of Education.* Faber and Faber.

[9] *Political Quarterly,* Vol. 26 (1955), p. 302.

pointments as advisers in the development of long range economic planning. One of these, the late Evan Durban, an Oxford economist, made some searching criticisms of the civil service.[10]

He said that in the first place the administrative capacity of Permanent and Deputy Secretaries was remarkably low. Though intelligent and charming, they were not men of imagination or action, rather, they tended to be slow, cautious, shrewd, but not wise; dependable but not creative; cynical rather than realistic. The average level of personal vitality in the lower ranks of the administrative class was not high and there was a tendency towards being too safe. He was also perturbed by the amateurishness and intellectual isolation of many administrators coupled with their lack of any specialised knowledge of either the social or natural sciences. This divorce of modern knowledge from the formation of policy was impossible to justify. There was no systematic training offered the young man about to enter upon his career and confronted with a dreary initiation period.

In assessing the criticisms which have been voiced by others, even if in less stringent tones, one must not lose sight of the fact that many of the top positions during the Second World War were occupied by men who had spent the best part of their professional careers under the several governments of the inter-war period. None of these governments were, nor for that matter was the country as a whole, dedicated to vital leadership or positive policies as a solution to the very grave domestic and international problems Great Britain faced in that period. It is probably true one also gets the administrators one deserves.

Nevertheless, there is the outstanding issue which underlies many of the faults and the criticisms of observers—the need for training in all aspects of administration for the British Civil Service. At all levels, from the most rudimentary tasks to the level where the most complicated questions of policy are decided, there is a lack of adequate training as well as a reluctance to provide any basic training in the art of administration or management, either within the service, or outside it through the universities. Both Greaves and Robson make this point.[11]

10 *Political Quarterly,* Vol. 15 (1944) , p. 95.

11 H. R. G. Greaves and W. A. Robson, *Political Quarterly,* Vol. 25, p. 363–p. 343.

It is also of some significance as an indication of the lack of flexibility of the service as a whole, that even in a highly developed society there is a great reluctance to use the obvious abilities of women in the British Civil Service except for the most menial duties.

CHART IV[12]

COMPOSITION OF CIVIL SERVICE, 1953

	MEN	WOMEN	TOTAL
Administrative class	2,415	179	2,594
Executive class	28,849	7,334	36,183
Clerical class	52,801	28,391	81,192

It seems unlikely that this state of affairs represents the maximum utilisation of available talent in terms of equal opportunity for both men and women.

This paper has given most emphasis to the problem of the administrative class within the civil service, a group which, though small numerically, does in fact influence the manner in which the other 117,000 civil servants will perform their functions. Much the same criticisms hold for the executive class, upon whose shoulders the major responsibility rests for the daily management of men and affairs. It could be said that the efficiency and effectiveness of the service is becoming more and more a responsibility of this middle management group. If this is the case, then it is equally important to treat its deficiencies, especially in the area of training with some degree of urgency.

LESSONS FOR NEW NATIONS

In the context of this paper, which emphasises only the most glaring and obvious problems of the British Civil Service, it is also true that useful comment and comparision in relation to the newer civil services must be somewhat restricted.

12 Frank Dunnill, *The Civil Service*. London: George Allen and Unwin Ltd., 1956, Appendix 3, 4 and 5, pp. 221–223.

Most of the newer nations, whether with an English colonial background or not, tend to retain the metropolitan model in both education and administration.[13]

It might almost be said that in their efforts to retain or reproduce the model, they are excessively concerned about minutiae but oblivious of the larger issues involved. This is all said by way of pointing out that newer civil services may at first be reluctant to accept the idea that for the two major groups concerned with administration and management, there should be some special training, either at the university, or as a continuing part of their career. This reluctance would be based upon the absence of this type of training in either British or French institutions of higher education. Also, to staff an adequate bureaucracy there must be a sound educational system from high school on up to university to provide a steady flow of recruits. To build a civil service not only requires able administrators, but also capable, literate and trustworthy clerks.

Because of the preponderant influence of the traditional in the newer nations there will be problems associated with tribal groupings. For example, the tendency to discriminate in recruitment and promotion by whatever is the ascendant group, could lead to problems which may provoke drastic political solutions. Apart from the possible influence of tribal discrimination, there could well be a reluctance on the part of the administrative *élite* to recognise the necessity to accept within their ranks through promotion, others who did not follow the same prescribed course of education and overseas experience they had followed.

Some mention must be made of corruption, a trait almost unknown in the British Civil Service, but one which has already manifested itself in a number of the new nations. It is of paramount importance that the civil administration be as Caesar's wife, above suspicion. 'Corrupt practices' in one context are often time honoured, traditional gestures and obligations. Several of the gaudier cases of corruption in Nigeria and Ghana have been fearlessly exposed and prosecuted. One may hope that the understanding of the need for an impartial and incorruptible administration is strong enough to ultimately permeate the society as a

[13] Eric Ashby, *Patterns of Universities in Non-European Societies.* London: Luzac and Company, 1961.

whole as well as to be strongly reinforced in the education of the youth of these nations.

Besides the question of corruptibility, there is also the independence of the judiciary to be considered as part of the total administrative climate. The recent case of Chief Enahoro[14] does not establish the political control of the judiciary in Nigeria, but does indicate a lack of sensibility on the part of government officials when they create situations which cast a doubt upon the integrity of justice.

In short, it could be said that the pursuit of modernity in a new state will in part rest upon the ability of the civil service to be dynamic rather than static, willing to make innovations and be flexible rather than overshadowed either by indigenous or cosmopolitan models.

Bibliography

APTER, DAVID EARNEST, *Gold Coast in Transition, 1955.* Princeton: Princeton University Press.

COHEN, EMMELINE, *The Growth of the British Civil Service.* London: George Allen and Unwin Ltd., 1941.

DUNNILL, FRANK, *The Civil Service—Some Human Aspects.* London: George Allen and Unwin Ltd., 1956.

GREAVES, H. R. G., *The Civil Service in the Changing State.* London: Harrap and Co., 1947.

LEWIS, R. and MAUDE, A. E., *The English Middle Classes.* New York: Knopf, 1950.

MCKENZIE, W. J. M. and GROVE, J. W., *Central Administration in Britain.* London: Longmans, Green and Co., 1957.

SMYTHE, HUGH M. and MABEL M., *The New Nigerian Elite.* Stanford, California: Stanford University Press, 1960.

YOUNGER, KENNETH GILMOUR, *The Public Service in New States; a Study in Some Trained Manpower Problems.* New York: Oxford Univerity Press, 1960.

Journals:

Public Administration.

Political Quarterly, Vol. 25, 1954, Vol. 27, 1956.

14 Reported in *Manchester Guardian Weekly* (March 28, 1963), p. 2.

The Parliamentary Ombudsman: Should the Scandinavian Scheme Be Transplanted?

DONALD C. ROWAT
Carleton University, Ottawa

EACH OF THE Scandinavian countries—Sweden, Finland, Denmark and Norway—now has an officer of parliament commonly known as the Ombudsman, whose job is to investigate complaints from citizens about the way they have been treated by government officials and, when he finds it necessary, to recommend remedial action. Recently, this Ombudsman scheme has gained widespread attention in other countries, particularly in the English-speaking world, and much discussion has taken place about whether it should be adopted elsewhere. In this article, then, we consider the history and nature of the scheme, the reasons why it is thought to be desirable in the modern democratic state, and arguments that have been raised against its transplantation to other countries.

I

The office of Ombudsman was first created by the Swedish Constitution Act of 1809, over 150 years ago. It has an even earlier prototype, however, the King's Chancellor of Justice, which extends far back into Swedish history. The Chancellor of

A revised and shortened version of "An Ombudsman Scheme for Canada," *Canadian Journal of Economics and Political Science,* November, 1962. The author wishes to thank the editor of the *Journal* for permission to reproduce portions of that article. Reprinted from *International Review of Administrative Sciences,* Vol. 18, No. 4 (1962), pp. 398–405, by permission.

Justice was empowered by the King to supervise the application of the law by judges and other officials. With the rise of parliamentary democracy in Sweden it became clear that the Chancellor's status as part of the executive made him too dependent upon executive authority. As a result, Parliament wrested the office from the executive by gaining power over the appointment of the incumbent. But Parliament lost its control over the executive after a short period, in 1772. When it regained control, in 1809, it decided to appoint an additional officer, the Ombudsman, as its own defender of the law. Just as the British Parliament's struggle for financial control over the executive laid the groundwork for the appointment of an Auditor General, the Swedish Parliament's struggle for political control laid the basis for the appointment of an Ombudsman.

Finland, too, has long had a Chancellor of Justice with powers of supervising the courts and the administration. Unlike Sweden, however, Finland, under its 1919 Constitution, made the Chancellor partially independent of the executive. In addition it created a parallel office of parliamentary Ombudsman. Thus Finland, like Sweden, has two public defenders, each with the power to receive and investigate complaints.[1] But because of the historic prestige and independence of the Finnish Chancelor, he is much more powerful than his Swedish counterpart, and is perhaps even more important than the Finnish Ombudsman as a defender of the law.

Impressed with the obvious advantages of the schemes in Sweden and Finland, Denmark decided to adopt the institution under its new Constitution of 1953, and its first Ombudsman was appointed in 1955. Although the Norwegian Committee on Administrative Procedure, headed by the Chief Justice, had recommended a civilian Ombudsman for Norway in 1958, it was not until 1961 that the Norwegian Government introduced a bill on the subject, and the Parliament did not actually adopt the institution until the summer of 1962. The new Norwegian scheme is patterned mainly upon its Danish counterpart.

As one might expect, there are some significant differences

[1] See Professor Kastari's article in this issue and my "Finland's Defenders of Law," *Canadian Public Administration,* IV, Nos. 3, 4 (September and December, 1961), 316–25, 412–15.

among the Nordic countries in the Ombudsman's powers and procedures. The jurisdiction of the Swedish and Finnish officers is more extensive than that of their Danish and Norwegian counterparts. In Sweden and Finland the Ombudsman supervises not only the administration but also the courts, and has the direct power to prosecute officials before the courts for illegal acts. In Denmark he may only order that a prosecution be initiated, while in Norway he may only recommend this. Finland used to be the only country in which the Ombudsman supervised local government officials, but Sweden extended his jurisdiction to include them in 1957, Denmark did likewise in 1961, and it is expected that Norway will do so too. In Sweden and Norway the Ombudsman's jurisdiction does not extend to the armed services, because these countries have a special Military Ombudsman, dating in Sweden from 1915 and in Norway from 1952.

Another significant difference is that in cases where administrative authorities have been given discretionary power, in Sweden the Ombudsman has no specific right to criticize the wisdom of a decision and rarely does so, while in Denmark he has been given the right to do so if he considers the decision to be unreasonable. The Norwegian Committee proposed a similar power for the Ombudsman. The Norwegian Government at first refused this recommendation, but then accepted the wording "clearly unreasonable." The importance of these differences should not be exaggerated, however, because the Danish Ombudsman has used this power sparingly, while the Swedish Ombudsman has usually managed to intervene on grounds of illegality where a decision was patently unreasonable. He may conclude, for example, that a decision not based on the facts should be considered illegal. Moreover, the Nordic countries provide opportunities for appealing discretionary decisions that are wider than in the common-law countries. Both Finland and Sweden have a system of administrative appeal courts, which in Sweden may deal specifically with the reasonableness of decisions, and the courts in all four countries may hear appeals on grounds of both law and fact.

In other respects the competence and practices of the Nordic Ombudsman are much the same. All of them can receive and investigate any written complaint, which can be submitted in a sealed envelope without reference to any superior authority. All can initiate investigations and make inspections, without first having received a specific complaint. All can call upon government agencies to give reports and all have the power to demand departmental records. All are appointed by Parliament, are entirely independent of the executive, and report annually to a special committee of the House. All can comment critically on official actions in their annual reports, and all can make a report on an urgent matter at any time. In the Commonwealth countries, the position of the Auditor General as an officer of Parliament is a close parallel, except of course that the Auditor General checks financial transactions rather than administrative decisions.

When the Ombudsmen find that a complaint is justified, in the less serious cases they make critical comments directly to the officers of the department or agency concerned. Many cases involve no more than explaining fully to the bewildered citizen the reasons for the decision of which he has complained, and warning the government office in question that in future it should give adequate reasons for its decisions. But the Ombudsmen's conclusions on important cases are given wide publicity and exert a profound influence on future administrative practice. Moreover, on questions of principle arising from cases investigated, the Ombudsmen can propose amendments in the regulations or the law.

The matters they investigate range all the way from official misbehaviour and outright illegality to less serious complaints of tardiness, inefficiency, or negligence. It is in the latter type of case that the Ombudsman comes into his own, for it is here that the biggest gap occurs in our systems of administrative control. Examples range from complaints about getting no answer to an application, leisureliness in replying to mail, tardiness or bias in making decisions, to giving insufficient information on a decision or right of appeal. Nevertheless, some of the Ombudsmen's most valuable work has been done on serious cases of illegality involving the liberty of the subject. Here are some recent examples from Sweden and Denmark: a mental patient complained that a male nurse had assaulted him; inadequate consent was given for mental patients to undergo shock treatment and brain operations; police unjustifiably recorded telephone conversations; a prison warden barred a magazine from his prison simply because one issue had criticized prison authorities; handcuffs were used unjustifiably; and the police refused to remove an acquitted person's photograph and fingerprints from police files. Nearly all of these are cases in which redress might have been given had they been taken to the courts, but in most of them the citizen could not be expected to know his rights, would not know what to do about it if he did, and very likely could not afford expensive aid. In several such cases the Ombudsmen have secured court action and free legal aid for the complaint. In others, they have simply demanded direct redress for the action and assurance that similar actions will not occur again. Where the authority refuses this redress, the Ombudsmen will of course report critically on the case to Parliament.

Some idea of the nature and extent of the Ombudsmen's work may be gained by considering the number and disposition of the cases with which they deal.[2] Each handles about 1,000 cases per year (not counting about 1,000 handled by the Military Ombudsman and the Chancellor of Justice in Sweden, and 1,500 by the Chancellor in Finland). Most of them arise out of complaints from the public, but cases initiated by the Ombudsman himself, as a result of inspections or reports in the press, account for a large proportion of the criticisms and prosecutions. In Finland and Denmark only 10 to 15 per cent of all cases require criticism, recommendations, disciplinary action or prosecution, but in Sweden the proportion is above 20 per cent. Probably the reason for the higher percentage in Sweden is the greater number of cases that arise from inspections, nearly all of which require criticism or remedial action. Another reason may be the long experience with the institution in Sweden and the public's better knowledge of which actions are likely to be condemned by the Ombudsman.

The total number of cases per year requiring criticism or remedial action is about 70 in Denmark, and in Finland is nearly

[2] Figures for Denmark and Sweden are given in Bent Christensen, "The Danish Ombudsman," and Stig Jagerskiold, "The Swedish Ombudsman," *University of Pennsylvania Law Review,* Vol. 109, 8 (June, 1961), 1105 and 1085; and for Finland, in my article, *op. cit.,* 414.

100 (not counting about 200 handled by the Chancellor of Justice). In Sweden, a country of about eight million, the total was close to 300 in 1960 (not counting about 200 handled by the Military Ombudsman and a few by the Chancellor). This will give the reader some idea of the number of cases of maladministration and injustice that may be going unnoticed in other countries each year. The number may even be proportionately greater in the common-law countries, because of the weaker role played by the courts and administrative appeal bodies, and also because the mere existence of the Ombudsman scheme is a powerful preventive influence. Yet a democracy should be ashamed of even one substantial case of unremedied injustice per year.

II

The success of the new Ombudsman scheme in Denmark, and the discussion and recent adoption of it in Norway have caused other countries to become interested in the idea. In 1957, Western Germany adopted the institution of the Military Ombudsman, patterned to some extent on the systems in Sweden and Norway, and it is reported to be working successfully there. Partly as a result of the Danish Ombudsman's willingness to write and lecture in English about his new office, the United Kingdom and New Zealand took up the idea. Widespread discussion has ensued in the United Kingdom, and in 1961 the British Section of the International Commission of Jurists, *Justice,* issued a report, the so-called Whyatt Report, recommending the scheme.[3] So far, however, the British Government has made no favourable pronouncement on the matter. The New Zealand Government, on the other hand, has pursued the idea enthusiastically, and in 1961 introduced a bill on the subject. This bill was re-introduced and passed in the summer of 1962, and Sir Guy Powles, former High Commissioner to India, has been appointed as Ombudsman. In Canada, too, the scheme is now being discussed widely, and in the United States several articles have

[3] *The Citizen and the Administration* (London, 1961); Director of Research, Sir John Whyatt.

appeared favouring its adoption, with suitable adjustments, at least by the state and local governments.[4] In 1961, a Committee appointed by the Mayor of Philadelphia and chaired by the Dean of Law at the University of Pennsylvania recommended the system for Philadelphia, and the Administrative Conference of the United States, which will report to the President at the end of the year, is now considering the idea for the national government. In the summer of 1962 the United Nations held a European seminar in Stockholm on protections against the abuse of administrative authority, at which the scheme was fully discussed.[5] Several Western European countries are now becoming more interested. In the Netherlands, for example, a semi-official committee under the chairmanship of A. D. Belinfante, Professor of Constitutional Law at the University of Amsterdam, is considering the scheme. Since the war, other countries of the world, such as Indonesia and the Philippines, have set up related schemes with similar functions. In the Philippines, for example, President Magsaysay appointed a complaints committee to receive and investigate complaints about official action.

The reason for this widespread interest in the Ombudsman type of institution is not far to seek: there is need for additional protection against administrative arbitrariness in the modern democratic state. All democratic countries in the twentieth century have experienced a shift from the laissez-faire to the positive state. The accompanying tremendous growth in the range and complexity of government activities has brought with it the need to grant increasing powers of discretion to the executive side of government. As one of Britain's great constitutional lawyers, A. V. Dicey, has warned, "Wherever there is discretion, there is room for arbitrariness." In other words, it is quite possible nowadays for a citizen's rights to be accidentally crushed by the vast juggernaut of the government's administrative machine. In this age of the welfare state, thousands of administrative decisions are made each year, many of them by minor officials, which

[4] See, for example, H. J. Abraham, "People's Watchdog Against Abuse of Power," *Public Administration Review*, XX, 3 (Summer, 1960), 152–157, and K. C. Davis, "Ombudsmen in America", *Public Law* (Spring, 1962), 34–42.

[5] *1962 Seminar on Judicial and Other Remedies Against the Abuse of Administrative Authority* (New York, 1962).

affect the lives of every citizen. If some of these decisions are arbitrary or unjustified, there is no easy way for the ordinary citizen to gain redress. In the preface to the recent Whyatt Report, Lord Shawcross expressed the situation in these words (p xiii):

> The general standards of administration in this country are high, probably indeed higher than in any other. But with the existence of a great bureaucracy there are inevitably occasions, not insignificant in number, when through error or indifference, injustice is done—or appears to be done. The man of substance can deal with these situations. He is near to the establishment; he enjoys the status or possesses the influence which will ensure him the ear of those in authority. He can afford to pursue such legal remedies as may be available. He knows his way around. But too often the little man, the ordinary humble citizen, is incapable of asserting himself . . . The little man has become too used to being pushed around: it rarely occurs to him that there is any appeal from what "they" have decided. And as this Report shows, too often in fact there is not.

In the past the courts were the bulwark of individual rights. But the ordinary courts have lost their flexibility and are no longer an effective instrument for remedying the wrongs of modern administrative action. The courts are too costly, cumbersome and slow, and in the English-speaking world the extent of their power of review is not at all clear, though certainly severely limited. Generally, they will review a decision only on a question of legality and refuse to review its content, wisdom, or even reasonableness. For these reasons, in most common-law countries special administrative appeal bodies have been created, to which an aggrieved citizen may take his case. But these bodies cover only a small portion of the total field of administrative action, and the vast majority of administrative decisions carry no formal right of appeal. The situation is better, of course, in those European countries that have developed a comprehensive system of administrative courts, where appeal is easy and cheap. But even administrative courts can be imperfect. Many of them are cumbersome and slow, so that the delay in deciding cases results in a denial of justice. It is significant that though Sweden and Finland have administrative courts, in recent years their

Ombudsmen have found it increasingly necessary to extend their supervision over administrative agencies.

The right to complain to one's Member of Parliament does not meet the problem. Citizens often do not know of this avenue of appeal, and it is usually unsuitable anyway. In countries with a parliamentary system of government, especially where there are only two major parties, the executive tends to dominate the legislature and to maintain a tradition of secrecy. Hence it is difficult to bring cases of maladministration to light. The Member's usual method of dealing with a complaint is to send an inquiry to the department concerned. Naturally the department is likely to put the best light on its own case, and the Member has no impartial source of information. If he is dissatisfied with the department's reply, about all he can do is ask a question of the Minister in the House. Even though the Minister may have had nothing to do with the original decision, he will naturally consider himself a party to the decision and will defend it as his own. About the only further recourse is for the Member, still with inadequate information, to debate the complaint in the House—in which case it will turn into a political battle with the dice loaded in favour of the Minister. The opposition party can of course demand a formal inquiry, but an inquiry is costly and cumbersome, and is accepted by a government only after enough public outcry has been raised. Clearly it is not an adequate device for remedying the average administrative wrong done to the little man. Even in countries where there is a multi-party situation and the executive is not quite so dominant, there is usually no adequate parliamentary procedure for handling complaints, sifting evidence or making recommendations.

In view of the shortcomings of all of these traditional protections against administrative arbitrariness, we may conclude that the office of Ombudsman has a number of desirable characteristics which argue for its adoption. In the words of the Whyatt Report (p. 52):

> First, there is the principle of impartial investigation. If a citizen makes a complaint against the conduct of a civil servant, the matter is investigated and reported upon by the Ombudsman, who is an impartial authority entirely independent of the Administration. Secondly, the impartial authority acts on behalf of

> Parliament although he is also protecting the interests of the individual complainant. Thirdly, the investigation is conducted openly . . . Fourthly, the method of submitting complaints and the investigation of complaints is very informal.

And one might add that, fifthly, since the great weapon of the Ombudsman is criticism, he does not interfere with day-to-day administration. Unlike appeal bodies, he does not substitute his judgment for that of the official, nor does he, like the courts, quash decisions.

III

Let us now consider some of the arguments that have been raised against transplanting the Ombudsman scheme. One reason the English-speaking world took so little interest in the institution before it was adopted in Denmark is that nothing was known of the Finnish plan, and of the Swedish scheme it was argued that the systems of government and law in Sweden were too different for the scheme to be applicable. Sweden has administrative appeal courts, a different system of court review, and a unique tradition of publicity whereby the press and the citizens may have access to departmental files at any time. More important, Sweden has an administrative system radically different from most others; Swedish departments resemble public corporations in their independence, and are not subject to detailed day-to-day control by the Ministers responsible to Parliament. Because of these differences, it was said that the scheme would not work elsewhere. However, its successful adoption in Denmark and its proposal for Norway exploded these claims. For the systems of law and cabinet government in these countries resemble those of the Commonwealth much more closely; neither country has a system of administrative courts, neither has a strong tradition of administrative publicity, and both have the system of ministerial responsibility for administration characteristic of parliamentary government elsewhere.

Too much has been made of the dangers of administrative publicity, in any case. Even in Sweden there are laws against revealing state secrets or information that would be injurious to private persons or commercial firms. The names of complainants and officials involved in cases are not ordinarily revealed, and the amount of publicity given to cases is partly at the discretion of the Ombudsman and is voluntarily controlled by the press. In the nature of things no publicity is given to minor cases of no news interest, and of course important cases *should* be discussed publicly.

A closely related argument against transplanting the office is that, in view of the revelations of the Ombudsmen, the need for a check on officialdom must be greater in the Nordic countries than elsewhere. The Nordic countries, however, are among the best-governed democracies in the world. The standards of their public services are extremely high, and their provisions for appeal of administrative decisions are certainly more ample than in the English-speaking countries. In adopting the Ombudsman system, Denmark and Norway have simply recognized that in the age of the welfare state, traditional controls are not good enough. As the Chairman of the Norwegian Committee on Administrative Procedure expressed it:

> [Our] recommendations are not based upon any assumption or allegation on the part of the Committee that the Norwegian administrative system is a bad one or that the civil servants are incompetent. The Committee states, on the contrary, that our administration may bear comparison with any other system of administration. This is also true of the guarantees and safeguards. The reasons behind the proposals to strengthen the means of control are much more far-reaching and go deeper. They have their origin in the characteristic development of the modern welfare state. It seems unavoidable at the stage of economic and technical development which, regardless of politics, has been achieved in all modern societies, that ever larger and broader powers shall be bestowed upon the administrative authorities . . . This is the background against which the Norwegian proposals—and the many efforts in other countries to introduce reforms in the same field—must be considered.[6]

Curiously, the opposite argument has also been raised—that the need is greater in the English-speaking countries, and is

[6] Terje Wold, "The Norwegian Parliament's Commissioner for the Civil Administration," *Journal of the International Commission of Jurists,* II, 2 (Winter, 1959; Spring-Summer, 1960), 24.

in fact so great that an Ombudsman would be overwhelmed with complaints. *The Times* warned (January 13, 1960) that in a large country like Britain the office might burgeon into something like the Chinese Control Yuan during the Han dynasty (206 B.C.–A.D. 220), which became a parallel branch of government constantly looking over the shoulder of the harried official. Instead of a public watchdog over the official's acts, the Ombudsman might become a bloodhound sniffing after his every decision. But as the *Economist* replied (January 31, 1960), this argument is to stand logic on its head. It is tantamount to saying that because the demand would be overwhelming the need should not be met at all. In any case, the fear is false. The Ombudsman performs his task in the Nordic countries with only five or six legal officers and a few office assistants, and he is certainly no super-administrator with power to substitute his judgment for that of other officials. In fact, he rarely comments on the content of a discretionary decision but rather on the *way* in which the decision has been made, to ensure its legality and fairness. That the bloodhound theory arises from a false fear is shown by the reversal in the attitude of civil servants in Denmark. Before the scheme was introduced they opposed it, but after its adoption they soon realized that the office was an aid rather than a hindrance. For in nine cases out of ten the Ombudsman vindicated their decisions and hence increased public confidence in the civil service. The scheme also shifted much of the task of handling the public's complaints from the civil service to the Ombudsman. Furthermore, minor officials soon found that the Ombudsman was an ally in their own dealings with arbitrary superiors. It is true, of course, that in the absence of a comprehensive system of administrative appeals, the work of an Ombudsman would be greater, but this problem must be attacked at its source.

It is frequently argued that to be the little man's defender the Ombudsman's office must be a highly personal one, while in large countries the size of the office would cause it to lose this personal touch. This argument has also been inverted: it is said that the office is *too* personal, too dependent upon one man's integrity, understanding and daily time; and that the nature of the office demands for its success a virtual impossibility—finding exactly the right man for the job, in particular one who combines a profound knowledge of the law with wide experience in various types of administration. These arguments, too, can be easily challenged. In the first place, there has been a lot of sentimental twaddle about the Ombudsman's personal touch. The principle of impartiality is far more important than the personal touch. Certainly citizens need to know that there is an independent authority to which they can turn for an impartial investigation, but this objective can be achieved without the paternalism inherent in a personalized office. Moreover, there are good grounds for the view that important and complex cases of a judicial nature should *not* be decided by a single person. (In fact, they are not so decided under the Ombudsman scheme. Although the Ombudsman deals with all important cases personally, naturally he and his expert staff discuss all such cases before he reaches a final conclusion, so that in effect they work as a group.) The old adage applied to the higher courts that two heads are better than one also applies here. For this reason I would recommend for populous countries a commission of three members, which might be called the Parliamentary of Administrative Complaints Commission. Commissioners would decide important cases together, but could decide minor cases individually. Each could specialize in a particular area or type of administration. The commission could include a judge and an experienced administrator (and perhaps also a representative of the public). In this way the proposal bypasses the argument that it is virtually impossible to find in a single man the qualities demanded by the office.

Having seen that most of the arguments that have been raised against transplanting the Ombudsman scheme may be effectively demolished, we should at the same time keep in mind that it cannot be a panacea. A number of people in Britain seem to regard "Ombudsman" as a kind of magic word that will cure all their administrative ills. But the age-old problem of the relation between the state and the individual is far too complex to be solved by one simple scheme. We need a whole variety of controls over administrative action, and the Ombudsman scheme must be accompanied by a number of other reforms that are needed to plug the gaps in our systems of control. Otherwise, the scheme may fail because we are trying to make it do too much.

We must remember that in the Nordic countries the scheme only supplements a battery of other effective controls, and that New Zealand is adding this scheme to an already well-developed parliamentary grievance system.

On the other hand, the danger in setting up a network of controls is that if the administration is surrounded with too many controls it will be unable to move. This is the danger in extending court review too far or in judicializing the administrative process too much. The United States has already gone too far in this direction, and recent British changes and proposals seem to point to the same danger. What we need is a fence along the administrative road, not a gate across it. The great virtue of the Ombudsman scheme is that its weapons are publicity and persuasion rather than cumbersome controls; it is in the category of the fence rather than the gate.

Staffing Procedures and Problems in the Soviet Union

Introduction

The signal importance of effective and orderly staffing procedures and criteria in the operation of the state has been recognized by Soviet leaders from very nearly the beginning of Soviet power. The early Bolshevik view that any worker or housewife could easily handle the affairs of government was quickly discarded when the new regime in 1917 and 1918 sought to cope with the complexities of state administration. From that time the Soviet leaders have concentrated heavily on a search for more effective organization and functions and better training and deployment of personnel.

The following description of the state system of the U.S.S.R. provides a useful preface.

Reprinted from a study submitted by the Subcommittee on National Security Staffing and Operations, U.S. Senate (Washington, D. C.: 1963), by permission of the Honorable Henry M. Jackson, Chairman. [Abridged.]

> The Soviet system is a dictatorship in which ultimate power is exercised by the leaders of the Communist Party. While the government apparatus is patterned after that of a Western political democracy, there is no system of checks and balances, and any concept of the separation of powers is definitively rejected. The functions of the government are dictated by the party, whose hegemony is explicitly acknowledged by the Constitution. The prerogative of the party to make state policy and supervise its implementation without direct popular controls or checks is unquestioned, and party influence and power pervade all phases of life from the lowliest private dwelling to the highest councils of state.[1]

Party and government in the Soviet Union, though structurally separate, are actually part and parcel of a single state system. The party Presidium, formally a part of the party structure, is the governing head of the entire system, and its power and authority are exercised through its two executive-administrative arms, the government bureaucracy and the professional party machine. The Soviet state system, moreover, is a totalitarian system embracing virtually every activity in the country. Except for a few minor jobs, all positions from minister to party clerk; from research scientist to streetsweeper; from party secretary to lathe operator—are parts of a single mammoth staff at the service of the Soviet rulers. [Thus, the men who bear ultimate responsibility for the security of the Soviet Union have the full manpower resources of the country at their disposal.][2] How these resources are organized and used in forwarding world Soviet interests is the central problem of this study.

Staffing resources

Official secrecy in the U.S.S.R. puts the Western student of Soviet politics and public administration at a great disadvantage. Practically nothing is being written in the Soviet Union, for instance, on how the governing organs of the party operate or how national policies are formulated. In this situation, there is

[1] U.S. Congress, Senate. Committee on Government Operations.

[2] Subcommittee on National Policy Machinery. *National Policy Machinery in the Soviet Union.* (Washington, U.S. Government Printing Office, 1960), 75 pp.

no public discussion of staffing at the highest levels and one can only guess at what proportion of the manpower pool the Kremlin would consider critical for formulating and carrying out Kremlin global policies.

If they elected to speak on the question, however, the Soviet leaders would probably present a rather broad estimate of their manpower needs in this field. The fact that the entire administrative mechanism—political, military, industrial, etc.—is closely woven together at all levels and operates as a single system makes it difficult to determine at what point the staffing function loses its critical importance. Only a small portion of the total manpower pool, however, is crucial. Soviet population figures will illustrate this point. (See Figure A.)

FIGURE A

MANPOWER RESOURCES IN THE U.S.S.R., 1959

	NUMBER OF PERSONS
Total Labor Force	109,100,000
Workers and Peasants	88,600,000
Intelligentsia	20,500,000
of which:	
Managerial and Professional Personnel	7,467,000

It is within the intelligentsia category that the people essential for "national security" functions will almost certainly be found. However, the intelligentsia includes not only management and professional personnel but also technicians, secretaries, typists, sales and restaurant employees, barbers, and other white-collar workers. The notion of the intelligentsia as a highly select, tightly knit group of intellectuals—as was the case in Russia in the years before the Revolution—is now almost entirely gone.

The nucleus of leadership in the U.S.S.R. is provided by the 390,000 persons who direct the Soviet government, the Communist Party and the various auxiliary organizations—such as the trade unions and the youth group, the Komsomol. Within the party side, there are the Presidium, the Secretariat, and the administrative organs of the Central Committee. On the government side, there is the Council of Ministers with its various ministries, state committees, and chief directorates. Also to be included are the leading party and governmental offices at the republic and regional levels. At the next stage are the nearly two million directors and managers of individual enterprises, including those who head bureaus and branches within factories. Leading members of this group are often promoted into policy-making positions—to the Council of Ministers, for example.

The professional personnel numbering some 5.5 million in 1959, are those persons who through education, experience, or a combination of both have mastered a critical speciality. This includes heads of scientific research establishments and other leading scientific personnel[3]—groups having a particular bearing to this study; it also includes physicians, lawyers, teachers and librarians—occupations generally outside the area under discussion.

Because the U.S.S.R. has no higher educational institutions that offer general education programs comparable with those offered by colleges and universities in the United States, the professional specialist has completely overshadowed the generalist in the U.S.S.R. and Soviet specialists are employed not only in the occupations for which they were trained, but to a degree unknown in the West, in managerial and administrative positions in the economic, social, and political affairs of the nation. Soviet engineers manage industry; physicians run hospitals and public health services; teachers are school administrators; agronomists administer agriculture; and scientists guide the research effort. In addition, a large and growing number of high-level positions in the Communist Party and the various government agencies are held by graduates who majored in engineering.

Staffing government agencies

Despite the crucial role of the party apparatus in supervising, controlling, and administering the regime's policies in the staffing field, the major share of work in staffing government

3 A soviet occupational category that has no U.S. counterpart. Includes faculty members at higher educational institutions, heads of scientific-research establishments, and selected individuals from all fields of learning who are engaged in research and have been awarded the title "scientific worker" by the state.

operations is performed by the government bureaucracy itself. Special government agencies develop tables of organization, job classifications and salary scales for all government agencies, activities, and installations. They administer personnel policies, and collect, process, and maintain statistical data relevant to the staffing process.

The government machinery, as a whole, shares in highlighting problems in the staffing field, and develops information reports and policy proposals for consideration by the Presidium. These functions channel through the Presidium of the Council of Ministers, the executive head of the government, which, within the framework of policies established by the party Presidium, makes decisions governing the operation of the government, interprets state policy, assigns tasks for its implementation, and resolves conflicts arising in the course of government operations.

The government Presidium supervises the staffing of upper echelon positions—down through heads of the major subdivisions of a ministry or state committee—and monitors the operation of the staffing mechanism throughout the government bureaucracy. Its decisions are normally final, just as if made by the party Presidium. The latter probably would take up a problem only if major policy shifts were at issue or if the problem cut across into spheres of interest and responsibility of the top leaders not on the government Presidium.

Each government agency recruits for positions in its own organization, and trains, assigns, promotes, transfers, or dismisses its personnel. Personnel actions in regard to all positions of responsibility within the agency require the express prior approval in each individual case of the appropriate party unit. For upper echelon positions, including all key "national security" positions, the approval must come from the central Secretariat in Moscow. The top 15–20 percent of all government positions are in this manner directly "controlled" by the party machine; assignments to the remaining 80–85 percent of the positions are "uncontrolled," i.e., are completely within the purview of the employing agency, subject to compliance with existing classification schedules, tables of organization and service regulations.

The Council of Ministers is composed of a Chairman (Premier), First Deputy Chairmen, Deputy Chairmen, heads of various Ministries, state committees and other agencies, and certain other individuals included on the Council because of either their position or their responsibilities. The Council is charged by the Soviet Constitution with directing the work of ministries and other governmental bodies, executing the national economic plan and the state budget, strengthening the monetary system, conducting foreign affairs, and supervising the general structure of the armed forces. It is far too large—on May 1, 1963, there were 82 members—for effective decision-making. The actual decisions are made by the much smaller Presidium of the Council of Ministers, with the full Council, which meets only rarely, giving *pro forma* approval.

None of the members of the government Presidium are personnel specialists, but throughout their careers all have had to devote a large share of their time to staffing problems and several of them have been involved in the staffing process not only as officials responsible for the managerial functions of the government, but also, at one time or another, as party executives.

The government Presidium does have a staff to assist it in the personnel work incident to the operations of the Council of Ministers. Little is known about the scope of authority or range of responsibility of this staff but it probably exists primarily to coordinate the work of the personnel departments of the individual agencies, ensuring uniform interpretation and application of existing regulations, and to keep the Premier and Deputy Premiers informed on the state of personnel work in the government. In addition, it would handle the paper work on those personnel actions which are formalized by decree of the Council of Ministers.

Functions related to staffing procedures are spread among several government agencies. The state budget, prepared by the Ministry of Finance, establishes the wage fund of the various ministries, state committees, officers and enterprises. The Central Commission on Staffs, an agency of the Ministry of Finance, is responsible for ensuring that the table of organization and salary schedule of each agency or institution meet the requirements of sound administrative practice and accord with existing legislation. The commission conducts an annual review of all staffing schedules and, if they are satisfactory, registers them for the coming year. An organization cannot draw upon its salary account in the state bank until the staffing schedule it has submitted has been approved. Approval of the commission must also be obtained for any changes in the table of organization or salary schedule desired by an organization during the year. The Control-Auditing Administration of the Ministry of Finance checks on all departments, offices, and institutions for adherence to authorized personnel staffs, salary rates, and wage funds.

The State Committee on Labor and Wages is responsible for working out uniform salary scales and preparing job classifications for all government positions. It is also charged with preparing drafts for government legislation in the salary and wage field.

The Central Statistical Administration gathers, collects, and disseminates manpower statistics, and it maintains the government's central personnel file. The latter includes information on all leading personnel and specialists, gathered by means of special censuses. A major census taken on December 1, 1956, by this administration listed a little over nine million persons in the "leading personnel and specialists" category.

The Party-State Control Commission, a joint control agency of the party and government, is charged with detecting violations of established laws, government regulations, and party directives. In the staffing field it duplicates some of the work of the Control-Auditing Administration of the Ministry of Finance, but the Party-State Control Commission has much broader responsibilities and it can levy administrative penalties for violations.

The Department for Planning the Training and Placement of Graduates, a department of the Ministry of Higher and Specialized Secondary Education, collects requests from government agencies for graduates of the higher educational institutions operated by the ministry. It matches the requests with the expected output of each educational institution and allocates the filling of the requests on the basis of priority need among the various educational institutions by means of a placement order. The responsibility of the department then ceases. All further contact is between the educational institution and the agency requesting graduates.

Each government agency has a personnel department to handle the routine functions involved in the staffing process and to advise the minister, chairman, or other head of agency on personnel matters. These departments maintain the records on personnel whose appointments, promotions or transfers are the direct responsibility of the top officers of the agency. The personnel department also supervises the work of the personnel units in the various offices and enterprises under the jurisdiction of the agency and works out plans for alloting new graduates among the agency's components. The head of the personnel department is usually one of the top officers in the agency—often times one of the deputies to the chief. Formal education in personnel administration has been conspicuously lacking; most personnel specialists have learned the work on the job. An effort has recently been made to improve the quality of personnel administration by assigning to personnel work graduates of juridical faculties who have concentrated on labor, civil and financial law.

STAFFING OPERATIONS IN THE GLOBAL POLICY FIELD

DEPARTMENTS AND AGENCIES. The head of a ministry or state committee enjoys fairly broad discretionary powers in hiring, assigning, promoting, and transferring the rank and file personnel of his department or agency. However, his power to pick his immediate subordinates—the positions of his greatest vital concern—is far more restricted. While recognizing that meaningful executive responsibility requires correspondingly meaningful authority, including that of selecting the subordinates upon whom the effective operation of an organization depends, the top Soviet leaders are reluctant to let direct control of important positions slip from their fingers. They are, moreover, concerned that the solution of large problems of national interest, including the allocation of scarce executive talent, be decided at a level relatively free from departmental rivalries. The result is clearly a compromise. The views of the departmental head are given considerable weight in the selection of his deputies, the heads of the more important divisions of his organization, and other key personnel, but the final decision is made in either the party or the government Presidium.

There is a second, somewhat larger, group of positions in the ministry or state committee, which, although still requiring prior party approval, are not normally the subject of personal attention by the top leaders. These include the lesser division chiefs, their deputies, and most of the positions in which technical control functions are vested, e.g., comptroller and inspector.

The agency has a relatively free hand in staffing the remaining positions. Assignments, transfers, promotions, and removals at the lower levels do not require prior party approval. . . .

Very little is known about the inner workings of the party's staffing units. As noted earlier they maintain personnel files on all party members in their jurisdiction—the central files in Moscow containing data on every Communist in the country—as well as full dossiers on personnel (party members or not) in "controlled" positions. From these records they may find likely candidates. Moreover, party units in all parts of the country can be checked for individuals with the desired qualifications. If the priority need of the "national security" agency is high, the party unit can arrange to transfer a qualified individual from an agency with less critical need.

Scrutiny of the candidate's qualifications by the party agency is apt to be more thorough when the Presidium is not directly involved in making the appointment. One fairly common requirement is that the candidate be personally interviewed by officials at party headquarters in Moscow. Although one of the purposes of the requirement for party approval of upper echelon appointments is to provide a mechanism for securing the most effective deployment of the party's personnel resources, there is some evidence that the party review is often limited in ensuring that the minimum requirements for the position under consideration, as set forth in legislation or in party decrees, are met. One of the frequent complaints about the staffing procedure voiced in the party press is that party officials too often base their decisions about personnel on formal records and do not evaluate the individual's performance in actual working conditions.

The requirement for party approval of upper echelon personnel actions appears, nevertheless, to be the major limitation on the agency head's exercise of executive authority in the staffing field. Government service regulations, to be sure, prescribe staffing procedures and set some limits to the arbitrary authority of the top executive in each agency, and he, like all other government executives, must operate within budgetary ceilings, tables of organization, and salary schedules over which he has no direct control. These limiting factors, however, do not appear an undue restriction on his executive authority. The government service regulations set minimum qualifications (higher education, for example), for particular jobs and provide an orderly system for advancement within the organization, but they grant only minimal protection to the employee against the exercise of managerial power. In the Soviet system individual rights are strictly subordinated to the operating needs of the state machinery. The Soviet executive, therefore, in attempting to improve the quality of his organization's performance does not have to wrestle with such knotty problems as veteran's preference or "bumping" rights. There are few administrative obstacles to removing incompetent or mediocre performers from "uncontrolled" positions, which even in the "national security" agencies may run as high as 80 percent of the total. It is the dearth of competent individuals and an endemic unwillingness to delegate sizable chunks of authority to lower echelons that has led most top executives to accept, if not prefer, the dispersal of functions among a number of mediocre employees rather than concentrating them in the hands of a few, more competent, officers closer to the top of the organization.

INCENTIVES. Staffing in the global operations field, as in other areas of Soviet life, is accomplished through a mixture of direct allocation procedures—assignment and draft—and incentives. During the Stalin era the emphasis in all fields was on direct allocation and restrictive control over job mobility. In recent years, however, the regime has shifted to greater dependence on incentive evidently believing that this gives better results in morale and efficiency than authoritarian placement. The state now depends on manipulation of incentives, coupled with extensive use of propaganda and indirect pressures, to take care of the greater part of its manpower allocation problem. Assignment still plays an important role, however—in the initial placement of most graduates of higher educational institutions, in filling "undesirable" positions, and in staffing executive echelons and critical functions. Information on the relative weight of assignment and incentive is lacking but it is clear that motivational factors are important considerations whether an individual is assigned a position or seeks it on his own.

Psychological incentives for work in the "national security" departments and agencies appear to be quite strong in the Soviet Union. The diplomatic, intelligence, and military (officer level) services have an aura of status and prestige, and they offer the lure of intrigue, travel, and stirring achievement, and a sense of close participation in the most important and critical of state functions. Patriotic motivations are strong and are assiduously cultivated.

High material rewards buttress and reinforce the psychological incentives. For comparable work, salaries in the military, diplomatic, and intelligence fields may run as high as 20 percent greater than in less critical fields. This advantage is shared with a number of agencies—such as Gosplan, for instance—which are also considered of "exceptional significance." Although comparisons are difficult due to the different nature of work, some fields—the scientific and creative arts—may even offer material advantages in excess of those enjoyed by the "national security" agencies. Nevertheless, the professional entering the "national security" field can look forward to a life relatively free of the financial worries that plague most Soviet citizens.

A career in this field offers other material advantages as well. Assignments within the Soviet Union are likely to be in or near Moscow, Leningrad, or the other urban centers where amenities and cultural advantages are to be found and where food and consumer goods are in greater supply. Another strong incentive is the likelihood of foreign assignment and the opportunity for obtaining Western goods. Other benefits include prospects for better housing and educational advantages for self and children.

Sharply differentiated salaries within the agencies provide

strong motivation for job performance and improvement of qualifications leading to promotion. A Soviet graduate beginning a career in one of the "national security" agencies, for example, has an opportunity for a salary increase of nine or ten times his entrance salary. Salaries for most officials in military, diplomatic, and intelligence work, scientific research and development, and a few other fields as well consist of two elements. There is rank pay intended as compensation for education, experience, etc., and appointment pay which varies according to the specific type of duty performed. The income is the sum of the two. In the military and possibly also in the other services, pay is also given for length of service. In addition, recognition of specific personal qualifications can be made in the form of a "personal salary" determined on an individual basis by the appropriate department or agency with specific approval of the Council of Ministers. The personal salary is a major source of the largest wage differentials, and can mean an increase of up to 50 percent of salary.

Moreover, upper echelon positions carry perquisites which may mean more than salary increases. Preferred housing, exemption from restrictions on the amount of living space allowed per person, a *dacha* (country house), greater opportunity for vacations at lavish resorts, chauffeur-driven limousine or private car, preferred medical care, and priority rights for scarce consumer goods are among the more important of these rewards. The net result is a fiercely competitive situation between individuals for advancement.

Orders, honorary titles, and other signs of official recognition are also used to reward outstanding public servants. Security requirements, however, by restricting publicity tend to reduce the effectiveness of this type of incentive.

Effectiveness of the System—An Appraisal

Judgments as to the effectiveness of the Soviet mechanism and procedures for staffing functions must necessarily be heavily qualified. Despite the undoubtedly freer atmosphere developed in the post-Stalin period, the relaxation of many controls, and the opening of the country to foreign visitors, a curtain of secrecy still shrouds most of the system and is, of course, most dense about the agencies and functions that are closely connected with global policy interests. The situation is further complicated by the fact that Soviet authorities have only recently begun to exhibit interest in the idea of teaching government administration and management. They have not in the past considered these important subjects for study and investigation, and as a result have developed very little literature detailing and analyzing their own administrative principles and procedures. Some of the basic features (as outlined in the preceding chapters) can be pieced together from the scraps of information available but these are insufficient for any real depth of understanding of the system. Nevertheless, a few observations may be in order.

The strength of the Soviet challenge in the world today, when the complexities of national and international life are greater than ever before, is in itself a measure of the effectiveness of Soviet staffing. The previous study[4] reached the conclusion that:

> [The machinery on which the Soviet leaders depend for policy formulation] appears to provide well-defined and clearly structured processes for getting policy questions before the Presidium in digested and manageable form, and to combine with this a degree of flexibility which prevents these processes from becoming a limitation on the Presidium's own initiative. The success of the system appears to depend less on its machinery, however, than on the capacity and energy of the men who run it.

The Soviet system appears to have been generally successful in developing and raising competent, often superior, individuals to positions of leadership. The top leaders in [the] regime are a shrewd, tough minded bunch, experienced over a wide range of subjects and capable of handling complex problems of national policy with reasonable foresight and dispatch. Each man on his way to the top has had to prove his worth in the crucible of deadly competition and is under continuing challenge to perform at peak capacity. The price of "failure" is no longer death or imprisonment, but in a society where private employment is

[4] *National Policy Machinery in the Soviet Union, Op. cit.*

almost nonexistent loss of high level position with its perquisites and privileges would appear to be a heavy enough price.

The nature of power in the Soviet Union—constantly subject to challenge, requiring daily maintenance, and shared only at great risk—creates a serious problem, however, in securing the most effective staffing of critical functions. The job of running the country is becoming increasingly complex and difficult. The alternatives in policy issues are more numerous, and the interrelation of functions so intimate that decisions in one field have effects, often deadly serious, extending into diverse other fields. The problem of making intelligent choices is beyond the ability of any one man; it requires the combined efforts of many.

On the positive side, however, the state has a virtual monopoly of employment and a highly centralized mechanism for selection and assignment of personnel. It can thus direct to the solution of critical operations the best the nation can produce in the way of superior, talented, competent, and experienced individuals. It is, of course, quite another problem to identify these individuals, to select the best man for a given job, to motivate him to superior performance, and to create organizational arrangements that will enable the greatest possible use to be made of his capabilities.

For identifying talented and capable individuals, providing the education, training, and work experience necessary for developing their abilities, and assigning them so as to make efficient use of their talents, skills, and experience, the staffing machinery appears to provide reasonably adequate process. The quality of staffing in the middle and lower echelons and in the low priority fields is rather spotty and probably rates only poor to mediocre, but in respect to the upper echelon positions and the more critical functions, areas which receive the closest high-level attention, the staffing appears generally good.

The U.S.S.R. still lacks enough generally capable individuals for staffing the middle and lower echelons of the administrative apparatus. The situation in this regard is improving with the steady expansion of education facilities and the efforts of the regime to promote promising young people to positions of responsibility but the needs of the state are far from being satisfied. The question might be raised, however, whether the Soviet regime is making most effective use of the able people it produces. There is little doubt but that it has been quite successful in concentrating its most capable individuals in the key leadership and other priority areas; but it may be that the effort to ensure adequate staffing in these areas has led to the assignment to them of more of the highly talented and capable individuals than they can use effectively. There is at least a hint that a number of individuals are being used in positions that do not permit full utilization of their capabilities, with promotions blocked by the presence of experienced personnel above them.

Overstaffing, a chronic problem in most bureaucracies, is especially marked in the Soviet Union. Nicholas DeWitt in his monumental study *Education and Professional Employment in the U.S.S.R.*[5] notes that:

> On the eve of Stalin's death, one of every seven Soviet workers and employees was administering or managing something or someone. During Khrushchev's administration, the managerial apparatus declined in size . . . and the proportion of managerial elite was reduced to one out of every ten workers and employees.

Even this sharp improvement leaves the Soviet Union saddled with proportionately one of the largest bureaucracies in the world.

Figures on which to judge the extent of overstaffing in the "national security" agencies are unavailable, but there is no reason to assume that those agencies are wholly free of something that so clearly afflicts other agencies of the state. When the eminent Soviet engineer-physicist P. L. Kapitsa a few years ago returned to the Soviet Union from Great Britain and a new institute was established for him, he was assigned four bookkeepers for his staff, although the institute was relatively small. Exercising his authority as director, Kapitsa dismissed three of them. On being queried about his action, Kapitsa replied: "I would have dismissed more, but unfortunately a bookkeeper, like an integer, is indivisible."

[5] National Science Foundation, Washington, D.C., U.S. Government Printing Office, 1961.

The causes of this overstaffing are too complex to be completely sorted out here. Many are common to bureaucracies the world over; others are grounded in the nature of the Soviet political system. One of the continuing factors has been the short supply of competent individuals and the uncertainty of replacement which has led administrators to hoard personnel like other resources. Then, too, the lack of an individual competent enough to do a particular job has forced the supervisor to parcel it out among two or more persons to get it done. The administrative attitudes and habits which these factors have engendered over a long period of time continue, even though, as in some areas, there are now enough generally competent personnel available.

This last point is part of a broader problem of revitalizing the government and party to meet the growing complexity of today's problems. Overcoming the bureaucratic stagnation that had developed during the Stalinist period was the main thrust of the de-Stalinization campaign launched in 1956 and pushed in varying degree since then. Old attitudes and habits die hard, however, and the ultimate solution to the problem of overcoming the Stalinist legacy probably demands the replacement of the older generation of state officials with younger, more imaginative and dynamic ones. The regime has been reluctant to tackle the problem in such a radical fashion, however, being clearly unwilling to accept the full implications of such a move and fearful of its own ability to control the rate and direction of the change it would engender.

The Relationship Between Collegial and One-Man Management in Soviet State Administration at the Present Stage of Development

IU. M. KOZLOV

UNDER THE CONDITIONS of the state of the entire people, we are witnessing an all-round improvement in the functioning of the state administrative machinery. The skill with which its organizing function is performed will largely determine the degree of success that will be attained in reaching the goals for the next decade set in the CPSU Program. The reorganization, on the party's initiative, of the system of central and local administrative agencies is making for an unmistakable rise in the economic component of the executive and administrative work of the state of the entire people. The principle of democratic volunteer activity in the organization and functioning of the government machinery is being advanced consistently. The techniques of Soviet administration are also being improved. As a consequence, considerable interest attaches to the problem of the interrelationship between collegial and one-man management techniques in the functioning of the administrative machinery. Certain aspects of this problem will be considered in this article.

We know that Lenin described collegial and one-man management as two forms of organization of Soviet governmental administration.[1] Consequently, collegial and one-man management are primarily organizational forms of government adminis-

Reprinted from *Soviet Law and Government,* Vol. 3, No. 2 (Fall, 1964), pp. 3–12, by permission.

[1] See V. I. Lenin, *Soch.,* Vol. 30, pp. 285–89.

tration. Board-governed and individually managed administrative bodies are differentiated accordingly.[2] Collegiality and one-man management are not only forms of organization; they are, essentially, the fundamental methods of operation of the administrative apparatus.[3]

Theoretically it is possible to draw a line of demarcation between them. But in practical affairs we see a close combination of the two principles in the operations both of board-governed and individually directed agencies. Lenin noted that "just as collegiality is essential for discussing major questions, so one-man responsibility and executive power are essential so as to avoid red tape and make it impossible to dodge responsibility."[4] In accordance with this, collegiality is the chief method of discussion and decision of the most important problems in agencies under collegial management, while some matters involving daily operations are resolved individually in these bodies by the appropriate guiding personnel. Here, individual decision-making is an auxiliary technique and is permitted for the purpose of eliminating the burden of discussion and decision on matters susceptible to solution in the course of actual operations. In agencies under individual management, we see the collegial principle at work as a method whereby basic questions of leadership are discussed until a decision is taken by the responsible indivdual. The collegial and individual-management principles may be encountered in this combination in any administrative agency of government. This promotes, on the one hand, improvement in the quality of the decisions taken on matters of principle and, on the other, the necessary flexibility in the work of the administrative apparatus. At the same time, this combination of techniques helps to establish "the most precise *responsibility of each* of the persons holding any Soviet post for *the execution of specific,*

[2] See *Sovetskoe administrativnoe pravo. Obshchaia chast'*, Gosiurizdat, Moscow, 1962, pp. 124–26.

[3] See V. A. Vlasov, *Sovetskii gosudarstvennyi apparat,* Gosiurizdat, Moscow, 1959, pp. 275–79; Iu. M. Kozlov, *Kollegial'nost' i edinonachalie v sovetskom gosudarstvennom upravlenii,* Gosiurizdat, Moscow, 1956, pp. 3–5; E. V. Shorina, *Kollegial'nost' i edinonachalie v sovetskom gosudarstvennom upravlenii,* Gosiurizdat, Moscow, 1959, pp. 7–12.

[4] V. I. Lenin, *Soch.,* Vol. 30, p. 222.

clearly and unambiguously outlined, tasks and *practical undertakings*."[5]

These are the points of departure that make it possible to analyze the problem of the interrelation between collegial and one-man management in Soviet government administration under the conditions of the state of the entire people.

During the period of the personality cult, Lenin's principle of collective leadership was forgotten. Having concentrated excessive power into his hands, Stalin personally decided numerous important economic and political questions. Under conditions in which centralization of state leadership was carried to its extreme, the role of the purely administrative machinery, in which the significance of group forms of leadership was significantly denigrated, increased. Nor did the creative initiative of the people acquire the scope it required. Meetings of activists in various branches of the economy and meetings in the villages were hardly held at all. Conferences and meetings that involved public participation were usually conducted as pure formalities, in an atmosphere of display, and so forth.

The CPSU, having led the struggle to overcome all the harmful consequences of the personality cult, gave its major attention to reestablishing Leninist standards and principles of life in the party and government and, above all, the principle of collective leadership. With respect to the system of Soviet state administration, the measures of primary significance were those directed, first, to expanding the existing collegial forms of organization and methods of operation of the administrative apparatus and, second, to assuring ever broader public participation in the discussion of major questions of administrative activity. These two processes, developed interrelatedly, make for not intermittent, but constant participation by representatives of the public in the functioning of administrative agencies. On this basis, a shift is being made, gradually but undeviatingly, from a situation in which various problems of the economy and culture were discussed jointly with the public to one in which they are decided jointly with it.

If we begin by recognizing the existence of an organic

[5] *Ibid.*, Vol. 28, p. 326.

interconnection between the two sides of the single process of development of collegial forms of Soviet administration, it appears to us that it is possible to identify the following major paths along which the collegial principle will develop under the conditions of the state of the entire people:

Expansion of the system of collegial agencies of administration. The past decade has seen the establishment of many bodies that function on the collegial principle (economic councils, certain administrative agencies in agriculture, etc.).

Emergence of new collegial forms of management in the system of local administration. As we know, the decisions of the March (1962) Plenum of the CPSU Central Committee resulted in a reorganization of the management of agriculture. The production administrations created on this basis have one-man management. However, all basic questions of guidance to the production and procurement of farm produce are resolved collectively. The organizational expression of this is the council of the production administration, which considers and decides the fundamental questions of agricultural production, the development and reinforcement of the economies of the collective and state farms, and the organization of labor and its remuneration. The proposals worked out by the council are carried into effect by the production administration.[6] Consequently, what we have here is a decision-making body, not a consultative group.

The appearance of new forms of collegial leadership in the central administration. In accordance with the decisions of the November (1962) Plenum of the CPSU Central Committee, new administrative agencies were established to perform functions of centralized planned guidance (the Supreme Economic Council of the USSR, the Economic Council of the USSR, and others), in which the collegial principle found specific expression. Thus, the USSR Supreme Economic Council has a Bureau of eleven members, and the Economic Council has a Collegium that may have up to fifteen members. Being organized on the collegial principle,[7] these agencies consequently have special subdivisions, also established on that principle, that are designed to consider and resolve corresponding problems of guidance to the economy.

6 See *SP SSSR,* 1962, No. 5, Item 38.

7 Thus, the USSR Economic Council may have fifty to sixty members.

Analogous forms of collegiality may be seen in the organization and activity of a number of the state committees (for example, the Academic Council of the USSR State Committee for the coordination of Scientific Research).

Enhancement of the role of existing forms of collegial leadership in administrative agencies under one-man management. This finds expression, for example, in the increased importance placed upon the collegial decision of important matters in the management of branches of the economy. Thus, with the object of further improving personnel work and adhering to the collegial principle in choosing and assigning people, it has been established that individuals in the categories subject to appointment by ministries and departments may be named and released at meetings of the collegia, after consideration of the appropriate presentations.[8]

The development of volunteer collegial forms in the administrative machinery. We have in mind the formation of various volunteer councils under local and central administrative agencies, their purpose being to discuss and consider problems whose resolution falls within the competence of the given agency. Councils of this type are being established under one-man and board-type agencies in the managements of enterprises and institutions (volunteer councils of departments of the executive committees, of ministries and their departments, councils on technical and economic matters under the economic councils, etc.).

Expansion of the membership of collegial agencies by adding representatives of public organizations.[9]

Development of forms of joint consideration of problems of guidance to economic and cultural development by administrative agencies and public organizations. Such forms have had intensive development during the past decade. This is vividly indicated, for example, by trade union experience. Thus, it has been established that consideration of problems of production,

[8] See *SP SSSR*, 1960, No. 6, Item 37.

[9] It is on this basis that one finds in the legal literature the emphatic assertion that administrative agencies of a new type—jointly governmental and civic—have arisen (see Ts. A. Iampol'skaia, "Aktual'nye problemy nauki sovetskogo administrativnogo prava," *Sovetskoe gosudarstvo i pravo*, 1962, No. 10, p. 16. It would seem, however, that the nature of the agency is primarily determined not by its composition, but by the authority it enjoys.

labor, and everyday life by ministries and departments must involve the participation of the central committees of the corresponding trade unions, and that their consideration by economic councils, councils of ministers of autonomous republics, and executive committees of local soviets must involve the participation of representatives of the regional and urban trade union councils.[10] The actual relationships maintained by factory and shop committees and production conferences with factory managements provide clear examples of joint consideration of problems in the organization of production.[11] This results in broad collegiality in the consideration of important problems of management and ensures that public opinion will be taken into account when final decisions are made.

Expansion of the practice of mass discussions of problems of government administration and draft decisions. In order to find the best solution to a given problem, administrative agencies have constant recourse to group experience and to the opinion of the broad Soviet public, which thus brings significant influence to bear upon the issuance of government decisions (USSR-side, republic-wide, industry-wide and local conferences, meetings, bodies of actively concerned people, as well as national discussions of drafts of the most important acts).

Development of forms of joint resolution of questions of government administration by government agencies and public organizations. In this area one may speak of the joint resolution of questions on the basis of the addition of representatives of public organizations to board-type administrative agencies (for example, commissions on the acceptance of buildings that have undergone major repair). Distinctive forms of the joint resolution of problems may also be seen in the everyday collaboration between administrative agencies and the public (for example, agencies of the Union of Athletic Societies and Organizations decide, jointly with ministries and departments, on the plans for training physical culture and sports personnel, etc.). A specific form of joint decision is the carrying out, by administrative agencies, of various measures on the basis of prior consultation

10 See *SP RSFSR,* 1958, No. 11, Item 111.

11 See *Vedomosti Verkhovnogo Soveta SSSR,* 1958, No. 15, Item 282; *SP SSSR,* 1958, No. 13, Item 101.

and agreement with the public. The degree and nature of this coordination vary, although there are cases in which no decision may be taken without this (for example, overtime work or the discharging of personnel). Finally, this category includes the issuance of joint acts by administrative agencies and the organs of public organizations.

Development of collegial forms of administration of government affairs on the basis of the transfer of certain functions or branches of government administration to public organizations. Any transfer of functions to the public involves change in the manner in which they are effectuated, as well as extensive development of collective leadership. This concept is emphasized, for example, in the joint resolution of the CPSU Central Committee and the USSR Council of Ministers "On Guidance to Physical Culture and Sports in the Country," of January 9, 1959, which pointed to the need for broad democratic principles in the development of the movement for physical culture and sports.[12]

Thus, examination of the major trends in the development of collegial forms of Soviet administration under the conditions of the state of the entire people permits one to conclude that the sphere of collegiality has expanded both with respect to the process of discussion and that of resolution of problems of guidance to economic and cultural progress. At the same time, the very diversity of these trends and the concrete forms of collegial guidance is evidence of the general enlargement of the role played by the collegial principle as a technique of Soviet administration. This is in full accord with the nature of the state of the entire people and Lenin's familiar precept that "collegiality is essential in deciding the business of the workers' and peasants' state," and that "only collective experience, only the experience of the millions is capable of yielding . . . definitive guidance."[13]

In connection with the foregoing, it is proper to pose the question of the relationship between collegiality as a method of Soviet administration and the principle of mass participation in the functioning of state agencies. What we have said provides

[12] See *SP SSSR,* 1959, No. 1, Item 1.

[13] V. I. Lenin, *Soch.,* Vol. 29, p. 403; Vol. 27, p. 374.

persuasive evidence of the role of the public in developing collegial forms of administration. However, a viewpoint holding that it is an unjustified expansion of the concept of collegiality even to post the idea that collegiality presumes the involvement of a broad mass of active citizens in the work of the agencies of government has been expressed in the legal literature. This view contends that collegiality is merely a particular organizational and legal form whereby certain government agencies function.[14] It would appear to us that such a conclusion is, in the first place, pedantic and, in the second place, does not reflect the objective process of development of collegial forms of Soviet administration under the circumstances of the state of the entire people, when the role of public opinion is rising steadily in all spheres of state and social life.

Under these conditions one cannot rely on a purely formal legal analysis of collegiality and not take into consideration the effect upon the concept exercised by the increasingly significant civic activity in the organization and functioning of the state administrative machinery. It appears to us that collegiality assumes participation in the discussion of a given question by the corresponding group of people, regardless of the specific nature of the group in the given case (paid staff personnel or volunteers). We know that Lenin also spoke of collegiality with reference to the period of "meeting-sickness," i.e., the detailed discussion by collectives of the working people of new tasks facing them ("random," "diffuse" collegiality).[15] And when we speak of collegiality in the work of administrative agencies, we have in mind not only forms, specified in law, of the organization of the functioning of a particular collegial-type or individually managed agency (for example, the quorum, the session, etc.) but also the opportunities available to these bodies for determining the joint opinion of the public on a given matter (conferences, groups of activists, etc.).

Collective leadership is expressed in the fact that all fundamental problems are discussed and decided jointly. It is precisely in this sense that it is said of collegial agencies that they exercise collective leadership. However, the principle of collec-

[14] See E. V. Shorina, *op. cit.,* p. 21.

[15] See V. I. Lenin, *Soch.,* Vol. 30, pp. 285–86.

tive leadership is most typical of public organizations. Therefore, we do not have sufficient grounds for asserting that the management of, for example, the individual enterprises and institutions is conducted on collective principles for, as we know, forms of one-man management are dominant here (at least as expressed in formal organization and law). But we can say confidently that collegiality does exist here, having in mind the various forms of mass or public discussion of fundamental problems of management. Naturally, we are not referring to discussion "in the line of command," i.e., among the personnel directly subordinate to the given official who has full responsibility, but of a broader type of discussion, which makes it possible to take into consideration the opinion of rank-and-file personnel of the given branch or enterprise, the opinion of public organizations.

Collective discussion is one of the elements of collegiality. Consequently, collegiality develops not only on the basis of the purely internal resources of the given agency of management, but by the involvement of the broad public in its work. This applies both to board-managed and to individually directed agencies. This concept was clearly expressed in N. S. Khrushchev's report to the November (1962) Plenum of the Central Committee of the CPSU: "The Leninist principle of one-man management is operative in the administration of our enterprises. And this is proper. However, certain comrades understand the principles of one-man management one-sidedly as a zeal for giving orders, high-handedness, and the control of production without the active participation of workers, specialists, and office personnel. These comrades forget Lenin's precept with respect to a proper combination of the principle of one-man management and the broadest involvement of the masses in the direct management of production." It is precisely when it functions in the closest possible combination with collegiality in the discussion of matters of fundamental significance (including public discussion), that one-man management constitutes a flexible, effective technique of Soviet administration.

What is the relation of one-man management to the principle of mass participation in Soviet administration? Basically, the question is that of what constitutes the essence of one-man management under present conditions. As we know, one-man management has always been most clearly manifested in the sphere of direct and operational management of production. The broad powers granted to the solely responsible executive make for successful direction of socialist production and assure the necessary labor discipline and organization. In the final analysis, they assist in unifying the personnel into a solid collective, bringing about combined efforts, and directing their joint activity to the solution of the problems facing the given enterprise, institution, or agency. Without this unity, the essential organization and discipline are impossible.

In addition, one-man management, considered on this plane, presumes the reinforcement and expansion of contacts between the manager and the collective being managed. "We must learn," Lenin pointed out, "to combine the 'meeting' democracy of the toiling masses—turbulent, surging, overflowing its banks like a spring flood—with *iron* discipline while at work, with *absolute obedience* to the will of a single person, the Soviet manager, during working hours."[16] Therefore, Soviet one-man management, as actual experience testifies, does not exclude but presupposes, as an essential, the broad participation of the working people in administration, in the discussion of questions of production and other matters, as well as the broad development of criticism and control from below and constant recourse to the experience, initiative, and support of the masses.

The CPSU Program points out that while there must be rigorous maintenance of the personal responsibility of each executive for the work assigned to him, it is necessary to effectuate collegiality consistently in the functioning of all links of the governmental and economic machinery. In accordance with this principle, it would appear to us that one-man management is presently acquiring, to an ever-increasing degree, the character of a technique of Soviet administration that operates most effectively in the process of execution of decisions collectively taken or discussed. It is precisely in this area that personal responsibility must be increased. At the same time, one-man management is increasingly associated with the solution of current problems of guidance, not only in board-managed agencies but in those under individual executives.

16 V. I. Lenin, *Soch.*, Vol. 27, p. 241.

Of course, it would be premature to formulate any rule on this basis, for it is by no means possible clearly to discern such changes in all branches of Soviet state administration (the military may serve as an example). However, if we were to analyze the relations between, for example, the executives of industrial and other enterprises, on the one hand, and trade union organizations on the other, which are regulated by the legislation now in effect and by other normative acts, it would not be difficult to arrive at the firm conclusion that all the major questions in the planning and organization of production at enterprises are considered, and are often resolved, by the management jointly with the unions and the collective of workers.

This situation is due to a number of factors, among which the central one is the constant enhancement of the role of the collectives of workers and office employees in deciding problems having to do with the everyday operation of the enterprises. In this connection it is important to note, for example, that the decisions of production conferences are carried into effect by enterprise managements. However, inasmuch as these decisions are adopted with the participation of management representatives, the conclusion may be drawn that one-man management is manifested specifically in the area associated with the effectuation of these collectively adopted decisions.

It is also necessary to take into consideration the fact that "no matter what abilities some figure may possess, no matter how much he contributes to the work, no real, lasting success can be gained without the support of the group, without the most active participation of the entire party and of the broad masses of the people."[17] This was also pointed out at the November Plenum of the Central Committee of the CPSU, when the need for a further increase in the role of the collectives of workers and office personnel in the management of enterprises was emphasized.[18] On this basis, one-man management is, under today's conditions, increasingly associated with the execution of decisions adopted or elaborated with the participation of the appropriate collectives, and this is particularly true in the sphere of day-to-day manage-

[17] N. S. Khrushchev, *Zakliuchitel'noe slovo na XXII s'ezde KPSS,* Gospolitzdat, Moscow, 1961, pp. 39–40.

[18] See N. S. Khrushchev, *Razvitie ekonomiki SSSR i partiinoe rukovodstvo narodnym khoziaistvom,* Gospolitizdat, Moscow, 1962, p. 72.

ment. One-man management finds its direct expression in heightened personal responsibility for the process of getting things done.[19]

At present it is actually difficult to contend that, for example, the director of an enterprise personally decides all the principal questions involved in the management of production, inasmuch as he decides these questions either jointly with the trade union or on the basis of obligatory consideration of its opinion or, finally, with consideration of the opinion of the production conferences, which constitute representative agencies of the workers and office personnel of the given enterprise. However, this does not mean that one-man management as such no longer exists here. It certainly continues, for executives not only make individual decisions on operational matters, but they organize, on the basis of strictly personal responsibility, the execution of decisions on major matters that have been arrived at jointly with the trade unions, etc. These propositions also have a direct bearing on the functioning of the central organs of government administration that are constructed on the basis of one-man management. Here, too, as experience has shown, one-man responsibility is associated to a great extent with the solution of operational and current problems, and with the execution of measures that have been determined collectively. All this gives expression to Lenin's formula with respect to joint discussion and one-man responsibility[20] and is in complete accord with the rising role of collective methods of work under the conditions of the state of the entire people.

In this connection it is legitimate to pose the question of the degree to which the one-man management of certain central agencies of administration (the state committees and ministries) meets the conditions of the day. It would appear that, with respect to these agencies, account must be taken of a number of important factors in describing their techniques of operation. If it is possible to suggest that even the director of an enterprise may not be in a position to cover all aspects of the work, and correctly and completely to decide all the questions that arise each day, then the problem is more directly applicable to the

[19] A similar viewpoint is held by A. E. Lunev (see *Sovetskoe gosudarstvo i pravo*, 1962, No. 7, p. 29).

[20] See V. I. Lenin, *Soch.*, Vol. 33, p. 47.

heads of agencies of the central administration who are entrusted with one-man management.

Further, the tasks which the central agencies for the various branches of the economy are called upon to fulfill today have to do chiefly with realizing overall national coordination, making decisions on basic problems of technological policy, and performing functions in the fields of science and technology, on the one hand, and the organization of operations on the other, i.e., matters that absolutely demand collective experience. However, analysis of the normative acts regulating the organization and activity of these agencies indicate that attention is centered primarily upon the techniques of one-man management. Yet the nature of the tasks involved in managing branches of the economy centrally, as well as the work of the existing collegia, provide definite grounds for a more flexible approach to the problem of the basic techniques of their operation.

If we consider the role of the ministerial collegia from this angle, our attention is immediately drawn to the fact that they are often described as advisory bodies to the minister.[21] In our view, such an approach cannot be supported today. The collegia of the ministries cannot be regarded as purely advisory bodies. This is testified to, particularly, by the instruction that decisions of a collegium are carried into effect by orders issued by the minister. The collegium resolves matters of administration pertinent to it, and its role in the decision of personnel problems is also great. It has the right to hear the reports of local agencies on their activity, etc. Obviously, such authority does not correspond to the nature of the ordinary advisory agency.

In a word, the regulations governing each ministry provide that the collegium shall participate directly in the decision of all the most important questions of practical guidance.[22] In cases in which the activity of a ministry is subjected to criticism, attention is always directed to the fact that the collegium has given poor guidance to the given field. This, however, is the factual state of affairs. Legally, as we know, the ministries constitute an area in which one-man management is firmly entrenched. This creates the impression that the minister alone has the right

21 See, for example, Ts. A. Iampol'skaia, *op. cit.*, p. 18.

22 See, for example, *SP RSFSR*, 1959, No. 20, Item 167.

personally to resolve all the major questions of leadership of the given branch of administration for the USSR as a whole, or for a republic. Is it not time to bring the factual and legal aspects of the question of the status of the collegia into accord with each other?

Under present conditions, when the scale of governmental management of the branches of the economy and culture has grown immeasurably, and the content of centralized planned leadership has become more complex, a one-man structure and one-man methods of operation in the ministries and departments do not, in our view, correspond to the tasks and content of this leadership. It must also be borne in mind that the USSR ministries have, as a rule, lost direct contact with the entities they guide. Many of them no longer have the responsibilities of direct management which typified them until 1957. Therefore, the ministries and departments must, under today's conditions, be organized and function as collegial organs. In this connection, an important role should be played by the official ratification of the status of the existing collegia as decision-making agencies.[23] The conversion of the ministries into collegial agencies would not, of course, change the usual relationship between collegiality and one-man management in executive operations, for the head of the collegium would be empowered individually to decide current questions (as occurs, for example, in the executive committees of local soviets). But it would codify those forms and methods of central branch administration that have in fact long since made a place for themselves and are in fullest accord with the conditions of the day.

There is yet another organizational matter that bears directly upon the problem under consideration. Experience has shown that the state committees are best suited to cope with the tasks of overall national coordination. This is illustrated most clearly by the measures taken on the basis of the decisions of the November Plenum of the CPSU Central Committee. However, these measures have not yet affected the entire system of central organs, among which there are ministries (for example, of culture and of higher and secondary specialized education for the USSR as a whole) that have, to a considerable degree, lost direct contact

[23] On this question, see A. E. Lunev, *op. cit.*, pp. 28–29.

with the individual institutions and are therefore expected basically to deal with problems of coordination and methods. Consequently, here too the necessary foundation exists for converting them into state committees for their fields. But this transformation involves, as does the organization and activity of the state committees already established, a decision on the question not only of the name of the agency (which is not, of course, fundamental) but of the manner in which its work is to be organized. A serious discrepancy exists in this field at present. Despite the fact that their names proclaim collegiality, the state committees actually function as bodies under one-man management. That is to say, the practices of the ministries, under which collegially adopted decisions, appeal procedures, and the like, are subject to the approval of a single individual, have been transferred automatically to the state committees, without consideration of that which is specific to their tasks. In our view, the state committees must be collegial not only in name and organization, but also in methods of operation. This is entirely determined by the nature of the functions of state agencies of this type. This would not involve a weakening of personal responsibility, as its existence is assumed not only within the framework of one-man management but also under collegial arrangements (for example, the responsibility of the head of a collegial body, the division of duties among the members of this body, etc.).

During the period of the comprehensive building of communism, collegiality in all spheres of governmental administration takes on particular importance. This is due primarily to two factors: the rising scale on which communism is being built, and the active participation of the people in the work of guiding economic and cultural development, and in managing the affairs of the state of the entire people. Under these conditions, collective leadership (and collegiality is one of its manifestations) makes for improved guidance to the development of our national economy, better organizational work on the part of the administrative apparatus, and proper training of personnel. It opens new possibilities for the all-round development of socialist democracy both in the sense of democratization of the methods of administration themselves, and in the sense of further active involvement of the citizens of our country in the activity of the agencies of government.

The development of governmental and civic forms of collegiality does not diminish the significance of the principle of one-man management, which is organizationally reinforced on the basis of expansion of the range of current problems subject to final decision on the part of the fully responsible executive, as well as the active participation of the working people in the consideration of fundamental problems of management. This goal is served, in particular, by the formation, at the enterprises, of broadly representative production committees. "The Leninist principle of one-man management," notes N. S. Khrushchev, "is not violated here but, given the changing circumstances, the role of the public in the management of production is increased in the period of the building of communist society."[24]

What we have said permits us to draw certain conclusions involving the further development of the techniques of collegiality and one-man management in Soviet governmental administration:

a) The agencies of government administration that perform tasks of centralized planned management today stand in need of a collegial structure because of their purposes, scale of operation, and the character of their specific functions. This applies both to the state committees and the ministries (departments). At present, however, collegial methods are expressed consistently and precisely only in the organization and functioning of the USSR State Committee for the Coordination of Scientific Research. In our opinion, it would be desirable to return to the former designation of the central agencies of administration of the branches of government—people's commissariats—or to make use of some other name, say, boards of public commissioners [*kollegii narodnykh upolnomochennykh*]. Such a designation would reflect the real essence of Soviet executive authority, for the fact is that all these agencies function on the authorization of the people, derived from the highest organs of the people's authority.

b) Under present circumstances, civic forms of collegiality are undergoing intensive development in Soviet administration.

24 N. S. Khrushchev, *op. cit. supra* 18, p. 73.

To stimulate them further, it would be desirable to carry out a number of measures aimed at expanding the participation of representatives of public organizations in the work of the collegial organs of management (the inclusion of larger numbers of representatives of the trade unions and the Komsomol in the boards of the ministries, departments, and state committees; the establishment of a broad system of various civic councils and commissions of a consultative and advisory nature under the agencies of administration, with the transfer to them of decision-making powers over particular problems, subject to final approval by the appropriate organ of administration; extension of the practice of the issuance of joint legal acts by branch agencies of management and the organs of public organizations, etc.).

c) The question of providing representation for public organizations in the local agencies of administration (the executive committees) merits attention. Perhaps it is permissible, with due consideration for the existing elective system, to add representatives of public organizations to the executive committees and to give them a consultative voice.

d) It would seem that various types of civic councils attached to local agencies of government administration (for example, the departments of executive committees) should be encouraged. This is particularly important if we bear in mind the exceedingly small paid staffs of these agencies of administration under one-man management. In actuality, opportunities exist to form such councils under any of the branch agencies of local administration. In addition, it is necessary to take steps to elevate the role of these councils. At the present time, there are no legal acts that fix, to any significant degree, their status in the system of local Soviet administration. It would seem to us that such an act is essential, and that it can be developed and approved by the presidiums of the supreme soviets of the union republics. In so doing, attention must naturally be given to expanding the functions of the civic councils, which today carry out monitoring functions for the most part. It seems to us that it would be mistaken to confine their activity to monitoring alone. Civic activity can be successfully utilized in all the major areas of activity of the local branch machinery of government.

e) The development and reinforcement of public participation in the consideration and resolution of the major problems of the functioning of enterprises and institutions is directly associated with the need to intensify the control exercised by the collectives of working people over the work of their managers, who exercise one-man management. In this connection, the prerequisites are already maturing for the associated personnel of enterprises and institutions to move from participation in the consideration and resolution of problems of management to direct participation in the selection of managerial personnel. Specifically, in those units of the administrative apparatus that are expected to provide direct management of the affairs of scientific and educational collectives, all the main administrative posts can even now, practically speaking, be made elective (the rector of a university, the director of an institute, etc.).

These, then, are some of the questions bearing on the relationship between collegial and one-man management in Soviet administration at its present stage.

Staffing Procedures and Problems in Communist China

Staffing the Government

The Chinese Communists conceive of the Government of the People's Republic of China as the executive instrumentality for carrying out policies decided by the party. The task they give the government is to help formulate and then execute plans for the implementation of the party's general line. This is a huge job since the government has to regulate not only such normal national security functions as defense, diplomacy and peace and order, but also a wide range of activities taken over by the communists, from industrial production to domestic and foreign

---

Reprinted from a study submitted by the Subcommittee on National Security Staffing and Operations, U.S. Senate (Washington, D.C.: 1963), by permission of the Honorable Henry M. Jackson, Chairman. [Abridged.]

trade, sports and even radio broadcasting. As a result, China's bureaucratic apparatus is immense.

The party organization remains separate and distinct from that of the government. The party as an organization stays clear of actual governmental administration. Party members are, however, spotted all through the government, from top to bottom. It is through their efforts that, in the words of a veteran communist, "the administrative agencies of the government are made to accept policies of the party and turn them into policies of the government."

STAFFING REQUIREMENTS FOR SENIOR POSTS. The nominal number-one job in the government, the Chairman of the Republic, is largely a procedural and ceremonial post. The Chairman is the formal chief of state. He has no direct control, by virtue of his government position, over the State Council or the ministries, which together handle the real administrative chores of the government. However, in Communist China, the chief of state has in fact been a figure of commanding importance by virtue of his party position. The first Chairman of the Republic, Mao Tse-tung, resigned in 1959 and was succeeded by Liu Shao-chi.

The chief executive is the premier, the principal officer of the State Council. The State Council includes 16 vice premiers and some 30 ministers and heads of commissions plus a secretary general. This group has such authority as is given the government to make high-level decisions necessary for carrying out national security policies. The premier and 12 of the 16 vice premiers are members of the Politburo; the other four are high ranking Central Committee members.

Broad functional control under the State Council is exercised by its six staff offices. These operate as more or less permanent coordinating committees, with a varying number of related ministries under their purview. They are the government counterparts of the party's central departments. Besides these staff offices, the State Council's Secretariat and the premier's office provide general coordinative functions. The Secretariat serves as the official link between the council and provincial and local administrations. The premier's office contains his personal staff performing such functions as he directs.

What does the party center look for in the men it assigns to jobs on the State Council? Mao Tse-tung and his confederates are doubtless looking for individuals who: 1) have a long and spotless party history; 2) have a demonstrated competence in the administration of complex problems and large numbers of people; and 3) have some acquaintance and experience with the specific affairs of the office.

The degree to which the first qualification predominates is illustrated by the fact that 75 per cent of the State Council membership is made up of party men. These are, for the most part, members of the party's Central Committee and are thus, in the party's judgment, its best career officers and administrators. Membership on the Central Committee identifies a man who has spent virtually all his adult life in the management of increasingly important affairs. Since 1949 this experience has, for some of them, included nationwide responsibilities in certain fields.

Non-Communists have been appointed to head ministries in the central government, but never to those involving national security functions. Non-Communists head ministries which handle things like water conservancy and postal services. Even then, the non-Communist minister will inevitably have a first vice minister who is a reliable party man and acts as a minister in everything but name. Some ministries, such as the ministries of foreign affairs, public security, and defense do not use nonparty members in any but the most menial positions.

Party members predominate even at the second level. Over 80 per cent of the 300 vice ministers and vice chairmen of commissions are party men. Party membership for the bureaucracy as a whole is more difficult to determine. An Tzu-wen reported that in 1956 one-third of the total number of cadres working at the country level or above were either party or youth league members. It may be that the proportion of party to nonparty cadres cited by An could apply to the bureaucracy as a whole; the same proportion has been noted in the U.S.S.R.

It might be noted that party membership accounts for only 4 per cent of the general population of over 15 years of age. The concentration of party members grows steadily heavier as you move up in the governmental machinery until it reaches 100 per cent at the level of the vice premier and above.

Structure for staffing government offices

The State Council. The 1954 constitution of the Chinese People's Republic declares that the National People's Congress is the "highest organ of state power." Its more than 1,200 deputies are elected. Sessions of the congress have been short, less frequent than called for in the constitution, and confined to rubber-stamping actions taken elsewhere. The Congress elects the Chairman of the People's Republic of China as well as a Standing Committee to be its "permanent working organ" when it is not in session. The present Standing Committee has some 60 members.

The chairman formally appoints the premier, subject to the approval of the National People's Congress. He appoints, on the recommendation of the premier, the other members of the State Council—the vice premiers, ministers, heads of commissions and the secretary general. After the premier's nominations have been "decided" by a congress (or its Standing Committee), they are formally appointed to their jobs by the chairman. The provisions for congressional approval are no more than window-dressing for decisions made at the party center.

The Second Level. Selection of the second echelon of government executives is legally the prerogative of the State Council. The second echelon includes the directors of the important staff offices of the State Council, the deputy ministers and assistant ministers, the commission vice chairmen and members, as well as all chiefs and deputies of the divisions, bureaus, and offices which make up the ministries. In the military field, the appointing responsibility of the Council extends to commanders and political commissars at the division level (more than 300 positions). In the foreign field it includes embassy counselors and consul generals. The State Council appoints all key personnel in the important financial, commercial, or industrial enterprises administered by the 25 economic ministries. Important administrative posts in the field of higher education are also controlled by the State Council. Altogether the State Council probably controls a minimum of 2,000 executive jobs in the government. All of them require reference to the party before being finalized.

In addition to specific responsibilities for appointing administrative personnel, the State Council is ultimately responsible for the government's staffing policies. The State Council, for example, as a part of each long-term and annual plan makes an allocation of manpower resources according to nationally determined priorities and, in effect, programs the development of new skills needed in China's industrialization.

The Secretary General and Secretariat of the State Council are key positions in the exercise of these council responsibilities. The Secretary General is Hse Chung-hsun, a high-ranking Central Committee member and a vice premier. He is assisted by ten deputies who are all party personalities. More than half of them have concurrent responsibilities in the party personnel machine. One of the them, Kung Tzu-jung, holds the following positions in the central departments of the party: head of the Committee for Central State Organs, member of the Control Commission, and deputy director of the Party Secretariat's Staff Office. Five of the deputies hold concurrent responsibilities in important State Council personnel offices.

The Secretariat has a special Personnel Division which appears to be responsible for enforcing personnel procedures, processing personnel actions, and maintaining personnel files on the employees working directly for the State Council. In addition, Premier Chou's own office assists him in making personnel and policy decisions.

Government personnel administration on lower levels is highly fragmented. The Ministry of Personnel, organized in 1950 shortly after the government was first established, had comparatively broad responsibilities for government personnel selection and assignment at a time when the new regime was busy filling its offices. It was closely tied with the party's Organization Department. Like the Organization Department, the ministry has been downgraded. In 1954 it was reduced to a specialized agency of the State Council; and in 1959 it was placed under the

Ministry of Internal Affairs. During the period, other, more specialized organizations were created by the State Council to handle aspects of personnel work, such as training, job allocation, or various specialized groups of personnel, such as scientists and technicians.

Today, the General Personnel Bureau of the Ministry of Internal Affairs performs the following functions for the government bureaucracy as a whole:

1. It implements the wage and welfare policies of the State Council and performs other personnel work assigned it by the council.
2. It drafts personnel regulations and supervises the establishment of tables of organization for offices of central government.
3. It processes personnel actions, including transfers, appointments and removals of personnel in government offices down to the country level.
4. It maintains personnel records.
5. It processes the transfer and job placement of demobilized military personnel.
6. It maintains liaison with and evaluates the work of personnel offices throughout the central government and in local governments at the provincial, automous region, and special municipality level.

The subordination of the Personnel Bureau to the Ministry of Internal Affairs in 1959 served to correlate the Bureau's general responsibility for control of the bureaucracy with the Ministry's responsibilities for veterans affairs, the mass mobilization of civilian labor crews for public works projects, and the administration of state welfare and relief programs. At the time of the merger, the Director of the Personnel, Chang Yi-pai, was made a Vice Minister of the Ministry of Internal Affairs, Chang has been associated with high level personnel work since the government was set up.

Specialized Personnel. In 1956 the administration of government personnel was compartmentalized in an apparent effort to improve upon the use of highly educated and trained Chinese—especially in high priority programs. The administration of two kinds of personnel with critical skills—"specialists" and visiting bloc technicians—was divorced from the general administrative system in 1956 and turned over to independent agencies of the State Council, the Specialists Work Bureau and the Foreign Experts Bureau.

The Specialists Work Bureau is today part of the Scientific and Technological Commission. It is responsible for the assignment, promotion and transfer of "specialists"—defined by the Chinese Communists as scientific workers, engineers, educators, doctors, and health technicians, as well as important cultural and artistic workers. The bureau may concern itself directly only with persons who have actual work experience. The bureau may also have been charged with carrying out a 1956 plan to register all scientific and technological personnel, and with keeping it up to date.

Advisory functions of the bureau include:

1. To investigate unemployed "advanced intellectuals" and place them in the state apparatus.
2. To investigate the assignment and working conditions of specialists and make recommendations to the State Council for improvement.
3. To investigate the implementation of policies and laws governing the use of specialists, and attempt to solve their problems and promote their fullest use.
4. To work out plans with government departments for the employment of students and specialists returning to China from non-Communist countries.

The second bureau established in 1956 by the State Council to handle special personnel requirements, the Foreign Experts Bureau, was designed specifically to take care of bloc experts. Prior to 1960 such personnel numbered in the thousands. The Soviet specialists left China over two years ago,[1] but a few hundred satellite technicians have remained. The bureau still functions. It investigates the technical and scientific specialization of foreign countries (both Communist and non-Communist) in the light of China's needs. It retains responsibility for engaging foreign specialists, arranging their assignment in China, providing living accommodations, and writing letters of commendation at the termination of their service.

1 [1961]

Another unit at the State Council level with important responsibility for personnel administration is the Bureau for the Administration of Government Offices. This agency provides living accommodations and security for top level government cadres, which probably includes the 50 officials of the State Council and may well include other important personnel in the ministries, commission, and special agencies.

MINISTRIES AND COMMISSIONS. Each ministry and commission has limited responsibility for locating, training, assigning, and promoting its rank and file. The ministries carry out this responsibility through personnel bureaus, the directors of which, like every important administrative office in a ministry, are appointed by the State Council.

The duties of a ministerial personnel bureau include the processing of personnel actions, maintaining personnel records, arranging leave and changes of assignment. They provide general services such as briefing newly assigned people and arranging for their housing, clothing, and travel.

In one of the most important national security ministries, the Ministry of Foreign Affairs, virtually all executive positions in Peiping (at least 100 and perhaps as many as 200 people) as well as responsible officials in the foreign service (an additional 200 positions at a minimum) are administered by the State Council.

The ministry's personnel unit controls appointments and assignments to middle- and junior-level posts as well as service positions. The ministry's general services department, rather than its personnel unit, negotiates with other government agencies for people trained in security work and assigns and transfers the more than 200 people working as couriers, code clerks, and physical security officers according to needs as fixed by the ministry.

GOVERNMENT PERSONNEL ADMINISTRATION

RECRUITMENT AND ASSIGNMENT. Although the staffing objectives and machinery of the U.S. and Communist China contain many similarities, placement procedures differ significantly. In a democratic system, the government must compete with other employers for an individual's services, and personal preferences play a large part in placement. In Communist China professional, semiprofessional, and vocational school graduates are given little alternative but to accept service in a job assigned by the state.

Professionals entering the labor force from higher educational institutions are assigned positions by the institutions on the basis of rosters prepared by the ministry which administers the institutions. The Ministry of Education administers general liberal arts schools, and the Ministry of National Defense and economic ministries run technical and scientific institutes.

Students earmarked for jobs in national security organs generally have had their course of study sponsored by a specific organization. Or they may have been hand picked before graduation for a special assignment. For those not so chosen normal placement procedure begins with the posting on its bulletin board of a roster of positions which the institution is responsible for filling. Each student is permitted to indicate three choices. In practice, however, the institution is guided primarily by other considerations, such as the state's needs, the student's class background, and his scholastic rating.

Although acceptance of state assignments is virtually mandatory, there is little need for compulsion. By the time a student graduates from an institute of higher education in Communist China, he has undergone a long process of mental preparation to put duty above personal considerations. He will probably be either ambitious or sincere enough to make personal sacrifices in the interest of furthering his career. Even if he lacks such motivations, a student has no ready alternative. The following account of a student's attempt to refuse an assignment was written by an intellectual who fled China:

> There was an actual case of a medical student who after graduation did not go to the frontier area assigned to him but went home instead to help his father keep shop. He was free to go home, of course: "No one could force him to do anything in a socialist country. . . ." He enjoyed several weeks of leisure with his family which he could financially well afford, but one

> day two classmates came to see him and, after tea and remarks on the weather, they explained that they thought he should "follow the leadership" and go to his assigned work. "In socialist societies," they told him, "no one should call his skill his own, because without the society a man could not be what he was. The Government spent so much money on the school we studied in. Therefore, . . ." The next day two other classmates came to persuade him: "In socialist societies no one can call his skill his own . . ."; the third day three others came: "In socialist countries no one can call his skill his own . . ."; the fourth day one of the two who came the first day came: "The government spent so much on the school we studied in. . . ." In any society there are some people with exceptional temperaments, and the Communists take care of them. This medical student persisted in shaking his head; and his classmates persisted in coming. Every afternoon he was subjected to a lecture which went on for hours: "In socialist societies no one can call his skill his own. . . ." At the end of two months he came to think that this was worse than any frontier region could be, and promised to report to the Committee of Party Members in the school.

Refusal to accept a job assigned by the state amounts to professional suicide, particularly for a young student just starting out. It results in automatic isolation from an employment system which controls all significant job opportunities in the entire country. Although an individual may eventually find some kind of employment, he has in effect placed himself under governmental "supervision," which itself can be a serious matter. His original refusal to accept a state assignment has become a permanent part of his personnel record. Even if he relents, as the reluctant medical student did, his future assignments, salary, and promotional opportunities have been irreparably blighted.

Offices directly involved in national security have the highest priority in personnel recruitment. The Ministry of Foreign Affairs, for example, usually has first call on students in the social sciences, in foreign languages, and in area studies. It takes the largest part of the graduating class from the country's basic foreign service training school. Those selected by the ministry from other institutions are generally out of the top half of their classes. An assignment to the ministry "must be complied with" and is accompanied by a thorough security check. Almost all professional employees are believed to be members of the party or the Youth League. The Ministry also enjoys a high priority in filling its personnel needs from other agencies.

TRANSFER AND PROMOTION. Once assigned to a critical job or agency, an individual has almost no horizontal mobility—at least not on his own initiative. The system which forces him into a niche, keeps him there. Transfers, like assignments, are arranged largely on the basis of the state's need and to refuse a transfer initiated by the state is likely to be detrimental to one's career.

Good performance or personal contacts can bring an individual to the attention of another agency with a clearly higher priority, and transfers can usually be arranged at the instigation of such an organization. Poor performance can result in a transfer either to less critical agencies or to less important responsibilities within the same agency.

There are also lateral transfers from agencies responsible for developing particular skills. This kind of transfer occurs frequently, in the national security field, from military to civilian agencies. Special police and security offices, for example, in the governmental structure are usually staffed by military veterans with special training in this kind of work. Organizations needing personnel trained in secure communications procedures recruit almost exclusively from the military. Other specialized agencies, such as the Bureau of National Statistics and the Ministry of Public Security, train specialists on a continuing basis and make them available to other government agencies as normal placement procedure.

Although it is not impossible to arrange one's own transfer in Communist China, such transfers are not common. The government does entertain requests from individuals for reassignment, though probably not from the national security field. The best reason for such a request, from the government's point of view, is that the individual's speciality is not being used. Misplacement does occur. For example, at one time a reported 10 per cent of the "advanced intellectuals" in the employ of one ministry were holding down jobs which did not utilize their specialized training.

Promotional prospects in the governmental service depend

on much the same criteria as in the party. The first concern of the authorities is in most cases likely to be political reliability. Like his colleagues in the party, the non-party professional has to attend regular study meetings. Though these are generally neither as frequent nor as intensive as for the party man, the non-party professional finds he must also express his opinions on the issues under discussion. This, of course, gives big brother in the party a chance to measure his political attitude. If it is judged inadequate, his other qualifications will have to be outstanding before he will have a chance to be recommended for promotion.

Still, professional excellence probably does count for more here than it does in the case of the purely party man. A man could conceivably advance quite high in an economic or scientific institution on professional merit. But he would find, ultimately, that he was closed off from the top posts unless or until he was accepted into the party.

VETERAN'S PREFERENCE. Veterans from the armed forces are employed in large numbers at all levels of responsibility in the Chinese government. Military retirement laws dating from the mid-1950's provide that all demobilized military personnel must, if they are physically fit and under 55 years of age, take job assignments arranged for them. These assignments, like those of civilian professionals, are virtually compulsory. High-ranking officers or personnel with special qualifications are usually assigned jobs before they leave the army. If an individual has no particular skills of use to the government or the party he is sent home. The personnel department of the government in his local area is responsible for providing him with a job. Some sort of employment is arranged, from a comfortable spot in an academic institution to difficult manual labor in factories or on farms.

Ex-soldiers also receive special salary considerations. Their military rank is converted to a roughly equal civilian grade. The actual salary paid a veteran is determined by a combination of this grade and his length of military service. A veteran can thus draw a higher salary than a nonveteran in the same job. One other factor contributes to veterans' preference in Communist China. The armed forces political indoctrination program is one of the regime's most effective. It tends to make veterans, many of whom are party members, especially reliable. Veterans are therefore likely to be considered for responsible positions ahead of nonveterans.

In-Service Training. Many of the ministries and commissions of the Chinese government run in-service training courses for their personnel, usually at specialized institutions in which they have an interest. One such institution is the Chinese Institute for International Relations in Peiping. Financed by the Ministry of Foreign Affairs and the Ministry of Education, it is under the operational control of the party. It provides training in international affairs, foreign languages, and area studies. Selection for study at the institute is considered a mark of distinction and the herald of higher positions to come.

Most of the Institute's 600 students are drawn from party cadres of the low and middle levels, foreign service officers who have already had a tour abroad, or employees of the ministry, and employees of other government and military offices—all of whom receive their salary while attending the school. It does accept some highly qualified middle school graduates. Entrance requirements read like the requirements for party membership—political reliability, a family background untainted by wealth or political ties with the Kuomintang, and no foreign connections.

The curriculum of the Institute is organized around a two- to three-year program for foreign ministry officers who have already served abroad, and a four- to five-year program for training language and area specialists. It is based on the study program of the Institute's Soviet counterpart. Studies include basic academic courses (geography, history, law), political theory courses (Marxism-Leninism, the history of the Chinese revolutions, dialectical materialism), foreign affairs (history of international politics and economic relations, international public and private law, the history of Chinese diplomacy), and foreign languages (English, French, Russian, German, Spanish, and Arabic). The major emphasis of the Institute is on political theory. The major language effort is on English.

Government Incentives. The promotional possibilities for professionals in Communist China range from an entering grade 21 for a college graduate to an effective ceiling at about grade 11. A handful of top executives hold the ten super grades.

The wage differential between grade 11 and grade 21 in Communist China is about the same as exists in the U.S. civil service system between the professional entering grade, GS–5, and the top regular grade, GS–15. Wage levels for professionals in the government have been generally stable and promotions slow. The government wage structure was last overhauled in 1956.

A government professional gets certain perquisites which determine his actual standard of living. Emoluments in housing, food, and clothing allowances are allowed high-level officials. Lesser officials in certain kinds of work such as personnel whose jobs bring them into frequent contact with foreigners receive better living allowances than the average employee of the same grade. Welfare benefits in the form of medical services and schools for dependents also are linked to professional status and grade.

Housing is at a premium in China. The higher one's grade the better the chance of being able to live with one's family, to obtain attractive accommodations, privacy, and enough equipment for relative comfort. For the many government employees whose jobs do not permit them to live with their families, the regime has a leave system which allows an individual to spend two to three weeks a year, or four to five weeks every two years with his family.

The Chinese Communist regime employes to advantage certain non-material incentives. It offers, for example, idealistic young people a chance to participate in the vital and challenging job of modernizing China. This factor is known to have played a large part in the return of hundreds of educated Chinese from the U.S. and Europe in the early 1950's. It is a factor heavily emphasized in university-level indoctrination programs.

A second non-material incentive is access to literature that has not been pre-masticated by the regime's propaganda apparatus.

The government's awards system seems designed more to promote loyalty to the regime than improvements in efficiency and performance. This system now in use provides for the granting of commendations, prizes, cash, grade raises and promotions on the following grounds: 1) loyalty to the job; 2) superior or model performance of duties; 3) observance of discipline; 4) suggestions, innovations, and inventions which contribute to the national welfare; 5) actions protecting government property or preventing loss to the government; and 6) fighting illegal activity. Four out of the six are reflections of political reliability rather than outstanding professional achievements.

These are also regulations on the books which are specifically designed to reward outstanding professional achievement. Under these, original contributions in both natural and social science are afforded national recognition and cash awards. The only publicized use of these awards occurred nearly six years ago.

Of course, there is the other side of the incentive coin. The government civil servant can fall afoul of the government's supervisory apparatus quite as easily as a party man can be enmeshed in his, and for equally capricious reasons. There is no legal code in Communist China. There is a system of courts in China, but the courts are not independent; they are only another arm of the executive. There is also a system of public prosecutors, whose chief task it is to check on government offices and employees to see that state regulations are observed by all administrative agencies, officials and the public at large.

The major responsibility for maintaining public order and policing the governmental apparatus, however, rests in the Ministry of Interior and the Ministry of Public Security. Interior is believed to take care of administrative cases involving government agencies and officials, to investigate how government decisions are being implemented, and to detect neglect of duty or violations of regulations. The Ministry of Public Security performs the general police function vis-à-vis the public. It has the largest and best trained investigative force, which is apparently used from time to time by other supervisory organs of party and government. These organs, primed to act at the whim of the central authorities, provide an important, if negative, slice of any government employee's incentive.

An appraisal of the system

The guiding principles of Chinese Communist personnel management were formulated in the less complicated world of the Chinese revolution and do not appear to have been markedly changed since. They include: 1) the absolute supremacy of the party, 2) a highly centralized management technique, and 3) a remarkable continuity and unity of purpose at the top echelons. They have produced a disciplined and dedicated elite, but at some cost in flexibility and individual initiative.

Mao Tse-tung and his closest associates are strong personalities, the result of rigorous Chinese Communist selection processes. The leading group has displayed high organizational and administrative capabilities. It has been able to move with dispatch on some issues confronting China. Its approach to others has been halting. It moved very quickly to exploit to Chinese advantage Soviet discomfiture as a result of the Cuban crisis in the fall of 1962. Communes were set up almost overnight in 1958, but the three-year retreat from these ill-conceived units has, on the other hand, been slow and painful.

Party personnel processes have brought to the second level of authority devoted, loyal men who share the aims and convictions of the top leaders and speak the same language. They are men who have had many years of administrative experience, men who have proven themselves to be tough and ruthless. Only true believers get this far in the system. As a group they are more likely to be versed in Marxism-Leninism and the teaching of Mao than in a technical specialty.

Many middle and lower level officials appear able, but there does seem to be a shortage of good administrators and managers. These lesser officials operate in a system which constantly preaches discipline. Naturally, many fail to develop an aptitude for vigorous, independent action. They become adept buck-passers, bureaucrats who check too many things with Peiping. This further overloads the top command in which key figures already hold several concurrent jobs. These officials can give less than full time and energy to any one of their posts. These men, whether in high party position or low, are in a sense the end product of Chinese Communist political indoctrination. This striking program has to a great extent created and maintained a unity of approach unthinkable in a democratic state. No real opposition is countenanced and no alternative courses are offered. There is relatively little wheel-spinning over objective or method.

The framework for recruitment, transfer, and promotion focuses a great deal of power and responsibility in a few hands. The dominant leaders indentify national security priorities and commit talent to favored programs in complete freedom. People selected for jobs have no real individual safeguards such as exist in the U.S. or Western nations. Most Chinese accept this sort of treatment, go where they are told to go by the authorities and do what they are told to do. There is no outside competition for talent. Recuitment and assignment of personnel present no problems; undesirable turnover is rare.

The system permits the authorities to channel the country's best talent, insofar as it is available, into key areas of national policy. Great efforts are made to stimulate work in approved scientific, technological, and economic fields, especially those related to the martial arts. This work is supported and directed by the party.

However, the system does try, all too frequently, to force round pegs into square holes. The over-all record of the assigning authorities might be termed fair to good.

Persons who have visited Communist China testify that the average Chinese Communist functionary is a hard worker. This is partly the result of the existing personnel system. Competition is fierce, and the individual must make his way within the mold in which the system has cast him. There is no opportunity to shift jobs, or even to resign. Advancement depends entirely upon pleasing the authorities above. The asceticism preached by the party helps produce individuals willing to devote themselves fully to their work. The sense of dedication today may not be what it was in earlier years, but enough remains so that it is a significant strength of the Chinese Communist system.

Material incentives are present and important in keeping the Chinese functionary bent to his task. His perquisites are small, but valued amidst the general poverty of China. These functionaries also work under the stimulus of a system of retribution which operates on abstract and shifting principles.

Overstaffing is a problem in today's China. Swollen staffs can be attributed in part to the Chinese Communist practice of giving on-the-job training to people who will be moved to staff other offices or factories when they are finished. A lack of mechanical aids means that many office and factory tasks, done elsewhere by machine, are done by hand in China. But the most telling reasoning is simply China's tremendous population.

Skilled manpower in China is strictly limited, yet the present leaders fail to make full use of what they have. They seem quite willing to fritter away some of the talent they do have.

Students who have been educated abroad are regarded, almost without exception, with suspicion when they return to China. They are viewed as having been infected by foreign ideas. It is up to them to prove otherwise, and over the long haul. Many returned students, even those afire with the desire to help build up a new China, find it hard to break through this shell of suspicion. They find that the party will not make full use of their hard-won skills.

The leaders in fact find it hard to rely fully on technically trained people, no matter where their education was won. There are in China competent scientists and economists who could contribute more than they do to the development of plans and practices. The people are, under the operation of the present personnel system, rigidly excluded from policy-making roles. The dominant figures—dogmatic, poorly educated and distrustful men—prefer to rely for advice on long-term associates who share the leaders' background, prejudices, and shortcomings.

Talent is also wasted in the party's obsessive drive for political conformity. Countless man-hours are devoted to political indoctrination and lost to production or the search for technical know-how. The authorities are willing to pay the price.

The personnel situation in Communist China today is in some ways like that in the Soviet Union during Stalin's dying days. The top strata, overworked, old and tired, forms an impenetrable roadblock for those below. The bureaucracy is stagnating. Advancement, even of able and trusted people, is generally slow and ponderous. Party seniority and personal relationships are still major factors in selection for responsible positions. What remains to be seen is whether the departure of the present leaders will rejuvenate the system.

SECTION 3

Development Administration

Developmental Administration: An Approach

V. A. PAI PANANDIKER
Planning Commission of India

THE EMERGENCE OF new socio-political forces in many of the developing nations like India has brought about pressing demands upon the State to provide a leadership to improve standards of societal living and participation in matters economic, social and political. In India the acceptance and the institutionalization of national planning have provided an apt recognition to the scale of the problem of national development. These and other allied forces have increasingly demanded new and improved conceptual and operational frameworks in the form of growth models, planning devices and programming of the total objectives so that national development is manageable and practicable.

However, while the need for planning and a plan frame has been well articulated, conceived and developed, less attention has been devoted to the basic operational characteristics of this endeavour and to the nature of the organizational system through which these end-goals are attainable. A conceptual framework encompassing this is particularly important to pro-

Reprinted from *The Indian Journal of Public Administration,* Vol. 10, No. 1 (January-March, 1964), pp. 34–44, by permission.

vide a major break-through in administrative theory and practice. The approach itself is not entirely new. What is necessary, however, is an articulation of the concept of developmental administration and giving it an operational framework. Such a development in public administration would be analogous to the growth of the concept of national planning in the field of economic policy. Despite the various industrial schemes and other kinds of projects undertaken till 1950–51, they lacked an integrated framework of economic planning which was subsequently provided by the Five Year Plans. Similarly, though the present administrative machinery performs essentially developmental work, there is a lack of a clear-cut integrated conceptual and operational framework. This paper is intended as an effort at providing a conceptual framework for operationalizing the end-goals of a national developmental system.

A pioneering effort in this direction was made by Edward Weidner in his paper on "Development Administration: A New Focus for Research."[1] Weidner reviewed the various uses of the term "development administration" and found one common element in all these uses: all seem to describe an action-oriented, goal-oriented administrative system. He himself defined it as the "means of selecting and accomplishing progressive political, economic and social objectives that are authoritatively determined in one manner or another."[2] However, Weidner did not proceed to provide an operational framework indicating the kinds and nature of administrative change that will be necessary to transform a non-developmental system into a developmental one.

The core of these end-goals of the national system can be expressed as "developmental." The word "developmental" is intended to indicate those bodies of thought that centre around growth and directional change. Basically, therefore, the framework of "development" gravitates around a planned change which is derived from a purposeful decision to effect improvements in a social system. Not until a decision is made to make a deliberate effort to improve the system does the process become "developmental." The decision itself entails setting up of specific goals whether in one sphere of national activity or another or all.

[1] *See* Ferrel Heady and Sybil Stokes (eds.), *Papers in Comparative Public Administration,* Ann Arbor, University of Michigan, 1962, pp. 97–115.

[2] *Ibid.,* p. 98.

Underlying developmental models there is an assumption that "there are noticeable differences between the states of a system at different time series; that the succession of these states implies the system is heading somewhere; and that there are orderly processes which explain how the system gets from its present state to . . . [wherever] it is going."[3] The direction may be expressed in terms of specific end-goals or the process of achieving them, or the degree of achievement toward these end-goals.

In the Indian context, the focus on planned change is clearly indicated by the various schemes detailed in and outside the Five Year Plans. The design of all these Plans and schemes is closely geared to bring about substantial transformations in the contents of our social, political and economic life. Improved educational facilities, removal of caste barriers, and opportunities for a higher standard of economic life that are being made possible by the rapid industrialization are all illustrative of these programmes of planned change.

The phrase "developmental administration" is intrinsically intertwined with this process of change. Here the word developmental is also intended to connote precisely the kind of planned changed that is intended in the Indian circumstance. And taken together with the concept of administration, the phrase developmental administration principally means administration of planned change. Essentially developmental administration refers to the structure, organization and organizational behaviour necessary for the implementation of schemes and programmes of socio-economic and political change undertaken by the Governments in India.

Underlying this definition of "developmental administration" is an assumption that where the functions of a government change largely from the law and order, revenue collecting, and regulatory type to those of socio-economic and political development, the role of administration changes from an "executive" to a "managerial" one. These two typologies used in this paper are strictly "model" types and do not necessarily indicate mutually exclusive patterns. They are primarily representative of the two

[3] For an excellent conceptual model, *see* Robert Chin, "Utility of System Models and Developmental Models for Practitioners" in Bennis, Warren B. *et al., The Planning of Change,* New York, Holt, Rinehart and Winston, 1961, p. 208.

kinds of "models" followed by the traditional and a new philosophy of administration. The "executive" type of administration is largely designed to carry out the directions given from time to time by the Government. These directions could be legislative fiats or executive orders. And even when the administrative hierarchies are somehow involved in the formulation of the policies, the emphasis of the "executive" oriented administration is principally to implement the policies and programmes.

Illustrative of this approach is the emphasis on the maintenance of law and order and collection of revenues. Following the general pattern of the "executive" type, the basic emphasis here is on the prevention of serious societal crises; the functions of the administration are to guarantee that the intent of the Government in this respect is clearly maintained. A similar approach pervades the revenue collection function. More is thought in terms of meeting the legal obligations of the revenue collection function than achieving any specific targets.

Another good illustration is the financial administration in the Indian Government. The primary emphasis in fiscal matters is on "appropriating" funds for certain areas of governmental operations accompanied by arrangements for executive and legislative control over public expenditures during the budgetary period. The entire system emphasizes negative expenditure controls rather than achievement of specific goals through fiscal means.

By and large, then, the traditional or "executive" type of administration is designed to fulfil all the legal requirements of governmental operations and to maintain social stability. In the main, this type of administration confines itself to the maintenance of law and order, collection of revenues, and regulating the national life in accordance with the statutory requirements.

In contrast the "managerially" oriented "developmental" administration is essentially programmatically inclined. It focuses its attention not merely on "carrying out" the dictates and directions of the governmental system but also on the crucial element of securing prescribed programmatic values. The emphasis here is not on appropriational authority or on preventing disequilibrating forces but on the attainment of goals and targets established in the planned programmes of the Government which in fact may have built-in forces disturbing social equilibrium. Because of this "managerial" orientation primary focus is placed on the assessment of total capital resources not only in terms of fiscal means but also by way of the general institutional resources and of the critical societal plus administrative behavioural values available. It is, indeed, this totality of programme inputs, both in financial and non-financial terms, which renders possible a greater degree of congruence between targets and actual output. Measurement of such inputs has traditionally been regarded as difficult. More recently efforts have shown that as a result of advances in performance budgeting, work measurement, and cost accounting sufficient internal data were available to permit construction of productivity measures.[4] Once such basic measurement is made, attention is largely concentrated on the appropriateness of programme goals and objectives in relation to national resources, on adjusting these financial and other resources within the set of priorities, and attaining the targets.

In the context of "developmental" administration, the functions of law and order and revenue collection are important to the extent they support the developmental programmes. The shift is on the emphasis placed between the primary developmental objectives of the administrative apparatus and the secondary objectives of merely carrying out governmental directions and requirements. The critical elements here are the clear-cut programmatic values expressed in operational terms which have to be attained by the administrative apparatus.

Characteristically these values of developmental administration are contained in a new series of socio-economic and political programmes. Since these programmatic values have to be secured in a planned fashion, the State has to act as the change-agent providing the necessary stimulus. In its role as the change-agent the questions relate more and more to the capacity of the instruments of the State to perform its function than to the objectives themselves. Above all, the approach of the State has to be based on a sound diagnostic orientation intended to pinpoint the change areas, methods of change, and the capacity both of

[4] For a good study on the input-output measurement in Government, *see* John W. Kendrick, "Exploring Productivity Measurement in Government," *Public Administration Review,* Vol. 23, No. 2 (June, 1963), pp. 59–66.

the people and [of] the governmental machinery to absorb and sustain change. And in translating the diagnostic interpretations into change goals and plans, it is crucially important that the administrative machinery of the State clearly knows what the end-goals of the process of change are, and what is feasible in terms of the application of change ideas and methods. The critical focus on the need for change has to be supported by means of the tools of applied social sciences to assess the capacity of the social system for change, and the capacity of the governmental apparatus for bringing it about.

Inevitably with the "developmental administration" so deeply concerned with introducing a new set of values, their integration into an operational framework implies that under the available conditions, the developmental administrative system may, in all likelihood, involve greater fusion of administrative roles. Such fusion of administrative roles may become inevitable because the content of change is more centrally decided, directed, and administered. Each of the administrative agencies and units may, therefore, need to perform a set of functions which in a non-developmental set-up are likely to be clearly differentiated and divided among several such agencies and units. In India such a fusion of roles in administrative machinery is evident at all levels beginning from the Planning Commission down to the District and Sub-divisional offices.

The single-minded focus of developmental administration on the achievement of programmatic values in terms of specific targets and goals introduces the need for institutionalization. The programmatic values have to be encased in terms of administrative values and institutional apparatus. In essence this implies that changes and modifications in the structural and behavioural patterns may have to be brought in line with the functional contents of developmental administration.

In its full dimension, the therapeutic administrative reorganization may involve redrawing of hierarchical arrangements, increase in programme and field units, shifting lines of reporting and communications, developing control mechanisms, and improved methods of data feed-back to top echelons of the administrative apparatus. Needless to add such developments inevitably imply complexities for co-ordinating and controlling functions at the higher levels of management. A key area of concern is the personnel; changes in the service structure and orientation and development of altogether new kinds of skills along with significantly improved personnel planning may inevitably become necessary. And, above all, the behavioural inputs of the entire civil service need to be seriously considered and weighted in the organizational planning for "developmental" administration.

II

A significant shift in the structural aspects of the organizational set-up may have to be in the current hierarchical arrangement. The Central Government offices have been designed into three main categories: secretariat, subordinate and attached offices. The secretariat is the headquarter, a kind of staff organization intended to assist the top management in matters of policy formulation, supervision and coordination of programmes. The subordinate offices are essentially the field of executive offices involved in the day-to-day application of the prescribed policies. As field agencies it is the subordinate offices which are directly confronted by the citizen clientele. The attached agencies are special advisory bodies whose function is either to regulate or to study and advise the Ministry in specific matters.

Much appears to have happened in the last few years to blur the distinction between the secretariat and the subordinate offices. The policy formulation job of the secretariat has increasingly been replaced by actual involvement in applications of policies. Such an administrative circumstance has inevitably confused hierarchical arrangements and has created additional factors responsible for decisional delays, thus leading to administrative propensities not conducive to "developmental" approach.

A single most important shift necessary in structural organizational aspects may be in terms of the institutions for achieving specific goals and targets which could go beyond the general scope of present field offices. In operational terms this implies the creation of what may be called programme agencies which would be built around a specific major objective in the forms of physical or service outputs. In order to form such programme units, it will be important to provide for a breakdown of the national plans and targets in terms of specific outputs which are administratively manageable.

The programme units would necessarily imply that the administrative apparatus must now be clearly related to the achievement targets and that a series of functions necessary for that purpose may need to be integrated in the single programme agency. Thus in the field of agriculture, it may involve a district-wise integration of transport, irrigation, fertilizer supply and such other vital agricultural inputs. Such a distinctly integrated programme organization may be in a better position to promote, direct, and secure the kinds of output targets assigned to it.

The design of the administrative apparatus in terms of programmatic schemes may involve increase in field units operating at the level of direct activity. These field units will need to express the organization's programme objectives in terms of the kinds of resources needed such as manpower and materials and weave them in a framework which will be directly involved in securing the specific objectives.

In turn such programmatically designed field offices may necessitate shifting lines of reporting and communication from departmental lines to programme organization; or it may involve dual reporting with primary emphasis on reporting to the programme office. Thus a district irrigation team may no longer find it desirable to report only to the Irrigation Ministry or Department, but also to the district agricultural production programme organization, if any. Communications in this case may flow directly between the programme agency and the office concerned with a single objective and the ancillary services which are essential to that objective. The remedial or corrective action can then be at the vital point without having the need to go through circuitous and dilatory double hierarchies.

Further organizational shifts may occur in the control mechanism. The traditional control in terms of expenditure of funds and highly diffused system of decisional authority may have to be replaced by a more active and fuller decisional authority and the controls geared more in terms of the programme values than in the traditional terms. Such controls could indicate the phased targets and goal objectives, whether in terms of production or services, their degree of attainments and the areas of shortcomings deserving immediate attention. These controls are more meaningful managerial components and they are conducive to directing and sustaining the crucial programme values.

The control mechanisms themselves may be closely intertwined with the kinds of data fed to the top management. More and more the data contained on the reports may have to be selective and intrinsically germane to the direct programme objectives, indicating the pattern of output schedules and the evolving cost structure vis-a-vis the projected costs and the causes of variance, if any. Such data have the advantage of being specific and geared closely to the attainment of programme objectives rather than to the problems of controls, checks and other considerations not pertinent to programme targets.

As the evolution of programme and field units continue, more and more problems may arise in the field of co-ordination. Systems may have to be devised at the headquarters to ensure that the execution of programmes follow the general prescribed pattern, also that the policies and practices of the various field units match those centrally prescribed as standard. And above all, it may be necessary to ensure that the progress of each operational unit maintains the balance necessary to ensure programmes in other units. More may, therefore, be necessary by way of a central co-ordinating office which can remain fully informed of the progress of each of the individual field units, and its compatibility with the progress of other supporting units. A continuous headquarter supervision, check, and direction to ensure the overall "line of balance" a kind of minimal performance rate in the programme projections of the organization as a whole will be critically important.

An area deserving special emphasis may be the system of financial administration. The traditional emphasis of financial administration has been on the treasury control, designed more to protect the public funds than to secure specific organizational objectives. For developmental administration the more useful role of financial administration lies in the variety of management tools it offers to exact performance and to establish responsibility centres. The financial system provides excellent devices, through the system of budgeting, internal auditing and the entire system of management accounting, to direct specific programmes or their objectives, to control the rate at which programmes move, and to pinpoint responsibility for performance. Because of the nature of the financial data, the analysis between phased programme objectives and their attainments are reduced to specific targets, and the shortcomings in individual areas are clearly pinpointed. In other words, it is important that under developmental administration, the system of financial administration may have to be more appropriately matched with the managerial needs of programme administration.

Another key area of concern of developmental administration is apt to be the personnel which mans the administrative apparatus. In the final analysis the effective conduct of developmental programmes becomes a function of the skills and ability of this personnel. The requirements of this achievement target oriented administrative system may be in terms of programmatic or functional service structure and a systematized personnel planning.

The traditional service structure in the Government of India is based on what is called as "career" staffing. Civil servants are essentially recruited to career services with a specific number of posts reserved for members of these services. While such a staffing system guarantees a certain degree of administrative continuity, members of these services have no commitment to the success of specific programmes. The approach leads to what has been called earlier as "executive" attitude concerned more with the handling of work as it comes up to a post rather than designing the work content to attain prescribed programme goals and objectives. A differently structured civil service system often referred to as "programme" staffing is precisely designed to sharpen the attention on the programme contents, and their attainment. Such programme personnel could be geared essentially to an organization without continuous shifts and transfers or deputations. Major advantages of such programme staffing, of course, are to provide a commitment on the part of the personnel to the goals and objectives of an organization, to create a pressure for maintaining work standards on the job, and to orient the personnel towards general "managerial" functions and responsibilities. Shifting a degree of focus from "career" to "programme" staffing may also appear significantly important.

Linked with this process of functional service structure is improved personnel planning. Once the programmatic personnel needs are specifically suggested, then recruitment and selection processes may become more amenable to programme considerations and requirements. Period or forward manpower planning becomes possible so that recruitment plans can be adequately worked out. Similarly the design of the examinations may also have to be structured to ensure a high degree of selectivity.

Lastly, the most crucial of all these would be the organizational behaviour. Social scientists and students of administrative sciences have increasingly realized that organizations are more and more led by the dynamic and behavioural components than by the formalized systems; that organizational effectiveness depends heavily upon the behaviour of its personnel. The essential ingredients of the bureaucratic behaviour are the various personnel values reflected in day-to-day operations. These would include attitudes to work, degree of professionalization, attitudes towards superiors, towards subordinates, attitudes to delegation of authority and acceptance of responsibility, and several others which have a direct impact on the operational aspects of an organization. These behavioural inputs of the bureaucracy play a vital part in shaping the character and the effectiveness of the entire organization. More and more, therefore, these behavioural inputs may have to be weighed in programme planning and . . . schemes of re-orienting the patterns of attitudes to fit more closely with programmatic needs will need to be considered.

All these implications are merely illustrative of the dimensions of the change which will increasingly become evident in the operationalization of a developmentally oriented framework. Actual impact of such a scheme is bound to be extensive and far more detailed than indicated here. But the effort made here is essentially to drive home some of the major changes that will occur under developmental administration.

III

The central theme of developmental administration is socio-economic and political change brought about through a series of programmes designed specifically to attain certain clear-cut and specified objectives and goals expressed in operational terms. This implies that the kind of administrative organization necessary to meet these objectives may require . . . [shifting] its base from the traditional structure and "executive" orientation to a definitely integrated "managerially" oriented programme organization. Various functions may need to be integrated in order to meet the objectives of a single programme organization; in other words, the structural organizational and behavioural elements may have to be carefully assessed, measured and incorporated in an administrative set-up designed to assimilate them and generate the requisite output.

Bureaucracy and Nation Building in Transitional Societies

S. C. Dube

National Institute of Community Development
Mussoori, India

Bureaucracy forms an important element of the modernizing elite in many of the economically less developed countries which have attained national independence during the last two decades. Trained in the colonial tradition, this organized and articulate segment of the native society functioned as a bridge

Reprinted from *International Social Science Journal,* Vol. 16, No. 2 (1964), pp. 229–236, by permission.

between the dependent indigenous people and the ruling power from the West. Although it had to work under the direction of the imperial power and had largely to carry out its policies, it was not without nationalist sentiments and aspirations. Held suspect during the days of the struggle for freedom, both by politically oriented fellow-countrymen and by the alien rulers, members of this class had, by and large, acquired a progressive orientation and the more sophisticated among them had definite ideas regarding the programmes of economic and social growth to be adopted by their country at the attainment of national independence. In many countries they were the only organized body of natives with considerable training and experience in administration; they naturally found themselves called upon to assume major responsibilities in the formulation and implementation of national plans for economic development and social change.

The general change in political climate, the assumption of power by the political elite, the changing alignments of power and pressure groups, and the emergence of new institutional and administrative patterns raised in their wake a series of complex problems for the bureaucracy. In consequence, it had to make some significant adjustments in its thought and work ways and to adapt itself to the new ethos. On the other hand, in many sensitive areas it found itself either openly resisting or accepting some of the new elements only theoretically. Thus, with or without the overt acceptance of the new patterns, it stood for continuity of some of the established norms. In meeting these intricate problems of adjustment and value-conflict, the character of bureaucracy in transitional societies is undergoing a rapid change. Since it occupies a pivotal position in these societies, and will possibly continue to do so in the foreseeable future, an understanding of the character and culture of bureaucracy is essential for those concerned with the programmes of economic growth and social change in the economically less developed countries.

Planning for economic growth is an extremely complicated business which involves highly specialized knowledge and developed manipulative skills; the implementation of these plans presupposes deep administrative insights and a keen evaluative perspective. In the context of the programmes of community development, it is common these days to emphasize the ideal of planning by the people but the crucial fact that this stage must necessarily be preceded by the stages of planning for the people and planning with the people is not given sufficient emphasis. The acceptance of these three stages means successively diminishing functions for the bureaucracy in matters of local and regional planning and in developmental administration, but it is essential to bear in mind that the gap between the first and the third stage is very considerable and that the transition to the final stage depends largely upon the manner in which the process is initiated and the first two stages are carried out. Both these stages involve considerable direct participation by the bureaucracy; the second particularly—which requires the initiation of a process of withdrawal—has critical significance. Optimism, bordering on wishful thinking, cannot alone diminish the importance of bureaucracy; its role in the process of planning and developmental administration is bound to figure prominently for several decades. The problem of the integration of local, regional and national plans demands knowledge and skills which perhaps only the bureaucracy possesses. Of course, as the process acquires greater complexity the technocrat is drawn into it more deeply, for without the utilization of his specialized knowledge planning for successive stages would become increasingly difficult. Nevertheless, much maligned and distrusted as it is, bureaucracy is not without a vital role to play in the process of planning for economic and social development. Modifications in its structure, values and work-ways are necessary to adapt it to the idiom of the fast changing situation, but the fact remains that it cannot be done away with. An understanding of its character and the initiation of imaginative plans for changing its structure and values so as to make it a more effective instrument for development must therefore be considered an essential prerequisite to planned change in these countries.

Discriminatingly recruited on the basis of specified criteria and carefully trained according to established and time-tested plans, bureaucracies in most of the former colonies and dependencies became efficient instruments of administration. Although they were oriented more to functions of law and order and the collection of revenues, they were also entrusted from time to time with some nation-building responsibilities. In discharging their responsibilities they showed all the classical characteristics of bureaucracies: they were formally organized with unambiguous demarcation of roles and statuses and were articulated to clearly defined goals; they were efficient and equipped with the required knowledge; they were well versed in formal rules of procedure and recognized their predominance; and finally they were trained to function in an impersonal manner under conditions of near anonymity.

In addition to the above, bureaucracies in these societies had certain special characteristics. In their respective countries they were perhaps the first large and organized group to enter the transitional phase between tradition and modernity—the twilight zone lying between societal types described variously in continua such as communal-associational, sacre-secular, status-contract, and *gemeinschaft-gesellschaft*. In other words, they were among the pioneers who sought to break away from the traditionally affective and emotion-based communal society and to set in motion the forces that were to contribute towards the emergence of a different type of society—a society characterized by affective neutrality and based on rational ends-means calculations for individual goals. As a distinct subcultural entity in the larger framework of their society, they were at least partly absolved from the traditional obligation of having to share communal attitudes, sentiments and repressive authority, and were among the first to constitute a group characterized by specialized division of labour, by different but complementary interests and sentiments, and by restrictive authority. It is not suggested here that they could break away completely from tradition to adopt the ideals and values of modernity; in the critical areas of choice making they had before them a wide zone of fluid values in which were present the elements of both tradition and modernity. The logic and rationale of selectivity in the process of choice making has not been analysed in depth, but the fact that, gradually and in an increasing measure, bureaucracy adopted several elements of modernity is not without significance.

It might be useful to describe here some special features of these bureaucracies, as they emerged and crystallized during the colonial phase.

1. Bureaucracy constituted a special sub-cultural segment—the high prestige strata of the society. Entrance to it was theoretically not barred to any section of the community, although in actual practice only the traditionally privileged could provide the necessary general background and the expensive education required for success in the stiff tests prescribed for entry into its higher echelons. In limited numbers others also gained entrance into the relatively closed group of higher civil servants. Middle-level and lower positions in it attracted the less privileged. Bureaucracy had a class bias and it tended to have a stratification of its own; its upper crust functioned as a privileged class. On the whole it symbolized achievement rather than ascription. Over time, it came to have distinct vested interests, and was sensitive to all threats to its position and privilege which it guarded jealously against encroachment from any quarter.

2. It existed largely in the twilight zone of cultures. Partly traditional and partly modern, it could and did in fact choose from the elements of both. In several ways it was alienated from the masses and uprooted from the native cultural traditions; significant differences in styles of living and in modes of thought separated the two. The Western rulers, on the other hand, never conceded equality to it. In consequence, bureaucracy maintained dual identification and was characterized by a dual ambivalence.

3. Besides offering security of tenure and relatively higher emoluments, bureaucratic positions carried vast powers which made them additionally attractive and important. The powers vested in a minor functionary gave him prestige, perquisites and privileges far beyond those justified by his emoluments and position in the hierarchy. Formally the role and status of functionaries at different levels were defined, but in actual practice the system of expectation and obligation between them tended to be diffused rather than specific.

4. Within the framework of the over-all policy laid down by the imperial power, in day-to-day administration the bureaucratic machine enjoyed considerable freedom from interference. Thus there were few hindrances to its exercise of power, which was often authoritarian in tone and content. Bureaucracy had, in general, a paternalistic attitude to the masses. The masses, on their part, accepted the position and looked to the administration for a wide variety of small favours.

5. Administration was concerned mainly with collection of land revenue and with maintenance of law and order. The general administrator under these conditions enjoyed supremacy. Subject matter specialists of welfare and nation-building departments were relegated to secondary positions and functioned under the guidance and control of the generalist.

6. Bureaucracy was carefully trained in formal administrative procedure and routine. Stereotypes in this sphere were well developed and were scrupulously observed.

7. In the limited framework of its functions and set procedures bureaucracy found a self-contained system. It resented and resisted innovations.

8. Its attitude to the nationalist forces within was most ambivalent. Few within the bureaucracy were devoid of patriotic sentiments and aspirations, but only in rare exceptions could they openly side with the forces of nationalism. Requirements of their official position made them an instrument for the execution of imperialist policies. This naturally aroused in the nationalist leadership feelings of anger and distrust against them. This rejection by the leaders of the nationalist forces as well as by the politically conscious masses was largely at the root of their ambivalent attitude towards the nationalist forces.

Bureaucracy welcomed the advent of independence as much as any other group in the former colonies and dependencies, but the first years of freedom were for it a period of great stress and strain. It had covertly resented Western domination, but in the first decade of independence it remained under the shadow of suspicion because of its former association and identification with the alien power. While its power and prestige were decreasing, its burdens and responsibilities were increasing. Attacked from several sides simultaneously and with mounting pressures, bureaucracy found itself in a difficult and uncomfortable position.

The more important areas in which it had to work for a redefinition and consequent readjustment of its position and responsibilities were (a) the culture of politics, (b) the emerging ethos, and (c) the expanding sphere of State activity and the new institutional arrangements.

The culture of politics

In the new order the supremacy of administration was replaced largely by the sovereignty of politics. Politics became the most important activity and the politician came to occupy a position of unquestionable supremacy in matters of decision making. Within the framework of this culture of politics, there was an unmistakable tendency towards the merging of political roles with personal and social roles; the expectations of the politician from his followers and administrative subordinates were diffused. Politics centered around individuals; informal factions or groups formed around key personalities were thus more meaningful units of political organization than the formal structure of political parties. Personal loyalty to politicians, under these conditions, played an important part in the process of political identification and decision making. Administration under such leadership could not remain wholly impersonal. The political élite was nurtured more in the politics of agitation than in the politics of nation building, and as a hangover from the past it persisted in its agitational approach. Nucleated around individuals, political processes lacked organic unity; communication was not adequately articulated. In general, political parties represented some kind of a revolutionary world view and philosophy, and on larger international and national issues they stood for an unlimited Utopia. On specific issues, especially of a regional or local character, the position was significantly different; political opinion on them was often narrow, sectarian and parochial. Thus political thinking regarding issues at different levels lacked cohesion and integration. The attitude of the political élite was characterized by ambivalence. They sought to work for modernization, without giving up their love for tradition; attempts to harmonize, synthesize and integrate the elements of the two, even on a conceptual level, were neither systematic nor serious.

In many countries the bureaucracy was trained well enough

to accept political direction, and only in a few exceptional cases did it try to gain the upper hand. Adjustment and adaptation to this political culture, however, was not without problems and difficulties. The new order posed a definite threat to bureaucracy's structure, values and interests. While its formal structure remained intact, the definition of roles and statuses within the hierarchy was disturbed by the emergence of the politician as the focal point of decision making. The personal nature of political decision making was another unsettling factor. It not only affected the internal status system of the bureaucracy, but also sometimes bypassed its special knowledge and side-tracked its procedural routine. In many specific contexts administration could not function in an impersonal manner. Interpersonal relations between the politician and the administrator tended to be uneasy. The politician recognized the value and importance of the bureaucracy, but he continued to have a definite antagonism towards it, to exhort and admonish it to change its ways, and to ridicule it for some of its modes of thought and action that were out of tune in the new order. Much of this criticism was valid, but the manner in which it was made was often irritating to the bureaucrats. Many members of the bureaucracy had silently admired the self-sacrificing patriots as heroes, but in close proximity they saw them without the halo that surrounded them during the days of the national struggle. Often, the gap between their profession and their practice particularly annoyed the perceptive members of the bureaucracy. The politician was himself adopting many of the ways which he criticized in the bureaucrat. Some members of the administration were all too willing to adapt, but their over-readiness to do so was viewed by the discerning administrator as a dangerous departure that could in the long run undermine the very character and role of the bureaucracy.

The emerging ethos

The emerging ethos also presented bureaucracy with a series of problems. In the new setting it could not maintain its image of power, nor could it continue to exist as a high-prestige class enjoying exceptional privileges. A closer identification with the masses was called for; the paternalistic and authoritarian tone of administration had also inevitably to change. On a theoretical and emotional level the desirability of this basic change was conceded, but a system of rationalization was developed at the same time to justify the maintenance of the *status quo.* Today a great contradiction persists between emotional awareness of the desirable and willingness to accept it in practice.

THE EXPANDING SPHERE OF STATE ACTIVITY AND NEW INSTITUTIONAL ARRANGEMENTS

The structure, values, and work-ways of the bureaucracy in almost all former colonies and dependencies were geared to laws and order and to revenue administration for which it was efficiently trained. Administration for nation-building necessitated a different approach involving a new value attitude orientation and modified institutional set-up. It is in these spheres that the failures of the bureaucracy are perhaps the most pronounced.

By and large the bureaucracy resists innovations in its structural arrangement. It appears to have a firm faith in the superiority of the pyramidal structure of administration and in the infallibility of the generalist. Efforts to nuclearize the administration for nation-building are resented, and there is great resentment if any attempt is made to dislodge the general administrator from his high pedestal. Concepts of inner-democratization, of administrative decentralization, and of delegation of authority and responsibility at best receive only lip service. Coordination becomes difficult because of faulty communication between the general administrator and the technical specialist. Effective utilization of the specialist is blocked by the accepted or assumed supremacy of the general administrator whose self-confidence borders almost on an arrogance. The latter perhaps realizes that he is not trained for certain jobs, but he rarely concedes this publicly. Innovations have been made in these spheres, but the marks of bureaucratic resistance are still evident.

Subconsciously the bureaucrat still perhaps believes in the efficacy of the traditional approach to administration. New approaches are discussed and half-heartedly accepted, but only in rare cases do they receive a fair trial. Extension and community development approaches, for instance, have encountered considerable resistance from the bureaucracy. Indeed, many members of the administration would be glad to revert to type, and would willingly reverse the process that has gained partial acceptance for these approaches after years of experimentation and persuasion.

It is generally recognized that the cumbrous administrative routine, good in its time, today practically immobilizes development administration. Yet, all attempts to change the rules of procedure result invariably in the formation of rules that are as complex as those they seek to replace, if not more so.

Efforts at deconcentration of power, such as the experiment of democratic decentralization for development in India, meet with even greater resistance. Doubtless the infant 'grass-roots democracy' is not without shortcomings, but its threats to the perpetuation of bureaucratic vested interests have alerted the administrator, whose approach to the experiment is extremely guarded, wooden and unimaginative.

Attempts have been made at reorienting the bureaucracy to the new philosophy of administration, but they have often been viewed as mere short-lived fads and fancies. Indirectly the new approach has made some headway, but there is little evidence to suggest that its utility has been generally accepted.

In the tasks of nation-building in transitional societies bureaucracy has a vital role to play. It consists, by and large, of people with progressive motivation, wide administrative experience, and a rich store of pooled knowledge. Far from being written off, it cannot be ignored. It must also be conceded that it has played an important part in the process of economic and social growth and has been willing to go part of the way at least to adjust to the new situation. It has functioned both as a model and as an instrument for modernization. But its effective utilization has been blocked by some of the paradoxes of the new political culture and by the inner contradictions within its own structure and ordering of values. In several respects the hard core of the bureaucratic culture has been unyielding, and has offered great resistance to innovation. The blame does not lie entirely at its own door, but at the same time the present state of uncertainty cannot be allowed to continue indefinitely. Lack of adequate understanding of its culture and values and of a balanced assessment of its past and future roles has been an important factor in the failure to utilize bureaucracy more effectively in programmes of economic growth and planned change.

Problems of Emerging Bureaucracies in Developing Areas and New States

S. N. Eisenstadt
The Hebrew University

I

In all developing countries, bureaucracies very rapidly tend to develop and extend their scope. As the post-colonial new states attained independence, and as some of the older states (e.g., Latin America or the Middle East) surged toward modernization and expanded the range of state activities, they took over many organs of public administration remaining from the former period; the scope of their activities greatly expanded, and new organs were created. Each became a very important part of the political framework in these countries. Since, in most of these countries, the government plays a great role in economic development, the bureaucracies also began to engage significantly in the activities of the economic sphere. The bureaucracy's activities could then have great influence on the direction and tempo of the country's economic development.

What will this influence be? What part will the bureaucracies play in the political life of these nations? Will they help in the establishment of viable modern political systems? Or will they contribute mostly to the development of unstable, tension-

Reprinted from *Industrialization and Society,* Bert F. Hoselitz and Wilbert E. Moore (eds.) (Paris: UNESCO, 1963), pp. 159–174, by permission.

ridden, and inefficient political structures? And what is the structure of the bureaucracies? How is it related to their functioning in these societies? To what extent is it similar to the major bureaucratic organizations that can be found in the West, and how does it differ from them? To what degree are the bureaucracies capable of efficiently implementing various social, political, and economic policies? Finally, how will they affect the process of economic development—will they facilitate or hinder it?

II

One of the striking facts about the bureaucracies of the developing areas is that, in most of these areas there exist not one but usually two or three, bureaucracies—or, at least, different layers of bureaucratic organization and structure. First, there is what may be called the "pre-modern" or "pre-development" layer, which had developed before the attainment of independence or the introduction of modernization. The second stratum has, as a rule, developed since World War II. It was engendered by the dual impacts of the attainment of independence and of modernization and of establishing new social, political, and economic goals.

In the post-colonial new states, the "old" colonial civil service still survives in remaining personnel, organizational structure, and tradition. The structure and organization of the old civil service provided the basic framework for the extension and development of bureaucratic administration after the attainment of independence.

Within these societies, the initial emergence of bureaucracies had been rooted in the need of the colonial powers for various resources and for the maintenance of law and order. The bureaucracy was based on over-all political control by the metropolitan powers; the administration participated minimally in the indigenous political and social life of the community. This necessarily limited its activities, confining them to the basic administrative services. It also dictated some of the bureaucracy's structural characteristics, such as the high degree of centralization, the great adherence to legal precepts and rules, and the relatively small internal differentiation. Thus the pre-independence bureaucracies helped establish the framework of modern, universalistic legal and administrative practices and organizations. On the other hand, they were highly apolitical. They did not meddle in politics, and they kept up the ideal of a politically neutral civil service. They were also apolitical in that they never really participated in the indigenous political life of the countries in which they served. Their very limited goals were prescribed by the colonial powers, who were not responsible to the political groups and opinions of the countries which they ruled. They did not perform any important functions in the regulation of internal political interests and activities among the "colonial" population, or in the articulation and aggregation of the political interests of that population.[1] Whatever "internal" political activities they undertook were perceived mostly in terms of administrative injunctions and enforcement of law. It is significant that the scope and impact of the activities of the colonial civil service were much greater in countries, such as India, in which "direct rule" was applied, than in countries governed according to precepts of "indirect rule," where the native population was left more or less alone to manage its own affairs, especially on the local level.

The second main layer of the bureaucracies in the new states consists of those departments and echelons which were developed after the attainment of independence. Here a new civil service—"new" in personnel, goals, departments, and activities—evolved. This stratum had to be staffed with new recruits—frequently with inadequately trained recruits whose chief claim to or qualification for office was their former participation in the nationalistic political movements. These new bureaucratic organs have had new types of goals, like economic development, social betterment, educational advancement, or community development.

Unlike members of the "colonial" civil service, most of the recruits to the new have usually had a clear and articulated political orientation and sense of political responsibility. They

[1] For the terms used here, see G. A. Almond, "A Functional Approach to Comparative Politics," in G. A. Almond and J. S. Coleman (eds.), *The Politics of the Developing Areas* (Princeton, N.J., 1960), pp. 26–58.

have very often perceived themselves as representatives of their respective movements, parties, or sectors. Moreover, they frequently have seen themselves as fulfilling chiefly political functions—either as implementing political goals, or as representing, articulating, and regulating the political interests and activities of different groups and social strata.

The relations between the older bureaucracy and the new echelons have not always been easy. In the first period after independence, particularly, the nationalist leaders' prevailing attitude toward the remnants of the older colonial services was distrust. In some cases, this led to the almost complete destruction of the older structure. In most instances, however, some sort of *modus vivendi* has been evolved between the older and newer echelon. One or the other is usually predominant; but necessarily the implementation of new social, political, and economic goals has been strongly emphasized, and the involvement in the political process has been much greater than before.

An even more explicitly politically oriented type of bureaucracy has tended to emerge in most of the new states. This type consists of the different "party" bureaucracies which grew out of the leading nationalistic movements which became dominant parties—e.g., the Congress of India, the CPP in Ghana or the Neo-Destour in Tunisia. These party bureaucracies have been oriented more to the political manipulation of groups of population and to the provision of political support and loyalty to the new regime than to the upholding of universalistic legal norms, the development of public services, or the creation of new public administrative services. In personnel or over-all political supervision, the party bureaucracy has often been very similar to the new echelons of the governmental bureaucracy, and has sometimes also been closely related to it, especially through the activities of prime ministers and cabinet ministers. However, the basic patterns of activities and orientations of the members of the party bureaucracy have frequently differed to a very great extent from those of the governmental bureaucracy, and have clashed.[2]

[2] See D. Apter and R. A. Lystad, "Bureaucracy, Party and Constitutional Democracy," in G. M. Carter and W. O. Brown (eds.), *Transition in Africa* (Boston, 1958).

III

The bureaucracies in developing countries which have not been under colonial rule exhibit a somewhat different, although not entirely dissimilar, pattern. Within each there existed, first, a traditional bureaucracy—whether "royal" (as in the Middle Eastern countries) or "oligarchical-republican" (as in most Latin American countries). These bureaucracies usually dominated the political scene until the end of World War II. Within them, some traditional elements were mixed with more modern ones. Frequently, the modern elements were copied from some European country—for example, the French pattern had strong influence in most Latin American countries.

These administrations were usually concerned with supporting the interests of the ruling oligarchies, and with implementing rather limited social and economic objectives. Whatever tendency to modernization they may have exhibited—e.g., in the fields of military affairs or education—their major political aim was to restrict modernization to those minimal spheres in which it was necessary to maintain the viability of the then existing system.

With increasing modernization, with the growing impact of internal democratization, and with the development of new social, political, and economic goals, these bureaucracies had to extend the scope of their activities and to recruit new personnel. However, the older pattern usually continued to leave its imprint on the new echelons and departments, in administrative training, organization, and to some extent also in social and political orientation.[3] Only in a few older countries, like Mexico, widespread, well-organized semi-revolutionary parties succeeded in upsetting the oligarchy and established a stable and viable modern political framework. There, a somewhat new pattern of bureaucratic organization was established, not dissimilar from those of new states.

[3] See the papers by G. Blanksten and D. Rustow in Almond and Coleman, *op. cit.* See also the papers by W. R. Sharp (on Egypt), A. Lepawsky (on Bolivia), F. Heady (on the Philippines), and J. N. More (on Thailand), in W. J. Siffin (ed.), *Toward the Comparative Study of Public Administration* (Bloomington, Ind., 1957).

In most of these older countries, the party bureaucracies were usually less important than in the new states. This was mainly because the oligarchical or monarchical elements were much stronger in the political structure, and because several major institutional interest groups, especially the armed forces, developed as important channels of political struggle and often constituted hotbeds of politics and influential pressure groups.

Both within the formerly colonial societies and in the states with longer traditions of independence, another distinct type of new bureaucratic organization has also emerged—the big economic or business corporation. Within the older countries, these corporations are usually more concentrated in the private sector; in the new states, more in the public or mixed sectors. In all these societies, however, the corporations play an important role in the economic and political life of the country.

IV

We see thus that, in each emerging country, the pattern of development of bureaucracies has been very mixed and heterogeneous. Each part of the bureaucracy developed under somewhat different conditions and in response to different types of needs and pressures. It was only after the attainment of independence, and/or the development of goals and programs of modernization, that these parts were brought together into a common framework and confronted with the need to find some *modus vivendi* in order to deal with the new tasks which they faced.

Perhaps the most important general problem which faced all the bureaucracies was the necessity to adapt themselves to the goals, new spheres of activity, and new social needs that arose from the growing differentiation and diversification of the social structures, the extension of the scope of social and political participation of many groups in the society, and the development of new social and political goals. In trying to adapt themselves, the merging bureaucracies developed several characteristics which were greatly influenced by their heterogeneous origins and by the conditions in which they found themselves.

In almost none of these countries has the bureaucracy evolved into the "classical" Weberian type of legal-rational organization or an entirely neutral civil service. True, in several of the post-colonial countries—notably in India and Ghana, and, to a lesser extent in the countries which were or are under French colonial rule—the ideal of such a service was transmitted and still has a strong hold on the developing civil service. But even in these countries, events have occurred that have greatly changed the major political orientation of the bureaucracy. Similarly, the structural characteristics and the patterns of activities of these bureaucracies differ in varying degrees, from those of the usual Western pattern.

The first and most important development in the social and political orientations of these bureaucracies is their high involvement in the political process in their respective countries. This is manifested in several ways.

In many of these countries, for example, the bureaucracy becomes not only the administrative arm of an executive, supervised by the legislature; it also constitutes itself as an effective executive or a component thereof, and plays a basic part in establishing, determining, and implementing political goals and major policy directives. In many nations, the bureaucracy may be the main or the only body which, apart from the head of the executive, is capable of formulating clear political and administrative goals and objectives.

The second major aspect of the bureaucracy's involvement in the political process is grounded in the fact that it tends to evolve as one of the principal instruments of political regulation—one of the main channels of political struggle in which and through which different interests are regulated and "aggregated"—and it tends to be very important, even predominant, in this facet of the political process. In some cases, e.g., in some Latin American countries, the bureaucracy also becomes a powerful pressure and interest group in its own right, strongly allied to other oligarchical groups.

Thus, in all these countries, the bureaucracy may tend to fulfill different types of political functions and—like parties, legislatures, and executives—become a center of various kinds of political activity. Although, through such activities, it may establish some of the basic frameworks of modern politics, it may also minimize the extent of differentiation of divers types of political roles and activities. In the latter case, it would greatly impede the development of autonomous and differentiated political activities, organizations, and orientations.

The second basic characteristic of the social orientations of emergent bureaucracies is that they are also major instruments of social change and of political socialization in their respective countries.

These bureaucratic organizations are (at least initially) based on universalistic and functionally specific definitions of the role of the official and the role of the client. The majority of the population of these countries, however, have a different orientation. In social life, their traditional orientations and structures, such as the extended family, are predominant. In these societies, most of a person's role relations are set within traditional groups; and rights and duties are defined in terms of personal relationships. Previous experience with bureaucratic organizations was restricted, and was rarely of any great significance.

Thus, the contacts of the public with governmental organizations provided a framework for a wider process of political socialization. The public's accommodation to the new political structure became, to a considerable extent, dependent upon its successful learning in these situations of contact. This has very often forced the bureaucracies to go beyond their proper specialized roles and to assume various roles of social and political leadership and tutelage—without which they could not have effected the necessary changes in the behavior of the population at large. This need to foster change often extended the scope of the activities of bureaucrats beyond their specific goals, and made them reach also into the realm of family, kinship, and community life of wide strata of the population.

V

What are the causes of these developments in the structure of bureaucracies? And what can be their possible impact on the processes of political modernization and economic development?

Generally, two types of causes can be discerned. One basic cause, often mentioned in the literature, is the difference between the general cultural values and social setting of the developing areas and those of Western countries where "modern" bureaucratic organizations originated. Presthus has illustrated these problems:

> In sum, the dominant educational philosophy tends to devalue practical training and this constitutes a barrier to bureaucratic evolution. Middle East youth prefer to become white-collar rather than blue-collar workers. This inapposite value has an immediate impact on technical and economic development, since it becomes difficult to build up the required force of skilled technicians. In the universities, subjects like statistics and research methods are resisted since they, too, tend to undercut the existing theoretical and subjective conception of learning. Such beliefs deny the demands of modern bureaucratic organizations for precision, specialization, and scientific method.[4]

For our purposes, the relevant point is that subjective, political values outweigh objective, bureaucratic demands of skill and experience.

In so far as recruitment and the locus of bureaucratic loyalties are concerned, it is well known in Middle Eastern countries that subjective, "particularistic" considerations compete strongly with objective standards in appointment and in policy determination. Western "universalistic" concepts of impersonality, technical supremacy, and loyalty to some abstraction, such as the "public interest," remain alien in societies in which primary loyalties are directed to members of one's family and to personal friends. A recent observer of the Egyptian civil service concluded that people in the Near East are not yet accustomed to looking upon others impersonally in any situation. They tend to regard others as individuals, with families, friends, and communities behind them; this trend is carried into realms where recent changes have established different formal requirements.

These general cultural values and social settings undoubtedly influence the nature of administrative structure and behavior in the new countries, and must be taken into account in their analysis. The cultural traits may explain many of the different

4 Robert V. Presthus, "The Social Bases of Bureaucratic Organization," *Social Forces,* XXXVIII, No. 2 (December, 1959), 103–09.

patterns of bureaucratic behavior which have been mentioned above. However, in themselves, they cannot explain the basic common political problems of these bureaucracies, nor the great variety of administrative structures and behavior that can be found in these societies.

It seems that consideration of these general cultural traditions and social orientations is not enough. It is necessary also to analyze some basic social aspects of the processes of political development and modernization in these societies.

VI

What are these processes? Perhaps the common central facets of the problem are the crucial role, in the process of modernization, of the state or of political leaders, and the internal contradictions which have necessarily developed in their activities in this context.

The first important fact in this respect is that—although the new ruling elites have attempted to establish frameworks of modern polities, have developed new political goals, and have tried to find the instruments for their implementation—the extent of general participation in the political process has been relatively small. There have existed few groups and strata capable of engaging in the process of modernization on their own, and able to articulate their political interests in a modern, differentiated way.

Many ascriptive (communal, tribal, and caste) groups existed. Their chief political orientations were traditional and restricted either to passive supplication and petition or to the old kind of court politics.

On the other hand, there were many small, splintered interests, such as divers small business groups, that were not able to articulate and aggregate their political interests. In some countries, especially in Latin America and the Middle East, there were also major institutional interest groups (churches, army groups) which monopolized most of the political positions and impeded the growth of modern independent political forces.

In general, in all of these societies, there developed only few and weak functionally differentiated groups and general responsible public opinion capable of generating an independent and diversified political leadership and organization.

Thus, the articulation, aggregation, and regulation of political activities and interests became mostly concentrated in the hands of the ruling elite—the leaders of the old nationalist (and military) movements. At best, they became concentrated in one major party which was able to establish a unified framework of modern polity. In other cases, they were splintered among different small parties and did not crystallize into more stable patterns.

With the attainment of independence, or with growing modernization, the elites faced several tasks in the area of political organization. They could not confine political participation to its former level; they had to extend it to the politically more passive or inarticulate groups from whom new types of allegiance, political involvement, and loyalties were being demanded. The new regimes could not maintain themselves entirely on the passive allegiance that had predominated in colonial times, since they themselves had undermined this allegiance. Through their emphasis on governmental activities in many spheres of society, they penetrated more and more into various social layers. Somehow, they had to foster the development of new social and political motivations and participation. Schemes for community development, for new industrial and agrarian organizations, and for agrarian reforms whenever these were undertaken—all implied the necessity for new orientations, incentives, and the development of many new motivational patterns.

By engaging in these, however, the new political rulers found themselves in a series of new dilemmas.

In most countries under discussion, a double contradiction developed in the activities of the ruling elites, and in their efforts to activate the various strata of the population toward participation in the common collective goals. First, there was the contradiction between the traditional forces and the development of relatively modern, "free-floating" resources and divers professional, economic, and cultural groups. Second, there was the contradiction between the tendencies of the more modern forces to coalesce in relatively independent and autonomous centers of power, and the aims of the ruling elites to control as many of these forces and centers of power as possible.

Simultaneously, the elites confronted another problem or contradiction. The new goals which they proclaimed often contained various implicit or explicit promises to the population, particularly in the economic field. Many social groups were ready to present this bill to the elite for payment, especially when their support was demanded. In this way, the government could, through the distribution of various goods and services—which it controlled—to its own supporters, maintain its position and attempt to control other social forces. However, the elite could thus arrive at an impasse, in which the implementation of the various societal goals, and its own ultimate claims to legitimation, would become seriously impeded by the necessity to spend many of its resources as emoluments for its supporters. The very need of the elite to control the traditional and, especially, the modern forces, and its ambivalent attitude toward many of them, can aggravate this problem.

VII

One of the main consequences of these contradictions—an outcome in which the political elites and the bureaucracies both co-operated—was the intensification of the inherent tendency of the political elite and bureaucracy to enhance their monopolization of power and prestige. This tendency is closely related to the social transformations attendant on the attainment of independence. It has manifested itself in: (a) attempts to create a strong hierarchy of status in terms of political power; (b) efforts to subject most processes of social mobility to the control of the political elites; and (c) efforts to subject a large number of economic, professional, and cultural activities to political control.

The political elite and the bureaucracy were inclined to belittle the importance and efficiency of purely economic activities and the claims of economic groups toward social autonomy. It tended to superimpose extraeconomic criteria on economic activities and on their bearers—not only by stipulating broad, general "social goals," but also by the daily regulation and direction of activity. Moreover, the political elites sometimes attempted to undermine the autonomous development of the middle and working classes, and of cultural and professional elites, and link their positions entirely to directives.

The efforts of the political elite and bureaucracy to direct and control all the main avenues of local mobility are closely associated to these developments. Through such efforts, they tend to maintain their hold on potential centers of power and to control their evolution. But these attempts are often self-contradictory; the close control exercised by the bureaucracy undermines efforts for economic development. More aspirants are created for new posts than there are posts available, and thus the bureaucracy itself is put in an insecure position.

This process took a somewhat different direction in the non-colonial countries. While the extent of political articulation and organization of wider groups and strata was relatively small and weak, the picture was different. In these countries, a much stronger competition between the older oligarchy and some of the new groups and parties usually emerged.

However, some modern political frameworks—even though born by a relatively restricted oligarchy—already existed. They were the main organs of political activity and regulation, and their very existence impeded both the "political" articulation of new social groups and, often, also any further political modernization. Hence the social and political predominance of these groups, which frequently also impeded the efficiency and rationalization of the structure of the bureaucracy.

VIII

These characteristics of the process of modernization were most influential in the development of bureaucracies in emerging countries. The most crucial facts are that this process was greatly fostered by the political elites; that political movements, and later the state, played such an important role in the breaking up of the framework of traditional society and in advancing growing social and economic differentiation; and that there were only a few other groups which participated autonomously in this process and were able to help in the implementation of new goals. These factors necessarily gave the bureaucracy a vital place in the political process and social structure of these societies: it had to become one of the major agents of change in all spheres of social life. But, just because it became such an agent of change, it had also to generate new types of interests and activities and to undertake many functions of political aggregation and articulation.

As a result, the bureaucracy in these countries was involved in dilemmas similar to those faced by the new rulers. Efficient implementation of goals and the establishment of viable frameworks of modern political institutions depended greatly on political stability and on the development of new political and administrative attitudes and activities. However, these same conditions could create pressure for certain kinds of activities on behalf of the bureaucracy that could easily undermine its efficiency and its ability to implement goals and services while withstanding the demands of many potential political supporters.

In this context, we also must analyze the relation between certain economic processes in these countries and their developing bureaucracies. The most important aspect is that, in these countries, the bureaucracies constitute one of the principal channels of economic and social mobility and advancement. Several factors account for this. One is the central place of the government in the sphere of economic development. Another is the great prestige of white-collar work that is widespread in most of these countries—a prestige which was only enhanced by political developments and the growing social importance of the political elites. The third factor comprises the growing aspirations to mobility that emerged under the impacts both of political and economic modernization and of the need of the rulers to satisfy the aspirations to mobility and to minimize their political explosiveness. The fourth factor is the structure of the educational system, with its strong emphasis on literary, as distinct from technical, education, and its influence on the structure of the labor force and occupational choice. For all these reasons, great pressure developed on governmental and civil service jobs. These pressures, obviously, potentially could have grave repercussions on the economic and the political developments. From the economic point of view, the demands and aspirations could easily create a lack of adequate manpower for technical jobs and widespread white-collar unemployment and underemployment. Politically, these tendencies created many potential pressures and tensions. Moreover, they could weaken the efficiency of the bureaucracy, by making it into a sort of system of sinecures in which there was little relation between job security and performance, and in which extraneous (political and personal) criteria could become the main determinants of recruitment and advancement. In these combined economic and political pressures, one can find the roots of the widespread tendency to corruption that has emerged in these bureaucracies.

IX

All these forces—the cultural orientations prevalent in these societies, the political and economic processes and pressures—necessarily have their repercussion on the structure of the bureaucracies and on their ability to implement major political and social goals and to provide continuous services to the population.

Among the most important of such structural problems, the following have often been noted:[5] (a) the low density of administrative structure, i.e., the relatively small ratio of officials to population and tasks; (b) the lack of fully qualified and adequate personnel; (c) the small extent of diversification of functions, and consequent overlapping between different echelons and departments; and (e) overcentralization, poor co-ordination, and lack of autonomy and initiative of the linestaff.

Riggs has aptly summarized some of these problems, especially as they apply to older independent countries:

> Obstacles to identification of personal with program goals are especially conspicuous in the way the work load and responsibilities of different officials are allocated, that is, in "organization

[5] See, for instance, J. L. Quermonne, "La sous-administration et les politiques d'équipement administratif," *Revue française de science politique*, IX, No. 3 (September, 1959), 629–67.

> and management." These often make it impossible for anyone to carry out a constructive project without waiting for the concurrence of many others, whereby many people have the power to block action. One result is often to elevate the level of settlement of even minor disputes to ministerial, cabinet, and chief executive levels. Top administrators become embroiled in continual interagency conflicts while subordinates piddle away their energies waiting for requisite approvals. Moreover, because many persons far from the scene of action become involved in decision making, questions are often referred to persons with only remote interest in them, it becomes difficult to assign responsibility for action, and final decisions hinge on the outcome of power struggles among individuals only indirectly concerned.[6]

In some countries, elaborate ministerial secretariats, staffed by generalists, who rotate frequently between headquarters and district assignments, have been placed in the line of communication and command between ministers and executive or administrative departments and divisions. Invariably, great delay ensues while secretariat officials review more and more of the work nominally assigned to and originating in the departments. We may quote the words of a distinguished former civil servant in India about the result:

> The head of the department is deprived of all initiative and instead of being allowed to attend to and make progress with his own work, has to spend a great deal of time submitting unnecessary reports, explaining the position in individual matters to the Ministry and getting its orders on points which lie well within his own sphere of authority.
>
> Because of overcentralization and lack of delegation, those close to the goals of action cannot easily cooperate with their colleagues in other agencies whose work directly affects the success of their own efforts. Characteristically, to overcome this stagnation, new agencies are often set up in the hope that, outside the bog of established structures, action may be possible. But the new agencies simply add to the intra-bureaucratic conflict and competition, increasing the burden on the top of the hierarchy to impose coordination.[7]

[6] F. W. Riggs, "Public Administration—A Neglected Factor in Economic Development," *Annals of the American Academy of Political and Social Science* (May, 1956), pp. 70–81.

[7] A. D. Gorwala, *Report on Public Administration* (New Delhi, 1951), p. 39. See also Paul H. Appleby, *Public Administration in India; Report of a Survey* (New Delhi, 1953), Sec. II, especially p. 21.

The relative importance of these problems naturally varies in different countries. In the post-colonial countries, the most critical problems seem to be lack of adequate staff, overcentralization, and too little diversification. In the independent countries, the most vital problems are the excessive control, rigidity, and lack of initiative of the officials, and their regarding their offices as sinecures. However, there is much overlapping between these different structural aspects. And beyond all these, there always hovers the double specter of corruption and growing inefficiency of the bureaucracy.

X

The patterns of activities, organization, and political and social orientations of the bureaucracies in developing areas differ greatly from those of Western countries. However, it does not suffice to stress the differences between the new emerging bureaucracies and the older bureaucracies of Western countries or to point out the former's structural deficiencies and problems. Except for their common characteristics, outlined above, the exact ways in which they will develop differ greatly between countries. These differences may be of crucial importance in their implications for political and economic development.

In evaluating the effect of these bureaucracies on political modernization and economic development, we must again stress the fact that they have become major agents of social and political change, and examine what influence they may have on such change. Generally, there are two major, and sometimes overlapping, possible influences the bureaucracies can have on processes of change and development in the developing areas.

The first major possibility is the development of relatively efficient frameworks of modern administration; the upholding of legal norms and rules and the maintenance of basic services, even if this is effected through the bureaucracy's extension of its scope of activities; and the assumption, by its officials, of many social, political, and leadership roles. These bureaucracies may generate through the establishment of new political frameworks and through the development of such activities, many new social organizations and activities on both the central and local level, and may contribute both to the establishment of viable political frameworks and to conditions conducive to economic development.

The evolution of this type of orientation and activities of the bureaucracy depends greatly on two conditions. (1) Some basic, unitary political framework, a relatively unified political elite, and a degree of political consensus must exist. (2) Purely institutional interest groups (e.g., army, churches, etc.) must be relatively weak in comparison to ecological strata and certain functional groups.

The main issues facing the elites are the extent to which they can overcome the pressures for a higher level of consumption, and the degree to which they can advance wider educational schemes capable of providing adequate training for personnel in technical fields and thus alleviating the pressures on the white-collar jobs.

The structure and patterns of activities of the bureaucracies which develop under these conditions differ greatly from those of "classical" bureaucratic organizations. However, the very fact that the scope of their activities is relatively wide, combined with a firm political orientation and a high measure of political consensus, may facilitate the maintenance of relative stability and continuity, induce and generate new types of economic entrepreneurship, and generate professional activities and political leadership on the local and even on the central level. Furthermore, the bureaucracy also may gradually generate diversification of functionally specific groups and independent public opinion and leadership. It is interesting to note that, in these cases, there usually exist also rather strong party bureaucracies. While, initially, there may be conflicts between them and the civil service, the very fact that there is some initial diversification of functions within a relatively unified political framework may help generate change and economic development.

The second important kind of possible bureaucratic development is characterized by the bureaucracy's contributions mainly to what Riggs has called "negative development."[8] Here the bureaucracy tends to monopolize some central political func-

[8] F. W. Riggs, "Economic Development and Local Administration," *The Philippine Journal of Public Administration,* III, No. 1 (January, 1959), 86–146.

tions; in addition, it tends to become a major interest group, usually closely allied with some institutional interest groups and with various oligarchical strata. Because of this alliance, the bureaucracy is inclined to become a center of attraction for various "white-collar" aspirants, and thus overstaffed. On the other hand, it necessarily becomes a "narrow" interest group, which tends to stifle any development of independent political action. It may easily obstruct schemes of economic development that threaten its level of relative income and other vested interests. In such cases, the bureaucracy usually becomes an active participant in the narrow political and economic struggle. Corruption usually becomes rampant; the stability of the basic administrative services, universalistic legal framework, and economic activities may be broken down. Such processes are facilitated when there is no unified political framework and consensus; when the rift between traditional and modern elites, or the lack of consensus within the modern elite, is very great; and when institutional interest groups, like a church, army, and other narrow oligarchical groups, predominate in the social and economic structure.

As indicated above, both possible developments within the bureaucracies are inherent in the basic conditions of economic and political evolution in the developing areas. In any concrete case, these tendencies can overlap, but the bureaucracy itself often influences, to some degree at least, the concrete outcome of these developments, through its own adherence to common political goals or through educational policies.

Improvement of Local Government and Administration for Development Purposes

EMIL J. SADY
United Nations

THIS ARTICLE COMPARES the approaches and summarizes the results of two meetings: the Cambridge Conference on Local Government in Africa (King's College, University of Cambridge, August 28th to September 9th, 1961) and the United Nations Working Group on Administrative Aspects of Decentralization for National Development (Palais des Nations, Geneva, October 16th to 27th, 1961). Participants at both were seeking, through a comparative approach, methods of improving local government. A comparison of their findings is of interest despite the fact that the meetings had different purposes, were constituted differently, and had a different area and subject matter scope. The Cambridge Conference was designed to provide refresher training and exchange of information for expatriate (British) and African administrative officers, and to advance knowledge on means of improving local government in English-speaking areas in Africa. The United Nations Group was convened primarily to assist in the preparation of a report for the use of governments of developing countries and technical assistance experts in devising forms of decentralization (whether through local government or other means involving participation by the people) which might

Comparative analysis of approaches and results of the Cambridge Conference on Local Government and the United Nations Working Group on Administrative Aspects of Decentralization for National Development. Reprinted from the *Journal of Local Administration Overseas* (published by H.M.S.O., London) Vol. 1, No. 3 (July, 1962), pp. 135–148, by permission. [Abridged.]

accelerate social and economic development. Exchange of information among participants was regarded more as a by-product, although an important one, of the United Nations Group. . . .

[B]oth meetings considered the following definition which we had developed in the United Nations: "The term local government refers to a political subdivision of a nation or (in a federal system) state which is constituted by law and has substantial control of local affairs, including the power to impose taxes or to exact labour for prescribed purposes. The governing body of such an entity is elected or otherwise locally selected."[1]

Both meetings expressed concern that the phrase "to exact labour for prescribed purposes" might be misinterpreted and lead to abuse. The Cambridge Conference, 'throwing out the baby with the bath water,' started afresh on a new definition which omits the phrase in question but otherwise differs little in substance from the definition quoted. The United Nations Group, on the other hand, accepted the definition with the understanding that the phrase in question would either be deleted or be more precisely worded to conform with international labour standards on the subject, that is limiting the exaction of labour in lieu of taxes to 'minor communal services' and calling for the progressive abolition of communal labour imposed on order of tribal chiefs.

It seems more fruitful to bring together in a meaningful way some of the more important results of the two meetings than to attempt further comparisons of arrangements for the meetings or a catalogue of items of agreement or disagreement. In view of the wider scope of the United Nations Group and the fact that the author was involved at all stages of its work, its conclusions will be summarized and important supplementary or contradictory conclusions of the Cambridge Conference noted. The views attributed herein to the 'United Nations Group' and the 'Cambridge Conference' represent the author's understanding of the consensus of the respective meetings and do not necessarily represent the views either of individual participants or of the organizations which sponsored the meetings.

[1] *Public Administration Aspects of Community Development Programmes,* (Sales No.: 59.11.H.2) page 2, paragraph 7.

Purposes of decentralization

Local government and other forms of decentralization involving popular participation contribute to national as well as local government by:

A. 'decongesting' government at the centre and thereby freeing national leaders from onerous details and unnecessary involvement in local issues, and facilitating co-ordination and expediting action at the local level;
B. increasing the people's understanding and support of social and economic development activities and, as a result, gaining the benefit of their own contributions to these activities, and of personal and group adjustments to needed changes;
C. making programmes to foster social and economic betterment at the local level more realistic and lasting;
D. training people in the art of self-government; and
E. strengthening national unity.[2]

Forms of decentralization

The United Nations Group found the following classification of systems of field administration and local government to be useful for purposes of comparative study;

A. Comprehensive local government system, in which most government services at the local level are rendered through multi-purpose local authorities. A concept of substantial unity of purpose of representative bodies at all levels underlies this system. Local authorities exercise some functions pursuant to general statutory authority and others on behalf of central ministries. There is, therefore, opportunity for locally as well as centrally initiated and controlled activities. The distinguishing feature of this system is that local authorities, instead of field

[2] This point was emphasized by the Cambridge Conference. While recognizing the argument that local government can be misused by the members of a particular race, religion, tribe or political party to promote disunity, the Conference felt that local authorities can and should be so constituted as to prevent this.

units of national agencies, render direct agricultural, education, health and social welfare services. This is the system in Yugoslavia, and is emerging in India, Pakistan and the United Arab Republic with the transformation of field units of central agencies into the executive arms of local authorities.[3]

B. Partnership system, in which some direct services are rendered by field units of central agencies and others by local authorities. The local authorities perform some functions more or less autonomously pursuant to general statutory authority and others on behalf of and under the technical supervision of central ministries. This system permits use of field administration and local authorities separately or jointly according to the needs of the particular function and situation. Field units are likely to be co-ordinated, if at all, only at the regional level. This is the predominant pattern in Ceylon and in English-speaking countries in Africa. The Cambridge Conference stressed the importance of co-operative relationships of central and local government and seemed to take for granted that the partnership system is the preferred form.

C. Dual system, in which central ministries administer technical services directly, with local authorities having autonomy *legally* to perform local services and to do what they can to foster local development but actually performing few if any technical services either directly or on behalf of central agencies. Suspicion and conflict rather than unity or co-operation characterize relationships between central government and local authorities. Local government under this system is more an instrument of political decentralization than of social and economic

[3] In these countries, local authorities are being established at district and other area levels where central field services were previously co-ordinated. In India, there are three tiers of local authorities; the council (*panchayat*) at the village level is directly elected by the people, while those at the other two levels (*panchayat semiti* and *zila parishad*) are formed by representatives selected by councils at the next lower tier. The arrangements in Pakistan and the U.A.R. are similar, except that both provide for appointed non-officials and officials to serve alongside elected members on the councils. In all three countries, field technical personnel of central government agencies are, with certain safeguards, being made the servants of the local authorities and the local councils are being given substantial responsibility and authority over planning, budgeting and administration of central government funds allocated to their areas. It is too soon to assess the results of these programmes but it is important to note that all three are designed to increase popular participation in and control over national development programmes in rural areas.

development. This is the predominant pattern in Latin American countries. Formal organization for field co-ordination of central government services is also rare where the dual system exists.

D. INTEGRATED ADMINISTRATIVE SYSTEM, in which central government agencies directly administer all technical services, with central government area co-ordinators or district administrators responsible for field co-ordination. Such rural local authorities as exist have little control over government activities and staffs in their areas. This is the pattern in most countries in south-east Asia and the Middle East.

The classification has, of course, limitations. The categories are very broad; the difference between the comprehensive and partnership systems lies largely in the extent of reliance upon local authorities as the channel for direct services. The categories do not reflect degrees of decentralization. There could conceivably be greater centralization of authority in a comprehensive local government system where technical personnel are weak than in an integrated administrative system where they may be given wide latitude for programme formulation and execution in consultation with people locally. Moreover, systems of decentralization are not static as might be inferred from the classification. They are constantly changing and, especially in developing countries, are subject to substantial changes as circumstances, ideas and needs change.

The classification is, however, useful. It highlights fundamentally different approaches to decentralization and the problems characteristic of each. For example, countries with comprehensive local government systems are likely to have special problems of technical supervision and support, a special need for an attractive local government career service or for an integrated career system for public employees at all levels, and special arrangements for financing. Under partnership systems, central agencies will have different financial and administrative relationship with local authorities—thus creating special problems of co-ordination. In the dual system, there are special problems in relations between central agencies and 'autonomous' local authorities, and of gaining popular participation in the development schemes of central agencies. Countries with an integrated administrative system may have to devise special methods for relating government programmes to local needs and interests, and also for enlisting popular participation in them. Certain problems are of course common to two or more systems but the classification is a useful tool for comparative study and exchange of information on problems of decentralization. Moreover, in the United Nations meeting at Geneva, reference to a particular system facilitated comprehension of the intended context for a remark or suggestion.

Size of areas and number of levels

The Geneva Working Group found that there is inadequate information on which to prescribe in specific terms the optimum size or sizes of areas for administration of agricultural, education, health and other technical services individually or as a group. It noted that widely differing standards are being used as a basis for demarcating boundaries of field administration and local government units which render most direct services (Egypt, for example, uses a population basis of 15,000 and India, 66,000). Having in mind the commitment of personnel and funds involved in applying such standards on a nationwide scale, the Group recommended that the United Nations and its specialized agencies attempt through further study to provide guidance on the optimum minimum areas for administration of technical services and general governmental functions under different types of situations. It noted important factors such as population density, facility of communications, social organization, and intensity of programming that would affect size of areas. It suggested, as a general rule of thumb in the absence of more specific guides, that where common areas are to be established for administration of technical services the size of the areas should be at least as large as required by the technical service having the largest area requirements for its activity at that level.[4]

[4] The papers prepared by Working Group participants from the United Nations and the specialized agencies provide some general guides on optimum minimum areas for administration of the principal technical services. These papers will, according to present plans, form part of the report on decentralization for national and local development to be issued by the United Nations.

The Group also made some useful suggestions on the design of regional planning, field administration and local government areas. For example, it favoured:—

A. establishment of common field areas and headquarters cities, rather than allowing each ministry to choose its own;

B. design of field areas large enough to accommodate the different needs of the several technical services but with the possibility in mind that they may be transformed into local government areas;

C. creation in large countries of planning regions by grouping field administration and local government areas, due account being taken of historical as well as planning and administrative considerations; and

D. establishment of as few tiers of field administration and local government as possible. Two levels of rural local authorities were considered ideal—the lower level covering the largest area at which a sense of community exists and direct citizen participation in local services is possible and the higher level covering the largest area from which most technical services can be provided efficiently but not so large that councillors cannot meet frequently.

Both meetings observed that local authorities established in an earlier era were generally too small for performance of technical services. Members from Western Nigeria mentioned a plan under consideration for creating special service authorities for major technical services within areas comprehending a number of local authorities. Representatives of the local authorities would serve as the governing bodies of the special service authorities and technical personnel of central agencies would be made available to them. There would be a separate authority for each technical service in a given area, but the same areas would be used by the several services and a single 'local government manager' would serve as secretary of all special service authorities in each area.

Area division of powers and functions

The United Nations Group emphasized that division of responsibilities between central government and local authorities, or between the various local authority levels, differs between countries and is constantly changing everywhere. However, it stated several principles that have wide acceptance:

A. functions that are plainly local in character (such as water and sewerage, refuse disposal, and local streets), should be allocated to local authorities wherever possible;
B. primary responsibility for execution of functions should be placed at as low a level as it is practicable to have the functions performed satisfactorily;
C. while the central Government should ensure that standards of performance do not fall below an acceptable level, it should not interfere with the operations of local authorities unless this is strictly necessary.

Both meetings recognized that central control over local authorities must be related to the powers and ability of local authorities. The Cambridge Conference, however, stated that its basic assumption was that "only local authorities which are capable of making *effective* use of discretionary power and financial *independence* are capable of fulfilling the purposes of local government" (italics are the author's). The United Nations Group's view, while not contrary to this, stressed the importance of maintaining the responsibility of central ministries for devolved functions of national interest and it listed control measures consistent with the status of local authorities to enable ministries to discharge their responsibilities through local authorities.

The Group classified the various methods of allocating powers and functions to local authorities as follows:

A. authorization to local authorities to do anything for the good of the locality which is neither forbidden them by law nor within the exclusive jurisdiction of another governmental unit (that is, an 'open-end' arrangement);
B. allocation of specific functions to local authorities by statute (maybe with provision for ministers to allot further functions at their discretion);
C. allocation to local authorities of functions by central government on the basis of a statutory list of subjects, the responsibility for which may be devolved in whole or in part;

D. constitution of local authorities as an integrated part of the machinery of central government.

The Group regarded *C* as affording the greatest flexibility because of the opportunity it offers for progressive delegation.

With respect to the mechanics of devolution pursuant to statute, the United Nations Group felt that while it is unnecessary to centralize the issue of warrants or instructions, there is need for a central office to see that a proposed action conforms reasonably with general practice; takes account of the funds required; provides for the consent of the local authorities in doubtful cases, especially where the action would impose an extra financial burden on them; and ensures that the communication is understandable and has been brought to the notice of all public and quasi-public bodies concerned.

The Cambridge Conference stated that local authorities should derive their powers directly from the central Government by statute and not by delegation from a higher local authority. It did not, however, object to delegation from one authority to another where it is done by mutual agreement and pursuant to law. The United Nations Group expressed a similar view. It recognized that a higher authority may have reason to devolve some power to a lower authority, or the lower authority may be justified in seeking some power possessed by a higher authority, but it felt that the proposals should be considered at a higher level than that of the authorities involved.

Popular participation and representation

The United Nations Group stressed the "critical need to associate the people with the government's development effort." Popular participation may occur at any level—from village to national; may be simply advisory, involve decision-making or extend to actual implementation; may cover all decentralized activities or relate only to a single service; and may be informal, organized on a voluntary basis, or formalized by statute. The initiative for organization may come from the people themselves or from the government, such as through community development programmes.

Popular representation is a special form of people's participation—more formalized, with legal backing and, at least above the village level, involves the principle of election. The extent to which a local authority is representative and therefore an instrument of people's participation depends on such factors as the qualifications for voters, nominating procedure, provision for minority representation, and the way the council functions.

The two meetings reached different conclusions on some points relating to the representativeness and methods of functioning of local councils. With respect to the qualifications for voting, the United Nations Group mentioned only age, and by inference, residence, whereas the Cambridge Conference subscribed to residence in harness with the ownership or occupation of property. Both opposed appointment of persons to local councils, but the United Nations Group mentioned the value of appointing officials of a higher authority as council members or advisers until elected members develop the necessary ability, provided that the elected element is not unduly diluted. The United Nations Group opposed extension of the vote to co-opted members whereas the Cambridge Conference reluctantly admitted the possibility of such members voting where necessary to ensure that co-option serves its purpose. It also commended the granting of *ex officio* membership, presumably with voting rights to recognized chiefs who "still occupy a traditional place in African local affairs and retain the allegiance of their people." Both meetings recognized the desirability of affording representation to ethnic minorities but doing so in a way that is consistent with the majority principle and avoids aggravation of group differences.

With respect to the functioning of councils, the Cambridge Conference was generally opposed to the separation of legislative and executive powers and "as a principle (could) see no reason why the committee system on the one hand and the delegation of powers to officers on the other should not serve as it has in the United Kingdom." The United Nations Group recognized the value of committees where the council is "too unwieldy in size," but favoured a chief executive, a career officer responsible to the council and its committees for 'implementation' of policies. Within these similarly worded conclusions lies opposition at Cambridge and approval in Geneva to the idea that the council-manager system in the United States is adaptable to local authority administration in many developing countries.

The Geneva Group noted that the methods for achieving popular participation and representation may yield any number of permutations and combinations, sufficient presumably to satisfy administrative needs in widely differing and rapidly changing circumstances. For example, where there is lack of popular response to needed changes community development workers backed by technicians skilled in community development methods might be introduced, followed by training of local persons with influence in the communities, the establishment of advisory bodies and eventually the entrusting of decisions and administration to multi-purpose or single purpose representative bodies which are subject to central controls depending, as mentioned earlier, on their powers and ability.

The United Nations Group noted that the criteria of 'representativeness' may be different for special purpose than for multi-purpose bodies, and indicated that it may be advantageous to establish special statutory bodies where:

A. local councils do not possess the technical competence to administer a service;
B. a special programme requires a greater intensity of attention and energy than the council can give it;
C. the minimum area or population for administration of a service differs substantially from that of local authorities; or
D. there is a special clientèle for a service.

Separate arrangements may be needed to co-ordinate the local activities of special purpose bodies that are organized on a national scale. Co-ordination of special purpose local authorities within a local authority area may best be achieved by the multi-purpose local authority.

Where a joint service for two or more local authorities is to be organized, a special board consisting of representatives of the councils concerned is usually formed or arrangements made within a higher level authority to perform the function.

Staffing decentralized services

The United Nations Group listed the following personnel requirements for effective decentralization: availability of qualified staff for sustained work in the area to be served; good *rapport* between the staff and the people; ability of staff members to work together; and adequate administrative and technical support and supervision.

It sketched the situation confronting developing countries as follows: critical shortages of qualified personnel, although paradoxically some countries have the added complication of over-staffing; difficulty of attracting qualified persons to work in rural areas due to the natural attractions of the capital city and higher salaries and prestige attached to work there, and the lack of amenities and public facilities in rural areas; lack of experience of community leaders in guiding and supervising technical services; a tradition of paternalism and authoritarianism in relations between government servants and the people; differences in compensation and allowances between field representatives of different agencies who are supposed to work together and substantially higher salaries paid to central government than to local authority employees.

The measures recommended to remedy these conditions regardless of a country's system of decentralization are noteworthy although few are novel:

A. acceleration of pre-entry and in-service training of technical and professional personnel, establishment of combined inspection and on-the-job training services, and orientation of local councilmen;

B. arrangements for training of auxiliaries who are from the area itself and training them in the areas;

C. more emphasis on training in administrative attitudes (for getting work done, for example), human relations, group dynamics, use of audio-visual aids, and rural development techniques;

D. establishing a career system under which young people would be started in rural areas, aided in their further professional development, and assured of advancement for meritorious service;

E. requiring those who receive training at the expense either of the government or of international organizations to accept employment for a certain period at such field posts as the government may determine or with local authorities;

F. giving special allowances (such as additional pension credit) for service in hardship posts;

G. enhancing the prestige attached to work in rural areas;

H. adjusting salary scales and allowances to eliminate any financial advantage from working in the capital and also to eliminate differences in compensation between agencies.

The Cambridge Conference expressed similar views. It probed more deeply into the financial and administrative implications of making central and local government conditions of service comparable but decided, as did the United Nations Group, that the advantages of making them comparable outweigh the disadvantages.

The United Nations Group intimated (and the author believes) that a good case can be made for a unified civil service system for both central and local government in a comprehensive local government system, at least in the early stages of development of such a system, provided of course that it is duly insulated from politics.

Both meetings favoured a unified civil service system for local authority personnel in preference to separate systems for each authority. A unified system offers greater career opportunities for personnel, facilitates standardization of qualifications, and reduces the danger of corruption and nepotism. The Cambridge Conference thought that the creation of a unified system had to be gradual, perhaps starting on a regional basis. It recommended that "appointments to the local government service should be the responsibility of an impartial statutory board which would not be subject to detailed control either by local authorities or by the Ministry of Local Government but would be bound by statutory regulations made by the Minister." The Cambridge Conference made other useful suggestions regarding the composition and functioning of the board.

It is the author's opinion that systematic comparative study of unified civil service systems is badly needed. Developed, as well as developing, countries stand to benefit from such a study and should be included within its scope.

The Cambridge Conference made a number of specific suggestions regarding local government training, including training abroad. A special organization for training is needed, with appropriate provision for local government training. The somewhat distinctive problems of in-service training of officers now holding higher posts and those expected to hold them in the future should be tackled concurrently. Despite the shortage of qualified local government officers and facilities for training them, the Conference urged that governments start on the basis of what is required rather than limit training perspectives to the funds that appear available at the moment. The Conference, addressing itself to training in English-speaking areas in Africa, expressed preference for training in other African areas with similar patterns of local government. It cautioned that only officers with advanced knowledge of their own system and a broad educational background should be posted to local authorities in Britain and only the most senior local government officers should receive training in other developed countries.

Financial aspects of decentralization

The United Nations Group pointed out how problems of financial policy and administration and approaches to their solution differ under the different systems of decentralization. For example, under the comprehensive local government system, there are special requirements and problems in supplementing local revenues and in satisfying both central and local interests in the formulation, approval, and execution of local authority budgets. A partnership system is likely to make considerable use of grants for specific purposes. In a dual system where central ministries administer direct services and do not have common areas, overcentralization of financial authority is often a principal problem. The integrated administrative system may also have problems of overcentralization as well as of gaining local financial support for local services.

The group developed general guides for dealing with problems of central-field financial relationships and of providing at the central level for the taxing powers of local authorities, grants-in-aid and loans to local authorities and supervision of financial operations of local authorities, without identifying the ramifications of these under different systems of decentralization. The Cambridge Conference covered much the same ground relating to local authorities, although the United Nations Group analysed in more detail the problem of corruption and measures to deal with it.

Both meetings recommended that local authorities be empowered to impose a variety of taxes. The Cambridge Conference suggested, however, that rural local authorities ideally should rely primarily for their revenue on a surcharge which they might levy on a graduated tax collected normally by central government, and should supplement this by special purpose taxes. The latter, sometimes called earmarked taxes, are especially useful in getting services started because people are often more willing to tax themselves for a specific service. Both meetings favoured one unit for collection of central and local government taxes in a locality; while recognizing the advantages administratively of having this as a central government unit, they were inclined to feel that local authorities should at least collect the special taxes they impose for specific purposes and might also, if given a commission for collection of central government taxes, prove effective as the single tax collection unit. The local authority should in any case levy local taxes even if a central government unit collects them.

The two meetings were generally in agreement on the uses of special purpose, block, and deficiency grants to local authorities: to finance services of national interest; to enable poorer areas, through equalization grants, to maintain essential services at the same level as those of richer areas; to improve and control the quality of services; and temporarily, to serve as an incentive to get services started.

As mentioned, the United Nations Group focused attention on the problem of corruption and methods of dealing with it. The main causes of corruption are: traditions which make it normal for officials to receive gifts for performance of a service; family favouritism and nepotism; low and irregularly paid salaries; the bad example of political leaders; the delays in official procedures which induce bribes to speed up the process; and laxity of controls inviting misappropriation of funds and contract irregularities.

The Group considered the following measures effective in dealing with corruption:

A. prepare clear and practical rules of conduct for public servants;
B. make it illegal for members of local authority councils to discuss a contract or other matter in which they have a special interest until they have declared that interest to their council;
C. regulate in other ways contract matters and other forms of purchasing to ensure open competitive bidding wherever possible and inspection of contract performance by an official other than the one who was involved in the award;
D. hold council meetings in public and open the record of proceedings to the public;
E. ensure the adequacy of the financial and administrative system by prescribing efficient procedures, providing for internal checks, helping to instal new methods where necessary, and training local personnel;
F. supervise those who handle public funds and make surprise checks on the internal audit system;
G. check the honesty and legality of transactions through regular post-audit by the central Government;
H. give citizens access to public accounts, subject to payment of a fee and other conditions to protect the public interest, and allow them to present inquiries or complaints to the auditor.

Central institutions required for rational decentralization and for the provision of central services to local authorities

The Cambridge Conference agreed that "it is a mistake—where rapid development is the primary objective—to maintain 'local autonomy' or 'freedom from central government interference' as the governing principle in central-local relations. Poor local governments, like poor people, are likely to get poorer if left to their own resources. They need help if they are to overcome their disabilities and realize their potentialities for useful service. Local government must . . . respond to the strong popular demand for social and economic progress."

The United Nations Group took a similar view and considered the question of what central agencies are required to foster rational decentralization of government powers and functions and to improve the capability of local authorities. It agreed on the following:

A. Central offices required for rational decentralization:

1. central organization and methods office and similar units in each major ministry are needed to work toward sound organization of government at the centre and rational decentralization to field areas and devolution to local authorities. Poor organization at the centre is an obvious impediment to effective organization of decentralized services;

2. central planning and budgeting agencies are needed to encourage local planning and to relate it to regional and national plans, to plan major public works and other national measures needed to accelerate local development, and to equalize opportunities for essential services between rich and poor areas;

3. a community development agency is usually needed to stimulate self-help effort of the people, to help in training technical and administrative personnel in community development methods, and in other ways to foster popular participation in government activities.

B. One or more central government agencies or other central institutions are required to render the following services to local authorities:

1. to exercise general surveillance over central-local government relations, to serve as an advocate of local authority interests among central government agencies, and to review all proposed legislation relating to local authorities;

2. to render technical assistance to local authorities in planning, legal matters, budgeting and accounting, taxation, procurement, organization and methods, research, and the functioning of local councils;

3. to advise and assist on personnel matters, including recruitment, promotion, pension schemes, and the establishment of a unified civil service system or, in its absence, individual civil service systems;

4. to audit and inspect local authority accounts and operations;
5. to loan money to local authorities readily and at reasonable rates;
6. to train staff and provide orientation for new councilmen.

Usually, several central government units and semi-autonomous or non-governmental institutions are required to perform these services: a ministry or department of local government; a national municipal bank; a local government public service commission; an institute of public administration with courses in local government administration or an institute devoted to training, research, and technical assistance for local authorities; a union of local authorities; and special offices in finance, public works and other ministries devoted exclusively to the support of local authority operations in their fields. The most important organization in developing countries, having comprehensive local government systems or partnership systems, is the ministry of local government; in countries having a dual system, it is more likely to be a semi-autonomous institute of municipal administration (as in Brazil) or a national municipal bank (as in Guatemala) ; in European countries where unions of local authorities developed strength before the dual system was replaced by a comprehensive or partnership system, it is likely to be the union of local authorities—as in the Netherlands.

International technical assistance

Both meetings recognized the potential value of the United Nations and other international programmes of technical assistance in helping governments to organize and staff central agencies and institutions for the provision of technical, financial and training services to local authorities. In addition, the group at Geneva suggested that the United Nations sponsor regional seminars for senior officers of ministries or agencies dealing with local government on 'Central services to Local Authorities,' using its material on decentralization and the study on this subject by the International Union of Local Authorities as starting points for discussion. It also suggested that the United Nations arrange study tours for the above-mentioned officers to visit countries in other regions which have had significant experience with decentralization for purposes of fostering development.

In conclusion, both meetings recognized the value of international exchange of information between administrators and scholars on methods of decentralization, especially on the use of local authorities, to accelerate social and economic development. They recognized the ending of an era of substantial isolation in the evolution of national governmental systems, one in which the emphasis in central-local relations has often been placed either on 'central control' or 'local autonomy.' Where central governments are willing and able to dedicate themselves to improving the living conditions of their people, the terms 'partnership,' 'interdependence,' and 'unity of purpose' are more suggestive of the principles which should underlie relationships between units at all levels. Thus in developing countries where representative governments replace alien or oppressive rule and are responsive to the surging desire of people for a better life, national entities —both governmental and non-governmental—are exploring ways of joining hands with local communities to foster national and local development. Through the United Nations and other agencies, they are able to tap the resources of the world community in this endeavour.

The Assessment of Staff Requirements in a Developing Country

Sir Richard Ramage, C.M.G.

Since the members of this Conference are concerned with the staffing of governmental organizations, I shall confine most of my remarks to that sphere. It is desirable to mention, however, that similar staffing problems are being faced simultaneously by non-government organizations, although generally in a much smaller and more restricted field; and that both groups will be in competition for some categories of staff who are likely to be in short supply. Any assessment of government staff needs must keep in mind the needs of industry and commerce, not to mention the various professions whose members operate outside government service. A country is just as unlikely to develop satisfactorily if all the emphasis is given to government staff to the detriment of commerce and industry—on which the country's economy must depend—than if the government staff are treated as the poor and relatively unimportant relations of commerce and industry—since the country would then probably lack the essential efficient machinery at the centre. In assessing needs, last but not least, due consideration must be given to the needs of education, covering all stages from primary to university status. In some countries, teaching is regarded as a part of the public service and in others there are different arrangements, but proper consideration must in either case be given.

Coming now to the assessment of public service needs, there are several separate but related basic matters which must be determined before an effective assessment is possible:

This paper was given before the R.I.P.A.'s Conference of Directors of Institutes of Public Administration in the Commonwealth. Sir Richard was Chairman of the Uganda Public Service Commission from 1955–9. Reprinted from *Public Administration* (Journal of the Royal Institute of Public Administration), Vol. 41 (Winter, 1963), pp. 325–333, by permission of the editor.

1. What standard of government organization is to be provided?
2. What is the educational output of the country and what is its form?
3. In the light of (1) and (2), how far can the public service fill its requirements and what steps are necessary to remedy deficiencies?

That process can be described as budgeting the manpower—and woman power—of the country. It is necessary to consider separately each of the questions posed and I propose, in order to complete the picture, to make some suggestions as to how the problems might be dealt with.

Standard of organization

First, what is to be the standard of organization? No developing country starts from scratch these days. There will already be an existing organization which, in the case of the developing countries represented here today, is likely to be a mixture of the stock-form Dependency organization, to which has been added a local version of the Central Whitehall model, scaled according to local taste and, ultimately, to the finance available. In the older territories something on the Whitehall model is more likely. We are concerned with the developing countries and the first questions are therefore is the existing form of organization suitable for the current and immediately foreseen phase of development, and is its scale—and consequently cost—appropriate in the circumstances of the country? I should venture a guess that in few cases would an objective review provide an outright answer of 'Yes' to either aspect. From some on-the-spot observations—not to mention Chairmanship of an Economy Commission—my personal view is that in a number of developing countries there has been a tendency towards 'empire-building,' not in the old Colonial sense, but in the more modern sense of building up one's own staff, plus a bit of Parkinson's Law. There is, of course, always an excellent justification for staff increases to put forward to a probably sceptical Treasury, but when it comes to highly technical matters the atmosphere of mystique—perhaps almost juju—is such that the balance between competing interests may be upset. What this is leading up to is that I advise strongly that a first step should be a review of the existing organization on a strict functional basis, taking account of approved development plans and the finances likely to be available. What exists doubtless serves some useful purpose, but is it *all* essential? If it were not there would the consequences be really serious—or merely rather inconvenient? There are frills on most organizations and when resources are not unlimited, whether in trained staff or finance, a bit of pruning of organization may do no harm. Quite the reverse, for it leads to economy in trained staff, which are certain to be scarce, and it saves money, which is also likely to be scarce. It also often gives more junior staff an opportunity to show their abilities and to qualify for promotion, which in turn helps to reduce the almost universal staff difficulties. The review must, of course, take account of approved development plans likely to materialize in the reasonably near future—again on the basis of essentiality and not merely desirability.

Educational output

While the review on a functional basis is proceeding the problem of providing the staff needed can be tackled. This has to be approached from two angles—what is needed and what is available—and in most developing countries there will be a considerable gap between the two, except probably in the lower grades. The key to the problem will, almost certainly, be education, which was the second question I posed. In general, education in most developing countries has developed primarily on an educational plan, not necessarily related to its economic or other needs, and certainly not specifically designed to produce public servants. Over a period it would doubtless, by and large, provide for the various categories required, as in this country. But in a developing country time is one of the scarce commodities. A closer relationship between educational output and the country's needs is more necessary than is likely to have existed hitherto. The most vital educational need in a developing country is secondary school pupils, those who have attained the School

Certificate standard or that of the General Certificate of Education at Ordinary level or an equivalent qualification. These are the pupils who, with some further education, will provide candidates for higher education leading to professional and higher administrative and the highest technical appointments. Those who do not go on to higher education will provide material for executive and technical posts, without which the usefulness of the professional or senior administrative officer may be seriously curtailed. An essential item in staff needs—and more important its fulfilment—will be a review of the output of secondary schools to see whether it is likely to produce the material required for development. I should remark here that I would not support any general scheme for speeding up secondary education by some form of cramming or other means. If education is to serve its most important function—which is training the mind and not merely memorizing various facts—time must be given for the mind to be trained and to develop. Experience has shown that for the average pupil that period should be about twelve to thirteen years from entering primary school. Undoubtedly the period could be reduced by cramming, but that must be at the expense of mind-training, on which further learning must depend.

I am, of course, well aware of the political pressures in developing countries for widespread—usually universal—primary education. In a developing country, however, the real interest of all may, in the earlier stages, lie in channelling into secondary education an apparently undue share of funds even if that means some slowing down of the expansion of primary education. That should, at least, ensure that the longer term needs of the country are met within the shortest time commensurate with 'real' education. The decision must, of course, rest with the political leaders of the country.

Staff needs

Having reviewed the form of organization and the material likely to be available for the public service, we can now consider staff needs. For convenience these can be divided into three very general groups:

1. Junior clerical and artisan staff, including the lowest technical grades.
2. Medium technical and executive grades.
3. Professional and administrative grades, and also the highest technical grades.

JUNIOR CLERICAL, ARTISAN AND LOWEST TECHNICAL GRADES. In most countries the requirements of the less responsible clerical types of posts and of artisans and the lower technicians can probably be filled by the existing primary or post-primary education. The survey of output should, however, give close attention to the output of technical and trade schools. These will vary between establishments which should produce an adequate artisan—possibly on a sandwich course basis—to those which are designed to produce staff of City and Guilds standard or higher. It is necessary here to give a warning: the assessment of needs must be on a long-term and objective basis, and not on possibly transitory boom conditions. It might be well worthwhile having an assessment by an expert. Departmental heads are apt to be over-optimistic, with the result that too many of one category might be produced at the expense of another less strongly pressed by its head of department. The result could be wasted resources in one case and shortage in the other. It is perhaps rather outside the scope of this lecture, but I might mention from fairly recent personal observation that in some areas at least an overhaul of the training of artisans—often wrongly called apprenticeship—seems desirable. The present British pattern is not necessarily the best model for automatic and literal copying. There is no natural law which requires five years' training for every trade, and organized training could probably be reduced by a year or more as in some foreign countries.

MEDIUM TECHNICAL AND EXECUTIVE GRADES. The next group is that of technical and executive staff, the latter in practice sometimes becoming a little blurred with senior clerical staff, although the real functions are quite different. In technical staff the scale of need is the existing provision plus that required for approved development plans. There is, however, another aspect. In some developing countries there has been a past tendency to inflate the number of professional staff and employ them on some duties not fully professional. As a result, insufficient attention has been given to the middle grades of technical staff, that is those between the lowest technical grades and the professional officer. Not only are professional officers expensive, but in developing countries there are never enough local qualified persons. The only other source is external recruiting, which is even more expensive than local professionals. I am convinced that to quite an appreciable extent the use of professional staff can be reduced by the increased use of technical staff. Professional staff are in short supply, are expensive to train, and take longer to produce than technical staff.

Assessment of needs here should, I suggest, be tackled by seeing first whether some of the work now done by professional officers could not be done by suitably trained technical staff. Obviously there are limitations to this, but one method is to see whether one professional job could not be broken down into several parts, each of which could be done by a technical officer of relatively limited training and experience. Another, and obvious, point of attack is to see whether professional officers are spending too much time on non-professional work which—without the breaking down process mentioned—should in any event be done by technical or executive staff. For example, by providing executive staff, even in some cases clerical staff, the time spent by the professional officer in his office can be reduced and more opportunity given him to supervise his technical staff or to do work for which only he has the qualifications. The aim should be that professional staff should concentrate on supervising and training their technical staff and in doing real professional work. By that arrangement a small number of professional officers can direct the work of considerable numbers of technical staff.

The Executive Class fulfil a most important function and one which in some countries at least was not properly recognized for a considerable time. The duties of the Executive Class were defined by the last Royal Commission on the British Civil Service as lying 'between those of the clerical class and the administrative class and may be summarized as the day-to-day conduct of government business within the framework of established policy.'[1] In other words, the duties are above those to be expected from clerical staff, but on which it would be wasteful to employ administrative staff. It is the latter aspect to which I wish to draw attention. Administrative staff, like professional staff, will almost certainly be in short supply and normally take a considerable time to produce. The review of needs of a developing country should therefore include a close inspection of the work now done by administrative staff to see how far it could be transferred to executive staff, who will be more numerous, less expensive, and easier to train. If the review shows that some duties could even be done by clerical staff, so much the better. I am definitely of the opinion that in this respect there is likely to be scope for better use of scarce material.

PROFESSIONAL AND ADMINISTRATIVE GRADES. I now come to the last two major groups, the professional and administrative staffs, who are normally regarded as a similar status in their respective spheres. As regards professional officers, I have already suggested the basis for assessment of needs—to do the professional work above the technical level and to supervise the latter. In this the word 'professional' must be given a strict interpretation. How are the required number of professional officers to be provided? Local resources will almost certainly be inadequate in the earlier stages. External recruiting will provide a short-term, if expensive, solution. For the long term we come back to the output of secondary schools. From that the Government should have machinery to pick out good material for training at local universities—if they exist—or to select good candidates from those already at universities. In some cases, training only available overseas will be needed. The machinery mentioned should select candidates for training for professional posts to fill the vacancies which have been established by the review of needs, which incidentally in all cases must include the replacement of normal wastage. Experience has shown that there must be adequate control over those selected for training. Once they get away from home a candidate may think that instead of being trained as, say, a scientist, which is badly needed for development, he

[1] Report of the Royal Commission on the Civil Service, 1953–5 (Chairman: Priestley), Cmd. 9613, 1955. p. 101.

would like to work for some other qualification more attractive to him, but not what the country needs: some may find that distractions are pleasanter than work. There should therefore be some organization which is in touch with students, through students' advisers or others, and which can act promptly and firmly if things do not seem right. Failing that, the production of professional, and similar, staff will almost certainly go wrong with adverse results to development plans. Even with the best supervision and the best of luck the going will be hard.

I have already indicated the basis for the assessment of the needs of administrative staff. It is convenient to give here a definition applied to such posts. They are those concerned with 'the formation of policy, the co-ordination and improvement of government machinery and the general administration and control of government departments.'[2] Obviously officers of high standard are required. In their highest ranks they provide the key staff for Ministries, other than in professional posts. In the past recruiting has been to a considerable degree from university graduates, but there has always been an infusion of non-graduates who have shown administrative aptitude. In developing countries, pressure of demand on available resources may make the non-graduate the more common appointment. I am, of course, aware of the various training schemes in existence for turning out administrative staff. It might be mentioned here that the holding of a degree, granted after a course of study at a university, has not of itself been regarded as an automatic qualification for higher administrative posts. The reason why the degree standard has been used is that the course of intellectual training and study required to obtain a degree—at least of the British type and particularly at the level of First and Second Class Honours—tends to produce a mind which is balanced and objective; and given the necessary personal qualities which are necessary, is likely to provide the best material for administration on which the development of a country must depend. Of course there are other factors besides the academic. Administrative candidates must show personal qualities of initiative and leadership, while practical experience will remain a decisive factor, which cannot be acquired in any training course.

[2] *Ibid.*, p. 92.

There is a point concerning scholarships for training staff which can conveniently be mentioned here. It is, should the grant of a scholarship from public funds be made dependent on signing a contract to take up a public appointment for a prescribed number of years? Some say 'yes' because public funds have been spent for a specified purpose. Others say 'no' because you are unlikely to get satisfactory work from an unwilling conscript—apart from the possible difficulty of enforcing a penalty clause in the contract. My personal view is that there should be a contract requirement to serve for, say, five years, just to create the right outlook of mind from the outset. The possibility of occasional difficulties should not offset the fact that the majority, if so warned, will fulfil the terms of their contract with satisfactory service. Doctors in particular may well afford to buy themselves out. The Government loses their services, but is at least partly reimbursed, and the country may gain them.

Interim arrangements

The suggestions I have made represent what I think could produce the best results over a period of years. They would, however, take considerable time and you cannot expect a developing country to sit patiently marking time until the training machine, after some years, begins to produce what is required. There must therefore be immediate but interim arrangements to cover administrative, professional, technical and executive posts.

For both administrative and executive posts there are two immediate sources: the staff serving in the lower grades of the public service and persons outside that service, particularly in commerce. Possibly neither category will have the full educational standards normally required, although that may apply less in the commercial group. Both categories, however, will have had an opportunity to develop and show ability since leaving school. In selection, therefore, the emphasis should be on experience and proved ability; and the normal educational standards can be diluted in direct relation to the standards attained of experience and proved ability.

There are no such interim arrangements possible for posts of full professional status. Doctors, scientists, professional agricultural officers, etc., are only produced by the full courses prescribed for training. In the inevitable period of shortage of professional staff, increased responsibility must be put on the technical staff with the hope that there will be not too serious a fall in efficiency. The supervision is bound to be much less than is desirable.

In the technical grades, the most promising source is likely to be careful selection of staff serving in more junior technical posts and giving them intensive training in the service to make them capable of more responsible duties. This may well have to be combined with the splitting of higher technical duties, so that two men of moderate status and training do, under supervision, the work previously done by one of higher status. This arrangement has already been mentioned as a long-term solution.

The arrangements outlined should provide means for tackling the most immediate needs but they will, almost certainly, create a further problem in due course. When the fully qualified officer appears after his scholarship or other training, he will find senior to him, older men of lower academic standing but of course with much more experience. When promotion or other official selection comes along, who is to be promoted or selected, the fully academically qualified or the less academically qualified but with the wide experience and proved ability? My personal view is that there should be no attempt to divide such officers into sheep and goats. There should be one standard and that should be efficiency in the widest sense in which practical experience must always be an important element. I have no reason to suppose that that is the sole prerogative of the fully academically qualified. I know that may well run counter to the views of the young men concerned and possibly of the political leaders, but it should provide the best machinery for the progress of the country which is the fundamental object of all planning. It should also help to maintain morale in the public service, a matter of great importance.

The mechanics of staff planning

Before I close it is desirable to mention a point of the mechanics of staff planning. If planning is to be effective, it must be detailed and it must be under close scrutiny. The most effective method I have seen is to set out, in table form, the totals of every grade of staff required, except the most junior, including graduate and other secondary school teachers whether they are, strictly, government staff or not. Against each grade you then insert a yearly target figure, giving an annual figure for anything up to eight or ten years. The targets must be realistic and related to the resources available or expected to become available. It is certain that this table will pinpoint some alarming shortages. To deal with them the organization for awarding scholarships should canalize candidates into appropriate courses, or, in some cases, the Government might set up special training schemes. The latter would be particularly useful for technical grades where both local technical institutes and external sources can be used. Having set out the needs and the annual targets, there must be running supervision of the results and annually there must be a full review of the results of the past year and a comparison made between the target and the actual result; in other words there must be an annual balance sheet. Almost certainly changes of emphasis will be necessary. They may arise from candidates failing or from changes in overall planning, but, with an annual balance sheet which takes account of what is in the pipe-line under training, there is a reasonable prospect of the needs of to-day being realized some years hence. Whether the needs then will be the same is the perennial headache of all responsible for plans, and requires that crystal-gazing ability which all good staffs concerned with training must cultivate.

The Introduction of Bureaucracy into African Polities

Raymond Apthorpe
Rhodes-Livingstone Institute (Lusaka)

At the thirteenth conference of the Rhodes–Livingstone Institute, on the adaptation of indigenous African political systems to modern circumstances, new data on political change were presented for the Luvale, the Ibo, the Somali and various peoples of Ruanda-Urundi, Tanganyika and Nyasaland. Data on the political structures of two peoples in Northern Rhodesia not previously studied by anthropologists—the Nsenga and the Soli—were also discussed in the preliminary form in which these and most other contributions to the conference were made. Some conclusions were reached about the introduction of modern bureaucratic elements into African policies. These are of particular interest, not least because they are not in support of the hypothesis advanced on the basis of investigations in an East African state (Fallers, no date),[1] which holds that western civil service conceptions are more likely to gain ground faster in African polities hierarchically centralized in their traditional form, rather than in societies which in the political sphere at least have non-centralized characteristics and are sometimes chiefless.

Before discussing some aspects of our findings it should be

Reprinted from *Journal of African Administration,* Vol. 12, No. 3 (July, 1960), pp. 126–134, by permission. This article is a version of the introduction to the proceedings of the 13th conference of the Rhodes-Livingstone Institute, which was published under the title *From Tribal Rule to Modern Government* (1959), pp. xix and 216. . . .

[1] The reading list from which all references have been cited appears at the end of this article.

stated first of all that most of the case studies discussed are in rural settings—only one is not and that is in a peri-urban area of Nyasaland. Secondly, the title under which the full report was published, *From Tribal Rule to Modern Government,* is not meant to convey any antithesis between 'rule' and 'government,' nor that only one kind of rule or government is in contact with one other, although the conference considered only one aspect of implanted modern government *viz.* its bureaucratic form. Still less should it be imagined that a list of criteria is at hand, acceptable to sociologists, with which to distinguish between 'tribal' or 'simple' and 'modern' or 'industrial' societies. The diversity in type of the former is scarcely less marked than that of the latter, and the sphere of polity is no exception to those of economy or land tenure, to take two random examples. It should also be stated that the unit 'tribe' is not a convenient one to emphasize for a series of case studies where sometimes a cultural—and not a political or governmental—delimitation is used, and when, even in these latter fields, it is often a cluster of 'tribes' which is in question, not a single one. I speak of polities, therefore, because in its customary usage this term comprises so-called stateless as well as state societies. Also, it emphasizes that our field of reference is political institutions and political change, which means social institutions and social change in general viewed in their political dimension. As the American sociologist Professor Talcott Parsons has expressed it, government is to polity as business is to economy: it is the focus but not the entire subject, and the same might be said for studies of political transition.

THE POLICIES OF ADAPTATION IN TROPICAL AFRICA

The first papers in the report describe in very broad terms the various colonial policy backgrounds against which individual case studies are to be seen. It should be stressed that these cases were considered mainly from the viewpoint of the indigenous not the implanted polities, and that the prime aim of the conference was to consider some political conditions, causes and consequences rather than to evaluate different policies themselves *as* policies. Nevertheless, some of our findings could be of use to policy makers as background information, and it is to be hoped that they will be.

In the various regions of Africa discussed, with the exception of Southern Rhodesia, indirect rule in one form or another is the policy of adaptation in force. It is fortunate to have in the scope of this one report the areas in which probably the most extreme variations in detail of indirect rule in Africa can be seen. In Eastern Nigeria all the emphasis is on village councils. In Northern Rhodesia there are practically no village councils with political or semi-political functions (although there is in the Eastern Province of that territory an incipient 'parish' system): all is concentrated in the hands of native authorities.

The description of Northern Rhodesia government policy for the utilization of indigenous political systems given on the opening morning of the conference by M. G. Billing (the Report, pp. 1–11) represents, I think it is fair to say, one of the classical forms of indirect rule, and this is confirmed by other statements recently made by officials (e.g. Jones, 1958). A recent lecturer on indirect rule, Air Andrew Cohen, has commented on what he calls (like Lytton, Lugard and Cameron, see the Report, pp. 50–53) "this essentially administrative system" that it "fits into the general British conception of relying on local institutions rather than a centralized bureaucracy." It failed, he said, "where the foundations of indirect rule in the classical pattern were not firm, where . . . the units were too small or the traditional leadership too weak, even if it existed at all," partly because the central governments had too rigid an approach and partly because the Colonial Office was generally encouraging governments in Africa—particularly in the thirties—to introduce indirect rule if they had not already done so, irrespective of local conditions. But the reason above all is because "the method of applying indirect rule was based on the assumption that we had indefinite time ahead during which the system could grow and develop under our guidance—an assumption accepted without question at the time by almost everybody" (Cohen, 1959: pp. 22–26). Moreover, indirect rule was a system which looked at the problems and interests of each given area or tribe. It was not conceived in the framework of building up a state or a nation;

still less—and this is very natural—did it take into account the tendencies and pressures appearing in the world at large, which at a later stage were to affect Tropical Africa." In the phrase of one of the conference participants (White, the Report, p. 195) indirect rule is "like an organism containing a lethal gene." Yet the conference considered bureaucratic elements in colonial governments in general to represent their main characteristic for a study of political change, and it was argued, for example, that the general preference for indirect rule in one form or another which has marked British colonial policy could be for the reason that colonial governments are themselves centralized and, sociologically speaking, authoritarian. Whereas "the 'natural reaction' of colonial governments is to recoil from recognizing chiefless societies" (the Report, p. 34) the emirates in Northern Nigeria, on the other hand, and *mutatis mutandis* the Lozi state in Northern Rhodesia, for example, offered ready-made societies to govern.

Truth lies in comparison. To conclude that bureaucratic elements especially characterize any one colonial government, requires that a comparative study be made of several from this point of view. This falls outside the scope of the present paper. Thus, unfortunately, it is not possible here to pursue this subject further. A subject of discussion which must also be postponed is the opposite argument to that advanced during the conference. It could be maintained that an authoritarian and centralized colonial government would tend to a system of direct rule in view of its own structure. This would require examination of such material circumstances of government as personnel and other resources available, in addition to a full appreciation of a point the conference stressed, namely that indirect rule is rarely *in toto* different from direct rule—indeed, it is very often true that any one system of government may be regarded as 'direct' or 'indirect' according to the point of view adopted.

The contribution of the conference in a field directly relevant to the policies of adaptation in tropical Africa lies in its degree of factual development of scientific knowledge about African political systems. The very introduction of policies of indirect rule has brought about an interest in indigenous political institutions, of which a noted land mark came in 1940 with the publication of *African Political Systems*, edited by Professors

Fortes and Evans-Pritchard. It was argued at the conference that of the indigenous polities in tropical Africa, it is the non-centralized and sometimes chiefless forms which probably represent the norm, not the centralized hierarchized systems with which Lugard for example, was so familiar. Perhaps the conditions in Northern Rhodesia form a microcosm of Bantu Africa as a whole for the study of indirect rule. In that territory, the Lozi system of government above all others seems to exert a political fascination and persuasion of its own over administrators who come into contact with it, to such an extent that Lozi conditions appear to be regarded by administrators as those which ought to exist throughout the territory merely with small variations here and there. But elsewhere in that area only the Bemba polity has a comparable intricate system of councils and councillors, and in the north-west, for example, political systems operate traditionally practically without the aid, for the most part, of chiefs. And where chiefs exist in other areas, often they have in the judicial sphere no prominent functions to complement their varying degrees of political authority, a subject which must be studied in the light of the conditions of immigration of chiefly lines, as some students of Northern Rhodesia have pointed out. Further, if the various tribal conditions of the interdependence of the judiciary and the executive in that territory are considered, 'paramount' is an appellation apparently bestowed by government on various chiefs randomly rather than systematically.

In Northern Rhodesia, and probably tropical Africa as a whole, centralized political organizations of the Lozi or Bemba types, or the inter-lacustrine examples, are deviations from the norm. And even in these areas, the type of centralization and hierarchy associated with the immigrant chiefly rule does not pervade society to such an extent that pre-existing alternative forms of political and social control have been all exterminated. More typical of the political conditions in tropical Africa at the time of European penetration are the non-centralized systems, such as we find in Northern Rhodesia among the Plateau Tonga and the Luvale, where power and authority lie in a system of lineages or comparable units, and not in a centralized state authority.

It would be misleading to end these introductory remarks

on the policies of adaptation without noting some innovations in 'indigenous' political organization which colonial government has brought about. Directly, it may be noted of Northern Rhodesia, for example, that government-termed senior chiefs may be nearly as much government creations as treasury clerks and managers of schools. Indirectly, the influence of colonial government in encouraging larger groupings and amalgamations of small units has interacted with the spontaneous upsurge of local loyalties which H. A. Fosbrooke, with many Tanganyika examples in mind, has described as 'neo-tribalism.'

Another aspect of innovation to be considered, in a more many-sided study than the conference was able to achieve, is the view, advanced by Dr. A. I. Richards with considerable force (1935), that not only does indirect rule create new political offices: also, and most importantly, not enough of the traditional offices of political importance are recognized and stipended by the colonial government under this regime to make it feasible for those which are, to function with their traditional authority. The economic opportunities which a cash economy and government support of the office of chief present may together enable chiefs to enhance both their prestige and status. In parts of the Eastern Province of Northern Rhodesia, for example, there is much reason to argue that some chiefs have taken advantage of these circumstances, so much that if the individual concerned also assumes office in an organization of peasant farmers, for instance, chieftainship may take on even a new meaning (the Report p. 95). In these eastern areas, however, the indigenous societies concerned are not hierarchically ordered to the extent that is characteristic of Bemba conditions, in which Dr. Richards was specially interested, and it is a feature of societies of this latter kind that government is usually through a multiplicity of councils and councillors.

The variety of types of African polities

As Dr. Richards implies, it is not only the conceptual or ideological position of the Bemba chief that is relevant to her argument. "Equally important" she says, as the functioning of a large executive in maintaining the chief's authority was "the chief's prestige, itself directly dependent on the size of his capital and the number of followers he could command and provide for." Thus the subject of the complexity in type of African polities is thrust sharply forward. From her argument it is clear that the Bemba, despite the strongly hierarchical nature of their polity by Northern Rhodesian standards, are surpassed in this character by other societies where such questions of personal prestige are by no means 'equally important' as the rights of office.

The matter is a delicate one for summary presentation but to elaborate sufficiently only for present purposes, one may say in theory at least political action legitimized by a person's office or authority, and such action issuing only from a person's prestige, are founded on opposite premises. The former is theoretically possible by a person of no prestige, since in this case it is the office which is obeyed, not its occupant. The latter may be independent of authority or office since, if a man's prestige is high enough, he need occupy no political office to wield political power. In actual societies, the two forms of political action, and the opposed types of polity they imply, mix to various degrees, but of the Bemba (and the Lozi and Ruanda-Urundi discussed in the conference) one may say the former is dominant. In these societies the size of a group or a similar source of stature does not confer on its head any greater degree of authority than he may possess according to ascribed qualities. The Yao of Nayasaland, for example, offer a great contrast. The following passage of Professor Mitchell, quoting an earlier writer in part, is selected by D. G. Bettison (the Report, pp. 138–9): "The (Yao) 'chief' may often have less influence than powerful headmen and we have known cases where he simply contented himself with grumbling when his headmen acted contrary to his desire. . . . A certain amount of ritual in terms of ancestor worship embellished his position: and he had some ascendance over village headmen to whom he had given land. Yet, in the last analysis, the 'chief' had to rely on his personal following and military power to subjugate headmen who were becoming too powerful. The chief was, therefore, in direct competition with his subject village headmen and involved in a constant struggle with them for followers." The dominant theme of Professor Mitchell's analysis is of the size of a unit giving it authority rather than the opposite.

To show another kind of African polity one may refer to W. J. Argyle's comment on Woli chiefs, that a significant reason why they continue to be respected is that they formed and still form almost the only foci of social identity for the Soli, whose social organization is but little formalized (the Report, p. III). Soli, like Luvale chiefs, have little political or judicial power traditionally. In many cases Soli chiefs and their assessors complain that people nowadays bring to them many trivial matters that would formerly have been settled by the village elders. Some associate this with what they claim is "a general tendency for the people to disobey their headmen, which makes the chief's own task more difficult, so that they may regard any accession of power which the courts have brought them as a mixed blessing" (the Report, p. 107).

Since 1940 practically the only successful large scale exercise in political typology is that of Professor Southall (1953), and this is notable mainly for its preliminary description of 'segmentary states.' The introduction to *Tribes Without Rulers* (Middleton and Tait, 1958) [2] adds nothing systematic to the subject because as one reviewer observed (Mair, 1959) their classification is "made on the basis of the type of arrangement of lineage and without reference to the way in which each society conducts its political business." And nothing is available in this sphere from the Rhodes-Livingstone Institute despite the excellent case studies it has sponsored in the field of political organization.

The conference did not aim at making any constructive contribution towards solving the problem of classifying political systems, but only to give such a summary description of the characteristics of states, segmentary states and stateless polities as was necessary for its main purpose. The main differences between state and stateless polities (segmentary states representing an intermediate form of structure) may be expressed as follows. An ascribed hierarchy of political status contrasts with a system in which elevated political status is open to all on the basis of individual achievements, determined through social competition. A centralized machinery for political control contrasts with a non-

2 See also J.A.A., Vol. XI, No. 1, pp. 45–46.

centralized mode of organization in which it may appear at first sight that there is no political machinery at work at all. A centralized court system contrasts with the maintenance of law and order by rewards and punishments laterally administered, by equals to equals. A social cohesion achieved primarily in terms of an ascribed hierarchy, and differentiated by dependence and respect, contrasts with the unity of competitors and differentiation by prestige. Instituted deputyship in the sphere of political office is associated to some extent with this division in type of polity, since in relatively inegalitarian societies this appears to be a more characteristic feature of the polity than in societies structured principally by means of a system of egalitarian relationships.

THE INTRODUCTION OF WESTERN BUREAUCRACY INTO AFRICAN POLITIES

In the concluding chapter of his *Bantu Bureaucracy,* Dr. Fallers observes that the general hypothesis which suggests itself from his studies of the introduction of western bureaucracy among the Soga, an inter-lacustrine state in Eastern Uganda, is "that the societies with hierarchical, centralized political systems incorporate the western type of civil service structure with less strain and instability than do societies having other types of political systems—e.g., segmentary ones" (n.d. 242). He suggests in qualification, however, that "there are inherent difficulties in applying the civil service conception of authority at the level of the local community. The stable local community is everywhere essentially a primary group: its members know each other as total persons as a result of long and intimate face-to-face contact . . . 'in the village, everyone is famous.'" The conference conclusion about the introduction of western bureaucracy into African polities was that it is in societies which are *not* hierarchically centralized that western ideas of bureaucracy can be more speedily adopted.[3]

To discuss this conflict of views one must first return to

[3] See also 'Civilizations,' Vol. X, July 1960 "Political Change, Centralization and Role Differentiation," by Raymond Apthorpe.

Fallers' study because the analysis which led him to his general hypothesis is not as uncomplicated as one might suppose. His study, specifically of the Soga state, emphasizes not only its element of hierarchy but also a tension in it between, on the one hand a corporate lineage organization, and on the other, the state, and he argues that this tension made the Soga peculiarly 'vulnerable' to western penetration. As far as is known only a minority of states in Africa contain this "structural antagonism" within them, and the states considered in the Report are not representative of this minority. And though Fallers describes the Soga state as "an incipient bureaucracy" he maintains that "in the state structure a client was his patron's personal dependent and servant. Furthermore, the state hierarchy was not a solidary group, but rather consisted of chains of dyadic relationships of subordination and super-ordination. Rights and responsibilities related to superiors and subordinates as individuals." A well known statement of Weber on bureaucracy may serve us as well as Fallers. A bureaucratic rule, he says, is "straightforward duty without regard to personal considerations . . . everyone in the same empirical situation . . . is subject to formal equality of treatment" (cited in Fallers, n.d. 18). Clearly then, Soga bureaucracy is not western bureaucracy as described by Weber, for example, and this is one reason why Fallers' conclusion is contradicted by that of the conference.

Other reasons are not confined to the peculiar features of the respective states discussed. It was argued in the conference, for example, that as "authority itself is diffused in these (non-centralized, politically acephalous) societies . . . there is a wider possibility for a number of people to accept new ideas. In more centralized societies, authority tends to repose in one or very few hands and so the introduction of modern bureaucracy is liable to be obstructed or made more difficult, according to the type of person who occupies that position" (White, the Report, p. 203). That 'one or a few hands' might be interdependent with an intricate council system does not essentially affect this argument if the extremity of variation in type of African polities is remembered. Another kind of argument is represented in such a view that any imposed system of authority might operate more successfully if it is kept completely separate from the indigenous one (the Report, p. 120 where there is also mention of expectations concerning the incidence of corruption in government in this connection). And there is the firm implication in D. G. Bettison's analysis for peri-urban Nyasaland that there bureaucratic administration is replacing the traditional system partly for the reason that in the latter there is no marked source of resistance to this kind of change such as ascribed hierarchical conditions present (see also the Report, p. 205).

Clearly such views need a more detailed and careful presentation than is possible in a brief conference, but of them it can be said at least that they all tend to lead to one conclusion. If the division of African polities made in *African Political Systems* may be expressed as between (*a*) polities dominantly constituted by competitive relationships, founded on egalitarian principles and diffuse political authority and power, and (*b*) polities based on ascribed status, hierarchically ordered into a centralized system, then (*i*) except for the element of non-centralization, the configuration of the former rather than the latter class of polity resembles that of modern bureaucracy, and (*ii*) to judge from the case studies presented during the conference, lack of centralization in an indigenous political structure appears to be less of an impediment to its reception of modern bureaucracy than lack of achieved status ideas and their correlate, an open form of social mobility. But it remains to be discovered whether there is a difference in application of bureaucratic techniques by politically dominant western government in the two types of society. Is there a difference in the ratio of legislative to executive powers allotted, for example, in the types of situations concerned? Another aspect of study required, as was suggested above, is the centralization component in bureaucracies. Perhaps in the context of political change being considered here, this component is not as pronounced as one might expect. A general consideration worth taking into account as a possible influence on the political (and social) change being considered here, is what might be a general tendency of administrations to speak of societies of the Lozi kind as productive of 'intelligent' people, whereas 'these Tonga,' to use an unfortunate local idiom, are so often described as 'an obstreperous, dissipated lot.' This is no more than an impressionistic observation of what appears to be a tendency of administrations in Central Africa. But if it is right, it suggests that a people may be judged in terms of that vital if elusive quality 'intelligence' merely on the evidence of their reaction to a foreign system of government. And this might considerably modify the type of bureaucracy introduced, with curious results.

Wider aspects and sources of political change

Lastly, a wider aspect of the subject of the conference may be introduced, if polities are to be considered the rule as well as the regime of societies (the Report, p. 187), and if bureaucracy is synonomous to some degree with western society in rural Central Africa. Further, the polity, perhaps more than any other aspect of society, is concerned with the mobilization of indispensable prerequisites for the attainment of that society's collective goals (for the beginnings of systematic sociological theory of the polity and society, see Parsons 1956, 1958). Here it may be mentioned from case studies presented during the conference that the general class of societies which is most adaptable to bureaucratic government may be that which in other respects is often the most adaptable in the direction of westernization, if not any social change on a very wide scale. A common feature of social change is that unless the social situation concerned is one of protest, or there are conditions for the interpretation of new institutions such as Professor Maquet is concerned with (the Report, pp. 207–9), dominantly hierarchically ordered societies tend in general to absorb new hierarchical elements as readily as a new form of competition is received in a society already dominantly competitively ordered: *la plus ça change* . . . And from such a point of view, the assimilation of cultures can be studied, as well as simply the adoption of new forms of government.

The conference concentrated on political change brought about from outside the political structure in question. But this must not lead one to suppose that there is no provision for protest aimed at political change of various kinds instituted in tribal societies themselves (the Report, pp. 87 ff). One may suggest here that Professor Gluckman's analysis on a connected topic,

Rituals of Rebellion (1954), could be further elaborated if the different forms of social (and political) mobility were considered in the states he mentions, and not just their common hierarchical form. With this proviso one may say of chiefs in traditional polities that they do not appear to be major sources of political change if they are compared with emergent middle classes, western educated bourgeoisie (see Mair, 1957), people, for example, who have returned to a rural environment from a period of work in the town. A survey in progress at the Rhodes-Livingstone Institute of the educational backgrounds of chiefs and other native authority personnel in Northern Rhodesia is now beginning to yield results.

The economic and political conditions in the rural areas of tropical Africa may well tend to form one nexus though the conference did not do justice to this. But for Northern Rhodesia at least it is difficult to get a clear impression of this from such sources as annual reports of provincial commissioners, as the two quotations which follow show: In the report on the Southern Province of Northern Rhodesia (1957:76) it is noted that "except for some localities . . . the Province enjoyed record harvests and the population were prosperous even by the high Southern Province standards. In some ways this is a disadvantage as it has resulted in needy political parties regarding this part of the world as a happy hunting ground and peddling their wares far and wide." In the 1956 report for the North-western Province one reads—about the Kawambwa district (p. 28) that—"fortunately the existence in the district of a flourishing industry and trade in the fish of Lake Mweru has encouraged some of the leading personalities to abandon politics for business which they have found far more rewarding and the politics have been left mainly to the disgruntled and the unsuccessful."

Finally, the student of political change must also look to the activities of organizations of expatriates which seek at a distance to reform the polity of their home countries. In Northern Rhodesia, the Barotse National Society is at work outside Barotseland, and one of the important acts of the Nsenga Young Men's Association, of which the headquarters are in Southern Rhodesia, has been to attempt to change Nsenga matriliny to patriliny. Time may show that in Africa as in Europe in the nineteenth century in particular, such organizations are most effective movements for producing political change.

References cited

Apthorpe, R. J., ed. (1959). *From Tribal Rule to Modern Government: based on The Adaptation of Indigenous Political Systems to Modern Circumstances,* being the proceedings of the 13th conference of the Rhodes-Livingstone Institute, held at Lusaka, February 1959. Roneoed. pp. xix, 216.

Billing, M. G. (1959). "Tribal Rule and Modern Politics in Northern Rhodesia." *African Affairs,* Vol. 58, No. 135–140.

Cohen, Sir Andrew (1959). *British Policy in Changing Africa,* Northwestern University, African Studies No. 2.

Fallers, Lloyd A. (no date) *Bantu Bureaucracy: a study of integration and conflict in the political institutions of an East African people.* Cambridge, Heffer, for the East African Institute of Social Research. pp. xiv, 283. 13 plates, 8 maps.

Fortes, Meyer, and Evans-Pritchard, E. E., eds. (1941). *African Political Systems.* London, Oxford University Press for the International African Institute. pp. xxiii, 301.

Gluckman, Max (1954). *Rituals of Rebellion in South-East Africa* (The Frazer Lecture, 1952). Manchester, Manchester University Press. pp. 36.

Jones, G. S. (1958). *Local Government Development (with special reference to Barotseland)*. Unpublished manuscript in Rhodes-Livingstone Institute Library.

Mair, L. P. (1957). "Representative Local Government as a problem in social change." *The Rhodes-Livingstone Journal,* XXI, 1–17.

Middleton, John, and Tait, David, eds. (1958). *Tribes without Rulers: studies in African segmentary systems.* London, Routledge and Kegan Paul. pp. xi, 234.

Northern Rhodesia, Department of African Affairs. (1957). *Annual Report for the Year 1956.* Lusaka, The Government Printer. pp. iv, 121.

——— (1958). *Annual Report for the Year 1957.* Lusaka, The Government Printer. pp. iv, 123.

Parsons, Talcott (1958). "Some highlights of the general theory of action." *Approaches to the Study of Politics;* ed. by Roland Young. Evanston, North-western University Press, pp. viii, 382.

——— and Smelser, Neil (1956). *Economy and Society,* Glencoe, The Free Press.

RICHARDS, A. I. (1935). "Tribal Government in Transition (The Bemba of Northern Rhodesia)." Supplement to the *Journal of the Royal African Society,* Vol. XXXIV, No. CXXXVII, 3–26.

SOUTHALL, A. W. (1953). *Alur Society: a study in processes and types of domination.* Cambridge, Heffer, pp. xviii, 397. Maps, illus.

Public Administration in Latin America

ROBERTO DE OLIVEIRA CAMPOS
Former Brazilian Ambassador to the United States

. . . WHEN I WAS first invited to give this lecture, I was understandably hesitant. What could an economist, victim of a fairly narrow professional training, say to people so well versed in broad problems of public administration matters and who, in addition, have taken specialized courses in economic development? I would like to say at the outset that my reason for accepting the task was not any romantic yearning for the cross-fertilization of social sciences. I have always believed that when a social scientist becomes too interested in interdisciplinary adventures it is because he no longer has anything to say on his own field of science.

My reasons were quite different. The first one is that substantial conceptual modifications have been introduced recently in the study of economics by what we call "developmental economics." This change has been the great emphasis placed on the so-called nonconventional inputs: organization, technology, management, and entrepreneurship. Until recently the emphasis of the economists was much more on the conventional factors of production under the general heading of land, labor, and capital. Looking now more closely at the intriguing and difficult problem of development, the economists are discovering that

Reprinted from *Public Administration: A Key to Development,* Burton A. Baker (ed.) (Washington, D.C.: The Graduate School, U.S. Department of Agriculture, 1963), pp. 41–54, by permission. [Abridged.]

they were guilty of having overemphasized the importance of physical investment in roads, dams, buildings, and the like, and underestimating the enormous contribution of qualitative improvements of the human factor of production through technology, organization, management, and entrepreneurship.

The second reason why economists are now much more inclined to discuss problems in other social sciences, particularly in the complicated and unreliable art of administration and governing, is the realization of the difference between the "spontaneous" type of development, which was characteristic of most cases of economic growth during the 19th century, and the present pattern of what we call "derived development."

In the first model of development, which was roughly the one according to which both the United States and great Britain evolved, development was very vigorously pushed by the entrepreneurship of individuals or groups or families possessed by a special demon, the need-achievement (to use a pedantic word of modern psychology). This special demon found its manifestation in the competitive spirit, in the acceptance of technological change, in the propensity to innovate. In the present-day pattern of derived development, it is the masses rather than the vigorous entrepreneur that, by applying pressure for increased consumption, impel the governments to take a leading function in promoting economic development.

This derived pattern of development leads to one important consequence. It necessitates a much greater degree of government intervention as an organizer and motivating force in the growth process. Accordingly, there is a much more important role for public administration and also a much greater emphasis on programming and planning which are aspects of public administration.

It is true, of course, that in addition to those basic questions of motivation and impulse, there are reasons requiring public administration to play a much greater role in the present-day developing countries than was the case in the countries of earlier industrialization. Among these reasons, I would cite the following: (a) imperfection and smallness of markets leading often to dangerous private monopolistic positions that may have to be averted or restrained by government intervention; (b) the abnormal uncertainty and risk in present periods of rapid economic and social transformation which act as a deterrent to private entrepreneurs; (c) equity considerations that impose the need for reducing income disparities, either between persons or between regions, a task for which the fiscal system is the only adequate instrument.

Thus public administration turns out, increasingly, to be one of the first chapters of any rational theory of economic growth. While relevant for all of the developing countries, the importance of public administration in the emerging countries of Africa and Asia goes beyond directing the organizational process in economic and social fields. It has the immense task of creating a national unity and a national personality capable of surmounting the centrifugal force of tribal and regional rivalries and, on the other hand, instilling the ferment of change in traditional societies.

In Latin America, where countries achieved over a century ago their political independence but still linger in the throes of underdevelopment, the task is narrower than in Africa and Asia, but no less important. The task is to organize the governmental participation in economic and social development and to launch the reforms designed for modernization of the societies.

In this lecture, I shall confine myself largely to public administration in Latin America. I shall not attempt any detailed list of techniques, flaws, or possible improvements, because I believe this already has been the subject of lectures here, and there are many competent public administrators who could enlighten you better on this type of problem. I shall therefore not dwell on individual malfunctions of the public administration system in Latin America, but concern myself largely with general economic and social questions, such as attitudes and motivations, which are both preconditions and conditioning factors of public administration. It will be thus more a disquisition on the economic and social background within which public administration has to operate in Latin America than on any specific field of public administration.

If we attempt to examine attitudes towards public administration in Latin America, we shall find a number of adverse psychosocial attitudes, which it is important to examine objectively.

The main drawback to improvement of public administration in Latin America is perhaps the tradition of State paternalism that is present in virtually all of the countries. There are several consequences of this traditional trait. It affects the recruitment of employees, which is more often than not conducted by the system of affiliation or allegiance to political clienteles rather than by systems designed to measure concrete achievement; it encourages padding of government offices; it tends to insulate state enterprieses from the winds of competition; and it explains the generally flabby nature of the control procedures over government operations and government enterprises.

The prevalence of paternalistic attitudes varies greatly from country to country and several of them have already made a dent in this tradition by objective systems of evaluation of performance and recruitment of personnel. By and large, however, there remains an unhealthy inheritance of paternalistic elements in the administration, which prevents an impersonal handling of public affairs conducive to impartiality of administration and efficiency of operations.

Another traditional flaw in attitude is what I might call the overcentralization in decision-making. This may manifest itself both at the regional level and at the sectorial level. At the regional level, there is an excessive weakness of provincial and local governments, leading to overconcentration of decision-making at the center. In fact, I recall that one of the most plausible rationalizations advanced in favor of the construction of Brasilia, the new capital, was that it might be the only way of preventing the President of the Republic from continuing to be in effect, though not in name, the mayor of Rio de Janeiro, compelled to take cognizance of minute problems of city administration.

At the sectorial level there is clear evidence of this same basic flaw in attitude. There is relatively little room for delegation of authority both because of the low level of competence of intermediate echelons of the public service and of the reluctance of the middle layers to take on or accept responsibility for policy decisions. This has led to a peculiarly perverse solution which in fact does not solve the problem at all. It is the excessive fragmentation of the administrative machinery by the creation of autonomous agencies which do manage to decentralize somewhat the decision-making process but at the cost of ruining the mechanism for centralized control, evaluation of performance, and establishment of working norms. Thus, some more flexibility in decision-making is attained only by impairing the mechanism for administrative coordination.

A third problem which is vital in the analysis of the present public administration picture in Latin America is the absence of an adequate and realistic theory on the role and limits of government intervention. Throughout the continent one finds complete disbelief in regulatory powers of the government. Parallel with this one finds overconfidence in the managerial performance of government enterprises as well as underestimation of the waste involved in the excessive and premature socialization of many enterprises.

Several distortions arise from the lack of a proper theory on the limits and role of government intervention. One is the continuous temptation of government organizations and enterprises to indulge in what we might call subsidy-pricing, namely, the charging for services at rates that are inadequate to cover the costs or to finance expansion. This leads to a wrong distribution of the financial burden of state services, which is transferred from the user to the general public through inflationary deficits or through general taxation, when specific taxation or levying of adequate user charges for the cost of services would be the correct solution. There is also the problem of giving a political tone or character to management, which is an almost inevitable consequence of often ill-concealed attempts to enlarge the area of government intervention prompted by the disbelief in the efficacy of government regulatory powers. Let us mention finally the old problem of absence or inadequacy of sanction against inefficiency and corruption in government enterprises.

There is, therefore, a great need for a correctly formulated theory of the role of government intervention in Latin America. I shall try to sketch a possible theory of government intervention applicable to countries in our stage and level of development.

Two premises must be recognized at the outset. The first one is that in the underdeveloped countries of Latin America, as well as in other developing countries, a much greater degree of government intervention is needed and desirable than is the case in mature, cumulative-growth economies, such as that of the United States. This need for greater government intervention exists even though admittedly the level of governmental efficiency tends to be much lower. The reasons behind this need are not only that traditional areas of investment—such as social overhead outlays for health and education as well as for the economic overhead in the form of flood control, irrigation, sanitation, and road-building—are of overwhelming importance in the early stage of development, but that even in the directly productive sectors there is need for special incentive and government action. A few cases can be cited to justify government intervention beyond the traditional area of investment.

First, there is the need for pioneer investment in the opening of new areas and in creating sources of power. Second, another motivation, which is somewhat more debatable but still important, is what might be called preclusive investment, arising from the need to implant government monopolies as a deliberate measure to prevent the creation of private monopolies. Third, there is the need for supplementary investment in cases where the technical lumpiness of the investment or technological progress necessitates changing the scale of investment. For instance in both Brazil and Argentina, government intervention was proved necessary when the problem was to change the scale of steel production from small characoal furnaces to modern openhearth steel-making procedures. This change required a greater accumulation of capital than private enterprise at the present level of private savings and investment could provide. There is, finally, what we might call expiatory investment, which is an attempt of the government to correct bottlenecks in several investment sectors, such as power and transportation. These bottlenecks are in many cases the result of inadequate incentives or punitive policies adopted in relation to private enterprise. This has been the case in virtually all Latin America, where privately owned railways, and in some cases, electric power companies, proved incapable of financing their upkeep and expansion in the face of rigid tariff rates in an age of inflation. The government had then to intervene to atone for the inequities visited on private enterprise and to undertake a job of its own. To these reasons I might add the need for assuring a better distribution of investment and income between regions. There are thus several powerful reasons why the scale, intensity, and frequency of government intervention in Latin American economies is bound to be much greater than that which would be considered as advisable or rational in this country.

There is a second important premise, which is often overlooked in Latin America; that is, that the only criterion for the division of roles as between public and private enterprise should be their respective suitability and efficiency for the assigned tasks. I am using the term suitability in a broad fashion to cover also political and security considerations of a paramount nature that make necessary or advisable the presence of the government. This second basic premise is often overlooked in Latin America where the debate between private enterprise and government intervention is carried along on ideological lines rather than based on a pragmatical evaluation of the relative efficiencies of the two sectors in fulfilling any specific task.

I would like to expatiate on those two premises in an attempt to develop some policy norms that might throw light on this emotionally debated problem of government versus private enterprise in Latin America.

The first norm would be that, whenever feasible, indirect controls through credit, taxation, and foreign exchange policies should be preferred to direct controls and to administrative rationing, basically for two reasons: (a) the technical and ethical problems inherent in the administration of direct controls; and (b) the desirability of preserving some of the basic allocating and guiding functions of the price system.

The second norm would be that regulatory controls should be in principle preferred to direct managerial control, and the latter to full ownership by the government. This principle is based again on two considerations: (a) that the government's financial and managerial resources are inadequate in Latin America even for those traditional tasks which are completely inaccessible to private enterprise; and (b) because the socially desirable controls can in most cases, though not in all, be enforced without either managerial control or full ownership by the government.

The third norm would be that government investment as a rule should concentrate on the economic and social overhead, with exceptions being made, however, to admit and encourage government intervention even in directly productive sectors, when the following conditions prevail: (a) there is "capital lumpiness," namely when the size of the investment effort is so capital-intensive that it exceeds the capability of private enterprise to mobilize resources; (b) there is need for pioneering either in a regional sense, the opening of new regions, or in a technological sense, the implanting of new techniques; (c) the maturation period exceeds the waiting capacity of private entrepreneurs; this often turns out to be the case in modern technology when the construction of large steel mills or large dams require four or five years, so that economic profitability is not reached until an exaggerated period elapses, a period which exceeds the saving capacity of private enterprise; and (d) there is need for avoiding the formation of private monopolies which may become a source of excessive private power or pirvate exploitation.

A fourth norm would be for government operational intervention, when needed, to take the form of mixed companies with private participation in financing, management, and control, rather than the form of state monopolies except when security or strategic considerations are paramount.

A fifth norm would be that government planning and investment should hopefully be based on noninflationary methods of raising resources through taxation, internal borrowing, or foreign loans, rather than on deficit financing, although the latter may be resorted to on a limited scale. Perhaps one could add another norm that experience has proved extremely difficult to implement, which is for the government to preserve its capacity and willingness to withdraw from a sector after the pioneering stage is completed. I say advisedly that this is a difficult norm to follow because having been a development banker, in charge of promoting government investment in several fields, I found it virtually impossible to withdraw state participation from many projects even after the child had well surmounted the weaning stage.

I expatiated a bit on the scope, limits, and rationale of

government intervention, because I believe they are at the very core of the problem of public administration in Latin America, where a comparatively small number of skilled administrators are saddled with quite impossible tasks. Not only do they have to conduct the normal operations of the government, but they also have to supervise a proliferation of government enterprises and entities, in fields that could best be handled by simple regulatory controls, if only our statesmen were less skeptical about the effectiveness of regulatory controls and more skeptical about the efficacy of government management.

It seems to be a peculiar twist of opinion that many people, while recognizing that a regulatory agency requires a smaller number of trained personnel, and therefore could be more adequately staffed than a whole host of different government agencies, still prefer somehow to face the awesome responsibility of direct administration instead of relying on a relatively small and effective body of regulators.

Let me now deal with another problem of public administration in Latin America which I would call "abnormal discontinuity." Discontinuity in administration takes place both at the operational level and at the policy-making level. At the operational level, the frequent succession of governments confronts a civil service that is floating without real roots, which does not benefit from regulated recruitment procedures and at times has no *esprit de corps*. This leads to excessive instability of the government machinery in response to changes of government. Of course, public administration is essentially a political task and the administrator cannot and should not be inert to political changes. But there is some intermediate point between complete inertia, creating a divorce between political orientation and administrative behavior, and complete upheaval with each change of administration resulting in complete disruption of the effectiveness of government operations. Fortunately, I think substantial progress has been made in most of the Latin American countries towards endowing the civil service with a greater degree of continuity. Certainly in Brazil, we have overcome a substantial part of the problem and perhaps indulged in the opposite excess by giving excessive stability to public officials, in the anxiety to overcome the problem of periodic disintegration of the government machinery at the occasion of government changes.

Discontinuity at the decision-making level is what an American economist recently called "the pseudo-creative response." Each new administrator, each new government becomes sometimes possessed of a convenient amnesia and forgets all of the progress made, the research and experience accumulated by the preceding governments. With unnecessary originality, it is decided that a fresh start must be made. This only too often occurs in our countries, although I might say that even in some much more stable and mature societies, such as the United States, one often finds succeeding governments embarking feverishly on unnecessary originality.

We might come now to what Professor Hirschman of Columbia University called the "dilemma of motivation versus understanding." In developed societies which have completed their process of maturation, technical creativeness and continuous adaptation lead them to incrementalist attitudes in problem solving. They usually tackle problems when they are ready for solution and when the solution is feasible. The so-called "latecomer societies," particularly those affected by the revolution of rising expectations, on the other hand, are in a hurry to develop and are often impatient in problem solving. (I find myself in great difficulty, I might add, to select appropriate terminology to describe the underdeveloped countries. Having been for the most part of the postwar period engaged in one way or the other in studies and debates on economic development, I found that the terminology develops much faster than the developing countries themselves. Originally they were called the poor countries, reflecting the rather fatalistic notion of the prewar days. Then a dynamic concept was injected—they were called the backward countries presumably because at some point they might be able to move forward. Then they were called, successively, the undeveloped countries, the underdeveloped countries, the emerging countries. Now that they are shaken by the wind of rising expectations, some facetious soul has called them the "expectant countries.") Well, one of the characteristics of the expectant countries is to attack simultaneously many-sided problems, which do not offer a real possibility of solution. Once failure results, they move to the other extreme and relapse into some sort of ideological fundamentalism, which is the attempt to seek a solution not by increments of reform but by drastic revolution.

This basic dilemma between motivation and understanding is a serious one and undoubtedly affects the direction, meaningfulness, and effectiveness of popular decision in Latin America.

Even in the conception of the Alliance for Progress one can find an acute manifestation of this syndrome. The Alliance for Progress is predicated on the notion that many-sided and multifarious reforms should be attempted for the modernization of society. But this poses immediately the problem of compatibility between short-run and long-run objectives. In the long run, there is perfect compatibility among the several objectives that make up the grand design of the Alliance, namely agrarian reform, fiscal reform, educational reform, creation of a suitable climate for profit investment, and reasonable price stabilization. In the short run, however, it is quite questionable that those objectives are reconcilable. So while there is nothing wrong in approaching these problems from many angles, the Alliance for Progress, as a catalog of evils to be cured and as an indication of desirable reforms, is apt to create more problems than it solves if this strategy is not implemented through incrementalist tactics. One ought to be satisfied at times with partial incremental reforms, rather than to be overly ambitious and to expect complete social transformation in one fell swoop.

Some of those dilemmas are already being felt in Latin America. If one presses, for instance, violently for agrarian and tax reforms, aiming at redistribution of income, it is unrealistic not to expect, at the same time, a deterioration in the climate for private investment, simply because private investors are precisely the property groups that are likely to get panicky at the reforms. So if one ascribes priority to reform—and that is probably a correct and desirable posture—then one ought not to be too sanguine in expecting an improvement in the private investment climate. In fact, one should be sophisticated enough to countenance its temporary deterioration. I think the executive branch of the American Government is probably conscious of the existence of this problem, but from speeches that I hear in certain quarters of Congress, there is very little if any awareness of the problem that there may be a short-run incompatibility between otherwise desirable objectives. One should not get impatient, discouraged, or otherwise irritated by the fact that, parallel with the push for reform, one has to sacrifice temporarily some other important objective. Similarly, price stabilization measures are desirable in themselves and useful for long-run development, but at times are rendered more difficult by the push for social equity and social justice. At the moment when the preaching of the gospel of social justice really takes hold, it is bound to stimulate claims for welfare benefits and wage adjustments which, though desirable in themselves, and perhaps nonpostponable, may render the achievement of price stabilization a still more complicated task than it normally is.

I think I have outlined some of the main problems that form the context within which the public administrator has to operate in Latin America. It is my hope that some limited usefulness will be derived from this analysis, which admittedly does not go into any detailed description of Latin American administrative procedures and problems. As an economist, I would like to conclude these short notes with a quotation from one of your economists, Kenneth Boulding, who has been pleading all along for a balanced approach to this problem of relationship between private enterprise and public administration. His way of formulating the problem brings perhaps a nice cautionary note on the way to approach those problems in Latin America. "The socialist," he says, "is likely to be too optimistic about the power of government to do good and the liberal too optimistic about the power of the market to prevent evil."

The Costs of Political Acculturation: The Administrator

Lucian W. Pye
Massachusetts Institute of Technology

We earlier observed that in well-established and stable societies it is possible to picture three more or less consecutive stages of involvement of the individual in his society and his polity: first, the process of socialization by which he is inducted into his culture; second, the process of political socialization out of which comes the understanding of citizenship and of membership in a polity; and finally, the stage of political recruitment when the few assume their active roles in public affairs. In transitional societies a sharp distinction does not exist between political socialization and political recruitment; for there is little sense of citizenship, only a division between observers and participants, and in place of a polity there is a realm of politics composed of principals and their followers. In a sense the process of political socialization in transitional societies takes the form of acculturation to the world culture. For, as we have noted, the political class usually represents the more acculturated elements of the society, and the process of learning about and relating to the modern world thus tends to become the essence of political socialization.

Of course, there need not logically be a political dimension to the acculturation process, and many people become members of the modern world without becoming sensitive to the realm of politics. Yet to an overwhelming degree acculturation has produced political responses. And certainly for members of the

Reprinted from *Politics, Personality, and Nation Building: Burma's Search for Identity* by Lucian W. Pye (New Haven: Yale University Press, 1962), pp. 211–220, by permission.

political class in societies seeking to build national institutions the experience of learning about the world culture has colored their understanding of the particular political roles to which they aspire.

We have already emphasized the fact that the complex reactions to the acculturation process provide the very dynamics of politics in most transitional societies. Here we turn to the genuine tragedy of that dynamics—that some degree of acculturation is necessary for a people to learn about the essentials of nation building, and yet the process of acculturation tends to produce psychological reactions which inhibit and frustrate the nation-building effort.

In the context of transitional politics this means that the more intense the acculturation the more will its influence be felt, until a point is reached at which there is a steep decline in political effectiveness even as the process of acculturation continues. And so in most transitional societies the more acculturated have tended to be replaced by the less, and this process has not stopped with the replacement of those trained by former colonial rulers. The more acculturated, even if they were nationalist leaders, have often lost out to those less in tune with the modern world.

The customary view of this phenomenon is that the leaders as they become more modernized lose touch with their people. This is the view that at bottom politics is an atavistic and unreasoning business in which the more civilized must always give way to the less. This is also the view that as people become more at home in the modern world they lose their capacity to communicate with their more tradition-bound compatriots. In essence, these views undoubtedly contain some elements of truth. However, there appears to be more to the process, for the decline in effectiveness appears even among those whose positions do not depend upon communicating with the general public. For example, in Burma British officials were surprised after independence to find that Burmese officials whom they knew well proved in time to be far less competent than they had once been. Similarly, some of the more modernized politicians seemed to be plagued with indecision, unsureness of commitment, and an inability to consummate political acts.

As we turn now to an examination of the recruitment of the Burmese political class, we shall be particularly concerned with how the process of acculturation may have tended to limit their full potentialities as creative and imaginative people and leaders. Treating first the experiences of the administrators and then those of the politicians, we shall observe how at different psychological levels they appear unable to conquer various forms of ambivalence that in their cumulative effect destroy the capacity for those forms of action necessary for nation building.

The performance of the Burmese administrative service

As in most other colonial countries, the passage to independence in Burma saw a decline in administrative politics and the emergence of popular politics. The future of the country, however, still depends upon the ability of the administrative class to perform effectively. As members of the bureaucracy they must manage the most significant structure in the political process, and their ability and skill are possibly the most crucial factors determining the pace of modernization and the course of nation building.

It would not serve our purpose to attempt to catalogue the various weaknesses in public administration in Burma; such a listing would have to cover practices commonly noted in most transitional political systems. We need only summarize them in terms of three general categories: first, ambivalence on the part of the administrators over the nature and forms of progress and modernization; second, profound confusion over the difference between ritual and rationality in bureaucratic operations; third, and most important of all, fundamental and all-pervasive lack of effective communication among officials.

Backward-Looking Modernizers. At present the civil service occupies a strangely ambiguous position in Burmese society. No matter at what level it is viewed, it offers contradictory impressions, for it seems to be pointing in two directions at once: it is peculiarly attached to the past and to conserving established practices, and yet it is also commonly identified as the principal agent for modernizing the country. On balance, the Burmese civil service represents the most modernized, the best educated, and the most skilled people in the entire society. It seems to be designed to fulfill modern functions of government; its standards of performance and its ideals of action are all taken from the modern world. Yet in spite of this apparent attachment to change and progress, it is in fact in the grip of tradition, and a tradition that reaches back not only to British colonial rule but also in some respects to the old East India Company and to the ethos of government of the Burmese kings. Thus, paradoxically, the logical agents for change seem in many ways to be as changeless as any aspect of a transitional society can be. The very men who should be champions of innovation and initiators of action if the country is to develop are to an alarming degree the victims of immobilism.

This ambiguous quality of the civil service is to be noted even in physical appearances. The Secretariat building is one of the most imposing structures in the entire country, but it is a memorial to the past and more particularly to a period of British, not Burmese, greatness. In the districts every physical aspect of administrative authority communicates an identity which is more modern than most other aspects of the setting but also unmistakably tied to a colonial past. Within government offices one finds the same divided world. The forms, the procedures, the files—all suggest an outmoded version of once modern procedures.

Even when speaking about new programs, senior Burmese officials convey a certain sense of nostalgia and a feeling that their golden age may belong to the past. Repeatedly in the interviews older civil servants would inquire whether we had ever been to Burma before and, on receiving a negative reply, would indicate that it was a pity because in various ways Burma was once a better, more presentable land. When pressed for an explanation for what had happened, they generally said that before the war they—meaning the civil service class—used to run the country but that now the politicians have their hands in everything.

To a striking extent, the administrative class tends to

picture itself in retrospect as a more powerful and influential community than it actually was during the colonial period. Men who have any form of official status are not prone to minimize their own significance, and sons tend to remember their fathers as powerful figures, even if they were no more than clerks. The Burmese administrative class is remarkably united in its belief that Burmese officials were important in helping to build up their country when it was under colonial rule. In actual fact much power did slip from the grasp of the limited numbers of Britishers, and the Burmese were not always outsmarted by the Indian officials in their land. Out in the districts, in particular, Burmese officials, even though of low status on the civil lists, still were important and authoritative people in their communities.

Regardless of the precise extent of Burmese influence and power before independence, senior officials now deeply resent the suggestion that they were insignificant before the war and that all credit for the orderly and efficient operations of government should go to foreigners, either British or Indian. Some have even expressed the opinion that the Burmese nationalist viewpoint that Burmese had no power in the colonial administration and that none were adequately trained was advanced by Burmese politicians in their efforts to discredit the entire administrative class. As one senior official has remarked:

> It is quite true that we began with a shortage of trained personnel, but we did have the cadres and orderly expansion was possible. It is not true, as our politicians and many foreigners have said, that we had no experienced people. The politicians were anxious to make everyone believe that we had no people about trained for the jobs, for all they wanted to do was to put their friends and workers on the government rolls. By claiming that there were no trained Burmese they could put their untrained and incompetent people in all the high jobs they wanted.

At the same time, however, the senior members of the administrative class cannot openly and forcefully insist upon their own importance before the war because to do so would raise questions about the extent to which they may have been lacking in true patriotism, serving as the "handmaidens of the imperialists." This touches on a deeper problem of guilt and anxiety about personal identity for the administrators which we shall be examining in a moment; it is enough to point out here that those who set the tone for the Burmese administrative class would like to be able to look back with more pride and to receive more recognition for their abilities, but they are also disturbed that their finest period may have occurred when foreign rule still existed. Thus the past is constantly with them, and, even though they have modern education and skills, they cannot forget what they once were.

Rituals in Place of Rationality. The Burmese administrative class suffers also from confusion between ritual and rationality. In characterizing the period of administrative politics, we noted the spirit of legalism and the reverence for procedure characteristic of the acculturated Burmese. That attitude now takes the form of believing that government can be strong only if all the proper procedures are carefully followed. There is thus an almost magical potential to government which can be tapped by a cautious respect for the proper.

This concern for ritual lies at the basis of the peculiar mixture of almost uninhibited optimism and complete cynicism which is the hallmark of the Burmese administrator. We have noted that in the calculations of Burmese politics there tends to be a constant vacillation between a sense of omnipotence and one of incompetence. At one moment belief and faith in the potentialities of ritual suggest that much is about to be accomplished; at the next moment a feeling for the decline of the entire administrative class and a sense of personal unsureness produces a bitter mood of cynicism about the government's ability to accomplish anything at all.

To a large extent Burmese anxieties about the importance of the rituals of administration can be traced to their experiences under colonial rule. The British sought to create a machinery of administration which could effectively preserve law and order, and thus appear as a stable and unchanging institution in a stable society—not as a force for change and innovation. Similarly, the British did not intend to imbue the individual Burmese recruited to the government service with initiative and a drive for change. Anxious to develop the most economical system of administration possible under existing conditions, they relied heavily on the initiative and talents of a few highly trained

British officials while depending for the maintenance of routine operations upon large numbers of Burmese and Indian subordinates. The British thus erected an extraordinary mechanism, indeed a mammoth machine, which operated impersonally and with easily interchangeable parts.

The Burmese were trained to see the machine as a completely impersonal structure within which communication must follow formal channels and set procedures. Their concepts of impartiality and justice became confused with the belief that security and wisdom—to say nothing of prudence—called for an inflexible adherence to rituals. In sum, the Burmese were trained in the spirit of the clerk while believing that they were being trained to take part in the decision-making process.

FORMALISM AND IMPERFECT COMMUNICATION. Under the British a gap existed between the formal and informal patterns of British administrative organization which was most conspicuous when viewed in terms of the flow of communication. Formal communications involved the activities of the Burmese and Indian clerks and had to follow set lines, while informal communications conformed to patterns of personal association among British officials. A British official could usually facilitate the communication process by dealing directly with other officials; then, informal commitments or decisions having been made, clerks could be instructed to draft the appropriate requests and the formal machinery could be called into play.

At present probably the main weakness of the Burmese administrative structure is that it rigidly adheres to formal procedures and does not utilize informal and interpersonal channels of communication. Indeed, the problem of the Burmese bureaucracy is almost exactly the opposite of what the student of prerational legal social systems might expect. The Burmese, instead of being unduly influenced by personal relationships in their administrative procedures, have gone to the other extreme. They have tried to operate their administrative machinery without the benefit of reinforcing and functionally compatible informal patterns of communication and association. They have assumed, as they were trained as clerks to believe, that all problems can be solved by finding a relevant regulation in an appropriate rule book.

As a consequence of this attitude, the machinery of administration has little capacity to discriminate among problems. Major problems are treated in the same manner as minor ones, and all tend to be moved up the hierarchy. The Burmese cabinet is called upon to resolve a hopeless array of issues. The operations of all aspects of the government seem to be excessively rigid and grossly overcentralized. The task of the administrative service becomes that of maintaining procedures, not solving problems and making decisions.

It is only at the point when the formal procedures are so overloaded as to produce paralysis that informal considerations enter into Burmese administrative behavior. At this stage, however, the informal considerations no longer reinforce the purpose and spirit of the formal procedures but become counterlegal in nature. For example, when the processing of applications or the granting of licenses overpowers the formal machinery, the question of whose application is to receive attention requires some personal act of persuasion, some means of attracting attention, which was not included in the formal procedures. There is no wonder that so many people seem to suspect the civil service of petty forms of corruption and graft.

Most of the difficulties of the Burmese civil service—its inflexibility, its passive rather than active posture, its overcentralization, its excessive reliance on the skills of clerks rather than the knowledge of specialists—can be traced back to the fact that the formal structure is not built upon and reinforced by informal patterns of communication. However, the crucial problem of communication involves far more than merely the formal training which the Burmese administrators had as clerks under colonial rule. It is also a manifestation of their deeper psychological reactions to the experiences of acculturation, reactions which have made them unsure of themselves and of each other and which take the form of distrust and suspicion which further reduce effective communication throughout the bureaucracy.

The background of administrators

Of those we interviewed who had had administrative experience before the war, the vast majority came from families in which the father at least was already to some degree acculturated to the modern world of his day. Of those who first became administrators after the war nearly two-thirds had the same kind of family background. These considerations may explain the extent to which the members of the administrative class tend to feel that they are confronted with an issue of collective rather than individual identity with respect to the entire problem of acculturation. They readily use "we" and "us" when speaking of the challenges they have felt to their own positions in Burmese society.

Two general experiences colored most of the attitudes of the prewar trained administrators, who still set the tone for the Burmese civil service, toward their political and social roles. The first was the formal education they received in a Western-styled school, and the second was their initial experience of informal apprenticeship within the service when they came under the direction of a senior British official.

FORMAL EDUCATION: SOURCE OF SOCIAL STATUS AND CAUSE OF INSECURITY. In almost all Asian cultures there is a profound faith in education and knowledge, in the Mandarin and the *Swami,* the sage and the Enlightened One. The mystique of knowledge and knowledgeability has in all Asian cultures been closely associated both with religion and with self-fulfillment. Education is thus a value in itself.

In Burma the elite status of the educated man is the cardinal article of faith of the Burmese administrative class. From low echelon clerks to senior secretaries, all seem acutely aware that their claim to superiority over the masses of their people can be justified most convincingly by their years of formal education. Many of our respondents indicated that their parents had impressed upon them from a very early age the relationship between schooling and getting ahead in life. Those who came from Anglicized families would naturally have been expected to go on to school, but significantly, even those who had extremely traditionalist parents said that their fathers wanted them to get a modern form of education because of its potential economic and social value.

The high value which the Burmese administrators tend to place on their years of formal schooling is not, however, combined with an equally high regard for either the skills of the specialist or the role of the intellectual. On the contrary, most of them still reflect the attitudes of their former British mentors, who, in the tradition of the British ruling class, had a well-articulated distrust of both specialized knowledge and any form of intellectual pretension. Some of our informants, for example, in discussing their experiences in England spoke of how hard it had been for them to learn the proper British custom of always appearing to be slightly less intelligent and less informed than one really is.

A Burmese judge remarked:

> I was very anxious to tell the guests [at a dinner party] all I knew about Buddhism in Burma and Ceylon, but I knew I shouldn't say anything on that subject because I had been told that English gentlemen discuss with animation only matters of common knowledge and of little import.

A university instructor said:

> Our Burmese students were often trying to display their intelligence. It didn't go down well with their classmates [in a British university].

However, the Burmese urge to display intellectual achievement is too powerful to have been checked by an awe of British forms alone. There seems to be a more basic inhibition reflecting the underlying doubt many officials have about their own intellectual abilities. School was for most of them the most intensely competitive experience of their lives, and the test of modern educational standards raised in the minds of many Burmese officials the question of whether they might not in fact be somehow inferior. Thus, although their modern education distinguished them from the great masses of their countrymen and justified their superior position, it also left them with a more precise awareness of their own deficiencies and inadequacies.

Hence, their extremely mixed feelings toward intellectual matters. On the one hand, the Burmese administrators have an endless need to extol the virtues and the inherent superiority of those who have passed the various stages of formal schooling and possess the appropriate degrees. In their thinking most of them divide all people between the educated and the uneducated; in the common vocabulary of the class, the usual way of attacking, denouncing, or belittling individuals or groups is to suggest that they are deficient in formal schooling. For example, in the interviews they made such remarks as these:

> They think they should run the district, but they haven't even been to a proper school.

> He is a minister, but he has never been to the university. Uneducated like all our politicians. What hope is there for us?

> The times have changed and even people without educations hold office and get rich.

On the other hand, the same people generally find it painfully difficult to discuss the details of their own experiences in school. They generally prefer to have it assumed that their credentials are in good order, that they belong, and that the rest can be left unsaid. Although some were among the best in their school classes, and all had to meet the minimum standards, most tend to display varying forms of hostility toward the idea of intellectuals and specialists. Those who came to the administrative class before the war easily direct this hostility against the new generation of Burmese—the "state scholars"—who have just been educated abroad at government expense and are expected to serve within the government on their return. In turn, most of these young men are quick to claim that the older generation fears their new and more specialized knowledge and thus seeks to neutralize their influence and impede their advancement. True to the traditions of the administrative class, the state scholars have expected that their formal education should be enough to place them within the circle of the inner elite. Yet at the same time their schooling experiences have left them feeling peculiarly vulnerable and defensive in their own country. The test of education has brought to them the same awareness of their own personal limitations as troubled the senior officials in their day.

In a sense, then, the state scholars find themselves confronted with precisely the same conflicts as their predecessors who are now their "obstructing" superiors. For both groups the easiest course has been to accept the status their education has given them but to minimize the content of the modern knowledge they supposedly have received. The need to cling to elite status, the risks of disappearing into the great anonymous mass of the nonelite, and the sense of personal inadequacies are all too great to permit ability in the application of knowledge to become the criterion of status.

Hence the paradox that is the common tragedy for so many underdeveloped countries: those who have been exposed to modern forms of knowledge are often precisely the ones who are most anxious to obstruct the continued diffusion of the effects of that knowledge; they desperately need to hold on to what they have and avoid all risks. The lasting consequence of their formal education has thus been an inflexible and conservative cast of mind. Modernization has bred opposition to change.

Bureaucracy and Environment in Ceylon

ROBERT N. KEARNEY
Duke University

and

RICHARD L. HARRIS
University of California, Los Angeles

FOR MANY OF the newly independent states of Asia and Africa one of the most significant legacies of Western colonial rule is the existence of a public bureaucracy organised

Reprinted from *The Journal of Commonwealth Political Studies,* Vol. 2, No. 3 (November, 1964), pp. 253–266, by permission of the editors and the publishers, Leicester University Press.

This article is a product of research conducted in Ceylon during 1961–62 under a Ford Foundation fellowship. While the Foundation's assistance is gratefully acknowledged, responsibility for the conclusions, opinions, and other statements contained in the article rests with the authors and not the Ford Foundation.

according to Western administrative concepts and incorporating to some degree Western notions of rationality, efficiency and impersonality. The colonial period was predominantly a period of bureaucratic rule in which the bureaucrats were often seen as constituting an elite of talent and wisdom, and in the areas under British control the colonial bureaucracies sometimes built admirable records of integrity and ability. Following independence, the bureaucracies have been forced to make occasionally painful adjustments to altered political conditions. At the same time the almost universal commitment to rapid economic development and the frequent desire to weld into national societies diverse ethnic and religious communities have greatly expanded the tasks of the bureaucracies. In these circumstances, the characteristics and effectiveness of the former colonial bureaucracies and their problems in adapting to the conditions of independence have become of critical importance to the future of most, if not all, newly independent states.

In the present study, an attempt is made to trace the impact of the social, cultural, and political environment on the contemporary bureaucracy of Ceylon.[1] The discussion of bureaucracy and environment in Ceylon, it is hoped, will contribute to the comparative analysis of the characteristics, problems, and prospects of non-Western, ex-colonial bureaucracies, particularly in those states which have emerged from British rule. Although parts of Ceylon were controlled in turn by the Portuguese and Dutch for three centuries, the modern bureaucracy was a product of British rule from the beginning of the nineteenth century to the grant of independence in 1948 and shared much of the heritage of the vastly larger and more famous bureaucracy of British India. While this paper is primarily concerned with the weight of external factors on the bureaucracy, it should be noted that the bureaucracy has simultaneously exerted a strong influence on its environment and played a major role in the process of modernisation in Ceylon.

[1] For the importance of indigenous social and cultural values and habits in influencing behaviour within non-Western bureaucracies, despite formal acceptance of Western administrative organisation and practices, see R. V. Presthus, 'The Social Bases of Bureaucratic Organization,' 38 *Social Forces* (1959), 103–9; and R. W. Gable, 'Culture and Administration in Iran,' 8 *Middle East Journal,* (1959), 407–21.

The prestige of the public service

As in many newly-independent and economically underdeveloped nations, government employment in Ceylon has an enormous attraction for the educated and skilled members of the nation's labour force. Studies of occupational preference consistently show that government employment is rated higher than any other occupation in Ceylon.[2] For the educated Ceylonese the public service is almost the only source of secure employment since the government dominates the small nonagricultural segment of the economy and has a virtual monopoly of white-collar employment. More than twenty per cent of all Ceylonese wage and salary earners are in the public service.[3] Pensions, employment security, and fairly high salary rates sharply distinguish government employment from the uncertainty and insecurity of private employment.

The great prestige enjoyed by the public servant has, however, probably contributed at least as much as material advantage or employment security to the attractiveness of a bureaucratic career. The social prestige of the modern bureaucrat is in large measure a heritage of Ceylon's feudal and colonial past. Traditional Sinhalese society was rigidly stratified by class and caste on the basis of status prescribed by birth. In this hierarchical society, government officials were drawn exclusively from families of the highest rank.[4] Hence, the belief developed that officialdom represented the 'best' families. This traditional outlook on officialdom was reinforced by the experience of European colonial rule. By their social exclusiveness and supreme confidence in the superiority of their own civilisation, the European colonial administrators helped to perpetuate the popular

2 Of the many indications of this preference, see M. A. Straus, 'Mental Ability and Cultural Needs: A Psychological Interpretation of the Intelligence Test Performance of Ceylon University Entrants,' 16 *American Sociological Review,* (1951), 371–5; and B. Ryan, 'Status, Achievement, and Education in Ceylon,' 20 *Journal of Asian Studies,* (1961), 463–76.

3 *Report of the Salaries and Cadre Commission:* 1961 Part I (Sessional Paper III—1961), 30.

4 R. Pieris, *Sinhalese Social Organization* (Colombo, 1956), 169–79. See also R. Knox, *An Historical Relation of Ceylon* (first published in 1681; Glasgow, James MacLehose, 1911), 106.

association of governmental position with superior social status.[5] The notions of tutelage and paternalism inherent in colonial rule reinforced the elitist conception of the colonial bureaucracy.

The first Ceylonese to enter the colonial service were recruited from among the Sinhalese low-country *Mudaliyars* (chiefs), and authority over the peasantry was exercised through feudal aristocratic *Mudaliyars* and Kandyan *Ratemahattayas* by the colonial regime until 1946. Headmen forming the base of the regional administration until 1963 were selected from the venerated, high-caste, landowning families of the locality. The presence of these feudal elements in modern administration has helped to establish a link in the mind of the Ceylonese villager between the contemporary bureaucrats and the exalted feudal nobility.

Social stratification and the bureaucratic hierarchy

Social and economic developments of the past century have significantly modified traditional Ceylonese social organisation, leaving in contemporary Ceylon a transitional society in which elements of the traditional exist alongside elements of the modern. While the rigid stratification of traditional society has been altered in a number of respects, social classes tend to be sharply differentiated on the basis of education, language, and manner of living, which are closely related to wealth and birth. For several generations, the island has been dominated socially and economically by those who were able to obtain an education taught in the English language. A wide chasm of social status and culture has separated the English-educated Ceylonese, commonly called the English-speaking elite, from the vernacular educated, producing one of the most profound divisions of Ceylonese society.[6] The members of this westernised elite enjoyed exclusive

[5] See Ryan, *op. cit.*, 467–9.

[6] On westernisation and English-language education as a source of class division, see *Sinhalese and Tamil as Official Languages*, Report of a Select Committee of the State Council (Sessional Paper XXII—1946); *First Interim Report of the Official Languages Commission* (Sessional Paper XXI—1951) G. C. Mendis, 'Adult Franchise and Educational Reform,' 2 *University of Ceylon Review* (1944), 37–44; H. A. Passé, 'The English Language in Ceylon,'

access to the higher positions in the colonial bureaucracy. They held political power at independence in 1948, but their political domination was broken in 1956, when resentment of the privileges conferred by education in English helped propel a more popularly-based and nationalist Government into power.

In the highly status-conscious environment of Ceylon, it is not surprising that the bureaucracy reflects the basic inequalities and sharp divisions of the social hierarchy. Like the society, the bureaucracy is stratified into highly differentiated classes or status groups. At the apex of this bureaucratic hierarchy is the administrative and professional officer class, constituting less than one per cent of the entire bureaucracy. The members of this group, called staff officers, are drawn from Ceylon's small number of university graduates and represent the narrow social stratum of the English-speaking elite.

Below the class of administrative and professional officers lies the middle segment of the bureaucratic hierarchy, the clerical class. Individuals in this class are also English-speaking but are socially inferior to the staff officers and have received English-language education only to the secondary level. The social distance which separates members of these two groups is much greater and more obvious than that which commonly exists in Western bureaucracies.

The base of the bureaucratic pyramid consists of a class of bureaucrats known in Ceylon as 'minor employees.' Eight out of ten public servants are members of this group of unskilled and semi-skilled maintenance and service employees.[7] The social and cultural gulf separating the top from the bottom of the bureaucratic hierarchy is suggested by the contrast between the sarong-clad and barefoot semi-literate minor employee and the university-educated staff officer attired in a western business suit. The distance is similarly visible in the obvious relationships between the two groups, characterised by obsequiousness on the part of the minor employee and haughtiness on the part of the staff officer.

1 *University of Ceylon Review* (1943), 50–65; and Hector Abhayavardhana, et al., *The Role of the Western-Educated Elite* (Colombo, 1962). It should be noted that what is usually called the 'English-speaking elite' does not include all persons with some command of English.

7 *Statistical Abstract of Ceylon:* 1960, 143.

The salaries paid to individuals in the different bureaucratic classes reveal the disparity between them in terms of standard of living and economic status. In contrast to the United States and Canada where the salary received by the highest paid public servant is about six times that received by the lowest paid public servant, in Ceylon the salary of the highest paid public servant is approximately forty times that of the lowest.[8] The economic gaps that exist between the different classes are further illustrated by the fact that the average starting salary of a government clerk is roughly twice that of a minor employee, while the average starting salary of a staff officer is five times that of a clerk.[9]

In some ways the clerical class has the least desirable position in this highly stratified bureaucratic hierarchy. Promotion from the clerical level to the administrative level is severely limited by the class structure of the bureaucracy. The educational and social distinctions maintained between the two levels impose a status barrier which few ever cross. Besides the bleak opportunity for advancement, the salaries of government clerks fall drastically short of supporting the urban standard of living to which they aspire. Frustrations arising from this dissimilarity between aspirations and economic and social status seemingly have caused the government clerks to be one of the principal sources of support for the left-wing political parties in Ceylon.[10]

Slightly more than 1,000 persons hold administrative positions in the entire public service of over 245,000 members.[11] However, until very recently this small cadre of administrative officers contained an even smaller administrative elite known as the Ceylon Civil Service, which enjoyed special prerogatives and immense prestige. The C.C.S., the Ceylonese counterpart of the Indian Civil Service, was formed in 1803 as the first overseas civil service responsible to the British Crown. Originally the Service included the highest British administrators sent to govern the island, and as late as 1927 two-thirds of the positions in the C.C.S. were filled by Englishmen. After 1948, the number of Civil Service officers remained around 200, although the public service

[8] *Report of the Salaries and Cadre Commission:* 1961, Part I, 49–50.

[9] *Ibid.,* 50.

[10] Ryan, *op. cit.,* 473.

[11] *Statistical Abstract of Ceylon:* 1960, 143.

doubled in size and the number of non-Civil Service administrative officers increased by more than fifty per cent.[12]

After independence, the C.C.S. continued to exist as a class apart from the rest of the administrative service. Civil Servants had different salary grades and promotion prospects from non-Civil Servants and a number of the top administrative posts in the government were reserved for Civil Service officers. In 1959, while the C.C.S. comprised only about thirteen per cent of all administrative personnel, its members held forty per cent of the top administrative positions and an even greater number of the next highest administrative positions.[13] The existence of this small and privileged group, which was felt to be a relic of colonial rule without purpose in an independent nation, was widely resented within, as well as outside, the bureaucracy. A government commission studying the public service referred to the C.C.S. as an administrative 'caste' which because of the special privileges and snobbishness of its members caused constant friction and discontent in the administrative level of the public service.[14] On May 1, 1963, the C.C.S. officially was abolished and the former Civil Service officers were incorporated into a Unified Administrative Service of 1,030 officers grouped in five grades.[15]

Influences of the educational system

Until recently, the prerequisite for securing a position in the government bureaucracy was an education taught in the English language. In fact, a primary purpose of the educational system in Ceylon in colonial times was to provide a supply of English-educated recruits for the public service. For most of the nineteenth century British colonial officers assisted by Ceylonese clerical employees formed the combination which governed the island.

The colonial system of education, geared to educating

12 Based on data from the *Ceylon Civil List* for the years 1948, 1952, 1955, 1957, and 1959.

13 *Loc. cit.*, 1959.

14 *Report of the Salaries and Cadre Commission:* 1961, Part I, 161.

15 *Ceylon News*, 9.5.63.

students for positions in the government service, exhibited the strong bias in favour of the humanities and neglect of technical studies which was characteristic of the 'generalist' preferences of the British colonial services.[16] This emphasis continues today and the educational system remains to a large extent committed to dispensing the same liberal education formerly required of recruits to the colonial bureaucracy. The public service officers of the Department of Motor Vehicles or the Irrigation Department today frequently hold degrees in Buddhist civilisation or English literature. Although the Government has repeatedly charged that the educational system inadequately supplies the nation's technical and scientific needs, the underproduction of graduates in technical subjects has been encouraged by the bureaucracy's practice of paying higher salaries and offering better promotion prospects to administrative officers than to technical and professional experts. This practice seriously discourages students from studying in the technical fields and forces technically-trained individuals in the public service to seek administrative posts in order to improve their financial position and obtain higher status.

Education is commonly sought in Ceylon as a means of securing a bureaucratic job and the dowry and status public employment commands.[17] The entire educational process reflects this orientation in that it is basically designed to prepare the student for passing the national educational examinations required for entrance into the different levels of the public service. Indeed, the key examinations in the school system are looked upon as stepping stones to positions in the public service. The present General Certificate of Education examination, for example, is generally regarded as the stepping stone to a post in the clerical grades, just as the University degree is thought of as the key to a post in the administrative and professional officer grades.[18]

16 A useful history of education in Ceylon during the British period which frequently mentions the connection between public employment and education is contained in H. A. Wyndham, *Native Education,* (London, 1933), 33–66.

17 Ryan, *op. cit.*

18 See C. R. Hensman (ed.), *The Public Services and the People,* (Colombo, 1963), 40.

THE IMPACT OF ETHNIC AND RELIGIOUS COMMUNITIES

Although westernising influences appear to have made considerably greater headway in the bureaucracy than in the society as a whole, the barriers separating Ceylon's ethnic and religious communities remain of considerable significance to the public service. Where strong consciousness of communal group membership lingers, the ethnic and religious composition of the bureaucracy becomes a matter of public concern. Almost inevitably, communal competition for the prized public employment develops and appeals are made to communal loyalties to support claims on public service positions.

The advantages of early establishment in the bureaucracy and access to English-language education have given certain ethnic and religious minorities a disproportionate share of public service posts. Among the first Ceylonese to enter the colonial bureaucracy were members of the small Burgher (Eurasian) community, whose swift mastery of English and recruitment to the public services was facilitated by their familiarity with European culture and concentration in Colombo near the first schools. The Tamils of Jaffna, faced with harsh economic conditions in the North, were quick to benefit from English-language educations made available by American missionaries and early entered the colonial bureaucracy in large numbers. In contrast, except for members of the Sinhalese low-country aristocracy, the Sinhalese of the majority community were slow to gain admission to the public service. Kandyan Sinhalese of the interior seldom acquired the requisite command of the English language and were almost totally absent from the colonial service. The share of bureaucratic posts held by the Burgher and Tamil minorities declined gradually and the Sinhalese, particularly from the coastal areas, improved their relative position in the later years of colonial rule. However, the Sinhalese, who comprise more than two-thirds of the Ceylonese population, have continued to be under-represented in the public service.[19]

[19] This discussion is bassed on S. J. Tambiah, 'Ethnic Representation in Ceylon's Higher Administrative Services, 1870–1946,' 13 *University of Ceylon Review,* (1955), 113–34.

Smouldering resentment over disproportionate minority representation in the bureaucracy has been fundamental to the communal strife which has plagued Ceylon since independence. A rapid expansion of vernacular education through the secondary level commencing in the 1930s led to demands for entry of the Sinhalese-educated into the public service, which remained the preserve of the English-educated following independence. At the same time, developing Sinhalese nationalism awakened mass Sinhalese political consciousness and sharpened awareness of communal differences. Communal loyalty was soon enlisted to utilise the political strength of the majority community in the competition for government employment.[20] To the Sinhalese, minority entrenchment in the public service has meant that 'the Tamil man is sleeping on the Sinhalese man's mat.'[21] The official language issue, originally designed to break the hold of the English-educated on the public service, developed into a demand by the Sinhalese for preferential access to the bureaucracy. The demand for *swabhasha* or the Ceylonese people's 'own language' was transformed into the call for 'Sinhalese only' as the official language of government.[22]

A new Government, brought to power in 1956 by the emergent nationalism and communal self-consciousness of the Sinhalese rural masses, immediately enacted legislation changing the official language from English to Sinhalese. After the passing of the Official Language Act, communal tensions exploded into violent riots in 1956 and 1958. A Tamil *satyagraha* campaign, intended to prevent implementation of the Official Language Act in the Tamil areas, paralysed administration in the North for three months in 1961.

The language changeover in the bureaucracy has been accompanied by considerable administrative confusion and bureaucratic demoralisation, since few public servants were proficient in Sinhalese. Despite incentive bonuses and threatened loss of regular salary increases unless an examination in Sinhalese

[20] For a perceptive discussion of communalism as a product of competition for public service employment, see G. C. Mendis, *Ceylon Today and Yesterday,* (Colombo, 1957), 97–107.

[21] Ceylon Senate. *Parl. Deb.,* vol. 10, 608.

[22] See I.D.S. Weerawardana, *Ceylon General Election:* 1956 (Colombo, 1960), 1–15, 98–109; W. H. Wriggins. *Ceylon: Dilemmas of a New Nation,* (Princeton, 1960), 228–70, 337–42.

was passed, at least half the public servants were believed to be unable to perform their duties in the new official language by 1961, five years after the enactment of the Official Language Act.[23] The requirement that entrants into the public service should develop a working knowledge of Sinhalese within three years of their appointment will presumably constitute a major obstacle to the securing of public employment by Tamil- and English-speaking Ceylonese and may be expected to alter the future ethnic composition of the bureaucracy to the advantage of the Sinhalese.

Parallel to clashes between ethnic communities for positions within the bureaucracy has been a rising concern for the religious composition of the public service. Ceylon's Hindu population is Tamil-speaking and the question of Hindu representation in the bureaucracy is indistinguishable from the question of Tamil representation. The Muslims commonly have turned to trade and have displayed slight interest in public employment. The sharp conflict is between the Buddhist majority, who are ethnically Sinhalese, and the Christian minority, composed of Sinhalese, Tamils, and Burghers. While the exact proportion of Christians in the public service is unknown, it almost certainly far exceeds the Christian proportion of the population.

Most English-language education was formerly in the hands of Christian missionaries, and Christian denominational schools dominated the field of education in English from the latter part of the nineteenth century until they were taken over by the government in 1960. The educational advantage of Christians is reflected in enrolments in the University of Ceylon. Until 1946 Christian students actually outnumbered Buddhists at the University, although the Buddhists constitute sixty-four per cent of the island population and the Christians only nine per cent. Although the proportion of Christians in the student body has since declined, it has remained well above the Christian proportion of the population.[24]

Buddhist resentment at the large number of Christians in

[23] *Report of the Salaries and Cadre Commission:* 1961, Part II, (Sessional Paper IV—1961), 11.

[24] Sir Ivor Jennings, 'Race, Religion and Economic Opportunity in the University of Ceylon,' 2 *University of Ceylon Review* (1944), 2–4; *Statistical Abstract of Ceylon:* 1954, 142.

the public service and the relative under-representation of Buddhists, intensified by the belief that the Christians benefited from favouritism in selection during the colonial period, have prompted repeated demands that the religious composition of the bureaucracy should more nearly reflect the religious composition of the society. In 1962, the influential All-Ceylon Buddhist Congress proposed that recruitment to the public service and army should be based on proportional representation of the island's various religious groups.[25] This suggestion was incorporated in the recommendations of the National Education Commission. The final report of the Commission urged that admission to the University and public service be regulated by quotas assigned to religious groups on the basis of their relative size.[26]

Caste and Family Influences

Caste attitudes and loyalties continue to influence the bureaucracy although for many years the government has formally opposed continuation of caste distinctions. Caste enters the bureaucratic recruitment and promotion processes through the preference higher officers grant members of their own caste. Although caste distinctions may be of declining significance in the society, caste members are still united by a strong sense of solidarity, based on caste endogamy, which suggests the possibility of kinship or of future family connections. Membership of the same caste, thus, is a convenient lever for evoking preference in the selection or promotion of public servants.[27] Although the magnitude of caste preference in the bureaucracy cannot be determined, privately made references to caste favouritism, particularly in the upper grades, are fairly common. Occasionally, charges of caste preference appear more openly. For example, the Permanent Secretary to the Ministry of Defence and External Affairs was recently charged in Parliament with favouring mem-

25 *Ceylon Daily News,* 28.5.62.

26 *Final Report of the National Education Commission:* 1961 (Sessional Paper XVII—1962), 152–3.

27 This phenomenon was noted in the *Report of the Kandyan Peasantry Commission* (Sessional Paper XVIII—1951), 37. A discussion of the impact of caste on administration is contained in B. Ryan, *Caste in Modern Ceylon* (New Brunswick, N.J., 1953), 323–9.

bers of the *Karava* caste in his ministry.[28] Caste lines are alleged to emerge in the present Cabinet when it considers projects which would create new government jobs, because of the fear that these new posts will be filled disproportionately by members of one caste. Ministers of the same caste as the Minister who is to have charge of the project frequently support the proposal, apparently expecting favouritism in employment to be shown to members of their caste. Similarly, Ministers of other castes may oppose the project because they fear that 'their people' will not receive adequate recognition in the distribution of jobs.[29]

Caste more openly influences bureaucratic assignments to posts exercising direct authority over the public. Popular reaction to low-caste persons in positions of authority over them apparently has not greatly changed in the hundred years since Emerson Tennent lamented: 'A reluctant conformity is exhibited on the part of high-caste persons placed officially under the orders of low-caste headmen; but their obedience is constrained, with no effort to conceal impatience . . .'[30] The low popular esteem of public servants of lower caste has seriously undermined their authority and imperilled the performance of their duties.[31] A colonial practice of tailoring certain appointments to local caste sentiments in the interest of tranquillity in administration is still evident. It is common knowledge in Ceylon that caste has been decisive in the appointment of headmen and teachers. Except for low-caste villages, headmen consistently were selected from among the high-caste landowners. Assignment of a low-caste schoolteacher to a predominantly high-caste village has commonly aroused the villagers to appeal to the local Member of Parliament to secure the teacher's transfer.

Widespread nepotism is not uncommon in Asia, where the family frequently holds the first loyalty of the individual and family welfare is accorded priority over such a shadowy concept

28 *Ceylon News,* 13.9.62.

29 This is based on the report of a well-informed and reliable informant, but by its nature cannot be confirmed.

30 E. Tennent, *Ceylon: An Account of the Island,* Vol. 2 (Third Edition, London, 1859), 157.

31 E.g. the plight of a low-caste Colonization Officer is described in B. H. Farmer, *Pioneer Peasant Colonization in Ceylon* (London, 1957), 303.

as the public interest. In contemporary Ceylon, family ties have retained considerable strength. The effects of family bonds are patently obvious in the private business practice of employing sons, brothers, cousins, and in-laws. In this environment, it is surprising that nepotism does not appear to be rampant in the bureaucracy. This may be explained by the persistence of strong colonial traditions of bureaucratic integrity and the wide acceptance of western values and attitudes among the senior Ceylonese public servants, resulting in less willingness to condone nepotism. Undoubtedly, however, individual public servants occasionally manage to give unsanctioned advantage to relatives.

Most of the charges of nepotism appearing in the nation's press relate to the semi-commerical government corporations, which are of recent origin and lack some of the formalism and integrity of the regular government departments. That nepotism does exist was revealed at a recent hearing conducted by the commissioners of the Salt Corporation. Among several examples of nepotism uncovered was the case of a typist who confessed that if her uncle had not been secretary of the Corporation she would neither have obtained nor been able to keep her position. The young lady was incensed at having been reprimanded during her employment for making errors in every line of letters she typed.[32]

The bureaucracy and the political environment

Rapid and profound political changes in Ceylon have had an impact of as yet uncertain magnitude on the Ceylonese bureaucracy. In the first decade after independence, resurgent Sinhalese nationalism, Buddhist discontents, and the language issue led to the political mobilisation of large sections of the formerly inert rural Sinhalese masses. The election of 1956 ended the political domination of the conservative, highly westernised, and affluent English-speaking elite and brought to power a political leadership more attuned to the aspirations of the Sinhalese villagers. The following years were turbulent. Communal violence flared, the governing coalition was plagued by instabil-

32 *Ceylon Observer*, 31.1.62.

ity, and in 1959 Prime Minister S. W. R. D. Bandaranaike was assassinated. After nearly a year of confusion and caretaker Governments, Bandaranaike's party, the Sri Lanka Freedom Party, scored an election victory and the nationalist and populist leadership headed by Bandaranaike's widow was confirmed in power, apparently with increased determination to effect fundamental social and economic reforms.[33]

Political interference in the public service, a common feature of Ceylonese public life at least since the Donoughmore Constitution of 1931–1947, appears to have increased considerably in recent years.[34] This rapid growth of interference seems closely related to the new political trends of the island. With the popular political awakening have come rising demands for and expectations of governmental action to alleviate social and economic discontents, particularly those of the rural villagers, who form eighty-five per cent of the island's population. The Ceylonese bureaucrat accustomed to the role of 'officer of the Crown' from the colonial era, has seemed little inclined to regard himself as a 'public servant' and has commonly been indifferent to the needs and convenience of the public. There is little notion within the bureaucracy that it exists to serve the society. Indeed, it is not improbable that a major portion of the public service believes that society exists primarily to support the bureaucracy. Poorly equipped by education, sophistication, or status to deal with the officers of the public service, the Ceylonese villagers have turned progressively to the politicians for assistance.

As a result of shifts in political power since 1956, the parliamentary candidate is no longer assured of election by the backing of the larger landowners and leading families in his constituency. He has become dependent for election on the support of the rural masses. Many politicians have concluded that this support can best be won by the performance of innumerable individual services for constituents, their families, or their villages. Thus, increasingly the villagers have sought political intercession with the bureaucracy and the politicians have

33 On political trends through the 1956 election, see Wriggins, *op. cit.* Recent political change is treated at length in R. N. Kearney, 'Ceylon: A Study in Political Change,' (unpublished Ph.D. dissertation, Department of Political Science, University of California, Los Angeles, 1963).

34 See *Report of the Salaries and Cadre Commission:* 1961, Part II, 101–2.

been receptive to these requests as a way of obtaining necessary electoral support. The result has been a striking shift in the role of the M.P. to that of an agent for his constituents in their dealings with the bureaucracy. M.P.s now accept as a matter of course that a constituent with a problem concerning the government will come first to his representative in Parliament. M.P.s are involved daily in such tasks as expediting pensions, securing rice ration books, arranging entrance into schools or hospitals, obtaining approval for the construction of village roads, and locating public employment for constituents.[35]

Political intervention is particularly prevalent in the transfer of government teachers. The M.P.'s aid is solicited to transfer from the village school a teacher who has run afoul of village opinion for personal, caste, or educational reasons. Teachers or their relatives ask M.P.s to intervene to halt impending transfers or secure transfers to desired schools. When a quorum cannot be found in Parliament, it is a standing joke that the majority of M.P.s are at the Education Department. In denouncing one instance of political interference in teacher transfers, an irate M.P. declared it to be 'disgraceful that the whole might and political power of the Government has been brought to bear on routine administrative transfers of the Department of Education.' The M.P. was enraged because other politicians had intervened to prevent transfers he had supported.[36] Service to local interests and responsiveness to constituents' desires were stressed in a defence of political intervention offered by one M.P.: 'We interfere in teachers transfers not to obtain any personal benefit but in the interest of the people in our areas.'[37]

The recent expansion of political interference is not, as has been said, simply a sign of degenerating public morals. While corruption and personal gain are not absent,[38] Basically this expansion represents the search for a new channel of popular

[35] These views of the changing role of the M.P. represent conclusions from lengthy conversations with several dozen M.P.s, confirmed by observation of contacts between M.P.s and their constituents in the lobby of the Parliament Building, government administrative offices, and the homes of M.P.s.

[36] *Ceylon News,* 10.1.63.

[37] *Ibid.,* 8.11.62.

[38] E.g. see *Reports of the Parliamentary Bribery Commission,* 1959–60 (Parliamentary Series No. 1, Fifth Parliament).

access to the bureaucracy. Political interference has grown in response to public demand.

The political changes which marked the election of 1956 created the conditions for a clash of interests between the upper levels of the bureaucracy and the new political leadership. The higher public servants are largely drawn from the affluent, urban, upper-middle class. Because of their westernisation and identification with the former colonial regime, they appeared, to many spokesmen for the growing Sinhalese nationalism to be an alienated group which had turned its back on traditional Sinhalese culture. The new political leaders won power with the support of the rural villagers, particularly members of the Sinhalese-educated rural lower-middle class.[39] The 'Sinhalese-only' official language issue which was instrumental in bringing the new leadership to power was a direct attack on the exclusiveness of the English-educated public servants, whose position and status depended on their command of the English language. The victorious politicians directed some appeals to the lower levels of the public service, but in their self-professed concern for the rural villagers and traditional culture there was little to attract the urban and westernised members of the upper levels of the bureaucracy. In addition, Government policies aimed at compensating for past disadvantages suffered by the Sinhalese and Buddhists alienated some of the numerous Tamil and Christian members of the public service.

Although conditions for a clash of interests seem to have existed since 1956, tensions between the higher public servants and the political leadership were not apparent until 1960, possibly because the entire country was preoccupied with the communal strife and political instability. After the elections of 1960, increasing evidence of tensions appeared.[40] Bureaucrats came

[39] See Wriggins, *op. cit.*, 326–69; Mendis, *Ceylon Today and Yesterday* 117–24.

[40] In addition to the indications noted below, see Hensman (ed.), *op cit.* An episode related in Parliament by one M.P. suggests an attitude toward the politicians which is not uncommon in the higher levels of the public service. When the M.P. demanded of a public servant the reason for a shortage of water buffaloes, he was told the shortage existed because 'the buffaloes are now in Parliament.' Ceylon House of Representatives, *Parl. Deb.*, vol. 48, 2738.

under attack by Government M.P.s for disloyalty to the Government and openly aiding the political opposition.[41] The 1960 election manifesto of the Government party threatened a thorough reorganisation of the public service.[42] A resolution at the party's 1961 annual conference urged the Prime Minister to eliminate 'sabotage' of the Government's programmes by the bureaucracy.[43] An article in a party publication claimed that the dismissal of all public servants who were disloyal to the Government was the most serious task facing the Government and asserted that 'our country can prosper only if we completely destroy the lazy, disloyal or corrupt public servant . . .'[44]

The response of the bureaucrats to the political interference in administration and mounting attacks by politicians has remained somewhat ambiguous. Many have attempted to placate the apparently hostile political environment and embrace the emergent nationalist and populist movement. Some have sought refuge in the glorification of the period of British colonial rule. A few of the most embittered have expressed regret over the failure of an attempted coup d'etat staged by a group of military and police officers in January 1962.[45] The most common reaction, however, has been what the Salaries and Cadre Commission called a 'general deterioration in the output and efficiency of the public service,' evident in 'absenteeism and unpunctuality, lack of interest, and indifference towards work.'[46] The present state of the public service led the Governor-General to speak in bewilderment of the decline in bureaucratic integrity and morale from colonial standards.[47]

41 *Ceylon Observer,* 5.11.61; Ceylon House of Representatives, *Parl. Deb.,* vol. 39, 375.

42 *Srī Lankā Nidahas Pakshayē Māthivarana Prakāsanaya:* 1960 [Sri Lanka Freedom Party's Election Manifesto: 1960] (Colombo, 1960), 18.

43 Resolutions Presented to the Sri Lanka Freedom Party Annual Conference on 2.12.61, at Ratnapura (mimeographed).

44 *Srī Lankā Nidahas Pakshaya Dasaväni Sānvathsarika Kalāpaya:* 1961 [Sri Lanka Freedom Party Tenth Anniversary Number: 1961], (Colombo, 1961), 174.

45 These varied reactions were encountered among public servants during 1961 and 1962. See also Hensman (ed.), *op. cit.;* and Abhayavardhana, *op. cit.,* 3–46.

46 *Report of the Salaries and Cadre Commission:* 1961, Part II, 100.

47 *Ceylon Observer,* 17.5.62.

Conclusion

Political animosity and interference appear to have damaged bureaucratic morale and impaired the effectiveness of the public service, although the depth of the effects is difficult to gauge. While lingering influences of caste, communal, or family loyalties have probably reduced the rationality and impartiality of the bureaucracy, adjustment to changing circumstances in the aftermath of independence has been the principal source of stress in the contemporary bureaucracy. Such adjustment has been made difficult because of the wide separation of the bureaucracy, at least at the higher levels, from the rest of the society.

Although traditional influences are observable in the bureaucracy, the extent to which public servants above the bottom levels adopted Western habits and the English language, discarding the outward manifestations of indigenous culture in the process, made the bureaucracy vulnerable to the force of growing nationalist and populist political currents. The official language issue, an attack against the exclusive hold on the bureaucracy of the English-educated, was both the first major manifestation of aroused Sinhalese nationalism and the first challenge to the privileged position of the westernised elite. The disproportionate representation within the bureaucracy of ethnic and religious minorities made the bureaucracy and the incumbent bureaucrats a natural target of the newly awakened demands for recognition of the Sinhalese majority. The isolation of the westernised bureaucratic elite was increased by the sharp horizontal cleavages within the bureaucratic hierarchy.

The exclusive and elitist tendencies of the bureaucracy have roots in traditional society and the colonial era. Traditional concepts of status and privilege combined with colonial notions of an elite possessing a superior wisdom to open a wide gulf between the higher bureaucrats and the masses of their countrymen. The necessity for a knowledge of English for public employment served to reinforce the idea of exclusiveness, and westernisation in language and manner of living became a symbol of elite status. It has been this exclusiveness and alienation which has, at least for the present, made difficult the adjustment of the Ceylonese bureaucracy to the political trends arising after independence.

Section 4

Toward a Conceptual Approach in Comparative Administration

How Bureaucracies Develop and Function

Arnold Brecht
New School for Social Research

Is it necessary to define bureaucracy? Everybody seems to know what the term implies. "Bureaucracy is a state of affairs where too much power is in the hands of appointed employees." This is twice ambiguous, however, because power has several meanings, and what type or amount of it is "too much?" Closer analysis will spare us a great deal of confusion.

Power may designate the constitutional or legal right to give or to enforce orders, as when the Constitution says, "The Congress shall have power to lay and collect taxes." For this sort of power I shall use the symbol P hereafter. Or power may mean the actual power to get things done or to prevent their being done. This will be designated by the symbol Π, the Greek equivalent of P.

"P-powers" and "Π-powers" may coincide, or overlap, or be entirely separate. The Supreme Soviet of the USSR has the P-power to pass laws, but not the Π-power to determine what laws will be passed; that power lies entirely with the party leadership. The same situation existed with Hitler's one-party Reichstag in Germany. The United States Congress had the P-power, together

Reprinted from *The Annals of the American Academy of Political Science,* Vol. 292 (March, 1954), pp. 1–10, by permission.

with the legislatures of three-fourths of the states, to forbid the manufacture and sale of alcoholic beverages, but not the Π-power to carry the prohibition through. The people in a democracy have the P-power to elect their representatives, but bosses may have the Π-power to "deliver the vote." Likewise, party juntas, pressure groups, or the press may, or may not, have the Π-power to make Congress use its P-powers in some specific manner.

Definitions of bureaucracy

Applying these distinctions, we find that appointed employees may wield either P-powers or Π-powers, or both, and that their powers may extend either to the entire sphere of public business or only to sections of it. It follows that we must distinguish at least four possible definitions, or types, of bureaucracy, namely:

B–1, where appointed employees hold all the P-powers of government;

B–2, where they hold some P-powers, though not all;

B–3, where they wield Π-powers over the entire sphere of government;

B–4, where they do so only over some sections of governmental activities.

In each of these four social patterns we may speak of "government by officials," and therefore of a bureaucracy, irrespective of the good or bad use made by the officials of their powers. We may, however, use the term bureaucracy also in a more limited sense, namely:

B–5 to B–8, only in such cases of the types B–1 to B–4 where the powers are exercised "improperly."

Yet what is an "improper" use? Are officials acting improperly (*a*) only when in excess of legal powers; or (*b*) also when, though staying within these powers, they act in conflict with the general welfare; or (*c*) even when their action is both legitimate and objectively sound, if it antagonizes the momentary desires of the people, or of some people, or of the people's representatives? Different answers are possible in different situations.

In view of the elusive vagueness of the criterion "improper" it is advisable to start out from the definitions B–1 to B–4. They are not only clearer; they are also realistic and in line with related concepts. For wherever human beings have power, they may abuse it. A dictatorship or an aristocracy remains one even when its powers are used benevolently in the interest of the people. Likewise, we can logically say, a government by appointed officials remains a bureaucracy even when it operates benevolently.

Actually, wherever we live in the modern world, whether under the most totalitarian kind of despotism or in the most liberal of democracies, we are being governed to a considerable, though varied, extent by appointed officials—officials who exercise both P- and Π-powers over us. Everywhere, then, we live under a bureaucracy of some kind. This we must realize at the outset.

P-BUREAUCRACIES

Bureaucracies of the B–1 type are obsolete today, it is true, at least in the public sphere. They were rare phenomena even in the past (see below). If one considers the cardinals of the Roman Catholic Church as appointed officials—since they are not elected by the people but appointed by the Pontiff—then it might be said that the hierarchy of the Catholic Church still today approximates the B–1 type of a bureaucracy, because the college of the appointed cardinals has the official P-power within the church not only to make governmental decisions but also to select the Pope, who in turn selects them. This rather extraneous example we may disregard here.

The B–2 type of bureaucracy, on the other hand, is found everywhere, because everywhere, at least in all major countries, appointed officials are granted extensive P-powers. Sometimes they are authorized to use their powers independently, as in law courts, or in administrative courts, or in quasi-independent boards and commissions. A voluminous body of law, frequently (though rather incorrectly) called "administrative law,"[1] originates in the P-powers of appointed employees. Sometimes their lawmaking P-powers extend even to reguar legislation, as they did for example in the Federal Council (*Reichsrat*) of the German Empire and of the Weimar Republic, where as a rule appointed civil servants represented the constituent states and, while bound by instructions, were permitted to act according to their own judgment in the absence of instructions.

But we need not refer to such particular cases only. Any delegation, by the legislature or by the chief executive, of P-powers to department heads, and through them or directly to their deputies, division chiefs, bureau chiefs, or field services, provides appointed employees with P-powers which are often of considerable importance. On the basis of P-powers delegated to them directors of internal revenue and their employees make decisions on tax returns, policemen interfere with disorderly conduct, consular officers grant or deny immigration visas—and so in almost every branch of public administration. While the employees are not independent in the use of these powers, but subject to instructions and to corrections after appeal, there is generally a wide margin of power left to their individual judgment and discretion. Appeals affect only a small minority of decisions and rarely question the fact that the subordinate official had the P-power to make the primary decision.

As it is considered one of the first virtues of a good administrator that he makes wide use of delegation of P-powers in order that he himself may be able to concentrate on the most important problems, well-administered countries offer at least as good illustrations of bureaucracies of the B–2 type as do countries with political leaders who jealously try to keep all decisions in their own hands.

[1] This term is better reserved for law whose subject matter is administration, irrespective of its source, i.e. the law *for* administration, not the law *by* administrators.

Π-BUREAUCRACIES

Just as in the case of P-powers, there is nothing necessarily wrong with the wielding of Π-powers by appointed employees. It is, to a considerable degree, their very function to exercise such powers. Employees are hired for the purpose of influencing both the making and the execution of laws by their expert knowledge and practical experience, won in or out of office. Their knowledge, their good judgment, prudence, and poise, are intentionally placed at the service of the government. When in the exercise of their official functions they try to make knowledge prevail over ignorance, the expert over the amateur, prudence over indiscretion, poise over imbalance, they are basically within their legitimate rights and may use them so as to deserve praise rather than blame. If the appointed employees failed to exercise such influence, a great deal of every country's legislation and an even bigger slice of its administration would only be the worse for it.

And yet, Π-powers contribute to the improper bureaucratic character of governments no less than do P-powers. More than a hundred years ago a critic of the British colonial administration wrote a classical description of how this happens. He charged that what the colonies far away received with awe as the decisions of the mother country on their complaints actually were decisions made by an anonymous official, satirically called Mr. Mothercountry. Although this story is well known to students of government because of Lowell's reference to it in his *Government of England,* I may be permitted to point out some details because they are still valid today as a competent analysis of thousands of similar situations. Mr. Mothercountry, so Charles Butler wrote in 1840,

> is familiar with every detail of his business and handles with unfaltering hands the piles of papers at which his superiors quail. He knows the policy which previous actions render necessary, but he never appears to dictate. A new Secretary . . . intends to be independent, but something turns up that obliges him to consult Mr. Mothercountry. He is pleased with the ready and unobtrusive

advice which takes a great deal of trouble off his hands. If things go well, his confidence in Mr. Mothercountry rises. If badly, that official alone can get him out of the colonial or parliamentary scrape; and the more independent he is the more scrapes he falls into.[2]

Every word in this description is significant and to the point. It is a *legitimate* right, even a duty, of the employee that is exercised when he uses his Π-power as adviser; it is exercised unobtrusively and without the will to dictate; it may be exercised well in most cases. And still, we have here a situation where the Π-power of an official has grown to such proportions that the stage of bureaucracy as an objectionable form of government is reached.

Naturally, Π-powers are not always used legitimately and in good faith for the general welfare. They are at times abused for selfish purposes, as when the officials of Russia's Peter the Great, or of Prussia's Frederick the Great, blocked the execution of laws that were in conflict with the interests of the class from which they hailed, or when modern civil servants have tried to influence the contents of civil service acts, the regulation of salaries, and the like in their own favor.[3] Yet these are exceptions rather than the rule. The situation most typical for modern democracies is one where the officials act in good faith and within the powers that they legitimately hold.

Historical extremes

The most familiar illustrations of strong bureaucracies are ancient Egypt, the later stages of the Roman Empire, and China.

[2] Charles Butler, *Responsible Government for Colonies,* London, 1840. See A. Lawrence Lowell, *The Government of England,* 2d ed. (New York, 1912), Vol. 1, p. 178.

[3] For illustrations see my article "Bureaucratic Sabotage," *The Annals of The American Academy of Political and Social Science,* Vol. 189, January 1937 (pressure against the heavy cuts in salaries in Germany in 1930, in Great Britain in 1931, in France in 1934, and somewhat less in the United States in 1933; pressure for increases in Germany and France in the late twenties); and my paper, "Personnel Management," in E. H. Litchfield and associates, *Governing Postwar Germany* (Ithaca, N. Y., 1953), p. 278 (pressure in favor of a conservative civil service act).

It was characteristic of all three that, at least outside of the respective capitals, the P-powers of appointed officials came to approximate B–1 proportions, that is, to encompass almost the entire governmental power within their administrative districts; and, secondly, that the use of their powers was not subject to any outside check based on freedom of speech, on a free press, on independent courts, or on parliamentary control. The only check was that exercised from the inside by superiors, or as we should say "through channels." The limited human "span of control" made it impossible for the despotic rulers themselves, even when they had the best of will, personally to control the use of the P-powers they had delegated to their field officials, such as *praefecti, vicarii, rectores,* and *curiales* in the Roman Empire. Sometimes they sent a second bureaucracy of secret agents to supervise the regular officials and to inform the emperor of their misdeeds, and a third one to supervise the second. When local officials tried to quit, because of the squeeze in which they found themselves between popular discontent and pressure from above, they were forced to stay, and their offices were even made hereditary. It has been said that people within the Roman Empire were better off under bad and selfish rulers who thought only of their personal pleasures than under well-intentioned emperors with a passion for good administration, because it was the latter who extended and intensified the centralized public administration to fantastic proportions according to uniform patterns imposed on the most divergent sections of the Empire.

SLAVE BUREAUCRACIES. Less well known, but no less extreme, is the historical illustration offered by slave bureaucracies which in the early Middle Ages arose in the southwestern parts of Asia under the Abbasides, the Samanids and the Ayubites (Saladin), in Egypt under the Mamelukes, and later in Turkey under the Ottoman Empire. Veritable slaves held great bureaucratic powers under all these regimes. The Samanids were finally overthrown by one of their slave administrators (about A.D. 1000), who took over, and whose successors, or imitators, later ruled as "slave kings" from Delhi in the thirteenth century, establishing a bureaucracy of the B–1 type. The Mamelukes, too, though originally slave administrators of the Ayubites—their very name being derived from a word meaning property—became actual rulers of Egypt under a nominal, faraway caliph. Hence they also can be said to have established a full-fledged B–1 bureaucracy. The governing positions were passed on, not from father to son but from slave to slave.[4] Closer to our time is the slave bureaucracy of the Ottoman Empire, as it was run from about A.D. 1400 to 1800 by the Osmanlis, whose ancestors had been nomads invading from the Asian steppes. The Osmanli padishahs, as Toynbee aptly puts it in his graphic description of the regime, "maintained their empire by training slaves as human auxiliaries to assist them in keeping order among their 'human cattle.' "[5]

THE PRUSSO-GERMAN BUREAUCRACY. The Prusso-German bureaucracy, which arose after the end of the feudal age to become hardly less proverbial than that of the Roman Empire, had a very different character. Although the P-powers of a Prussian *Landrat* (county executive), *Regierungspräsident* (district president), or *Oberpräsident* (provincial president) were likewise very strong, the use of these powers was not left unchecked from the outside, as it had been in the Roman Empire and in the slave bureaucracies. It was progressively subjected to public criticism by the free use of speech and of the press, to the review of the legitimacy of decisions by regular or administrative courts, and finally to parliamentary criticism as well. These outside controls facilitated a proper control from the inside, because the Prussian king did not have to rely only on complaints forwarded to him through official channels. But there was no guarantee that the king would respond to popular demands. The P-powers of the officials were thus enhanced by the authoritarian character of the regime. In addition to their P-powers, the Prusso-German officials wielded also very substantial Π-powers,

4 Arnold Toynbee, *A Study of History* (London, 1934), Vol. 3, pp. 22 ff.

5 *Loc. cit.* Toynbee's description of the Osmanlis relies primarily on A. H. Lybyer, *The Government of the Ottoman Empire in the Time of Suleiman the Magnificent,* Cambridge, Mass., 1913.

as illustrated by the influence the *Geheimrat* Friedrich August von Holstein, of the German Foreign Office around 1900, exercised in the rejection of British feelers in favor of an understanding. But this was, as the story of Mr. Mothercountry shows, in principle no peculiarity of the German bureaucracy.

Soviet Bureaucracy. The most formidable phenomenon of bureaucratic rule today is the Soviet Union, where three bureaucracies exert themselves side by side: one under the regular departments of the government; the second, the secret police, under the Minister of the Interior; and the third, the party bureaucracy, under the party leadership. The second and third control the first, but all three are controlled from the inside only, just as in the Roman Empire, without the outside help of freedom of speech, of freedom of the press, of independent courts, and of freely elected and freely operating parliaments. The size of these bureaucracies outdoes that of any previously known in history. This is chiefly due to the fact that all industrial activities within the Soviet Union are being operated by governmental officials or government corporations. With more than fifty federal ministries the problem of co-ordination must have assumed inconceivable proportions. It is almost a miracle that this threefold bureaucracy has not yet collapsed under its own weight. But that it is cracking under the bureaucratic stress is not an unreasonable thought. Once the records of this totalitarian enterprise are thrown open to an independent examination, we may learn unparalleled stories about bureaucracies of both the B–2 and B–4 types.

The use of appointed officials in the Soviet Union surpasses even that under the Hitler regime in Germany. There the number of government employees and other government workers on all levels soared to over four and one-half million, or about one out of twenty of the population, not counting the party bureaucracy.[6] But the economic sector, though closely controlled, was primarily left to private ownership and administration.

6 Figures of 1942; see my *The German Civil Service Today,* Office of the U.S. High Commissioner for Germany, 1950 (mimeographed). They include no soldiers.

Are there no countries without bureaucracies?

Bureaucracy was at its minimum in the feudal world of the Middle Ages. Countries were then governed through what may be called "feudal channels" rather than through large centralized bureaucracies. The rights of the overlords—such as the emperor of the Holy Roman Empire or the kings of England and France—and the duties of their vassals (the barons and the territorial princes) and of the latter's subvassals were strictly limited. The vassals and subvassals took care of the public interests—in the major Germanic principalities even of judicial matters—within their respective fiefs. Consequently, the emperor and the English and French kings had only relatively small bodies of public employees under them.

It has, therefore, sometimes been said that the feudal world was free from bureaucracy, as, for example, Max Weber has contended regarding the Holy Roman Empire.[7] But this is not entirely correct. In Ranke's history of the Reformation we are told that in the fifteenth century the German princes, nominal vassals of the emperor, repeatedly remonstrated to their overlord, Frederick III (1440–1493, great-grandfather of Charles V), against the influence he allowed his counselor, a man by the name of Prüschenk, to wield. The Emperor answered that he supposed "each of them also had his own Prüschenk at home" (*ein jeder von ihnen werde auch seinen Prüschenk zu Hause haben*).[8] Indeed, bureaucracies of both the B–2 and B–4 types may flourish within the smallest body of public employees. One single clerk may make a bureaucracy out of a government.

This is shown also by the postfeudal British administration, which until late into the nineteenth century remained one of

[7] See Max Weber, "Wirtschaft und Gesellschaft" in *Grundriss der Sozialökonomik,* 2nd ed., Vol. 3 (Tübingen, 1925), chapter on "Bureaukratie," pp. 650 ff., one of the pioneer studies on bureaucracy in the entire international literature.

[8] Leopold von Ranke, *Deutsche Geschichte im Zeitalter der Reformation* (Munich and Leipzig, 1914), Vol. 1, p. 95.

amateurs aided by clerks, especially on the county level. Such a government might appear a nonbureaucratic paradise. Yet actually every clerk became a sort of Prüschenk, whose bureaucratic power of influencing the decisions of the gentleman-administrator was considerable, and was felt by the public to be so. As always, this was not entirely unfavorable, since it served to maintain consistency in procedure and policy and to avoid whimsical, cadi-like decisions.

Even more effective than England in avoiding bureaucracy was the United States up to the Civil War, because of the deep-seated aversion against any type of government, whether bureaucratic or unbureaucratic, which has been so singularly characteristic of this country's history. The ensuing tendency to deal with matters of common concern through voluntary *ad hoc* associations rather than by setting up governmental agencies is one of the most effective antibureaucratic devices ever invented. Yet it has been actually a dispersion rather than an elimination of bureaucracy, since the individual associations often got their own, male or female, Prüschenks, who did gradually come to hold the reins tight in their secretarial hands. At any rate, to implement community undertakings in the old style has proved impossible under modern conditions. Thus the number of government employees has grown constantly. The absence of parliamentary control over them under the American system of separation of powers stirred Woodrow Wilson in the 1880's to write his *Congressional Government,* in which he suggested such control, without any tangible success. There were some hundred thousand federal employees then. There now are twenty to thirty times more, and with their numbers grew their powers, both P and Π.

Multipliers of bureaucracy

We have seen that it does not require many employees to produce a bureaucracy. A single clerk who serves an amateurish administrator may well gather considerable powers. But bigness surely has a multiplying effect. There is, first, the arithmetic impact of numbers; secondly, the increasing difficulty of reaching the head of the department owing to the jam in the bottleneck that leads up to him; and thirdly, the growing number of conflicts, both positive and negative, among officials whose numbers grow. As one European cabinet minister joked, a departmental headquarters that contains a thousand employees needs no outside world to be busy; they can keep busy all alone in intra-agency quarrels.[9]

REGULATIONS. But the most pernicious effect of sheer bigness is the increasing need for *regulations*. The mere number of employees makes it necessary for the responsible chief to resort to written regulations, which are intended to assure equality of treatment. Designed to make provision for all possible cases, they often fit none perfectly. For simple and clear situations they are too complicated because of their insistence on details that are obviously irrelevant; in the unusual case they rarely meet the situation accurately.

Regulations crush initiative and engender red tape, the ubiquitous disease of all big bureaucracies. They tend to transform all living, spirited, and flexible human impulse at the top into formal, dull, inflexible paper work at the bottom, and by this transfiguration may substantially impair the original plans.[10] The gravest shortcoming of "administration through regulations" is that, once established, regulations are hard to change. Therefore, they often remain in force long after they reach the peak of their usefulness, even though they may have become clearly inadequate and out of date.[11] The bigger the administration the greater the difficulty of getting regulations changed. If several departments have agreed on them and conse-

[9] Repeated from the article "Bureaucratic Sabotage," *supra* note 3.

[10] This implication often makes red tape appear as a kind of bureaucratic "sabotage" of good legislative intentions; but the sabotage is, as a rule, unwitting. See *ibid.*

[11] The famous directive JCS 1067, regarding the attitude expected of the occupation forces in Germany, presents an almost classical illustration on the highest level. Issued by the Joint Chiefs of Staff in agreement with the Department of State in April 1945, it was soon hopelessly out of date and definitely harmful to the execution of our changing policy; but it was not replaced until July 1947. See Litchfield and Associates, *op. cit.* note 3, p. 7, for details.

quently have to consent to the change, the difficulties can become unsurmountable in controversial matters, even those of little importance—yes, particularly in minor matters, because department heads cannot give their valuable time to little things, and much time is required merely to understand the issues. If the President himself approved the old regulations, how can he be incommoded with questions of minor changes on which the department heads fail to agree?

POOR ORGANIZATION. Poor organization stands out as another multiplying factor of bureaucratic defects, second in importance only to bigness. It increases the number and intensity of log jams. It fails to provide for co-ordination within bureaus or divisions, or between them, or between departments.[12] These defects may be made worse through overdepartmentalization. In addition, absence of regional co-ordination may unduly increase the number of matters that must be referred to headquarters.[13]

OTHER FACTORS. These two, bigness and poor organization, are the most general multipliers of bureaucratic defects today. Other multiplying factors, quite different in nature, are fortunately no longer so generally present. Where public employees enjoy particular privileges and prestige and where their enhanced position is associated with an authoritarian spirit, the bureaucratic character of the powers wielded by them will be the more marked. When, in addition, they are recruited exclusively from one class and when their *esprit de corps* welds them together into a kind of caste, then bureaucracy may stare everyone in the face. Such factors have played a considerable role in countries other than the United States, as they did for example in old Prussia, with many residues still perceptible in Weimar Germany, and some even today in the Bonn Republic.[14] How-

12 See my article "Smaller Departments" in *Public Administration Review*, Vol. 1 (1941), pp. 363–73, and the ensuing correspondence with Paul Appleby, *ibid.*, Vol. 2 (1942), pp. 61–66.

13 See the report of the Special Committee on Comparative Administration (organized under the Social Science Research Council) on *Regional Coordination*, 1943 (mimeographed).

14 See my chapter on "Personnel Management" in Litchfield and associates, *op. cit.* note 3, p. 263.

ever, it would be wrong to look only to such features in the search for bureaucracies. Bigness and poor organization operate as multipliers of bureaucratic shortcomings quite independent of authoritarian and caste factors.

American freedom no escape from bureaucracy

Bureaucracy, then, is not the same everywhere in every respect. There is a particular Prusso-German way of being bureaucratic, a particular English, French, or Soviet way; yet there is also a peculiar American way. Different as the American brand is from all others, it is bureaucracy all right, of proportions not to be belittled, with both bigness and imperfect organization operating as powerful multipliers.

Many Americans seem to be satisfied that the differences between the United States public service and that of countries with an older bureaucratic record are acting as a counterweight against any kind of bureaucratic pull. Such antibureaucratic factors are seen in (1) the absence of a rigid scheme of organization, especially at departmental headquarters; (2) the absence of a static career officialdom, at least in services other than the foreign service, the armed forces, and the police; (3) the practice of a thorough change in the leading personnel after a change of the party in power; (4) the continual high turnover of public employees on all levels.

Closer analysis reveals, however, that this greater "looseness," flexibility, and freedom of American administration is highly paid for by a number of bureaucratic evils that are peculiar to the American scene.

When after every change of the party in power all the top officials within a big administration are replaced, that does not necessarily produce an unbureaucratic type of government. The first result obviously is the lack of up-to-date departmental knowledge and experience at the top. Departments where all top officials have recently been replaced are like men without a memory. The new officials must either start anew from scratch or rely on subordinates to a far higher extent than old-timers had need to. This implies that it is now the departmental officials in the middle and lower brackets who gain a considerable influence (Π-power) in briefing their new superiors. Such lowering of the level in the bureaucratic reservoir is not altogether wholesome. There is likely to be more bureaucratic narrowness on the lower level than there was on the higher, and the memory of officials on the lower level is restricted to what has come to their knowledge. Public-minded citizens who had established fruitful relations with top officials have to begin anew. Whatever they did before, if still in the preparatory stage, is lost labor; the new man knows neither them nor the arguments and outcome of previous discussions. This is regrettable even when only one of the top officials has had to be replaced; where all have been, it implies a great deal of waste.

The one departmental memory that keeps going through all changes is that embodied in regulations—until they, too, are altered. Lack of a homogeneous civil service body and rapid turnover in personnel compel the American public administration to rely on written regulations rather extensively, more than countries with a less fluctuating personnel. Loose over-all organization makes co-ordination and control more difficult and tends to lead to overstaffing. It also hinders the ready change of defective and outmoded regulations. For all these and some other reasons poor organization, while looking pleasantly unbureaucratic, is likely to be a potent source of bureaucratic defects all over the field. As a result, no other western nation is so much in danger of seeing its public administration ruled by overdetailed, inadequate, and outmoded regulations as is the United States.

There is little to attract brilliant young men and women into services ruled by such regulations, and where the most attractive positions, that is, all those that permit the display of individual initiative, are exempt from the civil service and given to outsiders.

Remedies

The dream that one could have a public service in modern countries without a bureaucracy of the B–2 and B–4 types should be abandoned. We cannot improve the world by pursuing pipe dreams. Bureaucracy is here to stay. It may not be precisely endemic in human nature as such, but it certainly is so in large numbers of employees bound by detailed regulations. The problem is not how to govern without a bureaucracy but how to minimize its defects under democratic control.

As bigness is the number one multiplier of bureaucratic shortcomings great ingenuity should be employed to keep the number of public employees as small as possible. Restraint in the assumption of large-scale governmental functions and economical organization of all those services that must be run by the government are, therefore, the first postulates of an antibureaucratic campaign. Because of the multiplying effect of bigness it is also generally better to have several small bureaucracies than one big one. Dispersion of administrative functions among various units—such as states, municipalities, special authorities, government corporations, and private organizations—is, therefore, often healthier than centralization in one giant administrative machinery, provided that there is a clear distribution of functions and provided, further, that the dispersion does not lead to an increase in numbers. The American tradition of action through private associations rather than through government should not be allowed to die; it should be fostered wherever it can alleviate the burden of government and reduce its machinery. We should even take a new look at the use of trade associations for self-administration in appropriate areas under the ultimate control of democratic government.

But public administration in large countries will never again be reduced to proportions so small that the number of employees ceases to be a source of bureaucratic shortcomings. Next in importance, therefore, as a remedy for unnecessary bureaucracy is an organization so devised that it is able to control the bureaucrats and still to avoid the dangers of government by overdetailed, inadequate, or outmoded regulations. It follows that the best remedy for bureaucratic shortcomings in large administrations is not inefficiency, as the American myth has it, but efficiency; not poor organization but good organization, especially at the top, so that advisable changes can be brought about promptly. Efficiency in a democracy must include responsiveness, of course. But no big administration can be responsive unless it is efficiently organized and run.[15]

When we are annoyed by excessive bureaucracy the fault lies generally not with the employees but with the men at the top, who fail to give directives in clear and definite language or, worse, are not certain of what they themselves want the officials to do. If they know what they want and are able to issue clear instructions, they can generally make the appointed employees work satisfactorily, without undue bureaucratic shortcomings. Cases of conscious sabotage are very rare and can, as a rule, easily be taken care of where they occur. In particular, it is not the fault of the mass of employees but of their superiors if general regulations contain too many details or are impracticable or out of date, and if such faulty regulations cannot be changed readily.

Initiative, responsiveness, and friendly human relations should be cultivated on all levels of the public service by all suitable means.

Bureaucracies: Some Contrasts in Systems

WALLACE S. SAYRE
Columbia University

IN WESTERN POLITICAL systems there appear to be two important types of myths about bureaucracy. The first of these casts bureaucracy in the role of villain. Thus Harold Laski, writing thirty years ago on *bureaucracy* for the *Encyclopaedia of*

---

[15] For the postal service to be responsive means first of all to deliver mail promptly and frequently at low cost. This cannot be done unless the entire postal service is efficiently organized and operated. So it is with all services.

This essay is based upon two public lectures delivered on February 1 and 2, 1962, by the author at the Indian Institute of Public Administration, New Delhi, while he was a visiting Professor at that institution. Reprinted from *The Indian Journal of Public Administration,* Vol. 10, No. 2 (April-June, 1964), pp. 219–229, by permission.

the Social Sciences, describes bureaucracy as representing a passion for the routine in administration, the sacrifice of flexibility to rule, delay in the making of decisions, and a refusal to embark upon experiment. Laski saw bureaucracy as a threat to democratic government. His argument ran briefly as follows: the scale of modern government makes administration by experts inescapable, yet the power of these experts as bureaucrats is not easily controlled by democratic institutions. The bureaucracies continuously push the boundaries of their power, Laski asserts, while control over them becomes increasingly difficult and costly. Describing the problem in terms of the British parliamentary system, he says control takes the following form: (1) the legislature can only reject or accept the proposals of ministers, (2) the ministers are in turn dependent upon their bureaucracies, and (3) the bureaucrats urge the ministers toward caution, toward minimizing innovation. The net influences, then, are in the direction of reliance on precedent, of continuity, and of minimum risk or change. More recently Von Mises, too, in his book called *Bureaucracy,* has argued that bureaucracy cannot be efficient, primarily because the profit-and-loss criterion is absent from the work of governmental bureaucracies.

A second type of myth casts bureaucracy in the role of hero. Max Weber is perhaps the outstanding proponent of this view. Weber argues that bureaucracy is capable of attaining the highest degree of efficiency and the most rational form of administration. This is so, he believes, because it represents the exercise of control through knowledge. He presents an "ideal type" of bureaucracy in which activities are distributed in a fixed way, authority to command is distributed in a stable manner and is delimited by rules, the hierarchy of authority is monocratic, management is based on written documents, and membership in the bureaucracy is a vocation. In these terms bureaucracy is made virtually synonymous with rationality and objectivity in the administration of large-scale organizations.

We may describe these broad characterizations of bureaucracy as myths because they are persuasive mixtures of both fact and invention. As such they explain both too much and too little. A more modest version might simply assert that bureaucracy is necessarily neither villain nor hero, but rather a phenomenon found in all large-scale, complex organizations. This phenomenon has certain major characteristics: (1) specialization of tasks for the members of the organization, (2) a hierarchy of formal authority, (3) a body of rules, (4) a system of records, and (5) personnel with specialized skills and roles. In this view bureaucracy is a system for the administration of scale and complexity in human efforts to develop and accomplish purposes not otherwise attainable. In serving these purposes bureaucracy has both merits and liabilities. But we may assume that, within broad limits, these merits or liabilities are the result of choices made in constructing the bureaucratic system in a particular time and place. For bureaucracies are not all constructed in the same mould. Instead they vary greatly, one from the other, and they vary also over time. The American bureaucracies differ significantly from the British, and the British from the European, while presumably each of these Western bureaucracies differs importantly from the Eastern ones, which in turn must differ greatly from each other. And "new" bureaucracies apparently differ in many ways from "mature" bureaucracies.

It is with the choices about the forms and methods of bureaucracy that this essay will be concerned, not with the probably unanswerable and somewhat metaphysical question of whether bureaucracy is villain or hero. It will be assumed that it may, in some periods and some places, be either or a mixture of both. And the discussion will focus upon three specific questions about bureaucracies:

1. How are the bureaucrats to be chosen?
2. What is the role of bureaucrats in decision-making?
3. How are the bureaucrats to be governed?

II

How are bureaucrats—especially the higher-ranking bureaucrats—to be chosen? The full answer to this question involves several important choices in public policy, choices which have major consequences for the nature and behaviour of the bureaucracy which will be developed. That is, the ways in which the bureaucrats are selected from among the population will influence their representativeness, their skills and capacities, their responsiveness to democratic controls, and their attitudes toward change in public policy and in managerial methods. These influences are especially consequent in the case of the choices of those who are to hold the higher posts in the bureaucracy, for these higher bureaucrats usually set the tone and tempo of the whole bureaucracy.

The choices involved in the question of how the bureaucrats are to be selected may be concretely illustrated by describing the choices made in the building of the United States Civil Services, with some contrasts offered by the British system. The first choice may be described as *open* versus *closed* recruitment. The American option is for open recruitment; that is, to recruit from among all the talents available in the national labour market.[1] The British option, by contrast, is to recruit directly from the schools and universities, at the school-leaving or graduating age. The selection of those bureaucrats who are to hold the posts of higher responsibility in the bureaucracy presents an especially sharp contrast: in the American system these persons may be, and often are, recruited from outside the ranks of the bureaucracy at mid-career, or even later, stages. The American system has no counterpart of the British Administrative Class; the posts of the higher bureaucracy in the United States are filled by a wider system of recruitment that draws upon the talents available in the national pool of talent. These briefly described alternatives in deciding how the bureaucrats are to be chosen serve to illustrate that a deliberate and consequential choice can be made in determining the kind of bureaucracy a government wishes to have.

A second kind of choice can be made about the way in which bureaucrats are to be chosen. That choice is between the American preference for "programme staffing" and the British preference for "career staffing." The American practice is to

[1] The term "labour market" may require some explanation. The American labour market is somewhat distinctive. Career mobility is among its strong characteristics. Thus it is possible to recruit for the civil service experienced, highly trained, and successful persons from the general labour market, even though such persons are already well advanced in non–civil service careers. Other national labour markets may be less flexible in their response to such recruiting efforts.

recruit for particular programmes of the government, and secondarily for careers in the government generally. In the United States a new programme of the government usually means also a new agency and a new staff—a response often explained by asserting that "new ideas" require "new blood." The Tennessee Valley Authority may serve as an example. When the TVA was established in the 1930's it was not staffed from the ranks of the national civil service; instead, it was staffed primarily by newly-recruited experts from the professions and other relevant occupations in the national labour market. Two tests were paramount in the selection process: that the person recruited should have the knowledge and skills needed by the TVA, and that he should have a positive commitment to the objectives of the TVA. Thus programme-commitment, not neutrality, was deliberately sought in the recruitment process. More recent examples—the Atomic Energy Commission, the foreign aid and information agencies, the space agency—serve to support the TVA pattern as a major tendency in the American preference for programme-staffing.

These two choices in recruitment patterns are closely related to a third choice: whether one of the criteria of selection shall emphasize general capacity or specialized capacity. The British pattern is to select the junior members of the administrative class on the basis of their general knowledge and intelligence, demonstrated in examinations that test their mastery of a liberal-arts university education. These juniors are chosen at a young and plastic age; their training for advancement is provided by a variety of experiences within the bureaucracy, an experience pattern which continues to stress generalist capacities—a kind of amateur versatility within the frame of the bureaucratic tradition. The American pattern is a striking contrast. Although a growing number (but perhaps not an increasing proportion) of the bureaucrats are recruited by general examinations not very different from the British, the stronger preference is for specialized personnel often recruited after substantial experience has been acquired outside the bureaucracy. An example is provided by the recent history of the U.S. Foreign Service. In the 1920's the British model was in a general sense adopted as the recruitment method. World War II brought severe tests to this system, and it was in fact drastically modified by the creation of new agencies staffed by specialists. The Foreign

Service Act of 1946 was an attempt to restore the generalist pattern of the inter-war years, but the restored system turned out to be not viable. By the mid-1950's it was necessary to reorganize the foreign service personnel system drastically. A massive transfusion of "new blood" was accomplished by transferring into the foreign service corps practically all the specialized and professional personnel of the State Department, so that the U.S. Foreign Service again reflects the deep-seated American preference for the highly-trained and experienced specialist rather than for the generalist.

Yet a fourth choice also confronts the framers of bureaucracies: Shall the interchange of personnel between governmental careers and non-governmental careers be minimized or maximized? The British choice is to minimize the cross-flow of careers between the public and private sectors of employment. The American choice is to maximize the interchange, especially among members of the professions and among business executives and specialists. There are few high-ranking bureaucrats in the U.S. Civil Service who have not in their lifetime been both a bureaucrat and a non-bureaucrat. Exposure to the tests of success in a professional career or in some other private endeavour is more often than not one of the decisive standards in the recruitment of the higher civil service. These exchanges of personnel between public and private careers are not systematically organized, and are not always consciously sought by the personnel systems, but they are nonetheless one of the durable and prominent characteristics of the American bureaucracy.

These sets of choices, it will be apparent, are closely interrelated, in high degree interdependent. It will be apparent, too, that both Britain and the United States have made choices that give each of them a consistent series of choices; each of the two patterns is internally coherent. In a very real sense, also, the British set of choices arises out of the structure of British society, as does the American pattern out of its society. That is to say, each system of choices is indigenous. It is, therefore, doubtful that either is a neat package ready for export to other societies. The two systems of choices are accordingly less a problem in deciding which represents a preferable ideal than a demonstration that these persistent questions about the bureaucracy (Who are to be the bureaucrats? How are the bureaucrats to be chosen?) must be answered for each country in the context of its own society. The British answers, it may be hazarded, produce a more orderly and symmetrical, a more prudent, a more articulate, a more cohesive and more powerful bureaucracy; the American choices, it may be further hazarded, produce a more internally competitive, a more experimental, noisier and less coherent, a less powerful bureaucracy within its own governmental system, but a more dynamic one. The most perplexing question remains: for other countries, what is the relevance of these differences for their purposes?

III

What is the role of bureaucrats in governmental decision-making? We are all aware that the actual process of decision-making in governmental systems differs in some marked degree from the formal description of the decision-process. We have often observed, also, that the twentieth century has been especially hard on legislatures everywhere. Thus in Great Britain many commentators refer to Cabinet Government, as a way of noting the decline of the House of Commons, while some go a step farther, and speak of Prime Ministerial Government to emphasize an even greater distance between the House and the centre of decisions. Similarly in the United States observers often write of Presidential Supremacy to emphasize a trend away from Congress as a centre of power. In both countries these phrases are oversimplified descriptions of an important fact: there are trends and changes in the decision-making process in all governmental systems, and the reality of the process is not found merely in constitutional and other formal statements of the way in which power is distributed. The actual process is complex and subtle, and is not easily discovered or described.

In this actual and informal process of governing, it is worthwhile to ask: what is the role of the bureaucracy? The formal and official answer in most countries is that the bureaucracy is an agent of the decision-makers, not itself one of the decision-makers but rather their instrument, not an autonomous brain in its own right but rather the neutral executor of plans made by others. This formal theory of the bureaucracy is of course a myth. It is a myth which serves several purposes, but it does not help in a realistic description of the decision-making process. The fact is that in all countries the bureaucracy is one of the important actors in the making of governmental decisions; in some systems the bureaucrats are the leading actors, and in most systems their power as decision-makers would seem to be increasing. Our concern, then, is not with the formal, and now transparent, myth, but with the question of the roles that bureaucrats do in fact have in the decision-making process.

In a decision system does the bureaucrat take the initiative in making policy proposals, or does he wait upon the proposals of others? The answer appears to be that bureaucrats are increasingly the source of initial policy proposals, but that in most systems care is taken to obscure and to make ambiguous their initiating role. That is, the formal theory is deferred to, and a ritual is observed which masks the fact that bureaucrats are actually the source of many initiatives. The British system especially serves to mute the role of the bureaucrat as initiator and framer of policy. The American system, by contrast, pays less deference to formal bureaucratic theory; the higher civil servant is expected to initiate policy proposals, to do so often in full view of the other decision-makers and the public, and to take the career risks associated with such activity. There seems little doubt that the British bureaucrat makes a higher proportion of initial policy proposals than does the American bureaucrat, while the differing style and etiquette of the two systems create the opposite impression. One pattern protects the elected official by inflating his initiating role; the other provides the elected official with competition. One system cloaks the bureaucrat with the safety of anonymity; the other exposes him to equal risks with other decision-makers. The consequences are thus more substantial than they first appear to be.

Beyond the stage of initiation, is the bureaucrat an adviser on, or a protagonist of, policy and programme? The British system emphasizes the advisory and analytical functions of the bureaucrats, but this public posture obscures the more active roles pursued by bureaucrats behind the screen of ministerial responsibility. The American system also demands the advisory and analytical roles for its bureaucrats, but it gives equal or greater emphasis to the bureaucrat as champion of his programme—before Congressional committees, interest groups, and not infrequently with the communication media. This more open and visible policy role for the American bureaucrat is not unchallenged by other actors in the decision-making process (for example, by Congressmen, political executives, interest group leaders, and the communication media), but the role is widely and skillfully managed by the bureaucrats. In a large degree this practice is related to the fact that a substantial proportion of American bureaucrats are more fully committed to policies and programmes than they are to uninterrupted careers in the bureaucracy; many of them move in and out of the public service several times in a lifetime. The role of protagonist is a recognized and legitimate role for the American bureaucrat; risks attend it, but these are softened by the alternative careers open to the American civil servant and the genuine prospects of a return to the bureaucracy when the policy wheel has turned.

As one of the actors in the decision-making system is the bureaucrat cast as innovator and source of energy, or as guardian of continuity and stability? The British system emphasizes his role as prudent guardian; his task is to make the minister aware of risks and difficulties, of errors in fact and reason, of unanticipated and undesirable probable consequences. His most proper role is seen as the firm but deferential vetoer of amateur though perhaps popular enthusiasms. The American system is not free of these tendencies (probably common to the permanent staffs of all large and complex organizations, whether in the public or private sector), but the dominant characteristics of the system encourage the American bureaucrat to be an innovator, a source of forward-moving energy. The controlling expectations of the system are that new ideas, energetically expressed, will emerge from the bureaucracy. The system awards the rank of hero to these innovators, not to the guardians of continuity and stability.

These three aspects of the bureaucrat as policy-maker serve to underscore again the complexities and subtleties of the governing process, the gap between formal doctrine and structure and the realities of decision-making, as well as to emphasize the central role of the bureaucracy in governing. And this central role of the bureaucracy gives significance both to the question of how bureaucrats are to be chosen and to the question of the actual roles of the bureaucrats as initiators of proposals, protagonists of policy, and sources of innovation. These questions in turn lead to an even more crucial one: how are the bureaucrats to be governed?

IV

In any society that has as central institutions large-scale, complex organizations for the conduct of governmental business, the bureaucracy has perforce greater power. The bureaucrats thus become not merely a problem in administration but also an important problem in governance. How are the boundaries of bureaucratic power to be set, and by whom? What restraining rules are to confine the power role of the bureaucracy? What arrangements in the decision-making apparatus serve to make the bureaucrats visible and responsible actors in the exercise of their power?

Some commentators on these questions answer that the main ingredient of bureaucratic responsibility to democratic norms is a code of behaviour for bureaucrats which emphasizes deference to elected officials and other aspects of the democratic system. This "inner check," a democratic self-restraint to be exercised by the bureaucrats themselves, is regarded by other observers as an insufficient guarantee against bureaucratic domination. These skeptical commentators offer alternative answers, the more important of which can be examined by continuing to compare the characteristics of the British and the American bureaucratic systems.

There is first the proposal that the bureaucracy be made representative in its composition. The British system has given small emphasis to this criterion, while the American system has made it a major characteristic. Both systems recruit an elite group in terms of intelligence and skill, although these two terms are given different definitions in the two societies, but the American system has also been concerned to recruit a bureaucracy that is essentially a mirror of the nation—in social and economic class characteristics, in geographic, educational, ethnic, religious, and racial characteristics. To a very large degree, the American system does succeed in its aim to build a bureaucracy which is "representative," not an exotic elite. In fact, some students of the system declare that the American bureaucracy is more representative of American society than is the elected Congress. This is a large claim, and is perhaps not wholly relevant to the problem of a responsible bureaucracy, but it does reflect the degree of the American commitment to an open, mobile and representative bureaucracy, linked closely in its main characteristics to the American society itself.

There is also the proposal that the bureaucracy be made more responsible by making it more internally competitive, to make certain that bureaucrats compete openly with other bureaucrats for the exercise of power. The British system does not have this preference for a bureaucracy that is pluralistic and internally competitive in its structure and operations; instead, it values symmetry and a tightly meshed bureaucracy, especially in the monolithic characteristics of the administrative class at the top of the bureaucratic structure. The American system, by contrast, produces a bureaucracy that is so competitively pluralistic that contesting elements in the bureaucracy are compelled to seek allies outside the bureaucracy—in the Congress, in the interest groups, in the communication media. The American system accordingly does not often pose bureaucratic power against non-bureaucratic power; most often the contest in decision-making power is between opposing alliances each of which contains bureaucratic and non-bureaucratic elements. The American bureaucracy is not, as a consequence, self-contained as a centre of power, nor can it be self-regarding in its goals or strategies; each significant segment of the bureaucracy must be more involved with forces in its non-bureaucratic context than with other bureaucrats. And, to add to the pluralism of the system, most bureaucratic–non-bureaucratic alliances are vulnerable and impermanent, so that there is a constant reshaping and realigning, emphasizing still further the internally competitive nature of the American bureaucracy. Thus, one kind of answer to the problem of bureaucratic power is the American design for producing an internally competitive bureaucracy, a system in which bureaucrats restrain the power of other bureaucrats and each major group of bureaucrats must share power with non-bureaucratic allies.

There is a third approach to the governance of bureaucrats: personal responsibility rather than anonymity for the bureaucrat. In this respect the British and American systems also present contrasts. The British system emphasizes anonymity; the minister not only is required to take full responsibility but the bureaucrat remains a faceless unknown. (The establishment of this convention represents one of the great strategic triumphs of the bureaucracy, since anonymity is a method of exercising power without being required to pay the costs of error.) The American bureaucrat is not an anonymous, invisible actor in the decision-making process. He is, without any important limitation, held responsible for what he does. Presidents may on occasion try to shield him, or department heads may also; but in the end the Congressional committees, the interest groups, the communication media, or other actors, will usually bring home to the bureaucrat his personal responsibility for his own actions. This is not always accomplished with a fine sense of abstract justice—whether the bureaucrat is being praised or blamed—for this is competitive world of power in which no actor is regarded as either privileged or fragile. The American civil servant who earns high and lasting prestige in his society is usually one who most completely breaks the mask of anonymity and becomes a public figure. There are, of course, situations in which American bureaucrats would prefer the cloak of anonymity, and the convention is sometimes invoked by them or by allies on their behalf; there are also American observers who urge the adoption of the British model. But the system of personal responsibility prevails against these reservations, and appears likely to continue to do so. The visibility and personal responsibility of the bureaucrat is a characteristic built strongly into the American governmental system.

There is, finally, another aspect to the governance of bureaucracies: publicity versus secrecy. Here also the British and the American models stand in sharp contrast. In the United States there is a widely accepted code that the public is entitled to know everything about what the government is doing, even what the government is planning to do. The strongest exponents of this doctrine are the communication media, especially the newspapers, which have increasingly used their motto "the Right to Know" as if it were a part of the Bill of Rights. But every cross-section of American society tends to believe that there ought to be no governmental secrets except those which clearly affect national defence or the rights of individual persons to privacy. This general belief is encouraged and made effective by central features of the governmental system: the inquiry powers of the Congressional committees which open up executive branch secrets, the internally competitive bureaucracy which shares its secrets with its outside allies, and the zeal of the communication media in its daily probing to reduce the boundaries of secrecy. The bureaucracy is directly affected by this system of publicity because it is the custodian of most governmental secrets. In the American setting the bureaucrat's inherent preference for secrecy is sharply limited by the assumption of all the other actors that secrecy most often serves the convenience of those who hold the secrets, and that a strong case must be made against publication, the presumptions of the system being that publication is the norm. And, further, the operation of the actual decision-system compels the bureaucrats to share their secrets with non-bureaucratic allies; secrets thus shared are not secrets very long. The functioning of this system, with its strong preference for publicity over secrecy, is not devoid of difficulties. It is accompanied by complaints and counter-complaints, by rough exchanges between the contestants and by rough justice rather than mercy toward some participants, but the system does curtail the bureaucratic uses of secrecy and does make the American governing process one of the most highly visible in the world.

V

These brief and somewhat oversimplified observations on the contrasts between two important bureaucratic systems are intended mainly to suggest a few general hypotheses about bureaucracies. One of them is that in the building of bureaucratic systems there are many options, each choice having different consequences for the whole system; that is, these options are not merely technical issues in personnel management but more importantly choices affecting the nature of the governing process. Another implication is that the contrasting choices made in constructing these two bureaucratic systems were in the main determined by the matrix of the society in which they were each made; in other words, the nature of a particular bureaucracy is linked to the system of government and the society in which it operates. The options are thus limited by the social and political context of the particular bureaucracy, but this is not to suggest a rigid limitation—for example, the context of a parliamentary system does not dictate a particular set of choices. Instead, what is suggested is that the whole indigenous context—social and political and governmental—is the limiting factor. Bureaucratic models are not packages ready for export or import; they provide illustrations of options and styles for consideration in their separate parts, and for adaptation before acceptance in a different context.

Bureaucracy, Bureaucratization, and Debureaucratization[1]

S. N. EISENSTADT
The Hebrew University

IN THE LITERATURE dealing with bureaucracy we can often discern a continual shift between two points of view. The first point of view defines bureaucracy mainly as a tool, or a mechanism created for the successful and efficient implementation of a certain goal or goals. Bureaucracy is seen as an epitome

Reprinted from *Administrative Science Quarterly,* Vol. 4 (December, 1959), pp. 302–320, by permission of the author and the publisher.

1 This paper is a development of some of the analyses presented in a Trend Report on Bureaucracy and Bureaucratization, prepared by the writer for *Current Sociology,* 7 (1958), 99–163 (hereafter cited as Trend Report). I

of rationality and of efficient implementation of goals and provision of services.

The second point of view sees bureaucracy mainly as an instrument of power, of exercising control over people and over different spheres of life, and of continuous expansion of such power either in the interests of the bureaucracy itself or in the interests of some (often sinister) masters. This point of view tends mainly to stress the process of bureaucratization, i.e., the extension of the power of a bureaucratic organization over many areas beyond its initial purpose, the growing internal formalization within the bureaucracy, the regimentation of these areas by the bureaucracy, and in general a strong emphasis by the bureaucracy on the extension of its power.

This twofold attitude toward bureaucracy can be discerned, although in differing degrees, in most of the basic literature on the subject, whether that of the classical sociological approaches (Max Weber, Mosca, Michels) or that of public administration and the theory of organization. This twofold approach has in fact run through most of the discussions about bureaucracy since the end of the last century.[2]

Although the awareness of this problem of the twofold aspect of bureaucracy can be found in most of the literature dealing with bureaucracy, it is significant that these two points of view rarely converge. For those persons, as for instance the students of public administration, who see bureaucracy as a tool for implementation of goals, the power element is mainly seen as a stumbling block in the process of rational and efficient implementation of such goals. For those who see in bureaucracies mainly instruments of power and bearers of a continuous process of bureaucratization and of growing power of oligarchies, the

am indebted to the publishers, Messrs. Blackwell, Oxford, for permission to reprint some parts of the report. The reader will find in the Trend Report a more complete exposition of some of the points made here. The presentation here owes much to several discussions of this problem held during the fall of 1958 at the Universities of Oslo and Copenhagen and the Christian Michelsen Institute at Bergen. The general report has greatly benefited from the preliminary data of a research project on bureaucracy and new immigrants conducted at the Hebrew University under the supervision of Dr. E. Katz and the writer.

2 For a fuller discussion of this problem and of the literature see Trend Report.

implementation of the official or purported goals of the bureaucracy is but a secondary aspect, sometimes only an empty ideology.

And yet the very fact that these two points of view can be found in almost all the literature on bureaucracy seems to indicate that they are not two entirely separate and contradictory points of view, but rather that they point to various possibilities, all inherent in the very nature of bureaucracy. Thus the main problem seems to be not which point of view is right in itself, but rather the conditions under which each of these tendencies becomes actualized and predominant in any given bureaucratic organization.

It is the purpose of this paper, first, to show that both these tendencies are indeed inherent in the basic conditions of growth and development of any bureaucracy by its very nature as a social organization; and, second, to propose some preliminary hypotheses about the conditions under which each of these tendencies may become predominant in a given bureaucracy. In this way we hope to demonstrate that the convergence of various types of studies of bureaucracy and organizations that have developed recently can enable us to overcome the dichotomy developing between these two different points of view and some of the problems of the "metaphysical pathos" in the discussion of bureaucracy.[3]

Conditions of development of bureaucratic organizations

We shall start with an analysis of the conditions of development of bureaucratic organizations and see to what extent these conditions can explain the existence of different inherent tendencies in their development and their patterns of activities.

Although since Weber, there have been relatively few systematic studies of the conditions responsible for the development of bureaucratic organizations and processes of bureaucratization that could serve as a basis for a systematic comparative analysis, there exist numerous concrete historical analyses of the develop-

3 See A. Gouldner, Metaphysical Pathos and the Theory of Bureaucracy, *American Political Science Review,* 49 (June 1955), 496–507.

ment and functioning of different bureaucratic organizations.[4] On the basis of these materials and of current research it is possible to specify, tentatively, the conditions under which bureaucratic organizations tend to develop and which apply both to historical (Chinese, Byzantine, and Egyptian) bureaucratic societies and to modern societies or sectors of them.

The available material suggests that bureaucratic organizations tend to develop in societies when:

1. There develops extensive differentiation between major types of roles and institutional (economic, political, religious, and so forth) spheres.
2. The most important social roles are allocated not according to criteria of membership in the basic particularistic (kinship or territorial) groups, but rather according to universalistic and achievement criteria, or criteria of membership in more flexibly constituted groups such as professional, religious, vocational, or "national" groups.
3. There evolve many functionally specific groups (economic, cultural, religious, social-integrative) that are not embedded in basic particularistic groups, as, for example, economic and professional organizations, various types of voluntary associations, clubs, and so forth.
4. The definition of the total community is not identical with, and consequently is wider than, any such basic particularistic group, as can be seen, for instance, in the definition of the Hellenic culture in Byzantium or of the Confucian cultural order.
5. The major groups and strata in the society develop, uphold, and attempt to implement numerous discrete, political, economic, and social-service goals which cannot be implemented within the limited framework of the basic particularistic groups.
6. The growing differentiation in the social structure makes for complexity in many spheres of life, such as increasing interdependence between far-off groups and growing difficulty in the assurance of supply of resources and services.

[4] Parts of this material are now being used by the writer in a comprehensive comparative study of the political systems of historical bureaucratic empires, and some of the hypotheses presented here are based on this work. A preliminary presentation of some of the problems of these historical societies can be found in S. N. Eisenstadt, Internal Contradictions in Bureaucratic Polities, *Comparative Studies in History and Society,* 1 (Oct. 1958), 58–75; and see also S. N. Eisenstadt, Political Struggle in Bureaucratic Societies, *World Politics,* 9 (Oct. 1956), 15–36.

7. These developments result to some extent in "free-floating" resources, i.e., manpower and economic resources as well as commitments for political support which are neither embedded in nor assured to any primary ascriptive-particularistic groups, as, for example, monetary resources, a relatively free labor force, and a free political vote. Consequently, the various institutional units in the society have to compete for resources, manpower, and support for the implementation of their goals and provision of services; and the major social units are faced with many regulative and administrative problems.

The available material suggests that bureaucratic organizations develop in relation to such differentiation in the social system. Bureaucratic organizations can help in coping with some of the problems arising out of such differentiation, and they perform important functions in the organization of adequate services and co-ordination of large-scale activities, in the implementation of different goals, in the provision of resources to different groups, and in the regulation of various intergroup relations and conflicts. Such bureaucratic organizations are usually created by certain elites (rulers, economic entrepreneurs, etc.) to deal with the problems outlined and to assure for these elites both the provision of such services and strategic power positions in the society.

Thus in many historical societies bureaucratic administrations were created by kings who wanted to establish their rule over feudal-aristocratic forces and who wanted, through their administration, to control the resources created by various economic and social groups and to provide these groups with political, economic, and administrative services that would make them dependent on the rulers.

In many modern societies bureaucratic organizations are created when the holders of political or economic power are faced with problems that arise because of external (war, etc.) or internal (economic development, political demands, etc.) developments. For the solution of such problems they have to mobilize adequate resources from different groups and spheres of life.

Obviously, these conclusions have to be tested and amplified through detailed application to various societies and different institutional spheres.[5] But even at this preliminary stage of our analysis they are of interest in relation to tendencies of development inherent in bureaucratic organizations.

In sum, the development of bureaucratic organizations is related to certain social conditions, the most important of which are, first, the availability of various fluid, "free-floating" resources; second, the necessity for large-scale organizations; and, third, the development of several centers of power that compete for such resources. Thus two conclusions are indicated.

First, as a result of the very conditions that give rise to a bureaucratic organization, it is, almost by definition, obliged to compete for resources, manpower, legitimation within the society, general support and clientele, and, to some extent also, patrons and protectors.

The classical theories of bureaucracy recognized that a bureaucracy is always dependent on the outside world for its resources. Unlike traditional ecological, family, or kinship groups, the incumbents of its office do not receive direct remuneration from their clients nor do they own their means of production. But because many of these theories referred chiefly to governmental bureaucracies, they took the supply of the requisite resources for granted and only emphasized the fact that dependence on external resources assures the relative segregation and independence of the bureaucrat's role. In reality, however, the need to compete for legitimation and resources faces governmental departments also and can be considered as a basic aspect of every bureaucracy.

Thus from the very beginning a bureaucratic organization is put in what may be called a power situation, in which it has to cast its influence and to generate processes of power on its own behalf and in which it is under pressure from different centers of power in the society that would control it.

Second, this basic power situation in which a bureaucratic organization develops and functions is strongly underlined by the fact that any bureaucracy, not only implements different political and social goals and provides different services, but also necessarily performs regulatory and mediating functions in the

[5] A more complete exposition of this hypothesis will be presented in the forthcoming analysis of the bureaucratic empires.

society. This is because the rules governing implementation of goals and provision of services by a bureaucracy necessarily affect the distribution of power and allocation of resources to different groups in the society. These regulative and mediating functions enhance the potential power position of any bureaucracy, increase the competition of other groups for its services and for control over it, and generate many pressures both emanating from it and impinging on it.

Thus from its inception a bureaucratic organization is in a state of constant interaction with its environment and has to develop different ways of maintaining a dynamic equilibrium in this environment. The equilibrium results from adjustment of its own goals, structure, and interests in relation to the major forces in its social environment and to the power processes generated by each of them.

The bureaucratic organization as a social system

To understand more fully how different types of equilibrium are developed by different bureaucratic organizations, it is necessary to examine more closely some of the major characteristics of the internal structure of bureaucracies. A systematic approach to this problem is facilitated by the extensive data in the literature dealing with the problems of bureaucracy and of organization.[6] The major insights to be gained from these materials and analyses seem to be as follows:

1. Any bureaucratic organization constitutes a social system of its own; therefore its internal division of labor is determined not only by the technical problems of implementation of goals, but also by other needs and problems. Since special roles and activities geared to the provision of these needs exist within it, there can be no purely rational bureaucratic organization free from personal, primary, or power elements. On the contrary, some such elements (like primary groups of workers or identification between different participants) perform functionally important tasks in the organization.

6 For a review of this literature see Trend Report.

2. Each of the roles existing in any bureaucratic organization is systematically related to the outside world. The organization must manipulate several aspects of its external environment (e.g., directors must deal with boards of trustees and legislative committees, the sales managers with buyers and sellers, the manager with trade unions and labor exchanges). The necessary contact between the incumbents of such roles and parallel role incumbents in other organizations may establish professional, solidarity, or conflict relations and various reference orientations and identifications. The relations resulting from such contact may cut across any given organization and at the same time greatly influence the behavior of the incumbents in their organizations, consequently affecting the performance of these organizations. These contacts also distinguish the incumbents' bureaucratic roles within the organization from their other social roles in the family or community, especially the type of motivation for performance of their bureaucratic role that they bring from their social background. Finally, the relations with different types of clients and sections of the general public with which the incumbent of a bureaucratic role comes into selective contact might put him under pressure with respect to the performance of his bureaucratic roles. Such pressure may be exerted either by means of various professional or community roles and organizations in which both the bureaucrat and the client may participate, by specific organizations of the public or clients, or through direct interaction in the bureaucrat-client role.

3. Within each organization there develop various subgroups and subsystems (workmen, foremen, professional groups, departmental units, and so forth), and the organization is faced with the problem of co-ordinating these subgroups, of regulating their relations with each other and with the organization as a whole. Such subgroups may have different conceptions of and attitudes toward the organization's goals and needs, and these differences must be taken into account when studying the functioning of any bureaucratic organization.

4. Thus the interaction between the different subgroups or subsystems in any bureaucratic organization should be viewed as a continuous process of communication, of allocation of rewards, of mutual perception, a process by which some—but only some—fusion (the extent of which necessarily varies) is effected between the motives and goals of individuals and subgroups and the over-all organizational goals.[7]

5. The multiplicity of any organization's external relations and internal subgroups may lead to the development of many different types of activity that transcend the specific bureaucratic roles and relations both within and without the organization. Thus an organization interested in improving its internal human and public relations may help its members and their families integrate their activities with those of other social groups—all this to improve performance of the bureaucratic role.

Such activities, in turn, bring the incumbents of the bureaucratic role into various relations with other persons that may go beyond the basic relationship of the bureaucratic role. These might consequently lead (a) to development of new goal orientations by the organization and to processes of bureaucratization or debureaucratization; (b) to attempts on the part of the bureaucrats to impose the bureaucracy's conceptions and goals on these external activities and groups, or (c) to pressures of these groups on the goals of the organization and performance of the bureaucratic roles within it. These pressures may be directed toward changing or supervising the goals and activities of the bureaucratic organization, limiting their application, adding new dimensions to them, or taking over of the organization.

Here we are confronted with an aspect of the bureaucratic organization that is of major importance to our analysis, namely, the potential flexibility of its goals. We have seen that any bureaucratic organization evolves as a means of implementing a specific goal or goals. However, the very conditions responsible for its development, the multiplicity of its internal subgroups, its continuous dependence on external groups, and the numerous pressures to which it is subjected facilitate or perhaps even necessitate modification of at least some of its goals. Such flexibility is, as Thompson and McEwen have rightly stressed, almost

[7] Conrad M. Arensberg and Geoffrey Tootell, Plant Sociology: Real Discoveries and New Problems, in Mirra Komarovsky, ed., *Common Frontiers of the Social Sciences* (Glencoe, Ill., 1957), pp. 310–337.

a condition (especially in modern society) of the bureaucratic organization's survival.[8]

It is largely through incorporating new (mostly secondary) goals and attempting to assure the requisite resources for their implementation that a bureaucratic organization maintains its equilibrium with its environment. It thus exerts its influence on this environment, establishes various rules which influence the training of people aspiring to be enrolled into it, and indirectly may influence general educational standards and impose its own specific orientations on parts of its environment. It is through such processes, as well as those of competition for resources and power, that the different types of interaction and equilibrium between the bureaucratic organization and its social environment develop.

Bureaucratization and debureaucratization

It is through such continuous interaction with its environment that a bureaucratic organization may succeed in maintaining those characteristics that distinguish it from other social groups. The most important of these characteristics, common to most bureaucratic organizations and often stressed in the literature, are specialization of roles and tasks; the prevalence of autonomous, rational, nonpersonal rules in the organization; and the general orientation to rational, efficient implementation of specific goals.[9]

These structural characteristics do not, however, develop in a social vacuum but are closely related to the functions and activities of the bureaucratic organization in its environment. The extent to which they can develop and persist in any bureaucratic organization is dependent on the type of dynamic equilibrium that the organization develops in relation to its environment. Basically, three main outcomes of such interaction or types

[8] J. D. Thompson and W. J. McEwen, Organizational Goals and Environment, *American Sociological Review,* 23 (February 1958), 23–31.

[9] See, for instance, P. M. Blau, *Bureaucracy in Modern Society* (New York, 1956). Blau summarizes much of the available literature on this problem.

of such dynamic equilibrium can be distinguished, although probably each of them can be further subdivided and some overlapping occurs between them.

The first type of equilibrium is one in which any given bureaucratic organization maintains its autonomy and distinctiveness. The basic structural characteristics that differentiate it from other social groups and in which it implements its goal or goals (whether its initial goals or goals added later) are retained and it is supervised by those who are legitimately entitled to do this (holders of political power, "owners," or boards of trustees).

The second main possibility is that of bureaucratization, as it has been already defined earlier. This is the extension of the bureaucracy's spheres of activities and power either in its own interest or those of some of its elite. It tends toward growing regimentation of different areas of social life and some extent of displacement of its service goals in favor of various power interests and orientations. Examples are military organizations that tend to impose their rule on civilian life, or political parties that exert pressure on their potential supporters in an effort to monopolize their private and occupational life and make them entirely dependent on the political party.

The third main outcome is debureaucratization. Here there is subversion of the goals and activities of the bureaucracy in the interests of different groups with which it is in close interaction (clients, patrons, interested parties). In debureaucratization the specific characteristics of the bureaucracy in terms both of its autonomy and its specific rules and goals are minimized, even up to the point where its very functions and activities are taken over by other groups or organizations. Examples of this can be found in cases when some organization (i.e., a parents' association or a religious or political group) attempts to divert the rules and working of a bureaucratic organization (school, economic agency, and so forth) for its own use or according to its own values and goals. It makes demands on the members of bureaucratic organizations to perform tasks that are obviously outside the specific scope of these organizations.

Each of these possibilities entails a specific development of the bureaucratic role in relation to other social roles with which it has to interact—whether other social roles of the incumbents of the bureaucratic roles or other "client," public, or similar roles. Thus in the maintenance of a bureaucracy's autonomy and of its goal and service orientation the bearers of the bureaucratic roles maintain their distinctiveness from closely related roles but at the same time fully recognize the distinctiveness of these other roles.

In the case of bureaucratization the bureaucratic roles tend to dominate the other roles (both of the incumbents and of those with whom they interact) and to impose on them the bureaucratic criteria, so as to minimize the autonomy and distinctiveness of these other roles and maximize their own power over them.

In the case of debureaucratization the various outside nonbureaucratic roles impinge on the bureaucratic role to an extent which tends to minimize the specificity of the bureaucratic roles and the relative autonomy of the bureaucratic rules in the implementation of goals and in the provision of services.

Each of these possibilities may also involve, in different ways and degrees, the bureaucracy's orientation to new goals, its incorporation of new goals, and its diversion of activities to the implementation of such new goals. Many overlappings between these various tendencies and possibilities may, of course, develop. The tendencies toward bureaucratization and debureaucratization may, in fact, develop side by side. Thus, for instance, a growing use of the bureaucratic organization and the extension of its scope of activities for purposes of political control might be accompanied by deviation from its rules for the sake of political expediency. The possibility of these tendencies occurring in the same case may be explained by the fact that a stable service-oriented bureaucracy (the type of bureaucracy depicted in the Weberian ideal type of bureaucracy) is based on the existence of some equilibrium or *modus vivendi* between professional autonomy and societal (or political) control. Once this equilibrium is severely disrupted, the outcome with respect to the bureaucracy's organization and activity may be the simultaneous development of bureaucratization and debureaucratization in different spheres of its activities, although usually one of these tendencies is more pronounced.

We thus see that the problem of what kind of equilibrium

any bureaucratic organization will develop in relation to its environment is inherent both in the conditions of the development of a bureaucratic organization and in its very nature as a social system, in its basic components and its interrelation with the external environment in which it functions. Thus the dilemma of viewing a bureaucracy either as an instrument for the implementation of goals or as a power instrument is in a way resolved.

But this poses a new problem or question as to the conditions that influence or determine which of these tendencies will become actualized or predominant in any given case.

Some variables in the study of bureaucracy

It is as yet very difficult to propose any definite and systematic hypothesis about this problem since very little research is available that is specifically related to it.[10]

What can be done at this stage is, first, to point out some variables that, on the basis of available material and the preceding discussion, seem central to this problem, and then to propose some preliminary hypotheses, which may suggest directions in which research work on this problem may be attempted.

On the basis of those discussions we would like to propose that (a) the major goals of the bureaucratic organization, (b) the place of these goals in the social structure of the society, and (c) the type of dependence of the bureaucracy on external forces (clients, holders of political power, or other prominent groups) are of great importance in influencing both its internal structure and its relation with its environment. These different variables, while to some extent interdependent, are not identical. Each brings into relief the interdependence of the bureaucratic organization with its social setting from a different point of view.

10 Thus, for instance, in existing literature there is but little distinction between conditions which make for the growth of bureaucracy and those conducive to increasing bureaucratization. Gouldner's polemics against those who foresee the inevitability of bureaucratization are to some extent due to the lack of this distinction in the available literature. See his Metaphysical Pathos and the Theory of Bureaucracy.

The bureaucracy's goals, as has been lately shown in great detail by Parsons,[11] are of strategic importance, because they constitute one of the most important connecting links between the given organization and the total social structure in which it is placed. That which from the point of view of the organization is the major goal is very often from the point of view of the total society the function of the organization. Hence the various interrelations between a bureaucratic organization, other groups, and the total society are largely mediated by the nature of its goals. This applies both to the resources needed by the organization and to the products it gives to the society.[12]

But it is not merely the contents of the goals, i.e., whether they are mainly political, economic, cultural, and so forth, that influence the relation of the organization with its environment, but the place of the goals in the institutional structure of the society as well. By the relative place of the specific goals of any given bureaucratic organization within the society we mean the centrality (or marginality) of these goals with respect to the society's value and power system and the extent of legitimation it affords them. Thus there would obviously be many differences between a large corporation with critical products and a small economic organization with marginal products; between a political party close to the existing government performing the functions of a "loyal opposition" and a revolutionary group; between established churches and minority or militant sects; between fully established educational institutions and sectarian study or propaganda groups.

A third variable which seems to influence the bureaucracy's structural characteristics and activities is the extent and nature of its dependence on external resources and power. This dependence or relation may be defined in terms of:

1. The chief function of the organization, i.e., whether it is a service, market, or membership recruitment agency. (This definition is closely related to, but not necessarily identical with, its goals.)

11 See T. Parsons, Suggestions for a Sociological Approach to the Theory of Organization, I and II, *Administrative Science Quarterly*, I (June and September, 1956), 63–85, 225–239.

12 For additional discussion of this problem see Trend Report.

2. The extent to which its clientele is entirely dependent upon its products, or conversely, the type and extent of competition between it and parallel agencies.
3. The nature and extent of the internal (ownership) and external control.
4. The criteria used to measure the success of the organization as such and its members' performance, especially the extent of changes in the behavior and membership affiliation of its clients (as, for instance, in the case of a political party).
5. The spheres of life of its personnel that the activities of a given bureaucratic organization encompass.
6. The spheres of life of its clientele that the activities of a given bureaucratic organization encompass.

It is not claimed that this list is exhaustive, but it seems to provide some preliminary clues as to the possible direction of further research on the problem.

All these variables indicate the great interdependence existing between the bureaucratic organization and its social environment. Each variable points to some ways in which a bureaucratic organization attempts to control different parts of its environment and to adapt its goals to changing environment or to different ways in which groups outside the bureaucracy control it and direct its activities. The outcome of this continuous interaction varies continuously according to the constellation of these different variables.

Conditions of bureaucratization and debureaucratization

On the basis of the foregoing considerations and of current research like that of Janowitz,[13] of historical research on which we

[13] See M. Janowitz, D. Wright, and W. Delany, *Public Administration and the Public—Perspectives towards Government in a Metropolitan Community* (Ann Arbor, 1958), which is one of the few available works that have a bearing on this problem. We would also like to mention the work of J. A. Slesinger, who has worked with Janowitz, and who has recently proposed several hypotheses concerning some of the factors that might influence aspects of the development of bureaucracy that are of interest to us. See Slesinger, *A Model for the Comparative Study of Public Bureaucracies,* Institute of Public Administration, University of Michigan, 1957.

have reported already,[14] and research in progress on the relations between bureaucratic organization and new immigrants in Israel,[15] we propose several general hypotheses concerning the conditions that promote autonomy or, conversely, bureaucratization or debureaucratization. In these hypotheses we deal with the influence, first, of the structure, organization, and distribution of different goals in the bureaucracy's immediate social environment and, second, of the types of dependency of a bureaucracy on its clientele. As already noted, these are only preliminary hypotheses that do not, as yet, deal with all the variables previously outlined.

The first of these hypotheses proposes that the development of any given bureaucratic organization as a relatively autonomous service agency is contingent upon the following conditions obtaining in its social setting:

1. Relative predominance of universalistic elements in the orientations and goals of the groups most closely related to the bureaucracy.
2. Relatively wide distribution of power and values in the economic, cultural, and political spheres among many groups and the maintenance of continuous struggle and competition among them or, in other words, no monopoly of the major power positions by any one group.
3. A wide range of differentiation among different types of goals.
4. The continuous specialization and competition among different bureaucratic organizations and between them and other types of groups about their relative places with regard to implementation of different goals.
5. The existence of strongly articulated political groups and the maintenance of control over the implementation of the goals by the legitimate holders of political, communal, or economic power.

Thus a service bureaucracy, one that maintains both some measure of autonomy and of service orientation, tends to develop either in a society, such as the "classical" Chinese Empire or the Byzantine Empire from the sixth to the tenth century, in which

[14] See note 4 above.

[15] See E. Katz and S. N. Eisenstadt, Debureaucratization: Observation on the Response of Israeli Organizations to the New Immigrants (forthcoming).

there exist strong political rulers and some politically active groups, such as the urban groups, aristocracy, and the church in the Byzantine Empire, or the literati and gentry in China, whose aspirations are considered by the rulers.[16] It also tends to develop in a democratic society in which effective political power is vested in an efficient, strong, representative executive. In both cases it is the combination of relatively strong political leadership with some political articulation and activity of different strata and groups (an articulation which necessarily tends to be entirely different in expression in historical empires from modern democracies) that facilitates the maintenance of a service bureaucracy.

In some societies a group may establish a power monopoly over parts of its environment and over the definition and establishment of the society's goals and the appropriation of its resources. This group may use the bureaucracy as an instrument of power and manipulation, distort its autonomous function and service orientation, and subvert some of its echelons through various threats or inducements for personal gratification. Historically the most extreme example of such developments can be found in those societies in which the rulers developed political goals that were strongly opposed by various active groups that they tried to suppress, such as in Prussia in the seventeenth and eighteenth centuries, in many conquest empires such as the Ottoman, or in the periods of aristocratization of the Byzantine Empire.[17] Modern examples of this tendency can be found in totalitarian societies or movements. Less extreme illustrations can also be found in other societies, and it should be a major task of comparative research to specify the different possible combinations of the conditions enumerated above and their influence on the possible development of bureaucratic organizations.

The development of a bureaucratic organization in the direction of debureaucratization seems to be connected mainly with the growth of different types of *direct* dependence of the

16 For a more complete discussion of some of the problems of these societies see the references in note 4.

17 Hans Rosenberg, *Bureaucracy, Aristocracy and Autocracy: The Prussian Experience, 1660–1815* (Cambridge, Mass., 1958); A. Lybyer, *The Government of the Ottoman Empire in the Time of Süleiman the Magnificent* (Cambridge, Mass., 1913); and Eisenstadt, Internal Contradictions.

bureaucratic organization on parts of its clientele. At this stage we may propose the following preliminary hypotheses about the influence that the type of dependency of the bureaucracy on its clients has on some of its patterns of activity. First, the greater its dependence on its clientele in terms of their being able to go to a competing agency, the more it will have to develop techniques of communication and additional services to retain its clientele and the more it will be influenced by different types of demands by the clientele for services in spheres that are not directly relevant to its main goals. Second, insofar as its dependence on its clients is due to the fact that its criteria of successful organizational performance are based on the number and behavior pattern of the organization's members or clients (as is often the case in semipolitical movements, educational organizations, and so forth), it will have to take an interest in numerous spheres of its clients' activities and either establish its control over them or be subjected to their influence and direction. Finally, the greater its *direct* dependence on different participants in the political arena, and the smaller the basic economic facilities and political assurance given by the holders of political power—as is the case in some public organizations in the United States and to some extent also in different organizations in Israel[18]—the greater will be its tendency to succumb to the demands of different political and economic pressure groups and to develop its activities and distort its own rules accordingly.

As already indicated, in concrete cases some overlapping between the tendencies to bureaucratization and debureaucratization may occur. Thus, for instance, when a politically monopolistic group gains control over a bureaucratic organization, it may distort the rules of this organization in order to give special benefits to the holders of political power or to maintain its hold over different segments of the population. On the other hand, when a process of debureaucratization sets in because of the growing pressure of different groups on a bureaucracy, there may also develop within the bureaucratic organization, as a sort of defense against these pressures, a tendency toward formalization and bureaucratization. This shows that the distinctive character-

[18] See Janowitz *et al., op. cit.,* pp. 107–114, and Katz and Eisenstadt, *op. cit.*

istics of a specific bureaucratic organization and role have been impinged upon in different directions, and one may usually discern which of these tendencies is predominant in different spheres of activity of the bureaucracy. It is the task of further research to analyze these different constellations in greater detail.

Conclusions

The hypotheses presented above are necessarily both very general and preliminary and have as yet to be applied in detail to different types of societies and to their institutional spheres. Nevertheless, they make it possible to identify at least some of the major variables responsible for the development of bureaucratic organizations and to relate them systematically to the factors that determine the internal structure of such organizations and to types of equilibrium developing between bureaucracies and their environment. The preceding discussion points out that the type of dynamic equilibrium established at a given time depends largely on the forces in the immediate environment of the organization on the one hand and the type of power processes it generates in its environment on the other.

The interaction between these forces and processes engenders the continuous development of bureaucratic organizations and of processes of bureaucratization and debureaucratization. Whether a given bureaucracy will maintain its relative autonomy, whether at the same time it will be subject to effective "external" control, or whether it will develop in the direction of bureaucratization or debureaucratization is not precisely predeterminable but is largely contingent upon the concrete constellation of these various forces.

It is hoped that the preceding discussion—although preliminary—indicates possible ways of investigating various structural aspects of bureaucratic organizations and the nature of the processes of bureaucratization and debureaucratization. It has shown that with the development, systematization, and convergence of different fields of research it is possible to avoid the dichotomy of viewing bureaucracy as a service instrument or viewing it as an instrument of power. It is also possible to identify the conditions under which the autonomy of a bureaucratic organization and its service orientation is maintained or the conditions under which processes of bureaucratization and debureaucratization develop, and to relate them systematically to the analysis of the structure of bureaucratic organizations.

Bureaucracy East and West

Morroe Berger
Princeton University

Bureaucracy has been analyzed from two related sides. Studies of bureaucratic structures have examined the centralization of power and authority, the establishment of a hierarchy of offices with special requirements and prerogatives, and the existence of rules governing the exercise of function and authority. Studies of bureaucratic behavior, on the other hand, have examined the institutional or behavioral concomitants of these structures, such as caution in interpreting rules, self-interest among the corps of officials, their conduct toward the public, and (more recently) their informal relationships within the prescribed system.

The concepts and findings of these studies have, of course, been developed by Western scholars upon the basis of Western institutions. Their use as guides in a study of a bureaucracy in another culture—the civil service of Egypt today—points to their limitation for the analysis of bureaucratic behavior both in this non-Western setting and in our own society as well.

Although it is primarily agricultural and rural, Egypt has a long history of commercial and industrial activity and of urbanization. The early development of intensive agriculture through use of Nile waters was associated with the development of a

Reprinted from *Administrative Science Quarterly,* Vol. 1 (March, 1957), pp. 518–529, by permission of the author and publisher.

complex social and governmental organization. Thus, Egypt has a long tradition of bureaucracy. Differences between its bureaucratic structure and that of the West cannot, therefore, be attributed to Egypt's "underdeveloped" status in this respect; for in function its bureaucracy may be traced back to one that is among the oldest we know. This is not to say that Egypt's civil service has evolved in the way Western civil service systems have. The influence of the Islamic religion, the Ottoman Empire, and French and British culture and political control have left their special marks which distinguish the public bureaucracy of Egypt from that of Western countries. There is considerable emphasis upon obedience to superiors. Procedural delays have been as much a weapon as an inevitable concomitant of increase in size. A large proportion of university graduates seek to enter the civil service. These characteristics are so much more marked in Egypt than in the West that they make its public bureaucracy considerably different from most Western types.

In recent years, nevertheless, Egypt has made many changes in its civil-service system, including the creation of a Civil Service Commission charged with introducing modern personnel policies, eliminating waste, and improving administration. Its efforts have been successful in some degree but, of course, the legacy of centuries is not easily altered.

Although the civil service has long been a career for the middle and upper classes, despite traditionally low salaries, it has also been open to the lower classes. In a sample of 249 higher civil servants interviewed in 1954 (and comprising a 16-per-cent sample of all civil servants in their grades in four ministries), the distribution of their fathers' employment was as follows:

civil servant, white collar	39%	*independent professional*	6%
landlord	24%	*army officer*	4%
peasant	16%	*white-collar worker*	3%
small merchant	8%		

Have structural differences between the Egyptian and Western civil-service systems produced differences in their bureaucratic behavior as well? Is there, indeed, a difference between types and degrees of bureaucratic behavior that will permit us to say that one way of doing things is more or less bureaucratic than another? May we say, for example, that one official is more bureaucratic than another because he is more dependent upon his superiors and is quicker to throw upon them the burden of a decision that is properly within his own competence? May we say, in other words, that the more willing an official is to use the full measure of discretionary power that his post permits, the less bureaucratic he is?

What is involved in these questions is the degree to which personal initiative is related to bureaucratic behavior. The exercise of such initiative is not structurally excluded from bureaucracy, yet it is usually characterized as unbureaucratic behavior in scholarly studies as well as in popular discussion. Similarly, its opposite, extreme caution, "playing it safe," "covering" oneself by getting a decision from the official on the next level of the hierarchy, is thought of as the typical behavioral concomitant of bureaucratic structure.

The uncertainty surrounding this aspect of bureaucratic behavior in the West is compounded when one looks to notions derived from studies of such behavior for guidance in the analysis of bureaucratic patterns in another culture. If, for example, one wants to determine to what degree Egyptian bureaucratic behavior resembles its Western counterpart and to explore the socioeconomic background of those Egyptian civil servants who behave most like Western civil servants, there must be a firm idea of what actually constitutes Western bureaucratic patterns. Suppose, then, we ask whether the Egyptian official who displays great dependence upon his superiors is more or less bureaucratic than one who is more willing to rely on his own judgment in affairs within his competence. If our model of bureaucracy, so to speak, implies that the tendency toward caution in this respect is typically bureaucratic, then the more cautious official is the more highly bureaucratic. If, however, the model implies that typically bureaucratic behavior does not exclude the full exercise of such personal initiative as is permitted by the rules, then the more cautious official is not necessarily the more bureaucratic.

To add to our difficulties, suppose we find that we must consider not one but two models—one Western and one Egyptian. Suppose, further, that the Western model implies that the more bureaucratic official is the one who is more willing to exercise the permitted degree of personal initiative, while the Egyptian (or Eastern, or preindustrial) model implies that the more timid official is the more highly bureaucratic. We should then have to say that the more timid Egyptian official is the more bureaucratic one if measured along the Egyptian scale but the less bureaucratic one if measured along the scale of Western bureaucracy we have just postulated. We now confront our problem in its full extent: we are limited by the shortcomings of the theory of bureaucracy.

In this study of Egyptian bureaucratic behavior we used documentary data; historical accounts; and a questionnaire concerning socioeconomic background, attitudes, and opinions which was answered by 249 higher civil servants in the three grades below the highest one. By means of the questionnaire we hoped to learn the socioeconomic characteristics of those higher civil servants whose attitudes toward the government, the service, and the public most closely resembled what we could assume, from such studies as have touched this matter, to be the Western bureaucratic norm.

In a widely quoted paper Robert K. Merton has summarized some structural and behavioral patterns of bureaucracy that have generally been viewed as constituting the Western (if not the universal) model. In this model bureaucratic structure is a

> series of offices, of hierarchized statuses, in which inhere a number of obligations and privileges closely defined by limited and specific rules. Each of these offices contains an area of imputed competence and responsibility. . . . The assignment of roles occurs on the basis of technical qualifications which are ascertained through formalized, impersonal procedures (e.g., examinations).

Behaviorally, the model describes bureaucracy as tending toward "a high degree of reliability of behavior, an unusual degree of conformity with prescribed patterns of action." Emphasis is placed upon "discipline," which becomes an end in itself and "develops into rigidities and an inability to adjust readily." The very structural devices (such as grading, seniority regulations, pensions) that promote conformity to the rules, however, "also lead to an overconcern with strict adherence to regulations which induces timidity, conservatism, and technicism."[1]

The usual description of bureaucracy, like this one, implies that the various components of the structure or the behavior are always found together, that they are harmonious parts of a whole. Our study of the Egyptian higher civil service, however, emphasizes the need to determine whether this is indeed the case. We expected that those Egyptian officials highly exposed to Western influences through travel, study in the West, and familiarity with Western mass media of communication would come closest to the Western norms. We expected, then, that the most highly exposed respondents would have the highest score on a Guttman scale of items touching bureaucratic behavior. We found something different. The results, as may be seen in Table I, showed that the most highly exposed respondents were concentrated at the mid-point of the bureaucratic scale rather than at the high point.[2] This outcome suggested a re-examination of the items that went into the scale purporting to measure bureaucratic attitudes. Upon analysis it appeared that these items did not all touch the same aspect of official behavior, that what we

TABLE I

RESPONDENTS' SCORE ON BUREAUCRATIC SCALE, CLASSIFIED BY SCORE ON EXPOSURE SCALE

SCORE ON BUREAUCRATIC SCALE	HIGH EXPOSURE (106 CASES)	LOW EXPOSURE (143 CASES)
	%	%
High	32	43
Medium	42	37
Low	26	20

1 Robert K. Merton, *Social Theory and Social Structure* (Glencoe, Ill., 1949), pp. 151–152, 154–156.

2 Tests of statistical significance are not mentioned here because no claim is advanced regarding this aspect of any relationships upon which this discussion is based. The relationships form a pattern that suggests the questions raised.

had assumed was a unitary, irreducible predisposition had to be analyzed into several components. Significantly, too, these components, we learned, did not necessarily vary together. Rather, since they seemed to be different aspects of what we call the bureaucratic pattern, they might vary differently when related to a given variable. It was this differential response to the same independent variable that had resulted in the finding that the respondent with high exposure to the West was more likely to be in the moderately bureaucratic group than in the highly bureaucratic one.

Re-examination of the items led to the consideration of three dimensions of bureaucratic behavior that accompany corresponding structural features of bureaucratic organization.

1. Rationality and universalism: the degree of emphasis upon efficiency in getting a task performed and upon recruitment based upon competence rather than upon other considerations such as need or loyalty to family, religion, or community.
2. Hierarchy: the degree of emphasis upon the prerogatives of position, upon the authority of the superior official and the obedience of the subordinate.
3. Discretion: the degree of emphasis upon the official's area of free judgment and personal initiative; the degree of willingness to accept responsibility and to exercise the full measure of discretionary power permitted by the regulations.

These three components are, of course, intimately related to one another. The first, rationality and the emphasis upon efficiency, involves the second, the maintenance of a system of division of labor and authority. The second, hierarchy, permits varying degrees of the third, discretion. And discretion or personal initiative often is demanded if the first, rationality and efficiency, is to be realized. They may, however, be considered separately to see just how far a high degree of each of these aspects of bureaucratic behavior is associated with a high degree of any of the other two.

Although the questionnaire answered by our sample of Egyptian civil servants was not designed as such a test, the responses do throw some light upon this problem. As already mentioned, we had expected that high exposure to Western influences, for example, would place a respondent in the group high in predisposition to bureaucratic behavior. But the data concerning the three components of such behavior do not entirely fulfill this expectation. On one clear item of the questionnaire touching the first component, rationality and efficiency, respondents highly exposed to the West indeed scored high, indicating a high predisposition to this particular quality of bureaucratic behavior. The respondents were asked: "As you know, the government, in employing people, considers their degree of education and experience. Do you think the government should consider other factors in making these appointments? For example: social position?—family connections?—wealth?—religion?—political belief?" Of those highly exposed to the West, 61 per cent say only education and experience should be considered in recruiting civil servants, whereas only 57 per cent of those less exposed say so. Another way of looking at the answers to this question yields a similar result. Of the 249 respondents, 44 mentioned two or more of these qualifications other than education and training; the proportion giving this response was only 14 per cent among the two most highly exposed groups compared to 19 per cent among the less exposed ones.

On those items touching the second component, hierarchy, the respondents highly exposed to Western patterns scored low, indicating a low predisposition to this element of the bureaucratic pattern of behavior. One item described an imaginary situation in which a government economist is asked by his superior to prepare a memorandum defending a policy with arguments that contradict what most economists, in and outside the government, accept as valid. The respondents were then asked: "Can the department head expect this civil servant to prepare such a memorandum?" Of 248 who replied, 53, or 21 per cent, revealed less loyalty to the hierarchy by saying that the department head could not expect his subordinate to do his bidding under these circumstances. As Table II shows, the proportion of respondents who took this position was much greater among those highly exposed to the West than among the others —28 per cent compared with 16 per cent. Another imaginary situation sets up a conflict between loyalty to the hierarchy and

TABLE II

OPINION AS TO WHETHER SUPERIOR CAN EXPECT ECONOMIST TO PREPARE MEMORANDUM, CLASSIFIED BY EXPOSURE TO THE WEST

	HIGH EXPOSURE (106 CASES)	LOW EXPOSURE (142 CASES)
	%	%
Superior cannot expect it	28	16
Superior can expect it	72	84

to the public. A fieldworker assigned to study ways to promote village cooperation and to improve sanitation recommends a program that his superiors discard; they propose a different one, which the fieldworker believes would not be in the interests of the villagers, and they ask him to carry out this program. The respondents were asked: "Can his superiors expect this civil servant to carry out this policy?" Of the 248 respondents, 65, or 26 per cent, said they could not. Again the proportion who decided against the hierarchy was, as shown in Table III, higher among those highly exposed to the West—30 per cent compared with 23 per cent.

Finally, on the items concerning the use of discretionary

TABLE III

OPINION AS TO WHETHER SUPERIORS CAN EXPECT CIVIL SERVANT TO CARRY OUT POLICY, CLASSIFIED BY EXPOSURE TO THE WEST

	HIGH EXPOSURE (106 CASES)	LOW EXPOSURE (142 CASES)
	%	%
Superiors cannot expect it	30	23
Superiors can expect it	70	77

power and personal initiative, the results are unfortunately not clear.

Let us consider the way in which another variable, age, affects the data. On rationality and efficiency, the older respondents scored higher than the younger. On hierarchy the reverse obtains. On discretion and initiative, the evidence is again inconclusive. Still another variable we tried was location of the place where higher education was obtained, that is, the responses of civil servants who took their baccalaureate or higher degree in Europe or the United States were compared with the responses of those who studied in Egyptian institutions. On rationality and efficiency those educated in the West scored higher. On hierarchy, those educated in Egypt scored higher. On discretion and initiative the Western-educated again scored higher.

Thus none of these three variables—exposure to Western influences, age, and place of higher education—uniformly yields high or low scores on the three components of bureaucratic behavior we have postulated. What emerges is a picture of the older, Western-educated, and Western-exposed civil servant as more highly predisposed to emphasize rationality, efficiency, and universality and less predisposed to emphasize the power of position, the authority of the superior official, and the propriety of obedience by the subordinate. That these three independent variables, incidentally, should affect the data in the same way is not surprising, for they are all related to one another in our sample.

The questionnaire data are relevant to professionalism, another aspect of bureaucratic studies. A. M. Carr-Saunders and P. A. Wilson, in their classic study, have stated the generally accepted features of professionalism. Professionals, they say,

> by virtue of a prolonged and specialized intellectual training, have acquired a technique which enables them to render a specialized service to the community. . . . They develop a sense of responsibility for the technique which they manifest in their concern for the competence and honor of the practitioners as a whole. . . . They build up associations, upon which they erect, with or without the cooperation of the State, machinery for im-

posing tests of competence and enforcing the observance of certain standards of conduct.[3]

This statement, like the usual one on bureaucracy, does not suggest that the various components of professionalism may be found in varying degrees of strength and that emphasis upon one may be accompanied by disregard of another. This concept, too, we found to be susceptible of analysis into three component parts. We were led to this point by the same reasoning as in the case of attitudes on bureaucratic behavior. We had expected to find that the respondents most exposed to the West would also score high on an index of items touching professional loyalties. They were, instead, concentrated among the moderately professional group, as Table IV shows. Surprised by this result, we again examined the items making up the index and concluded that they seemed to bear upon predispositions that did not necessarily respond uniformly to a given stimulus. We saw three components of what we had been taking to be the irreducible concept of professionalism.

1. Skill: emphasis upon technical competence as the chief characteristic of an organized professional group and upon self-discipline and self-regulation in the group to maintain its standards of skill.
2. Self-protection: emphasis upon self-interest of the professional group through monopoly of function, secrecy, and exclusion.
3. Service: emphasis upon service to the public or clientele as the main feature of professional activity and upon protection of the public's interest.

As in the case of bureaucracy, these component parts are of course related to one another. The first, emphasis on skill, is promoted by the second, the power to exclude those not meeting the standard. The goal of the second, obtained by means of licensing and control of recruitment, ostensibly accomplishes the third, protection of the public. Again, however, these components may be separated to enable us to see whether they uniformly accompany one another or whether they vary in the degree to

[3] A. M. Carr-Saunders and P. A. Wilson, *The Professions* (London, 1933), p. 284.

Table IV

Respondents' Score on Professionalism Index, Classified by Score on Exposure Scale

SCORE ON PROFESSIONALISM INDEX	HIGH EXPOSURE (106 CASES)	LOW EXPOSURE (143 CASES)
	%	%
High	28	33
Medium	54	43
Low	18	24

which they respond to a given variable. Our data on these matters are less satisfactory than the data regarding bureaucracy, but they do indicate that this line of analysis is worth pursuing. Exposure to Western influences, for example, affects two of the three components differently. The respondents who are highly exposed to the West tend to emphasize the skill component of professionalism but not the self-interest component. On the service component, however, the results are less clear.

Although bureaucratic and professional predispositions vary similarly in the ways that we have just reviewed, they are not at all related to each other in our sample of Egyptian higher civil servants. Table V shows that among those high on professionalism, 38.5 per cent are also high on the bureaucratic scale,

Table V

Relation Between Bureaucratic and Professional Predispositions

BUREAUCRATIC-SCALE POSITION	PROFESSIONALISM-INDEX POSITION	
	HIGH (78 CASES)	LOW (171 CASES)
	%	%
High	38.5	38.6
Low	61.5	61.4

and among those low on professionalism, virtually the same proportion, 38.6 per cent, are also high on the bureaucratic scale. Thus the respondents who are high in bureaucratic tendencies come in equal proportions from those high and low on professionalism. Further evidence of the differences between these two qualities in our sample appears in the fact that, for more than thirty items in the questionnaire, the characteristics which distinguish the highly bureaucratic respondents from those less bureaucratic are different from the characteristics that mark off those high on professionalism from those low in this respect. Finally, the data reveal that there are many significant relationships between the respondents' position on the bureaucratic scale and such characteristics as age, civil-service grade, social mobility, and job satisfaction. Professionalism, however, is not significantly related to these characteristics, which suggests that it is less rooted than are bureaucratic tendencies among the respondents in our sample. Although professionalism and bureaucracy are usually said to be closely related in the West, this relationship does not necessarily hold in other cultures. The differences between the two qualities in Egypt show that bureaucratic tendencies *precede* professional loyalties in point of time; there is evidence that these are different types of loyalty in the West,[4] and our data show which one develops first.

Bureaucratic and professional predispositions, our evidence suggests, may not be unitary tendencies. Each has several components that do not accompany one another in the same degree when considered against certain independent variables. It may be that these differential effects would be found in Western studies as well, that bureaucracy and professionalism are more complicated attitudes and behavior patterns than we have assumed. The individual member of a public or private bureaucracy, the individual independent or salaried professional, may display a high degree of one quality and low degree of another quality of either of these institutional complexes. When we try to compare bureaucratic and professional predispositions in the

[4] Wilbert E. Moore, "The Nature of Industrial Conflict," in *Industrial Conflict and Dispute Settlement* (Montreal: Industrial Relations Centre, McGill University, 7th Annual Conference, 1955), pp. 1–15; and Dwaine Marvick, *Career Perspectives in a Bureaucratic Setting* (Ann Arbor: Institute of Public Administration, University of Michigan, 1954), esp. ch. ix.

East and the West, we find that there may be differences of attitude and behavior in spite of the similarity in structure. As in other realms, similarity of structure and form, often the result of cultural diffusion, does not mean similarity of institutional or behavioral patterns.

Bureaucratic Theory and Comparative Administration

FERREL HEADY
The University of Michigan

WORKERS IN THE developing field of comparative public administration have been much concerned with questions of methodology, conceptualization, and model building. As a precaution against aimless accumulation of information this has much to be said for it, but some apprehension has been expressed that this concern may delay the field research necessary to test the varied proposed methodologies.[1] Certainly we should try to avoid the danger pointed out by Merton of having many "approaches" but few "arrivals."[2]

At this early stage, however, these attempts at conceptualization seem useful and valuable, for a traditional approach to

Reprinted from *Administrative Science Quarterly,* Vol. 3 (1959), pp. 509–525, by permission.

1 The best summary of these developments is in the introductory essay by William J. Siffin in Siffin, ed., *Toward the Comparative Study of Public Administration* (Bloomington, Ind., 1957). He comments that at this particular point "the major explicit problem of methodology consists of applying it. . . . A great deal of work has been done in the realm of conceptualization. . . . If there is to be much truly significant progress in comparative studies in the years ahead, it can occur only through emphatic attention to the application of approaches which have by now reached a fair degree of refinement." (pp. 12–13).

2 Robert K. Merton, *Social Theory and Social Structure* (rev. ed.; Glencoe, Ill., 1957), p. 9.

such a complex area of study as this would be unfortunate and probably unproductive. On the other hand, too early an adoption of any particular new approach, however fresh and promising, would cut off much-needed investigation in what is still largely unexplored territory. What is needed for the comparative study of administration is a trial of each of several possible conceptual frames.

One of the research designs proposes to focus upon the comparative study of public service systems of bureaucracies as major social entities functioning in given social environments.[3] The model presupposes that the public bureaucracies of selected countries can be identified and that a body of bureaucratic theory exists which will provide a basis for comparative analysis. Our primary concern in this essay will be to inquire whether such a supporting body of bureaucratic theory does in fact exist.

In a provocative article, "Bureaucracy East and West," published in the March 1957 issue of *Administrative Science Quarterly,* Morroe Berger has expressed some serious doubts about this which merit careful and thorough consideration.[4] Berger's observations grew out of his recent study of Egyptian bureaucracy.[5] He notes that bureaucracy has been analyzed from two related sides, through studies of bureaucratic structures on the one hand and studies of bureaucratic behavior on the other. He properly points out that the concepts and findings of these studies have been developed "by Western scholars upon the basis of Western institutions." After trying to use these studies as guides in his investigation of the current Egyptian bureaucracy, he concludes that they have decided limitations "for the analysis of bureaucratic behavior both in this non-Western setting and in our own society as well."[6]

[3] See Jonathan A. Slesinger, *A Model for the Comparative Study of Public Bureaucracies* (Papers in Pub. Adm., no. 23, Bur. of Govt., Inst. of Publ., Adm.; Ann Arbor, 1957). "This model, judiciously used, has the attractiveness of broadness and relative simplicity. It points toward the tentative formulation of hypotheses concerning the content of public administration as defined for comparative purposes and concerning certain general patterns of interaction between public service systems and their social environments" (Siffin, *op. cit.*, p. 11).

[4] Vol. 1, no. 4, pp. 518–529.

[5] *Bureaucracy and Society in Modern Egypt* (Princeton, N.J., 1957).

[6] "Bureaucracy East and West," p. 518.

If these doubts are justified, the prospect for success in developing comparative administration through the comparative study of bureaucracies is much reduced. Selection of public bureaucracies as a worth-while point of focus can be justified only if a fairly systematic theory exists to provide a basis for comparison. Is there such a body of bureaucratic theory? How exclusively does existing theory relate to bureaucracies in highly industrialized western societies? Are current concepts as to the characteristics of bureaucracy applicable to economically underdeveloped nonwestern societies? On one point, at least, everyone is in agreement as to methodology. This is that a suitable methodology must facilitate comparative studies which include both nonwestern, economically underdeveloped societies and the highly industrialized societies of the West. That is why it is crucial that the issues raised by Berger be explored before a choice is made among alternative frames of reference for comparative research.

In order to assess Berger's doubts we will first summarize the empirical findings which have led him to his conclusions. Then we will review existing formulations of bureaucratic theory as a background for analyzing and evaluating the theoretical assumptions upon which Berger conducted his study. Finally, we will suggest a theoretical orientation concerning public bureaucracies which might open the way to fruitful comparisons involving both western and nonwestern bureaucratic systems, based upon further empirical research along the paths Berger has used in his study of the Egyptian bureaucracy.

Berger's conclusion as to the inadequacy of existing theory for the analysis of bureaucratic behavior is based mainly on the fact that responses to the questionnaire which he used in his study did not conform to his expectations. In his research he found it necessary to make certain assumptions about "Western norms" of bureaucratic behavior. Since he wanted "to determine to what degree Egyptian bureaucratic behavior resembles its Western counterpart and to explore the socio-economic background of those Egyptian civil servants who behave most like Western civil servants," he saw that "there must be a firm idea of what actually constitutes Western bureaucratic patterns."[7] This

[7] *Ibid.*, p. 520.

led him to devise a bureaucratic scale designed to measure "the respondents' degree of approximation of Western bureaucratic norms."[8]

The scale was constructed on the assumption that "the usual description of bureaucracy . . . implies that the various components of the structure or the behavior are always found together, that they are harmonious parts of a whole."[9] Three items on the questionnaire were used to construct the scale. One question asked what the respondent disliked about civil service employment; he was permitted to say anything he chose rather than asked to select from a suggested list of answers. Responses mentioning "favoritism, inefficient use of personnel, and the absence or killing of initiative" were considered "Western," any others "non-Western." Another question posed an imaginary situation concerning a civil servant engaged in factory inspection who orders a factory owner, under protest, to close the factory on the ground that a floor is about to give way under the weight of a machine. The respondent was asked a number of questions about this situation under varying assumptions as to the basis in fact for the closing order given by the factory inspector. Two responses to one of these sets of assumptions were used in constructing the bureaucratic scale. On the assumption that the inspector's judgment turned out to be wrong, the respondent was asked (1) whether he thought the civil servant acted properly in closing the factory and (2) whether the civil servant's superior should discipline him for taking such a step. An affirmative answer to the first question and a negative answer to the second one were considered "Western" responses.

From these items four positions along the bureaucratic scale were possible, ranging from no western answers to three western answers. Respondents who answered all three items in what was presumed to be the western manner were rated high on the bureaucratic scale. The scale was used for the purpose of determining what proportion of Egyptian higher civil servants showed "a high degree of Western bureaucratic predisposition." It was assumed, but of course not proved, that "Western civil service

[8] Berger, *Bureaucracy and Society in Modern Egypt,* p. 217. For details concerning the methodology, refer to App. 4, pp. 217–228.

[9] "Bureaucracy East and West," p. 522.

groups would, on the same questions, emerge with a larger proportion in the high group."[10] Berger also used four items in the questionnaire dealing with professionalism to produce a professionalism index. Here again he assumed that certain responses were "professional" and "Western," and would be more likely to occur among western than Egyptian higher civil servants.[11]

What Berger discovered upon analysis of the questionnaire data was that the Egyptian civil servants most highly exposed to western influences did not, as he had anticipated, come closest to what he had assumed to be the western norms, either on the bureaucratic scale or the professionalism index. Instead, the most highly exposed respondents were concentrated at the midpoint of the bureaucratic scale, and among the moderately professional group on the professional index.

"This outcome," Berger reports, "suggested a re-examination of the items that went into the scale purporting to measure bureaucratic attitudes. Upon analysis it appeared that these items did not all touch the same aspect of official behavior, that what we had assumed was a unitary, irreducible predisposition had to be analyzed into several components."[12] The re-examination led to identification of "three dimensions of bureaucratic behavior that accompany corresponding structural features of bureaucratic organization." These three behavioral components were designated as (1) rationality and universalism, (2) hierarchy, and (3) discretion.[13] Likewise, what had been taken as "the irreducible concept of professionalism" was analyzed into three component parts, identified as (1) skill, (2) self-protection, and (3) service.[14]

For each component in each category it was assumed that a high rating indicated conformity to the western model of bureaucracy. Thus the western bureaucrat was presumed to place

10 *Bureaucracy and Society in Modern Egypt,* p. 219.

11 Details concerning construction of the professionalism index are in App. 4, pp. 219–220.

12 "Bureaucracy East and West," p. 522.

13 *Ibid.,* pp. 522–523.

14 *Ibid.,* pp. 526–527.

great emphasis on efficiency in performance and competence as a basis for recruitment, to emphasize the importance of hierarchical arrangements and to favor the exercise of initiative and discretionary power. As a professional he was presumed to emphasize skill or technical competence coupled with self-regulation as the mark of professionalism, to insist upon self-protection by the professional group of its own interests, and to emphasize at the same time service to the public or clientele as the main feature of professional activity.

Questionnaire items were then re-examined for relevance to each of these components, including items which had not been used in constructing the bureaucratic scale and professionalism index in the first instance. For example, under the heading of rationality and efficiency a question had been asked as to factors other than education and experience which should be considered in making appointments. Mention of other factors such as social position, family connections, wealth, and so on were regarded as showing low attachment to the trait of rationality and efficiency. Two items were analyzed relating to hierarchy, involving preparation by a professional economist at the request of his superior of a memorandum defending a policy not regarded as valid by most economists and the carrying out by a fieldworker in public health of a sanitation program proposed by his superiors which he believed would not be in the interests of the villagers concerned. Responses that the expectations of the superior officials should be met were regarded as showing emphasis on hierarchy.

The respondents highly exposed to the West tended to conform to the supposed western bureaucratic norm on the criterion of efficiency and rationality, but not on the criterion of hierarchy. The results were not clear on the third criterion of initiative and use of discretionary power. With regard to professionalism it was found that respondents highly exposed to the West "tend to emphasize the skill component of professionalism but not the self-interest component. On the service component, however, the results are less clear."[15]

Berger's conclusion from analysis of this evidence, as already stated, is that bureaucratic theory developed in the West has decided limitations for the study of both western and non-western bureaucracies. A brief resume of the voluminous litera-

[15] *Ibid.*, p. 527.

ture on bureaucratic theory[16] will help provide a basis for evaluating the soundness of this judgment.

A bureaucracy is "an organization marked by certain structural features that cannot be readily called either desirable or undesirable *per se*."[17] The perspective here is on "bureaucracy as structure of organization."[18] Bureaucracy is "the type of organization designed to accomplish large-scale administrative tasks by systematically coordinating the work of many individuals. . . . Since complex administrative problems confront most large organizations, bureaucracy is not confined to the military and civilian branches of the government but is also found in business, unions, churches, universities, and even in baseball."[19]

Max Weber made fundamental contributions to the systematic development of bureaucratic theory along these lines.[20] Essentially he advanced the view that demystification and rationalization are distinctive features of modern society that are manifested in bureaucracy. He developed the concept of an "ideal type" of bureaucracy and described the characteristics which would occur in such an ideal type. Although acknowledging the seminal nature of Weber's contributions, commentators have recently been expressing reservations about some of his assumptions and conclusions.[21] These re-evaluations of Weber have in turn stimulated numerous reformulations of bureaucratic theory.

Although differing in details, these reformulations show a

[16] A valuable collection of this literature is contained in Robert K. Merton, ed., *Reader in Bureaucracy* (Glencoe, Ill., 1952).

[17] Robert A. Dahl and Charles E. Lindblom, *Politics, Economics and Welfare* (New York, 1953), p. 234.

[18] Fritz Morstein Marx, *The Administrative State* (Chicago, 1957), pp. 21 ff.

[19] Peter M. Blau, *Bureaucracy in Modern Society* (New York, 1956), p. 14.

[20] For summaries of his views, see Weber, "The Essentials of Bureaucratic Organization: An Ideal-Type Construction," in *Reader in Bureaucracy*, pp. 18–27, and Blau, *op. cit.*, pp. 28 ff.

[21] For examples, refer to Carl J. Friedrich, "Some Observations on Weber's Analysis of Bureaucracy," in *Reader in Bureaucracy*, pp. 27–33; O. D. Corpuz, "Theoretical Limitations of Max Weber's Systematic Analysis of Bureaucracy," *Philippine Journ. of Pub. Adm.*, 1 (1957), 342–349; and Blau, *op. cit.*, pp. 21 ff.

close similarity. Recent examples may be found in Friedrich,[22] Dahl and Lindblom,[23] Dubin,[24] Blau,[25] Slesinger,[26] and Morstein Marx.[27] All agree substantially on such central elements as a rational orientation toward goal attainment, a hierarchy of authority, work specialization, professionalism, and systematic rules as a basis for operations. Except for Blau, all of them seem willing to consider structural characteristics as the proper point of focus for defining bureaucracy. Blau has suggested a somewhat different approach to the concept of bureaucracy as the result of studies during the last generation of actual conduct in organizations as contrasted with formal expectations. This concern with "bureaucracy's other face"[28] and the "irrationality of rationalistic administration"[29] has suggested to Blau and others "a revision of the concept of bureaucratic structure."[30] Such a revision would stress purpose, adaptability, and suitability.[31] Even this emphasis, however, assumes that bureaucracy involves the presence of such fundamental structural characteristics as those enumerated above. The focusing of attention on "achievement of purpose" does not mean abandonment of organizational characteristics as typical of bureaucracy, but rather it has far-reaching implications for the behavioral aspect of bureaucratic analysis.

Theories of behavior in bureaucracy have been relatively

22 Carl J. Friedrich, *Constitutional Government and Democracy* (rev. ed.; Boston, 1950), ch. ii.

23 *Op. cit.,* pp. 227–271.

24 Robert Dubin, *Human Relations in Administration* (New York, 1951), pp. 151–161.

25 *Op. cit.,* ch. ii.

26 *Op. cit.,* ch. ii.

27 *Op. cit.,* ch. ii.

28 The phrase is that of Charles H. Page, quoted by Blau, *op. cit.,* p. 46.

29 *Ibid.,* p. 58.

30 *Ibid.,* p. 60.

31 "Bureaucracy, then, can be defined as organization that maximizes efficiency in administration, whatever its formal characteristics, or as an institutionalized method of organizing social conduct in the interest of administrative efficiency. On the basis of this definition, the problem of central concern is the expeditious removal of the obstacles to efficient operations which recurrently arise" (*ibid*).

neglected, probably in large part because of the obvious complexity of the matter. It is naturally assumed that the structural traits of bureaucracy considered as a sociological concept will be accompanied by behavior patterns associated with these structural characteristics. The range of these behavior patterns and the question of which particular pattern, if any, should be considered most "bureaucratic" have received much less attention and have produced much less of a consensus.

Three views or approaches to the issue of bureaucratic behavior emerge from a survey of existing literature. The first of these is best represented by Friedrich.[32] Of the six elements which he finds recurring "in a developing bureaucracy in demonstrable institutionalization," three are organizational and three are behavioral. The behavioral elements are objectivity, precision and consistency, and discretion. According to Friedrich, these behavior aspects of bureaucracy are just as normal, proper, and appropriate as are the organizational or functional aspects with which they are grouped as primary criteria of bureaucracy. They "embody rules defining desirable habit or behavior patterns of all the members of such an organization," and they were originated by "men of extraordinary inventiveness who were laying the basis of a rationalized society by these inventions."[33]

A more common tendency among writers on bureaucratic behavior is to concentrate upon behavior which is "dysfunctional" or "pathological." This refers to tendencies of bureaucracies to develop behavior patterns which, although linked to the rational base of bureaucratic organization and related structural devices, inhibit the attainment of the legitimate objectives of bureaucracy. In his influential essay, "Bureaucratic Structure and Personality," for example, Robert K. Merton has analyzed these "dysfunctions" and "negative aspects" of bureaucracy.[34] He is concerned with the fact that "the very elements which conduce toward efficiency in general produce inefficiency in specific instances"[35] and "also lead to an overconcern with strict adherence to regulations which induces timidity, conservatism,

[32] Friedrich, *Constitutional Government and Democracy*, pp. 44–57.

[33] *Ibid.*, p. 44.

[34] Reprinted in *Reader in Bureaucracy*, pp. 361–371.

[35] *Ibid.*, p. 366.

and technicism."[36] Stress on "depersonalization of relationships" leads to conflict in relations with bureaucratic clientele and so on. Behavior of this sort is typical of the "trained incapacity" of the bureaucrat.

Specific behavioral orientations often mentioned are "buck passing," red tape, rigidity and inflexibility, excessive impersonality, oversecretiveness, unwillingness to delegate, and reluctance to exercise discretion. The implication is that behavior which is most typically bureaucratic is behavior which develops from overemphasis on the rationality of bureaucratic organization and which is dysfunctional in its effects. This suggests a model for bureaucratic behavior which would stress these contradictory or self-defeating traits connected with bureaucracy considered as "ailment of organization."

A third method for dealing with bureaucratic behavior suggested by Blau is that bureaucracy should be conceived of primarily in terms of achievement of purpose. In modern society, with its necessities for large-scale operation, this probably requires that certain basic organizational characteristics be present. These would include hierarchical arrangements, specialization, professionalization to some degree, a set of operational rules, and a basic commitment to rational adaptation of means to ends. Although Blau recognizes the tendency for bureaucracies to develop behavior patterns which detract from the attainment of legitimate objectives, he does not accept the view that all behavior that deviates from the formal expectation or seems irrational is in fact dysfunctional. He suggests a category of behavior of a somewhat different kind, which he terms "irrational but (perhaps) purposeful."[37] Behavior having its source in undercommitment to rationality may be dysfunctional, but this must be judged by results rather than by reference to a preconceived set of behavioral traits which are assumed to accompany the structural components of bureaucracy. The test as to the propriety of behavior would be its contribution to fundamental bureaucratic goals. Behavior which is pathological in one bureaucracy might be healthful in another.

36 *Ibid.*, p. 367.

37 Blau, *op. cit.*, p. 58: "To administer a social organization according to purely technical criteria of rationality is irrational, because it ignores the nonrational aspects of social conduct."

The preceding resume indicates that considerable agreement exists as to the basic organizational characteristics of bureaucracy, but there is much less certainty as to the behavioral traits associated with it. Three alternatives have been presented for designating a pattern of behavior as "bureaucratic." One points toward normal, functional, desirable behavior to be expected and accepted as natural in bureaucratic operations. Another stresses dysfunctional behavior which is likely to develop from the rationalistic orientation of bureaucracy and the structural features designed to maintain it. The third alternative relates the propriety of behavior to the bureaucratic environment and results in a more flexible standard as to what behavior is bureaucratic in the sense of being functional.

To return to Berger, we find that he pays relatively little attention to the structural side of bureaucratic theory. Apparently he would accept a listing of basic structural elements such as those previously referred to and would expect them to be present in both western and nonwestern civil service systems. His concern is with theories and models concerning bureaucratic behavior rather than with structure. He implicitly assumes that a "model" of bureaucracy, either of a general type or one confined to western patterns, would combine identifiable structural *and* behavior features. He quotes Robert K. Merton as summarizing "some structural and behavioral patterns of bureaucracy that have generally been viewed as constituting the western (if not the universal) model."[38] The behavioral attributes quoted by Berger are those that Merton discusses as "dysfunctions of bureaucracy."

The implication is that on the behavioral side a model for bureaucracy would stress "dysfunctional" or "pathological" tendencies, along the lines of the second alternative discussed earlier. Since existing bureaucratic theory has been built largely upon study of western bureaucracies, such behavioral traits presumably would be part of a "model" for western bureaucracy if one were to be formulated. This impression is strengthened by Berger when he discusses the question whether "one way of doing things is more or less bureaucratic than another."[39] He illus-

[38] "Bureaucracy East and West," p. 521.

[39] *Ibid.*, p. 520.

trates this by referring to the issue of the degree to which personal initiative is related to bureaucratic behavior. "The exercise of such initiative is not structurally excluded from bureaucracy," he comments, "yet it is usually characterized as unbureaucratic behavior in scholarly studies as well as in popular discussion. Similarly, its opposite, extreme caution, 'playing it safe,' 'covering' oneself by getting a decision from the official on the next level of the hierarchy, is thought of as the typical behavioral concomitant of bureaucratic structure."[40]

Nevertheless it is puzzling to note that his western model does not seem to be built upon the combination of behavioral traits which he cites as commonly propounded by bureaucratic theorists. In particular, he assumes that the western bureaucratic norm is one emphasizing the exercise of personal initiative and discretion. For instance, in constructing the bureaucratic scale already described, two of the three questionnaire items used dealt with "the degree to which the respondent felt it proper and safe for a civil servant to use his initiative."[41] A respondent had to favor the use of initiative in each item in order to be rated "high" on the bureaucratic scale (the equivalent of "the ideal Western manner").

This same ambivalence toward acceptance of the behavioral pattern suggested by the quotation from Merton as "typical" or "Western" appears in the breakdown of bureaucratic behavior into components. A behavior profile which would be labeled "most bureaucratic" by combining "bureaucratic" ranking for each trait is one which shows high degrees of emphasis on efficiency and competence, on the prerogatives of position, and on the exercise of initiative and discretion. Of these, only the second behavioral component, the one stressing hierarchy and its claims, is rather clearly in the pattern of behavioral traits often considered pathological or dysfunctional.

In short, Berger's assumptions as to "the bureaucratic pattern of behavior," which he apparently equates with "the Western bureaucratic pattern of behavior," seem not to conform with his own citation from bureaucratic theory as to the behavioral components of bureaucracy. Instead, he seems to have modified

40 *Ibid.*

41 *Bureaucracy and Society in Modern Egypt,* App. 4, p. 218.

this pattern to what he regards, for reasons not clearly explained, as a model for "Western" as perhaps contrasted with "non-Western" bureaucracies. This leaves attitudes toward "hierarchy" as the only phase of "Western" bureaucratic norms most likely to prove dysfunctional. It may be significant that it is on items touching this component of hierarchy that the Egyptian respondents highly exposed to western patterns scored low, indicating either that these supposedly westernized Egyptian bureaucrats did not actually conform in this respect to the western norm or that the norm itself was inaccurate as an indicator of the actual pattern of behavior of western bureaucrats regarding hierarchy.

Thus Berger does not seem to have done what he started out to do. He began by asserting that the usual description of bureaucracy, like that of Merton which he quotes, "implies that the various components of the structure or the behavior are always found together, that they are harmonious parts of a whole." This model, on the behavioral side, stresses tendencies toward dysfunctions which interfere with the attainment of bureaucratic objectives. Since he emphasizes that this model is based upon western bureaucratic experience, Berger would be expected to use such a model in making his assumptions as to "Western bureaucratic predisposition." Instead, without explanation and indeed in direct contrast with what he refers to as the usual characterization of bureaucratic behavior, he chooses to abandon this model in some very important respects when he makes his assumptions about normal western behavior, to which his Egyptian respondents most highly exposed to western influences will presumably conform. Thus Merton's "typical" bureaucrat who is inclined to "timidity, conservatism, and technicism" becomes Berger's "Western" bureaucrat who will respond to a problem situation by feeling that it is "proper and safe for a civil servant to use his initiative." The weighting of items for the bureaucratic scale made this inclination toward use of initiative decisive in achieving a high score on the scale.

On the other hand, Berger does go along with the typical model in other respects, especially in dealing with the component of hierarchy. Here he labels as "bureaucratic" a pattern of behavior which puts emphasis "upon the prerogatives of position, upon the authority of the superior official and the obedience of the subordinate."[42] This certainly implies a tendency toward dysfunction and raises a serious doubt as to the consistency of calling bureaucratic this attitude toward "hierarchy" when combined with the attitude already discussed toward "discretion." It would seem rather unlikely that these attitudes would be found together.

The problem, Berger says, is that "we are limited by the shortcomings of the theory of bureaucracy." It may be that the main problem is the hybrid or bifurcated model of bureaucracy which he uses and the confusion which results. If his model had been consistent in specifying dysfunctional behavioral traits as those to be termed "bureaucratic," this would have provided a standard against which to measure existing patterns of bureaucratic behavior, both in western and nonwestern bureaucracies. If his intention was to postulate a western model of bureaucratic behavior which reflected less of a tendency toward dysfunction, then it is not explained why he chose to retain a high regard for the prerogatives of hierarchy while calling "bureaucratic" a willingness to exercise personal initiative and discretion. He does not support on any empirical evidence a finding that such a combination is normal in western bureaucracies. Therefore data collected tending to show that western-exposed Egyptian civil servants do not conform to a supposed western or bureaucratic regard for hierarchy do not prove that this category of Egyptian bureaucrats is less like western bureaucrats as a group. It may instead indicate a misjudgment as to the actual behavioral orientation of western bureaucrats toward hierarchy. It may well be that surveys of bureaucrats in western bureaucracies would show them to rank high or "bureaucratic" in Berger's terms on rationality and universalism and on discretion, but low or "unbureaucratic" on the component of hierarchy.

Of course, as Berger suggests, we could end up with two or more "models" of bureaucracy, such as a western model and an eastern or preindustrial model. His discussion implies that this may be necessary,[43] but this seems to create more difficulties than

42 "Bureaucracy East and West," p. 523.

43 "To add to our difficulties, suppose we find that we must consider not one but two models—one Western and one Egyptian. Suppose, further,

it solves, and it is not necessary. The meaning of "bureaucracy" and "bureaucratic" is a matter of definition. What would be gained by labeling "more bureaucratic" or "highly bureaucratic" each of two contrasting behavioral traits, depending on whether the measure is the western or nonwestern model? Both an unusual willingness to show initiative and excessive timidity would then be "highly bureaucratic." The same might be true concerning attitude toward hierarchy, with both a small degree and a large degree of emphasis on the prerogatives of position qualifying as "highly bureaucratic." To complicate the matter further we are hardly prepared yet to say what behavior would be "bureaucratic" in either the western or nonwestern sense. Berger raises considerable doubts as to his own success in postulating norms which conform to actual patterns of behavior in either the West or the East.

An escape from some of these semantic snares, which might at the same time open the way toward progress, would be to define bureaucracy in terms of certain essential structural characteristics that are already generally accepted and understood, without attaching the label of "bureaucratic" to any particular pattern or combination of behavioral traits. It would then be possible to classify bureaucracies by behavioral patterns into whatever number of types seem required by the data available, without having to decide which behavior is more bureaucratic and which is less bureaucratic. (This is comparable to classifying societies into types such as industrial and agrarian, without having to call either type more "societal" than another.)

By making the structural aspect central to the concept of bureaucracy, we can provide a conceptual framework on which there is already a substantial measure of agreement and which offers a basis for comparison in both western and nonwestern states. A decision against incorporating a particular pattern of behavior into the concept of bureaucracy has several advantages.

that the Western model implies that the more bureaucratic official is the one who is more willing to exercise the permitted degree of personal initiative, while the Egyptian (or Eastern, or preindustrial) model implies that the more timid official is the more highly bureaucratic. We should then have to say that the more timid Egyptian official is the more bureaucratic one if measured along the Egyptian scale but the less bureaucratic one if measured along the scale of Western bureaucracy we have just postulated" (*ibid.*, p. 521).

It avoids a premature theoretical commitment in an area where too little is known, although the complexities are obvious. It would not interfere with, and should facilitate, the identification and analysis of the various patterns of behavior traits to be found in existing bureaucracies. It would not hamper efforts to distinguish normal from pathological or dysfunctional bureaucratic behavior. Without requiring discussion as to what is more or less bureaucratic, hypotheses could be formulated and tested to explain differences in behavior between western bureaucracies in industrialized societies and nonwestern bureaucracies in transitional societies.

To illustrate, Blau's treatment of bureaucracy suggests that some behavior traits which would be considered dysfunctional in western bureaucracies are functional in nonwestern bureaucracies. Blau points out that behavior which appears irrational may further the attainment of organizational objectives, even in western bureaucracies. This may be much more likely in nonwestern bureaucracies. For example, in a perceptive discussion of the connection between administrative leadership and culture in the Philippines,[44] Carlos Ramos has stressed that here, as in other Asiatic nations, there is "a mixture of Western cultural influences superimposed upon an oriental agrarian mode of living," which affects the characteristics of successful leadership behavior.

> Studies in the Philippines indicate that willingness to recognize and accept leadership depends in part upon family ties, common geographic backgrounds and relative social status. Workers often prefer to follow relatives, especially relatives of higher social status than themselves. . . . The leader is effective to the degree that he can induce others to cooperate in the direction of the organization's functional purposes. But if he is able to do that because of an understanding of family ties, geographic backgrounds, and the outward symbols of social status, he enhances his functional usefulness as well.[45]

Research directed at such problems, relating to the propriety of behavior to the character of the bureaucracy and the society in which it functions, would be of great value.

44 "Developing Administrative Leadership," *Philippine Journ. of Public Adm.,* 2 (1958), 9–19.

45 *Ibid.,* pp. 10–11.

Another hypothesis worth testing is that pathological behavioral tendencies in nonwestern transitional bureaucracies often have a different origin than the behavioral dysfunctions commonly associated with bureaucracy in the West. Most self-defeating tendencies in the West are blamed upon an overcommitment to rationality and the structural devices designed to ensure rationality. On the other hand, much dysfunctional behavior in transitional bureaucracies may be caused by an undercommitment to rationality as a basis for operation and a failure to relinquish in a bureaucratic setting behavioral patterns inherited from a still-potent preindustrial, nonrationally oriented society. Moreover, there is a possibility that extreme dysfunctions may be produced when the same behavior pattern is reinforced from both sources. For instance, exceptional deference to superiors may be due to recognition of hierarchical claims grounded in the rationality of bureaucracy, plus a deep-rooted pattern of respect for age and social status. Or unusual emphasis on tenure rights may be traced both to a desire to protect the objectivity of the bureaucrat and to an attempt to maintain civil servants whose jobs should be eliminated in the interests of efficiency.

Bureaucratic theory which defines bureaucracy in terms of essential structural features found in all modern public service systems but encourages empirical research to test hypotheses concerning behavioral patterns in various bureaucracies should resolve Berger's misgivings concerning the adequacy of theory for the comparative study of "bureaucracy East and West." The pioneering data which he has collected in Egypt give us a start and point up leads for future research. Shortcomings of bureaucratic theory are not as serious as he fears and are of a different character than he suggests. These shortcomings do not cloud the prospects for advancing the comparative study of administration through systematic analysis of public bureaucracies. Instead the existing conceptual framework is at least as well developed as any alternative design for advancing our knowledge of comparative administration.

The Major Traits of Prefectoral Systems

ROBERT C. FRIED
University of California (Los Angeles)

Prefectoral systems have certain common characteristics.

1. The national territory is divided into areas variously called "provinces," "departments," "governments," "prefectures," etc.
2. In each of these areas there is appointed a high functionary representative of and responsible to the central government (and in particular to a Minister of the Interior, or Justice, or Government) to carry out the following kinds of functions:
   a. political and social representation of the central government;
   b. maintenance of law and order;
   c. supervision of central government officials operating in the area;
   d. supervision of minor units of government in the area.
3. This official is a civil functionary operating independently of the military and the judiciary.
4. He does not enjoy the security of tenure enjoyed by other officials and may be dismissed or transferred at the pleasure of the central government.
5. He is not a resident or native of the area which he governs.
6. He may be either a career functionary or a "political" appointee from outside of the career service.
7. And he is usually supervised by a specialized central department—a Ministry of the Interior—which is nationally responsible for such matters as public safety and local government.

Reprinted from *The Italian Prefects: A Study in Administrative Politics* (New Haven and London: Yale University Press, 1963), pp. 301–314, by permission.

THE DIFFERENCES BETWEEN PREFECTORAL AND FUNCTIONAL SYSTEMS

STRUCTURE. The structural differences between prefectoral and functional systems may be summarized in the following chart:

PREFECTORAL	FUNCTIONAL
1. The national territory is divided into areas of general government and in each of these is placed a general representative of the central government (Prefect).	*1.* There is no general representative of the central government in the various regions of the national territory.
2. Each of the central ministries issues commands to its functional counterparts in the field via the Prefect.	*2.* Lines of command run directly from the central ministries to their field units.
3. Most state services use the areas of general government presided over by the Prefect.	*3.* State services use varying sets of administrative areas in accordance with their particular requirements.
4. The Prefect's area of general administration also constitutes an area of local self-government.	*4.* There is no necessary identity between field administrative and local government areas.
5. Central government control over minor units of government tends to be (a) more penetrating than in functional systems; (b) administrative rather than legislative; and (c) unified under the Prefect.	*5.* Central government control tends to be (a) less penetrating; (b) legislative rather than administrative; (c) and dispersed among several central and field institutions.

ORIGINS. It is much more difficult to ascertain and generalize about the factors that account for the establishment and maintenance of a prefectoral, rather than a functional, system of field administration. Such a broad question has yet to be studied and certainly cannot be answered on the basis of the foregoing historical study of a single prefectoral system.[1] The basic factors involved would seem to be the nature of the political system; its prevailing ideologies; its relative degree of consensus, internal security, and national cohesion. Functional systems, with their greater diffusion of administrative power, are more apt to develop within liberal political systems, in states with a high degree of consensus, security, and cohesion. The various areas of such states tend to be regarded as units deserving of some degree of autonomous decentralized power, rather than as dependencies and "wards" of the central government. Prefectoral systems are rarely to be found where there are strong and *generally accepted* centrifugal or decentralizing tendencies.

Conversely, more authoritarian systems and those with greater political fragmentation, dissension, and insecurity tend to develop prefectoral systems—primarily as instruments of centralization. The dominant political groups tend in such systems to view decentralization as potentially destructive of the political unity of the state. They are not averse to the concentration of administrative power in a single official within each area. They consider regional interests as dependencies requiring on-the-spot tutelage by the central government. Prefectoral systems will rarely, if ever, be found within genuine federal unions or highly decentralized unitary states. It would seem (although this remains to be tested) that the choice of a prefectoral, rather than a functional, system depends less on considerations of how the central government bureaucracy is to be organized than on what is to be the distribution of power as between the central and minor units of government. In other words, the choice hinges less on the desired pattern of *deconcentration* within the state administration as between central and field officials than on the desired pattern of *decentralization* as between central government and local government officials.

Prefectoral systems seem to suit best the purposes of absolutist governments and the traditions of those emerging from a period of absolutist, especially colonial, government. In Western

[1] On this question, see James W. Fesler, "The Political Role of Field Administration," in Ferrel Heady and Sybil L. Stokes, eds., *Papers in Comparative Public Administration* (Ann Arbor, Institute of Public Administration, 1962), pp. 117–43.

Europe, prefectoral systems evolved from the institutions devised by absolute monarchs in order to centralize power and control of economic resources within their kingdoms at the expense of the nobility and medieval communes. They constituted a basic arm of monarchy in conflict with domestic feudalities and foreign dynasts. They were the major element in the royal administrative machinery designed to deprive feudal lords and communes of their privileges and functions, to transform feudal serfs into royal subjects, and to elaborate and implement the economic policies of mercantilism. Mercantilist policies had, in turn, been devised to promote national unification and national power. They called for active state intervention in social and economic life: they required and made possible the development of the royal bureaucracy.

In an age of growing overarching allegiance to the Crown and of primitive bureaucratic specialization, the prefectoral system provided for the unified symbolic representation of the Crown in the provinces of the realm; for the reliable enforcement of royal commands; and for the reproduction in each province of the unified and theoretically absolute authority of the monarch. The same purposes were served in the Napoleonic model, which rationalized and modernized the prefectoral institutions of the old regimes, abolishing venality and inheritance of office. The Napoleonic system clarified the division of functions as between civil, military, and judicial officials. It strengthened prefectoral control over minor units of government, now uniform in structure and functions and subject to nationally uniform rules. It exalted the Prefect to clear supremacy over other government officials in his province. And it emphasized monocratic as opposed to collegial forms of administrative power and responsibility.

Prefectoral systems were part of the heritage of the old autocratic regimes, together with institutions such as the monarchy, which were accepted by and adapted to the purposes of the liberal constitutional regimes established in Scandinavia, the Low Countries, and Italy during the nineteenth century, withstanding the liberal attack upon both centralization and mercantilism. Retention of the prefectoral system—as of the monarchy—may indeed have been one of the prices paid by the liberal movement to secure the acceptance of the new regime by the older ruling elements.

Types of prefectoral systems

One of the major conclusions of this study is that there are at least two polar types of prefectoral systems: the integrated, exemplified by the classical French system of the nineteenth and early twentieth centuries; and the unintegrated, exemplified by the contemporary Italian system. The difference between the two systems lies in their structure, origins, and functions.

STRUCTURE. Structural differences between the integrated and unintegrated systems can be seen in the following chart.

INTEGRATED	UNINTEGRATED
a. locus of authority	
Authority is exclusively or largely deconcentrated from the central ministries to the Prefects, who become a link in all or most chains of command. The Prefect is the hierarchical superior of the technical field directors in his province.	Authority is largely reserved to the specialist functional officials in several purely functional chains of command.
b. communications	
The Prefect is the sole channel of communication between the functional departments in the capital and those in the field.	The Prefect is neither the normal nor the exclusive channel of communication between central and field functional units.
c. auxiliary services	
The prefecture houses all or most of the state field offices and provides them with the administrative services needed to accomplish their technical programs.	The technical services in the province do not depend upon the prefecture for accounting, supplies, secretariat, or space, which are instead provided by the central ministries or by the technical field units themselves.

INTEGRATED	UNINTEGRATED
d. areas	
Most state services use the prefecture's area of operations.	The functional services, organized independently of the prefecture, use varying sets of areas.
e. echelons	
Regional offices, standing between the prefecture and the central ministries and/or using interprovincial areas, are exceptional.	Regional offices, with direct operational responsibilities and/or supervisory authority over provincial offices, are common.
f. local government	
The Prefect is chief executive of the provincial self-government unit, the staff of which is organized within the prefecture.	The provincial self-government unit includes a directly or indirectly elected executive authority, with control of separately organized provincial staff.

ORIGINS. Given these types of prefectoral systems, why is one type adopted rather than another? . . . In the case of the best known *integrated* prefectoral system, that of the French, the reasons for making the Prefect the undisputed hierarchical superior of the various state services in the department probably include the clear supremacy of the chief of government, the King and later Napoleon, over his ministers; a desire by the ruler to reproduce this clear supremacy in his direct representative, the Intendant and the Prefect; the absolutist conceptions of the ruler which legitimized monocratic administrative forms; and Napoleon's military conception of responsibility, authority, and efficiency as requiring one-man direction.

FUNCTIONS. One type of prefectoral system is maintained presumably because of its relative advantages over the other type, because of its functions or consequences, because of the costs of changing over to the other type. The Italian system remained unintegrated after unification for many reasons, including the continuance of several of the factors initially responsible for the adoption of such a system. Once going, the unintegrated system acquired the force of customary behavior. Ministries enjoyed and defended the almost complete control that the unintegrated system afforded them over their particular field services. Separate technical offices were established in a growing number of sectors and each of these offices was vested with an interest in self-preservation as an autonomous entity responsible only to its technical superiors in Rome.

The relative *advantages* of the unintegrated Italian prefectoral system, as opposed to the integrated system, seem to be the following:

1. Theoretically, at least, the authority of the Prefect can be adjusted to allow him to control or coordinate some programs or activities where the case for such coordination is particularly strong, rather than a general desideratum. It may, however, prove difficult to insert prefectoral control in the traditionally strong vertical hierarchies, given the absence of a countering tradition of prefectoral control such as has long existed in France.

2. The unintegrated system gives free rein to all the functional services which may carry out their nationwide responsibilities in accordance with their particular, technically informed judgment, allowing for the necessary geographical adaptation within their respective services.

3. The system does provide for a natural coordinator within each of the major areas of the country, a natural chairman of interagency committees, a neutral arbiter for the adjustment of interservice difficulties. It may, however, be difficult for the Prefect to coordinate the activities of services using various areas, enjoying varying amounts of deconcentrated authority, such as the unintegrated system tends to produce. The Prefect's area, moreover, may not be the appropriate level for interagency coordination in some or most matters.

4. The unintegrated system avoids the serious problem of dual supervision, of defining satisfactorily the respective spheres of authority of the central ministries, Prefects, and technical specialists in the field—or it does so long as the Prefect's authority over the technical specialists is restricted to the submission of recommendations and excludes final decision-making. Thus avoidance of the problem of dual supervision hinges upon the maintenance of a high degree of concentration in matters to be coordinated by the Prefects. Actually, the problem is not avoided but merely shifted to each of the separate field services, in some of which it may become highly acute.

The relative *disadvantages* of the unintegrated system would seem to be the following:

1. It is relatively uneconomical since, unlike the integrated system, it does not provide for common housekeeping services. The administrative overhead expenses involved in running several distinct offices is greater presumably than in running joint services in the prefecture.

2. It tends to place administrative burdens on technical field directors which distract them from their specialized tasks. They are forced to be generalist office managers and to attend to matters for which they have little aptitude, liking, or training.

3. It requires a greater over-all number of talented administrators capable of directing independent offices.

4. It tends to de-emphasize the interrelations of various technical programs within particular areas and communities.

5. It fosters a tendency toward undue concentration of administrative authority, since there are no strong generalist Prefects pressing for and defending larger amounts of authority.

6. It requires constant negotiations among the services with no hierarchical arbitrator short of the Prime Minister or Council of Ministers.

Challenges to prefectoral systems

What are the major challenges to the survival or stability of prefectoral systems?

The Political Challenge. The prefectoral system may become identified with a regime or with the policies of a regime and accordingly share its fortunes. If the regime falls, as Fascism fell, there is apt to be a drive to abolish the prefectoral system as an accomplice in the regime's activities.

The prefectoral system may also become identified with

some of the policies of a regime or rather, with one element of the system, such as centralization, and if a drive develops to change those policies or to change one element of the prefectoral system, the whole system may be placed in jeopardy. The prefectoral system in Italy has become identified with centralization. Hence, the drive for greater local self-government has brought in its train a demand for the abolition of the prefectoral system—despite the fact that a prefectoral system is not necessarily tied to any particular level of centralization.

A political challenge of another sort may develop in a revolutionary situation in which not so much the *legitimacy* as the *effectiveness* of the system is challenged. The loyalties of the Prefects may be subjected to severe strains in a situation, such as existed in 1919–22, where the Prefects are required to act against groups to which they are socially allied and politically sympathetic. Rapid renovation of the prefectoral cadres may not prevent the undermining of prefectoral discipline.

THE TECHNICAL CHALLENGE. Prefectoral systems may also be undermined by processes of social and technological change, leading to the expansion of state functions into new and highly technical fields of activity. Separate central units are established to take care of the expanding functions of central administration and each of these is apt to press for an autonomous field service under its complete control. The newer technical departments in the capital, based on changed social expectations and new technological possibilities, project their drive for autonomy in the central administration into field administration as well. They will also press for the organization of their field service along lines suited to their particular function.

The prefectures are apt to be bypassed in this process of administrative growth and ramification for three reasons: (1) they will tend to lack the necessary expertise or the appropriate geographical jurisdiction to perform the new functions; (2) they cannot be as uniformly responsive as can distinct field services to the needs and desires of the newer technical central agencies; and (3) they may be the victims of a long-standing process of institutional decline, involving the routinization of duties, the flagging of esprit de corps, the petrifaction of customary ways of thinking and acting.

PREFECTORAL SYSTEMS AND POLITICAL SYSTEMS

The question of the relationships, if any, between prefectoral systems and stable democracy is as interesting as it is difficult to answer. There appears to be no simple or necessary relationship between the two. Some stable democracies have no prefectoral systems; some stable democracies do.[2] Prefectoral systems, moreover, vary considerably among themselves in at least three ways: (1) the level of centralization they sustain, (2) the degree of integration in the state field administration they permit, and (3) the policies administered through them and with which they may become identified. Of these three variables, only the first (the level of centralization) and the last (the policies administered) seem relevant to the stability of the political system.

Yet just how relevant centralization is to the stability of democracy has still to be demonstrated. It is frequently asserted that stable democracy requires a considerable degree of decentralization, of local self-government. It may be, however, that there are stable democracies that are highly centralized. If there *are* no stable democracies that are highly centralized, if all stable democracies are highly decentralized, then it will follow that those stable democracies with prefectoral systems must all permit considerable local government power and autonomy. This has yet to be tested.

Possibly there is a necessary relationship between the level of centralization and stable democracy. It seems reasonable to expect that political cultures that tolerate the dispersion of power involved in decentralization may more readily support the other forms of dispersed social and constitutional power that constitute pluralistic democracy. It is often asserted, however, that centralization leads to *incivisme* and "widespread public disaffection from governmental authority."[3] One might, on the basis of

[2] Seymour M. Lipset in *Political Man* (New York, Doubleday, 1960) lists thirteen European and English-speaking countries as stable democracies (p. 49). Of these thirteen, six have prefectoral systems: Belgium, Denmark, the Netherlands, Norway, Sweden, and even Luxemburg.

[3] Nicholas Wahl, "The French Political System," in Samuel Beer *et al.*, *Patterns of Government: The Major Political Systems of Europe* (New York, Random House, 1958), p. 331.

this study, invert the terms and assert that it is *incivisme* and widespread disaffection that lead to centralization.

Does a prefectoral system facilitate the establishment of dictatorship, provoke the downfall of a democratic regime, or facilitate the conquest of power by undemocratic forces? It may just as easily be maintained that a prefectoral system may be used to defend a democratic regime, to bolster democratic forces, to provide a sense of security and order, and to dissolve or alleviate the tensions that might undermine a democracy. A prefectoral system is basically a neutral device which can be made to serve a wide range of purposes. Like other formal structures of government, its function in the political system may be derivative and of marginal importance.[4] It is rather the social and ideological forces that work through and upon political and administrative structures that are the autonomous and decisive factors in determining the fate of a democracy.

The "Sala" Model: An Ecological Approach to the Study of Comparative Administration

FRED W. RIGGS
Indiana University

THE NEED FOR NEW, ECOLOGICAL MODELS

As we move toward an empirical science of public administration—as distinguished from a normative doctrine intended to guide us in administrative reform or development—we will need two kinds of knowledge: first, increasingly clear and relevant information about administrative practices, organization and

[4] This institutional skepticism seems to be shared by Lipset in *Political Man*, pp. 90–92; see also Robert A. Dahl, *A Preface to Democratic Theory* (Chicago, University of Chicago Press, 1956), pp. 134–37.

Delivered at the 1961 Annual Meeting of the American Political Science Association, St. Louis, Missouri, September 6–9, 1961, and reprinted from *Philippine Journal of Public Administration*, Vol. 6, No. 1 (January, 1962), pp. 3–16, by permission.

history in particular countries; and secondly, more testable and tested hypotheses about causal relationships among administrative variables. Both types of knowledge should be useful in the practice of administration, but in the present context they are viewed as contributing to the growth of social, and especially political, science.

A basic tool in both kinds of inquiry—area study and theory formation—is the "constructed type" or "model." Everyone uses such models, whether implicitly or explicitly, to provide a frame of reference, "criteria of relevance," in order to select from the undifferentiated universe of sense experience the data which contribute to an organized body of knowledge. They provide the outlines around which we assemble descriptive country or area information—whether American, British, Indian, Cuban or Congolese—and they suggest relationships which we link together in our propositions, statements of causal interdependencies.

Hitherto the models upon which we have relied in political science and public administration are predominantly those derived from the study of America, Britain, and other Western countries. Because of the relative uniformity of environmental factors in all these countries, it is possible to study administrative institutions and practices as though they had an autonomous existence, apart from their environment or setting. Yet the "ecology" of public administration is as much a limiting factor as in the ecology of biological species or cities. When administration in non-Western countries is studied with the help of our non-ecological models with their implicit assumptions of institutional autonomy, or when generalizations taken from these models are applied to situations in the "underdeveloped" countries, they tend to crumble away. Hence I suggest that we need to construct alternative, ecologically based models to help us in the study of administration abroad. I make this suggestion in all modesty, quite aware that much research of value can be accomplished within the framework of the available models, especially if one makes full use of those developed by our sister disciplines, notably anthropology and sociology in which a "holistic" or ecological approach is used. However, I am persuaded of the utility of trying to supplement the existing models by attempting, consciously, to create some alternative types.

Our greatest strength lies in concepts and typologies designed for use in American and the relatively similar Western systems of government, where environmental influences are generally ignored. The social anthropologists and comparative sociologists have given us models particularly suited to the study of traditional or "folk" societies. But neither fit very well the conditions in developing countries with their mixture of tradition and industrializing-modernization. Hence I suggest our chief need is for an explicit model of transitional societies and their administrative sub-systems.

"Prismatic society" and the "sala model"

I call one model for this purpose a "prismatic" system, not for the joy of using a new word, but because it enables me to impute to the model a limited number of characteristics, and hence to eliminate the clustering connotations that adhere to more familiar words like "underdeveloped" and "transitional."

The word itself is part of a larger system, in which polar types are used, based on definitions taken from structural-functional analysis. These terms are explained at some length elsewhere, and it would detract from this paper to repeat the discussion here.[1] Suffice it to say that the prismatic model is intermediate between a "fused" model, useful in studying traditional or primitive societies, and the "refracted" type, useful for analysis of government in advanced industrial Western societies.

Within the prismatic society one can construct sub-models for its various structures, e.g., its political, administrative, economic, social, religious. I call the administrative sub-model in a prismatic society, a "sala." The word is taken from current usage in much of Asia where a *sala* often means an office, but also a pavilion, drawing room, or place for religious meetings. I wish thereby to symbolize the resemblance of a sala to the "office" or "bureau," which may be taken as the typical locus or "ideal

[1] See, for example, "Prismatic Society and Financial Administration" in *Administrative Science Quarterly,* Vol. 5, June 1960, pp. 1–46, and *Ecology of Public Administration* (Bombay, Asia Publishing House, and N.Y., Taplinger, 1961.)

type" of administrative behavior in the "refracted" model. At the same time the diffuse uses to which the sala is put suggest the multi-purpose, undifferentiated character of the "home" or "court," as locus of administration in a "fused" society, where, indeed, we cannot find a separate structure for administrative as contrasted with other functions of the society.

HETEROGENEITY. One of the characteristics of a prismatic society is a high degree of "heterogeneity," which is to say, a mixture of traditional, "fused" characteristics, on the one hand, and modern, "refracted" traits on the other. Hence a modern city with a sophisticated, intellectual class, Western-style offices, modern gadgets of administration, is typically found in the same country with rural villages run by "chiefs," "headmen," or "elders" whose political, administrative, religious, and social roles may be quite undifferentiated and traditional in character. The significant administrative features of a prismatic society, however, would not be brought to our attention if we merely looked for this mixture of traditional and modern institutions, even though we found plenty of examples of both.

Even more significant in the mixture might be a set of new administrative structures, different from both the traditional and modern, and a product of the mixture. This new set of administrative phenomena is what I choose to call the "sala model." To repeat, the most characteristic administrative features of a prismatic society are to be found in the sala, but in the heterogeneity of a prismatic system, we will find the modern "bureau" and the traditional "court" as well as the sala. One problem of analysis in a particular situation is to find the proportions in which these structural features are mixed, and to explain the mixture. I believe that only afterwards can we manipulate intelligently, i.e., re-shape the mixture to match our goals and aspirations.

FORMALISM. What, then, are the essential features of the sala itself? Some are suggested by a second major feature of the prismatic model, i.e., a high degree of "formalism." By "formalism" I refer to the degree of discrepancy or congruence between the formally prescribed and the effectively practiced, between norms and realities. The greater the congruence, the more realistic the situation; the greater the discrepancy, the more formalistic.

In both traditional or fused societies, and in modern industrial or refracted societies, a relatively high degree of realism prevails. Not that complete realism ever exists. The degree of formalism in our own society is a measure, perhaps, of the extent to which we are not fully refracted, to which prismatic conditions are to be found here. Indeed, one conclusion to which I have come is that the American administrative system, especially in local government and in the more "underdeveloped" parts of the United States, is quite prismatic.

For the prevalence of formalism, to repeat, is a distinguishing mark of the prismatic system. In other words, the laws on the statute book are one thing, the actual behavior of the official is another. Not that the law is irrelevant to behavior. Indeed, the official may insist on literal performance of the law or he may disregard it utterly. What permits formalism is the lack of pressure toward program objectives, the weakness of social power as a guide to bureaucratic performance, and hence great permissiveness for arbitrary administration. Whether an official chooses to enforce a law to the letter or permit its total violation depends, presumably, upon his inclinations and his advantage.

It is easy to see that administrative discretion of this type opens the door to corruption. The client may have to pay the official to carry out the law—as in the issuance of permits, licenses, quota allocations—or to overlook violations—as in the payment of taxes.

Some implications for administrative reform should also be evident. If reform is based on a change in the law, a reorganization, re-definition of positions and duties, etc., probably no effective change in behavior will follow the change in norms and prescriptions. In a refracted model, by contrast, where a high degree of realism prevails, clearly, acceptance of a change of law or regulation can be taken as equivalent to corresponding changes in administrative behavior. Reasoning from the refracted model, the administrative specialist may conclude that similar changes in a basically prismatic system will have similar results. Were the specialist familiar with the sala model, however, he might consider such formal changes useless, and seek first to achieve a higher degree of realism, i.e., to bring about a closer approximation of practice to prescription.

Overlapping. A third feature of the prismatic model suggests even more implications for the sala, namely the phenomenon of "overlapping." By "overlapping" I refer to the extent to which formally differentiated structures of a refracted type co-exist with undifferentiated structures of a fused type. In other words, it is typical in a prismatic situation for new structures—government offices, parliaments, elections, markets, schools—to be set up, but the effective functions of administration, politics, economics, education, continue to be performed, at least to a considerable extent, by older, undifferentiated structures, such as the family, religious bodies, caste and communal groupings. New norms or values appropriate to the differentiated structures are given lip-service, but the older values of an undifferentiated society still retain a strong hold. Thus overlapping implies a social schizophrenia of contradictory formal (conscious) and informal (unconscious) behavior patterns.

In neither the fused nor refracted models do we find substantial overlapping. In the refracted model, insofar as the structures realistically perform their "manifest functions," there is no overlapping. In the fused model, since there is only one major set of structures for all functions, there is also no occasion for overlapping. The concept is, perhaps, not an easy one to grasp in the abstract. I will try to illustrate it by several applications to the sala model.

Nepotism: the sala and the family

The sala is, formally, a locus for governmental administration. In a relatively refracted society, considerations of family loyalty are effectively divorced from the conduct of office. Indeed, the American administrative expert typically takes such a divorce so much for granted that he scarcely looks for it in studying or manipulating administrative behavior. In the sala, however, many administrative functions which were once performed openly under the aegis of familial or kinship institutions continue to be performed on this basis, but clandestinely. The new formal structures of an office are superimposed upon the family, and lip-service is paid to a new set of official norms.

One characteristic administrative result is the phenomenon of "nepotism." I do not think it appropriate to speak of nepotism in a fused society's administration. Here the family provides the formal basis of government. Positions are typically filled on a hereditary or "patrimonial" basis. It is scarcely appropriate to speak of nepotism when a king takes over by virtue of hereditary succession, but if an elected president or prime minister were to replace himself by a son or nephew, the epithet would be properly used. Similarly, we don't think of the inheritance of a small business by the son of the owner as nepotistic, but the appointment of close relatives to office in a large firm may be called nepotism.

My point is that in a fused society, hereditary succession to office is not nepotism; and in a refracted society, familial influence on appointments is negligible. Nepotism, however, is a characteristic mode of recruitment in the sala: characteristic because here patrimonialism is officially proscribed but actually practiced.

Overlapping of the family with the office occurs also in other aspects of sala behavior. The formal rules of the sala prescribe universalistic norms for the administration of the law, the general programs and policies of a government agency. However, family influence prevails, so that the law is applied generously to relatives, stringently against strangers. This becomes a matter of importance in law enforcement, the administration of contracts, purchase of supplies, enforcement of taxes, granting of licenses, foreign exchange control, import and export permits, etc. To the outside observer, the typical sala official appears "individualistic" or "anarchic" because he ranks his private and familial goals higher than the corporate goals of his agency, government or country.

"Poly-communalism" and "clects"

In speaking of the family and kinship groupings I have oversimplified the basis of group solidarity. It is characteristic in a prismatic society for minority ethnic, religious or racial groups to become relatively "mobilized" for mass communications without, at the same time, becoming fully "assimilated" to the elite.[2] Such a condition produces several "communities" that live side by side in a relatively hostile interaction in the same society, "differentiated" in Deutsch's terms. Furnivall calls this a "plural society," but I prefer to speak of it as "poly-communal."

The development of poly-communalism has a characteristic impact on the sala. Whereas in principle a government office administers the law impartially as between or among all citizens, the sala official discriminates in favor of his own community and against members of other communities. Such discrimination affects recruitment. In other words, perhaps more significant even than nepotism is the tendency to fill positions in a sala only with recruits drawn from a dominant community. Alternatively, different offices may be apportioned on a "quota basis" to the several communities, leading to mutual hostility, or noncooperation between the several agencies staffed by members of rival communities. When members of the different communities are mixed in the same office, obstacles to cooperative action also arise.

This characteristic feature of the sala is, in fact, found in America, especially in local administration in the South. The relations of the white and Negro communities of the South to each other are typical of poly-communalism. In the sala of the South, as in the sala in other countries, administrative recruitment and law enforcement predictably favor the "dominant" against the "minority" communities.

A further consequence of poly-communalism occurs in the organization of "interest groups." The refracted model leads us to picture interest groups in the form of functionally specific associations, open on a universalistic basis to all who share the group's primary goals. Such associations interact with political and administrative agencies to propose and help implement public policy in diverse functional fields.

An implicit assumption of such associational patterns, however, is open participation on a universalistic basis. In a poly-communal situation, however, group membership is typically

[2] These concepts were developed by Karl Deutsch in *Nationalism and Social Communication* (N.Y., Wiley, 1953).

restricted to a single community. Consequently, instead of a single chamber of commerce or trade union federation, a different chamber and federation appears for each community. The result: interest group activity is designed not only to encourage a particular policy but to apply that policy "selectively" for members of the favored community, against members of disfavored groups. Or, considered from the viewpoint of the sala, administrative recruitment and policy is oriented positively toward groups based on dominant communities, negatively against groups drawn from deviant communities.

Because these interest groups exhibit characteristics different in crucial respects from the associations of a refracted society, I think it is useful to have a special term for them. They share some of the characteristics of cliques, clubs, and sects, but none of these words exactly identifies the category I have in mind. Consequently, I have coined an expression based, mnemonically, on sounds common to these three words, i.e. *clects*. A clect may be defined as an organization with relatively diffuse functions of a semi-traditional type, but organized in a modern, associational way. Sectarian oppositional political parties and revolutionary movements in a prismatic society are typically clects. They provide their members with an alternative solidarity system to replace extended family, caste, village and religious units. They stand for a total way of life, and typically demand unconditional loyalty of their members. Whereas one may belong to a variety of associations, he can belong to only one clect. Of course, not all members of a prismatic society belong to clects. Typically, only a minority do. But the clect provides a disciplined core for economic, political, religious and social action. Clects tend to be uncompromising and hostile in their relations to each other, and to the sala.

Thus we find the sala often involved in close relations with clects, or itself taking on clect-like characteristics. A particular government office or agency may be captured by a clect. Then overlapping manifests itself in unofficial orientation toward the dominant clect, despite an official mandate to serve the general public interest. An example would be an agency to regulate business conditions which favors a chamber of commerce and business men of the dominant community, at the expense of traders in "outsider" communities. Often this means that the dominant group gets special privileges, licenses, permits, foreign exchange, tax rebates. However, the recipients of these favors often do not use them, since an easier road to wealth lies in blackmarket collusion with members of the outside or "pariah" business community.

Officials in the sala also profiteer from this situation, either receiving a "rebate" or "kick-back" from the privileged clientele, or taking a "bribe" from illicit entrepreneurs in the pariah community. Thus the clect-sala relationship serves to advance the special interests of an in-group as against the interests of an out-group in the same functional field, contrary to the ideal association-bureau relationship in which policy is shaped so as to advance the interests of all members of the society who share a particular functional goal or technique.

Sometimes a particular agency in the sala becomes itself a kind of clect. Once admitted, a member is treated as though he were part of an enlarged family. It becomes impossible to discipline or discharge a member, for example, just as a family would not consider expelling a member except for the most extreme reasons. Thus clect formation within the sala contradicts the achievement and universalistic norms, typical of a refracted government bureau or office. Here again overlapping means effective behavior contradictory to the prescribed norms of the sala.

ECONOMY—THE "BAZAAR-CANTEEN"

Elsewhere I have characterized the typical features of the "bazaar-canteen" as the economic sub-model of the prismatic society.[3] The bazaar-canteen is the prismatic counterpart of the refracted "market." Here typical price mechanisms are used for the exchange of goods, but they overlap with more traditional "reciprocative" and "redistributive" institutions,[4] resulting in

[3] See "The Bazaar-Canteen Model," *Philippine Sociological Review,* Vol. VI, July–October, 1958 [1960], pp. 6–59.

[4] These concepts are based on Karl Polanvi, *et. al., Trade and Market in the Early Empires* (Glencoe, Ill., Free Press, 1957).

behavior quite different from that expected in formal economic theory.

One of these characteristics is "price indeterminacy." Although there are other important typical bazaar-canteen traits, this one will illustrate the phenomenon of overlapping. In the refracted model, market conditions are assumed. Hence such aspects of administrative behavior as budgeting, salary determination, purchasing and price decisions are based on market costs and equalitarian assumptions. By this I mean that a government service which is for sale to the public is sold at the same price without distinction of persons to all citizens. The salary of officials is based on the relative value of work performed and the market cost of labor without regard to the personal identity of the incumbent.

In the sala model the same assumption is made formally, but it does not work in practice. As we have already seen, poly-communalism is typical. Hence public services are sold at preferential rates to members of the dominant community or inside clects, but at higher rates to outside clects, to members of deviant or minority communities. Often, however, a formal price is announced, from which secret deviations are made. Victims sign a contract for purchase, but pay an under-the-table bonus. Those selling to the government may receive the official rate, have to "kick-back" an unofficial percentage.

In salary determination or appointment to office, the family considerations which I have already mentioned lead to the creation of "sinecures," i.e., an official is named to a salaried position without having to perform corresponding duties, or with only minimal duties. Again, substantial "fringe-benefits" are offered to privileged incumbents beyond the official salary. Others who lack "influence" or "pull" find themselves assigned to lowly posts, denied promotion or salary increases, unable to obtain fringe benefits.

Corruption is institutionalized in the sala model. Some officials are in advantageous positions to extort bribes and other favors from clientele groups. Part of this extra income must be passed on to superiors or influential members of the bureaucracy who protect the "rackets." Outside positions as "consultants," the privilege of concurrent employment in private firms, plus other devices for augmenting income through the exercise of influence mean that the effective income and living costs of officials diverge strikingly from that officially sanctioned.

These are administrative counterparts to the economic bazaar, in which the actual price paid by a customer, after protracted bargaining, reflects not only prevailing supply-demand conditions, but also a super-imposed set of inter-personal relationships between seller and buyer. A wide fluctuation in the price of a commodity, depending upon the identity of the buyer, tends to prevail.

The canteen model refers to a situation in which uniform prices are actually charged, but prices vary widely between market-places. In some, the "subsidized canteens," prices are kept low for privileged members of an in-group; in others, the "tributary canteens," prices are raised for captive members of the out-groups.

Similarly, the sala makes its privileges available to in-group members at bargain prices, as when it seeks foreign exchange at the official rate to privileged businessmen of the dominant community. Penalized entrepreneurs of the "pariah" community are forced to buy at inflated prices in the "black-market," or obtain funds at official rates only after making informal bonus payments through extra-legal channels.

In a sense, the whole bureaucracy is privy to a subsidized canteen. Its privileges and status are a prize eagerly sought by ambitious individuals in the dominant communities. The proliferation of governmental functions, encouraged both by the first stages of industrialization and the rosy attractiveness of the "welfare state," give rise to rapid expansion of agencies, increase of offices, and conspicuous overstaffing. Yet at the same time, the economy as a whole remains poor, the national budget hopelessly unable to provide adequate salaries for all. The pitifully low salary schedule which results provides an economic incentive for capitalizing on every opportunity each incumbent encounters to augment his official salary from unofficial sources.

Whether in the bazaar or canteen form, then, price indeterminacy pervades the sala at all points where money is involved, in salaries and "fringe-benefits," contracts for purchase and supply of goods and services, in regulation of public utilities, customs and tax administration, budget making, accounting and auditing procedures, and the like.

Any analysis of the economic aspects of sala administration which accepts, at face value, the formal price structure will miss completely the effective price structure. The difficulty for analysis, of course, arises not only from the use of inappropriate models based on the assumptions of a refracted administrative bureau, but also on the formalistic discrepancy between the formally approved behavior, which is like that of the bureau, and the officially disapproved behavior, which is quite dissimilar. This consideration takes us to value systems in relation to overlapping.

Poly-normativism and lack of consensus

The refracted bureau presupposes a set of "ground rules" or a "formula" which is generally agreed to by all participants, the officials in the bureau as well as the various clienteles served or regulated. Although there is often opposition to any particular policy or rule of government and administration, there tends to be unanimity on key rules governing adoption of norms, and on procedures to be followed to get them changed. Even those who oppose a particular rule, tax, or official procedure, generally concur in obeying the norm, even while protesting and seeking to have it changed through legal means.

In the prismatic society, however, these conditions do not exist. Here a new set of norms, political formulae and myths, based on experience in more refracted settings, are superimposed in a society which continues to adhere, in large measure, to older traditional norms, formulae and myths. The result is substantial lack of consensus.

Different individuals are involved in this lack of consensus in different ways: some adhere to traditional norms, others embrace the modern substitutes. But a substantial body of intermediate or transitional individuals are attracted ambivalently to both sets, sometimes adhering to one, sometimes to the other, sometimes to an attempted syncretism of both, and sometimes violently rejecting all norms. For these typically prismatic individuals we may speak of "poly-normative" and even of "normless" orientations.

The administrative implications of poly-normativism may be traced in the behavior of both officials and members of the public.

An official, while publicly adhering to a modern set of norms, may secretly reject them as meaningless or not binding. Hence the overlapping behavior of the sala becomes comprehensible in terms of the value system of the incumbent. For example, he can adhere publicly to the norm of objective, achievement oriented standards of recruitment, equality of status and universalistic norms, but privately subscribe to more subjective, ascription oriented standards, to a rigid hierarchy of status and particularistic norms. He can publicly castigate bribery and corruption, but secretly encourage it. He can insist, one moment on a strict and literal enforcement of regulations, but the next moment work at their open violation.

Another contrast between the formal and effective norms in the sala model may be discerned in the "status-contract" distinction. The formally prescribed norm of the sala is based on contractual assumption: obligations and rights are voluntarily undertaken by the public servant in an agreement between himself and the "government." But in the overlapping status system, officials have privileges and duties which stem from their personal identity, their family and social position, their station in life.

The sala bureaucrat seeks to maximize the advantages to himself to be gained from both the contract and status systems: to minimize the disadvantages. The typical manifestation of this status/contract mix is heavy stress on "rank." Rank differs from ascribed status in that it is not inherited or claimed as a matter of right but must be "attained." Typically, a school or university degree or an examination, lays the basis for a claim to rank. But unlike the achieved position of the bureau model, in which performance validates official rewards, in the sala model attained rank becomes its own justification. Thus one who has been granted a particular rank on a semi-achievement basis can thereafter claim its corresponding perquisites on a semi-ascribed basis. In other words, he seeks entry to rank by contract, but then rests on his laurels by status.

Another manifestation of the overlapping between refracted and fused norms may be discovered if we reflect on the relationship between ends and means. In the refracted model a "scientific" or "rational" orientation is stressed, by which I mean careful study and testing of the adequacy of any given means to accomplish specified ends. Administratively, the ends are prescribed by political processes, and the bureaucrat takes them as given. Within limits, therefore, he strives for optimum utilization of scarce resources to achieve these specified goals. His goal is "efficiency;" his approach "rational."

By contrast, the official in a fused society focuses on ends as intrinsically important. He cannot test the efficacy of the means. This basic orientation is "ritual." Not that his ultimate ends are philosophically any less justifiable than those of refracted man. Moreover, he is also quite aware that his chosen means are not in themselves ends. A rainmaking ceremony, for example, is clearly intended to bring rain, but its efficacy for this purpose cannot be demonstrated.

In the sala, the intrusion of rationalism has sufficiently discredited old rituals to throw doubt upon their effectiveness, but it has been insufficiently assimilated to provide satisfactory proof of alternative procedures. Hence the sala bureaucrat resorts to methods which are neither truly rational nor ritual. On the one hand, he may try to discover and revive ancient and presumably corrupted rituals—a procedure we can call "ritualistic." Alternatively, he may borrow techniques from the administrative repertoire of a refracted society without knowing how they can really help him solve his problems—a procedure we may call "rationalistic." The two approaches, looking to the historic past and the external present, the ritualistic and rationalistic, both imply an element of copying or imitation which we can term "mimetic." Hence another example of the characteristic overlapping in the sala model is a high degree of mimesis. This, incidentally, may help to explain a relatively high degree of receptivity to largely irrelevant technical advice from abroad in many countries today.

The same ambivalence of orientation characterizes the public in its dealings with the sala. On the one hand, the enraged citizen makes unreasonable demands and censures the administration for its failure to abide by modern, refracted norms. But the next moment, without any sense of contradiction, he busily works to undermine these norms by collaborating with corruption to secure special privileges for himself. Indeed, he lacks any strict sense of principle and the implications of a "rule of law." Rather, he takes advantage of opportunities to "break the law" when that serves his interest, but demands rigid "law enforcement" when that happens to fit his convenience. Ultimately, the public is cynical about law and administration. The official is viewed as a leech, and the accepted attitude toward government is normless. One abandons attempts to reform and seeks rather to "cope" with situations as they arise, pulling wires, paying what must be paid, hoping somehow to survive and, if possible, gain entré to some of the spoils of the system. Objectivity and truth as criteria of information tend to dissolve, and the victim is left with no option but to judge information by the status of its source, its usefulness as a means.

POWER DISTRIBUTION: AUTHORITY VS. CONTROL

In closing this discussion of the sala model, I wish to note the phenomenon of overlapping in the power distribution system. A widespread observation of experts visiting "underdeveloped" countries is the tendency to extreme "over-centralization," inability to delegate authority, to decentralize. One of the most frequent recommendations made is to strengthen field offices, to train intermediate and subordinate personnel so they can take over more powers, induce superiors to delegate functions to others, in general to loosen up the bottleneck at the center which keeps the administration in a perpetual state of crisis.

Unfortunately, these recommendations mistake the formal aspects of sala behavior for the effective. If we bear in mind the concept of overlapping, we may see that other institutions than the prescribed office actually govern, to a greater extent, effective administrative behavior. Indeed, our whole discussion of corruption, nepotism, poly-normativism, clect influence, etc., suggests that effective power is widely dispersed in the sala model. If the central authorities had the highly over-centralized power attributed to them, all these deviations from the rules could scarcely be permitted.

The reality, as I see it, can only be understood if we distinguish clearly between officially sanctioned or legitimate power, i.e., "authority," and unofficially permitted or illegitimate power, i.e., "control." In both the fused and refracted model power includes both the elements of authority and control. Indeed, this linkage is so much a part of our thinking that we have difficulty making this distinction, or describing a situation in which the two are divorced. Yet one of the salient characteristics of the prismatic model, as noted above, is a high degree of formalism. Translated in terms of power structure, this means a separation of authority and control.

Or, in terms of overlapping, it means that the authority structure of the sala overlaps with a different kind of control structure. I have already pointed to the roots of the control structure in the prevalence of poly-communalism, the rise of clects, the pervasiveness of poly-normativism and normlessness. I suggest that in practice control in a prismatic society is highly dispersed. Traditionally-oriented groups in the hinterland resist central government control. Deviant communities and their clects also cannot be brought within the control system of the official government. Normlessness makes many, even members of the elite, surprisingly unresponsive to official norms, as reflected in widespread violation of tax and other laws. Even members of the bureaucracy itself, as our argument has shown, are singularly unwilling to subject themselves to effective regulation by the agencies of which they are nominally a part, at least in their formal requirements.

Viewed from this perspective, centralization of authority can be understood as a desperate attempt to bring the government and society under control. Indeed, when effective control weapons are so notably lacking, the cheapest and most apparent remaining weapon is the power of formal authority. Unfortunately, this nominal power turns out to be without potency, resulting, often enough, in a final resort to violence.

Centralized authority is largely formalistic. Hence recommendations to decentralize are greeted with fear as a threat to that limited power base which remains to the central authorities;

or as irrelevant, since those on the inside already know how limited is their effective control.

The power structure of the sala model, then, may be said to consist of a highly centralized and concentrated authority structure overlapping a control system that is highly localized and dispersed. Here again, unless one has this model in mind, he is likely to rely on the refracted bureau as a model, and hence to look upon the formal authority system as a sound clue to understanding the effective power structure.

The paradox of overlapping may be viewed from another point of view, the relationship of bureaucratic to non-bureaucratic power. The formal administrative bureau in a refracted society is regarded as a purely instrumental "apparatus" for the execution of policies formulated by a separate political system, as institutionalized in legislative bodies and elected executives. Hence the formal model, in terms of which public administration in a prismatic society is both understood and evaluated, presumes that power is concentrated in directing centers outside the bureaucracy.

But the traditional locus of power in relatively fused systems is in the hands of officials working with an hereditary ruler. Here any distinction between "administrative" and "political" structures is quite arbitrary, since the same men and offices perform both types of function without even being aware of the distinction.

In the sala, the official continues to exercise the undifferentiated political-administrative functions of the fused model, but behind a façade of administrative institutionalism borrowed from industrial, relatively refracted societies. Hence he can scarcely admit to the public, or even to himself, that much of his actual behavior is essentially political, involving a struggle for power and participation in the making of whatever decisions are made for the society. The Western-trained observer who tries to identify the locus of decision-making in such a system comes away baffled, convinced that decisions are made surreptitiously, conspiratorially, clandestinely.

Thus the sala official who exercises control often lacks authority, first because it has not been formally delegated to him by his status superiors, and secondly because, as a bureaucrat, he is not supposed to make decisions according to the formally announced constitutional system. There are two characteristic responses for the sala official caught in this paradoxical situation. We may view these responses as polar opposites on a scale, typical behavior involving some combination of both, though in varying proportions.

At one extreme, the official takes the initiative and assumes the mantle of "tutelage." He announces that, in the long run, he will serve as an "instrument of the people," but in view of their present lack of education and political sophistication, he will teach them, help them prepare to assume real political power. Thus he openly admits the exercise of power, but at the same time he gives lip-service to the view that his ultimate role, as a bureaucrat, should be instrumental.

The other extreme is suggested by the word, "sinecure." This is the posture of officials who give up the attempt to make decisions. The formal power holders—the people and the "politicians"—cannot guide or control him, and he abandons the attempt to seize the initiative himself. Rather, he accepts and clings to the privileges of office, but rejects any serious attempt to exercise the duties of office. While refusing to delegate responsibility, he is unable to exercise it effectively himself. This posture, of course, is not one to be rationalized but rather to be concealed, and so the sinecurist makes a pretense of busy-work, while in essence abandoning the tasks of government.

The extent to which officials in a sala make policy or reject responsibility may be disguised by the extent to which such policy is weakly oriented toward an agency's program goals. Where nonbureaucratic power is substantial, bureaucrats are provided with a strong incentive to promote program goals since success is well rewarded. Often, indeed, they "identify" to a great extent with these goals. When this happens, efforts by public servants to promote policy decisions are directed toward the realization of "principled interests," the manifest ends of the agency concerned.

However, when non-bureaucratic power is weak, bureaucratic achievement is poorly rewarded. Indeed, an official who "identified" with a public goal and sought its achievement would court punishment by his colleagues as a "rate buster." Familiar "feather-bedding" techniques come into play. Hence bureaucratic influence in policy is directed rather more to safeguard strictly bureaucratic interests—such matters as security of tenure, recognition of seniority, fringe benefits, enhancement of status and prestige, toleration for violation of formal norms. In other words, bureaucratic policy-making is oriented chiefly toward "expediency interests" in the sala.

The observer who sees in every bureaucrat a man carrying out politically framed policy can only choke with indignation when he discovers officials who either arrogate to themselves the policy-making role, or meekly refuse to carry out any policy. Yet, if he were to analyze the situation in terms of the sala model, he might come closer to understanding the reasons for what he saw and perhaps even to discovering a way to stimulate the kinds of change he wanted to induce.

Conclusion

In closing, I should like to repeat the statement made in opening this paper that a model, like that of the sala, is not intended to serve as a description of any particular society or system of government. Rather, it serves an heuristic purpose. It gives us a tool by which we can better describe and, hopefully, understand, situations in real life. It seeks to relate administrative behavior to ecological factors typical of transitional societies.

In other words, with this tool one should be able to go into a particular country and study its administrative system more illuminatingly. The model suggests possible ecological relationships to look for, relationships which would not be suggested by the more familiar, non-ecological administrative bureau models based on the relatively refracted situation in the United States. One might also be able to describe the country or governmental system studied as being highly prismatic, semi-prismatic, relatively refracted, etc. Indeed, one consequence of this exercise might be to enable students of American administration to recognize in a more systematic way the "prismatic" elements of our own government. I am convinced, for example, that we will understand much of our system of county and township administration better in terms of the sala rather than the bureau.

Finally, the analysis of relationships suggested in the sala model may enable us to formulate hypotheses or propositions about possible relationships between variables in administration. Such hypotheses, growing out of observation in a variety of settings and linked to the elements of the sala model, can be further tested by looking at new settings, or re-examining those first studied at a later date. In so doing, of course, the concepts could be refined and made more operational. As the hypotheses become stronger, they should give us a better basis for explaining and predicting actual administrative behavior. This, in turn, will provide us with a more powerful weapon for administrative action, since it will help us to establish demonstrable cause-effect relationships, and hence to change phenomena by modifying their causes rather than by attacking only the symptoms or manifestations of administrative pathology. In this sense, I submit the sala model primarily as a contribution to the development of empirical, ecologically-oriented research in comparative administration, but also as a potentially useful weapon for those more particularly concerned with administrative development.[5]

[5] The relationship of the approach outlined in this paper to the general development of research in comparative public administration is discussed in my paper "Trends in the Comparative Study of Public Administration," prepared for the American Society for Public Administration conference, April 1961.

Japanese Administrative Behavior and the "Sala" Model

James R. Brady
The University of Michigan

I. Objectives

During the past decade, increasing numbers of American scholars and officials have been studying the role of public administration in the economic growth of "underdeveloped" countries and considerable new information and theoretical concepts have been developed. However, we still lack comprehensive theories or models which are supported by objective, empirical data and, consequently, we are still far from identifying the best type of administrative system for facilitating economic development. A significant amount of experimentation in transplanting or adapting Western administrative concepts has occurred with inconclusive results, so there may be some gains in exploring other approaches. For example, the writer felt it might be interesting to examine an Asian country which has already achieved a relatively high level of economic growth—Japan—to see how its administrative system compares with that found in underdeveloped countries.

Some descriptions of Japanese officials indicate that their behavior resembles that of their counterparts in less developed countries more than that of Western administrators. To explore this contention, we have hypothesized that Japanese administrative behavior should be similar to that described in Fred Riggs'

This article appeared in a slightly different form in the *Philippine Journal of Public Administration,* Vol. 8, No. 4 (October, 1964).

"sala" model of administration in the developing areas.[1] Testing this proposition should provide some insights into Japanese behavior and provide a basis for future comparisons using the "sala" or other models. If the behavior of Japanese bureaucrats *is* similar to that which Riggs says is present in the developing countries, we may need to re-examine the assumption that Western, "modern" or "rational" administration is essential to economic growth. In pursuing our main goal, we should also benefit by 1) testing the utility of the "sala" model for identifying and classifying salient behavioral characteristics in a given administrative system and 2) becoming more familiar with Japanese administrative behavior.

To achieve our objectives, we will compare statements about Japanese official behavior in selected English-language studies with behavioral patterns described in Riggs' "sala" or deductive model of an administrative system of a developing, transitional, or "prismatic" society.[2]

II. Frame of reference

The primary purpose of this section is to make more explicit some of the writer's personal values or interests which may influence his selection and interpretation of data. A broad distinction has sometimes been made between students of comparative administration who tend to be prescriptive, normative, or policy-oriented, and those who are more descriptive, objective, or interested in the study of administrative phenomena as an end

1 We are attempting to use the model as described in Fred W. Riggs, "An Ecological Approach: The 'Sala' Model," in Ferrel Heady and Sybil Stokes (eds.), *Papers in Comparative Public Administration* (Institute of Public Administration, University of Michigan, 1962) pp. 19–36. However we have arbitrarily condensed some of the elaborations of terminology—hopefully without altering the basic concepts. Riggs' article is reproduced in the present volume on pages 412–432.

2 Those who are interested in Riggs' models of transitional societies should see Fred W. Riggs, "Prismatic Society and Financial Administration," *Administrative Science Quarterly,* Vol. 5, No. 1 (June, 1960), pp. 1–46; Riggs and Edward W. Weidner, *Models and Priorities in the Comparative Study of Public Administration,* American Society for Public Administration, 1963, pp. 1–43; or Riggs, *Administration in Developing Countries: The Theory of Prismatic Society* (Boston: Houghton Mifflin Company, 1964).

in itself.[3] While this type of dichotomy may be useful to justify contrasting approaches to the same subject areas, it appears that the ultimate concern of both sides is quite similar: to predict behavior.[4] Some academic researchers seek this goal in order to alleviate guilt pangs about the designation of the study of politics and administration as political *science* while the practitioners hope to raise their odds for successful decision-making closer to unity. The writer's own prejudices probably place him closer to the policy-oriented group because of his recent extended exposure in the American foreign aid program to the problems of inducing rather than studying administrative change. However, the myopic analysis resulting from constant confrontation with operational problems should encourage any practitioner to inquire if his academic friends have something of value to offer. To be more specific, the present project stems in part from a dissatisfaction with the results of trying to transplant administrative structures or procedures developed in the West to Asian societies as a *sine qua non* of economic development. Technical assistance activities in administration have often appeared to be based on the following types of assumptions: (1) certain administrative structures or procedures were important in Western economic growth; (2) consequently, they are necessary in the development of non-Western countries; and (3) their adoption will produce behavioral patterns similar to those associated with the (often idealized) Western administrator. While we still lack a comprehensive evaluation of technical assistance activities in administration, there is probably sufficient validity in the criticisms raised to warrant exploration of alternative or additional appoaches for improving administrative systems in underdevel-

[3] A more precise treatment of the different motivations for studying comparative administration is given in Ferrel Heady, "Comparative Public Administration: Concerns and Priorities," in Heady and Stokes, *op. cit.*, pp. 1–18.

[4] Karl Deutsch observes that an adequate theory of politics should link the "is" and the "ought." ". . . It should show the effect of specific facts and policies on the main values that men have held in Western culture; and it should show the significance of some of our major values for specific policy choices. Beyond this, it should show which policies are likely to prove compatible with the pursuit of a wider range of values, and what values are likely to prove in political science more compatible with others . . ." *Nerves of Government* (New York: Free Press of Glencoe, 1963), pp. vii-viii.

oped areas. Similar sentiments have been expressed by David Brown:

> Even among those who should have been most concerned with it, the teachers and researchers of public administration, not nearly enough has been done, and often the wrong things. We have spent far more time, for example, with the tactics of public administration than we have with the strategies, with techniques rather than with constructs. We have concerned ourselves with what we think ought to be done—usually in the American image—rather than with learning why some of the things we have done have not worked. All too often we have permitted our hopes to influence our judgments. Now, belatedly, we must face the fact that we do not really know what we need to know about public administration technical assistance.[5]

There are thus many possible ways of approaching the problems of administrative change and economic development, but we have arbitrarily decided to pursue our interests in Japanese administration and Riggs' sala model.

III. Applying the sala model

The sala represents one type of administrative system found within a transitional society. The term "sala" is used in many Asian countries to refer to an office, but it may also be a pavilion, drawing room, or place for religious meetings. Riggs contrasts the sala with the "bureau" or "office" in modern societies and the "court" or "home" in traditional societies.[6] The primary elements identified in the sala are nepotism, poly-communalism and clects, bazaar-canteen economic features, poly-normativism and lack of consensus, and centralized "authority" with decentralized "control." We will examine these elements and try to find out how prevalent they are in Japanese administration.

[5] "The Key to Self-Help: Improving the Administrative Capabilities of the Aid-Receiving Countries," *Public Administration Review*, Vol. 24, No. 2 (June, 1964), pp. 67–77. Brown advocates that the U.S. Agency for International Development do some internal soul-searching and reorient its own administration to make the technical assistance activities in administration more effective.

[6] Riggs, "An Ecological Approach: The 'Sala' Model," *op. cit.*, pp. 20–21.

A. Nepotism. Family loyalties play a very important part in "sala administration, particularly in the recruitment of officials and the provision of public services. While formal rules may prescribe impartial or universalistic norms, relatives of officials actually receive favored treatment *vis à vis* other members of the society.

In Japan, it appears that nepotism is of less direct significance in national administration. After the Meiji Restoration (1868), recruitment for the higher bureaucracy came to be centered around a competitive examination system. However, about 90% of those entering the higher civil service were graduates of the Tokyo University Law School.[7] The fact that this university's professors and alumni helped prepare the civil service examination no doubt ensured the continuity of its status as the best institution to attend if one wanted to obtain a top government position. Although Tokyo University attracted very capable students from all over Japan, most of these were from the higher and upper-middle classes since a university education was rather expensive. Consequently, some pre-selection of officials took place within the education system. Masamichi Inoki reports that the higher civil service examination itself became the basis for ascriptive selection of top bureaucrats. In prewar days, considerable favoritism was shown those who had passed the higher civil service examinations and other bureaucrats had great difficulty in reaching top positions. Inoki believes that this discrimination was a principal cause of the development of radical public employee labor unions after the end of World War II.[8]

It should also be noted that after passing the entrance examination in prewar times, candidates were placed on eligibility lists from which appointments were made by the individual ministries. At this point, sons or brothers of top officials or other influential persons could and sometimes did receive preferred treatment.[9] In spite of these problems, the examination

[7] Robert E. Ward, "Japan" in Robert E. Ward and Roy C. Macridis (eds.), *Modern Political Systems: Asia* (Englewood Cliffs, N.J.: Prentice-Hall, Inc., 1963) p. 100.

[8] Masamichi Inoki, "The Civil Bureaucracy—Japan," in Robert E. Ward and Dankwart A. Rustow, *Political Modernization in Japan and Turkey* (Princeton University Press, 1964) pp. 294–95.

[9] See Nobutaka Ike, *Japanese Politics: An Introductory Survey* (New York: Alfred A. Knopf, 1957), p. 146f.

system did provide an avenue of social mobility for the more ambitious youths from rural areas who could somehow finance a higher education.

The American Occupation (1945–52) succeeded to some degree in broadening the social composition of the civil service by expanding educational opportunities and by altering the examination system to place less stress on legal studies. The impact of these and related reforms on the bureaucracy probably were not as significant as was anticipated. Robert Ward reports that a 1954 survey showed that about 76% of the higher civil servants were still graduates of the Tokyo University Law School.[10]

One's family connections are probably useful in being admitted to a particular school, but of less direct value in being appointed to the higher civil service. Access to the ±4500 positions in the top three grades is open only to those who have passed the higher civil service examination which is now under the centralized control of the National Personnel Authority.[11] Once in the service, advancement appears to be dependent on seniority and the cultivating of superiors or faction leaders within the dominant Liberal-Democratic Party. (More will be said below about party-bureaucracy relations.)

B. "POLY-COMMUNALISM" AND "CLECTS." In addition to the element of kinship or family solidarity which accounts for nepotism in the "sala," there occurs the mobilization of ethnic, racial, or religious minority groups to provide internal favors and protection against outside groups. This means that several "communities" are living side by side in a relatively hostile interaction in the same society. The "sala" official discriminates in favor of his own community and against other communities. In some cases, official positions or even entire agencies may be distributed on a quota basis among the various groups, usually the more dominant ones. A related element is the development of interest groups whose membership is typically restricted to a single community. Since these groups do not resemble Western-

10 Ward, "Japan," *op. cit.*, p. 101.

11 A summary of recent activities of the National Personnel Authority appears in Ardath W. Burks, *The Government of Japan* (New York: T. Y. Crowell Co., 1961) pp. 143–48.

type interest organizations as much as they do cliques, clubs or sects, Riggs prefers to label them as "clects." Sectarian oppositional political parties and revolutionary movements in a transitional society are examples of clects. "Sala" officials may operate in close relationship with certain clects or even form a clect themselves. Privileged clects get special treatment from officials and the latter in turn may receive rebates from the various transactions. Members of pariah clects or communities are discriminated against if they are not willing to bribe the officials. Achievement of formal organizational objectives thus comes to have little significance in the sala.

Turning to Japan, we find that "poly-communalism" was an important factor in the Meiji Era when the various local clans competed for power. However, as nationalism developed, the clan apparently declined as a political organization and it does not seem to be a significant element in current national administration. Ward observes that the Japanese population is remarkably homogeneous with only 0.7% belonging to registered minority groups (in 1959).[12] The largest minority group is the Koreans, many of whom came to Japan when Korea was a Japanese colony (1910–45). Koreans have been subjected to private and official discrimination, but there was little specific data about the problem in the materials surveyed.

Divisions in Japanese society appear to be based more on differences between younger and older generations, between urban and rural groups, or between capital and labor than between groups organized along ethnic, racial, or religious lines. (One exception may be the increasingly influential and militant *Soka-Gakkai*—an avowed offshoot of Nichiren Buddhism.)[13]

Although some of the prescribed characteristics are absent, the Japanese higher bureaucracy bears a close similarity to the "clect" of the sala. The relatively stiff competition for access to the civil service and the traditional role of the civil servant as an agent of the Emperor created an extreme elite or in-group orientation which still exists to a great extent. The present

[12] Ward, "Japan," *op. cit.*, pp. 46ff.

[13] A good general discussion of contemporary Japanese social problems appears in E. O. Reischauer, *Japan—Past and Present,* 3rd Ed. (New York: Alfred A. Knopf, 1964) Chap. 14.

constitution declares that "All public officials are servants of the whole community and not of any group thereof," but the concept of "public servant" remains strange to most Japanese citizens as well as the bureaucrats. In fact, the often-repeated phrase of prewar days, *kanson minpi* or "official exalted, people despised," still has some currency in many peoples' minds. As Nobutaka Ike points out:

> The situation has changed somewhat in recent years, and there are even signs that some agencies are becoming aware of "PR" or public relations; but it is true to say that as yet the notion that the bureaucrat is a "public servant" is somewhat alien to the Japanese mentality. When an individual becomes an official, he has, according to the prevailing scale of values, achieved status and prestige, and he tends to show it. By the same token, the expectation which seems to prevail among the general public is that bureaucrats are an arrogant and haughty lot who look with scorn upon the citizenry. . . .[14]

In spite of the gulf which has existed between the officials and the public, it should be noted that many of Japan's modern social welfare measures were introduced through bureaucratic initiative. Even the agrarian reform legislation passed during the Occupation reportedly originated in the Agriculture and Forestry Ministry.[15] John Maki contends that today's officials are ". . . no longer representatives of an omnipotent executive with all its authority and force behind them. They are now subject to the pressures of the legislative branch and of a diligent public opinion."[16] However, there is still some disagreement about the

[14] Ike, *op. cit.,* p. 149. A Japanese business executive has expressed similar sentiments: ". . . Bureaucrats here tend to be arrogant and superior. They habitually treat callers like bothersome pests. One of the most common occurrences when you call on a Government office is to find most of the staff out and the rest playing *Go.* Callers who may be there on extremely urgent business are regularly ignored for half an hour or more. Unless you have an 'in' with the top man it is virtually impossible to get any matter taken care of within a reasonable period of time." Boye DeMente, *How Business Is Done in Japan* (Tokyo: Simpson Doyle & Co., 1963) p. 13.

[15] Inoki, *op. cit.,* pp. 193–95.

[16] John M. Maki, *Government and Politics in Japan—The Road to Democracy* (New York: Frederick A. Praeger, 1962) p. 109. For an analysis of the bureaucracy's role during the Occupation, see pp. 69ff.

effectiveness of these pressures in influencing administrative behavior.[17]

C. The Bazaar-Canteen. Riggs uses "bazaar-canteen" to refer to the economic system of a transitional or "prismatic" society, but some of the same features are found in the administrative system. For example, prices of public services vary according to the relationship between the official and his clientele. Friends or relatives might have to pay less than the formally prescribed rate while outsiders may have to pay more. There is thus a bazaar-like atmosphere where considerable bargaining may occur over the amount of fees, taxes, rebates, bribes, etc. Moreover, jobs or even whole offices in the sala are sometimes regarded as canteen commodities to be distributed or sold by those in power. The person acquiring his position in this manner is essentially concerned with using it to recover his investment plus "interest." These factors again indicate that official program goals may have little significance and that corruption becomes institutionalized in the sala.

Opinions on the significance of partiality and corruption in current Japanese administration seem somewhat mixed. Perhaps speaking from an historical perspective, Edwin Reischauer concludes that ". . . government services in general show a relatively high degree of honesty and efficiency."[18] Nevertheless, the dominant role played by the government in economic affairs has resulted in various unofficial channels of influence being developed. In exchange for favors, some businessmen offer bureaucrats promises of sinecure jobs upon retirement (which comes relatively early), gifts of stock, lavish entertainment, or outright bribes. For the year 1958, the governmental watchdog—the Board of Audit—reported 355 cases of misappropriation of public funds totaling about US $3,333,333.[19] Relations between

[17] Professor Chitoshi Yanaga claims that attempts to carry out reductions in force or to simplify administration through reorganization have been failures because of the united opposition of the bureaucracy: "The truth of the matter is that the politicians and Diet members are completely at the mercy of the bureaucracy since without the help and support of the career officials and ex-bureaucrats they are unable to operate at all." Cf. *Japanese People and Politics* (New York: John Wiley and Sons, 1956) p. 307.

[18] Reischauer, *op. cit.*, pp. 247–48.

[19] Ward, "Japan," *op. cit.*, p. 101f.

members of the dominant (conservative) Liberal-Democrats and the higher civil servants have also become sufficiently intimate to raise questions about administrative impartiality. In contrast to prewar days, bureaucrats cannot normally be appointed to the Cabinet unless they resign and stand for election to the Diet. It has become increasingly common for top civil servants to resign or retire to join the Liberal-Democrats and thus gain access to Cabinet and Diet positions. Inoki says that the ex-bureaucrats have contributed to the expertise of the Liberal-Democratic Party, but, on the other hand, the party has also sought to gain control over higher civil servants through partisan promotions and demotions. Inoki concludes:

> Thus, there is a tendency toward the fusion of high civil servants and leaders of the conservative party. This tendency both threatens the neutrality of the civil bureaucracy which is a *sine qua non* of parliamentary democracy, and makes careers in the civil service less attractive to able university graduates . . .[20]

It might be asked whether the Liberal-Democratic Party is trying to take over the bureaucracy or vice-versa. Ike and others have pointed out that ex-bureaucrats have been assuming an increasing number of party leadership positions and that control of the party may rest with them rather than the professional politicians who have worked their way up winning local and national elections.[21] However, it is perhaps more accurate to say that the bureaucrats may be gaining control over a majority of factions within the party, since the party is a rather loose-knit coalition of groups owing political allegiance to individual leaders. The short life of Japanese Cabinets (the average lasts ten months) is at least partially due to the demands of the various faction leaders for rotation of the portfolios among "deserving" members of the party. Finally, it should be noted that the normal carry-over of the aloof, if not arrogant, attitudes of the bureaucrat from his civil service role to his parliamentary position has not helped the Diet or the Cabinet to create a very democratic public image. According to Ward, ". . . the bu-

20 Inoki, *op. cit.*, pp. 299–300.

21 Nobutaka Ike, "Political Leadership and Political Parties," in Ward and Rustow, *Political Modernization in Japan and Turkey, op. cit.*, p. 405.

reaucratic, and allegedly, undemocratic background of so many Cabinet Ministers is perhaps the most common and bitter complaint against political leadership encountered in Japanese circles today."[22]

D. "Poly-Normativism" and Lack of Consensus. In the sala, there is no basic set of ground rules for administration to which the officials and their clientele agree. Riggs explains that this lack of consensus results when a new set of norms, political formulae, and myths, based on experiences in more modern situations, is introduced into a society which largely continues to adhere to older traditional norms, formulae, and myths.[23] Consequently, some persons are using modern norms, some traditional, and some a mixture of both. For example, an official may publicly adhere ". . . to the norm of objective, achievement-oriented standards of recruitment, equality of status and universalistic norms, but privately subscribe to more subjective, ascription-oriented standards, to a rigid hierarchy of status and particularistic norms . . ."[24] The overlapping of norms is sometimes reflected in the official's acquisition of rank through achievement (in education or in an examination); but once he obtains the position, advancements and other perquisites are claimed on an ascribed basis. The mixture of norms also appears in the vacillation between traditional or "ritualistic" and modern or "rationalistic" approaches to problem-solving. For example, some citizens criticize the administration for not being honest or behaving according to modern or objective norms and then they turn around and undermine the norms by using corruption to secure special benefits for themselves.

The American Occupation of Japan represented a whole-

[22] Ward, "Japan," *op. cit.*, p. 85. Sometimes, however, even the more powerful ex-bureaucratic politicians go too far in their tactlessness. Hayato Ikeda was reportedly forced to resign as Minister of Finance because he told the Diet that "It can't be helped if five or ten small businessmen involved in blackmarketing commit suicide because of bankruptcy." See Theodore McNelly, *Contemporary Government of Japan* (Boston: Houghton Mifflin Company, 1963) pp. 93–95. Nevertheless, this *faux pas* did not prevent Ikeda from becoming Prime Minister in 1960.

[23] Riggs, "An Ecological Approach: The 'Sala' Model," *op. cit.*, p. 29.

[24] *Ibid.*

sale attempt to impose new norms upon a society from outside. Evaluating the extent to which Japanese values were altered will keep scholars occupied for many years to come. Kazuo Kawai's *Japan's American Interlude* is considered one of the better studies published thus far on the Occupation.[25] Some of his observations on bureaucratic recruitment and advancement are similar to those made in earlier sections of this paper. Like the sala official, the Japanese bureaucrat may obtain his initial appointment via examinations, but subsequent advancement depends more on non-competitive factors such as seniority and support of one's superior. Each important ministry official has a collection of protégés whom he tries to help and from whom he may request future favors (e.g., as when he retires and enters politics). Consequently, there is considerable intrigue and politicking among rival cliques of senior officials and their followers. It is politically safer to put in one's time shuffling routine papers than to take the risk of doing something significant which may fail and provide ammunition to rival cliques. Kawai points out that these practices are largely carry-overs from prewar days.[26] The National Personnel Authority, an Occupation creation, did introduce some performance tests and a scheme for position classification, but only limited implementation has been achieved.

In spite of the negative qualities attributed to bureaucrats, they are reportedly still seen by most Japanese as being technically competent, impartial, and powerful.[27] This may also be a reflection of the average Japanese's conception of government in general as part of the fundamental order of things, as natural perhaps as the family itself. Although there are minority elements who challenge the government's authority in certain areas, Ward concludes that:

> [It] is still probably fair to say that most Japanese accept and usually endorse a very wide range of governmental action and control. The seeming prominence of private enterprise in Japan, therefore, is decidedly misleading. The government is

25 Kazuo Kawai, *Japan's American Interlude* (The University of Chicago Press, 1960).

26 *Ibid.*, pp. 119ff.

27 McNelly, *op. cit.*, pp. 93–95.

heavily involved in a great variety of ways in what seem to be private operations in the economic and social spheres.[28]

We can perhaps speculate that the Japanese citizen may not personally like to deal with government officials but, at the same time, he looks to the government to solve many of the economic, social, and political problems which affect his own welfare. It is also misleading to try to measure changes in postwar Japanese society in terms of changes in the bureaucracy. The latter may have changed less than many other national institutions in Japan. It should be remembered that the American Occupation purged only the very top officials of the bureaucracy and that many administrative structures were retained intact as instruments through which other reforms were effected. There is little reason to believe that the bureaucrats who moved up to replace their purged seniors held very different views on administration since they had gone through essentially the same processes of political socialization.

E. Power Distribution: Authority Versus Control. In the sala, officially sanctioned or legitimate power, i.e., *authority,* may be vested in a given body or organization, while unofficial or real power, i.e., *control,* lies elsewhere. For example, a central government office may have *authority* over its field offices or local government units, but in reality the latter are largely autonomous. Or, elected officials may have *authority* over administrative organizations but little real control. However, Riggs points out that the sala officials' behavior may sometimes range from an obvious open exercise of control (perhaps under the guise of "tutelage") to a complete abandonment of initiative or decision-making (the "sinecurist"). The influence of political leaders (or others with *authority*) on the administrator varies with their ability to reward or punish him. If the formal leaders are weak, achievement of public or organizational goals is poorly rewarded and the sala administrator may devote most of his efforts to safeguarding his own interests (security of tenure, fringe benefits, and personal exploitation of official contacts).[29]

[28] Ward, "Japan," *op. cit.,* pp. 56–57.
[29] Kawai, *op. cit.,* p. 125.

Prior to 1945, both authority and control over Japanese local administration were concentrated largely in national agencies. In spite of efforts by Occupation authorities to decentralize control over many functions to local levels, these changes were often more formal or legalistic than real. There also seems to have been considerable recentralization after the Occupation ended. The local governments were often willing to relinquish their new postwar functions because of traditional reliance on the central government and because they lacked the needed revenue sources to finance the added activities. Consequently, a significant degree of both *authority* and *control* may still be located in the national ministries.[30]

Relationships between elected officials and bureaucrats in Japan show more similarities to those described in the "sala" model. As mentioned earlier, Japanese civil servants have apparently not been too successful in converting their former loyalty to the Emperor into allegiance to the citizens or their elected representatives. From the official's viewpoint, it is difficult to replace the more concrete image of the Emperor with vague abstractions such as "the people as a whole or the peoples' welfare."[31] Given the increasing complexity of national administration, the instability of Japanese Cabinets, the organizational weakness of the Diet, and the loose party structure, political control in Japan seems to be primarily shared by the Prime Minister, other faction-leaders in the Liberal-Democratic Party, and the top bureaucracy. This does not mean that other groups or interests are ignored in decision-making. Although the Japanese public is generally regarded as politically apathetic, Ward believes that there is an increasing awareness that politics is amenable to some degree of popular influence and control and that political change is natural or at least possible. Political leaders are becoming alert to this more activist attitude and are

[30] Cf. Ward, "Japan," *op. cit.,* pp. 102–3. For a brief study of Tokyo and its role in local government, see James R. Brady, "Governing the World's Largest City," *The National Chengchi University Journal,* Vol. 6, December 1962, pp. 11–22.

[31] Cf. Yoshinori Ide. *Trend of Public Administration in Japan: A Note on the Postwar Development* (Honolulu: East-West Center, 1964) mimeographed, 58p.

beginning to adjust their policies and actions accordingly.[32] If active participation in politics becomes more widespread, increasing pressures may be exerted to make the bureaucrat more responsive to popular attitudes. Also, as the higher bureaucracy becomes more involved in party politics, its internal cohesion may tend to be weakened. Kawai observes that more younger officials are starting to cooperate with non-conservative elements, such as the Socialists, thus breaking up the monopoly of bureaucratic support enjoyed by the Liberal-Democrats.[33]

IV. Concluding remarks

Now that our rather impressionistic *tour de force* of Japanese bureaucracy and the sala is concluded, what can be said about the utility of the "sala" model for empirical studies? Quite frankly, our attempt to operationalize the model was less rewarding than anticipated, although this does not mean that the model itself is the only problem. The following observations may be of interest:

1. Any attempt to examine the administrative system in isolation from other systems in the society is too restrictive, if not impossible. Riggs himself makes several references to factors outside of the "sala," and we were thus forced to examine other elements, especially the political system in which the bureaucracy functions. Brief mention was also made of the economic system, but the important relationships between the economy and Japanese administration were not developed. However, keeping any research effort within manageable boundaries may require the omission of variables which later turn out to be important.

2. While the "sala" model does seem logical and internally consistent when examined in the abstract, comparing its basic characteristics or elements with real situations is rather difficult:

a. The basic phenomenon being analyzed is the extent to which various traditional and modern characteristics *overlap* in a given society. In Riggs' terms, the problem is therefore to ascer-

32 Ward, "Japan," *op. cit.*, pp. 60–61.

33 Kawai, *op. cit.*, p. 125.

tain the proportions in which the characteristics are mixed and to explain the mixture.[34] The elements analyzed in the "sala" (poly-communalism, lack of consensus, etc.) are also found in traditional and modern societies although usually to a lesser degree. Thus, precise comparisons between the "sala" and other administrative systems would require the isolation and weighting of the examples given under each element in the "sala" and then the identification and weighting of like elements and examples in the other systems. Given the numerous variables in the model, the effort required to do this was deemed too great for the anticipated returns. We thus made only very crude comparisons of the basic elements which are summarized in Chart I.

CHART I

DEGREE TO WHICH SALA ELEMENTS ARE FOUND IN JAPANESE ADMINISTRATION

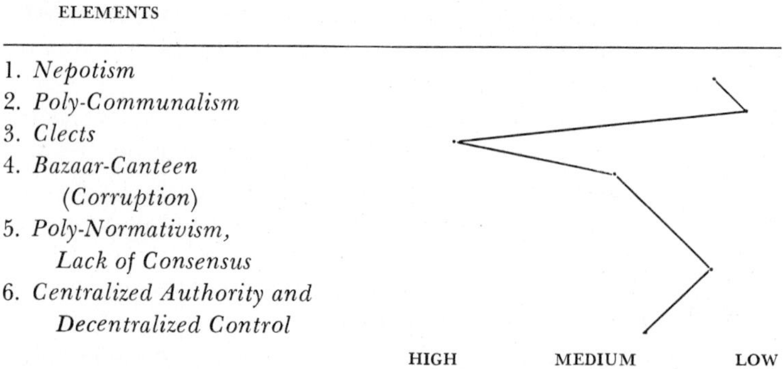

b. Comparisons were also made difficult because the precise and abstract terms developed by Riggs for deductive manipulations were often too restrictive to relate to real phenomena. Furthermore, some of the elements which seemed bound together in the "sala" model had to be separated before they could be applied to the Japanese situation. Hence, we did not find "poly-communalism" to be significant, but we found the related item "clect," useful for describing the Japanese bureaucracy. How-

[34] Riggs, "An Ecological Approach: The 'Sala' Model," *op. cit.*, p. 21.

ever, were we describing a "clect" or the more mundane "clique"? Perhaps the basic question is whether the extensive abstracting out of references to real entities does not sometimes place the model-builder so far out in space that re-entry into the terrestrial realm becomes impossible without disintegration of his vehicle.

3. There is, of course, the possibility that we would have achieved better results by comparing the "sala" with an administrative system in a country less developed than Japan. Alfred Diamant has observed that the sala actually represents a rather static situation in which little development is occurring.[35] We used the model because of our assumption that the administrative system in Japan was developing more slowly than other systems in the society. Our rough evaluation probably indicates that Japanese administration is considerably more modernized than the sala. While our hypothesis about the similarity of the two administrative systems was not supported by the evidence, our assumption about the bureaucracy lagging behind other Japanese institutions may still be correct. However, the literature we surveyed—and thus our conclusions herein—may have been more negative toward the status and performance of the Japanese bureaucracy than the situation warrants.[36] Because Japan does exhibit many modern characteristics, there is perhaps a tendency by Americans to evaluate its administration in Western terms and this may be inappropriate. Moreover, we devoted little treatment to the specific role (negative or positive) played by the bureaucracy in Japan's rapid economic growth since 1949. It seems difficult to believe that the bureaucracy is a completely negative factor, given the dominant role of the government in the economy.

In short, we acquired several insights into Japanese admin-

[35] Remarks made at the 1964 Summer Seminar of the Comparative Administration Group (American Society for Public Administration) held at the University of Michigan.

[36] Although Japan reportedly has more social scientists than any country in the world except the United States, relatively few scientific works have been translated into English. A legalistic approach still predominates in Japanese research, but interdisciplinary and behavioral studies have been increasing. Cf. Yasumasa Kuroda, "Recent Japanese Advances in the Human Sciences," *The American Behavioral Scientist,* Vol. 7, No. 6 (February, 1964), pp. 3–8.

istration by using the "sala," but we still have many unanswered questions, especially about causal relationships between the elements examined. Additional research is still required to classify the Japanese administrative system and to evaluate its potential value for emulation in the developing areas. It might also be interesting to identify specific barriers to economic growth in certain underdeveloped countries and then see how these were handled in Japan. This somewhat limited problem-oriented approach might not generate comprehensive theories as rapidly, but its empirical foundations might be firmer than some of the broad-scale models being developed.

Toward an Empirical Framework for Ecological Studies in Comparative Public Administration

John Forward
The University of Michigan

Introduction

In recent years, increasing interest has been shown in the ecological approach to the study of comparative administration. The basic premise of this approach is that bureaucracy may be regarded as one of several basic institutions in a society and that in order to fully understand its structure and function, it must be studied in the context of its interrelationships with other institutions. In system theory terms, bureaucracy as a social institution is continually interacting with the economic, political and socio-cultural systems in a society and is both a modifying influence on these systems as well as being modified by them.

Many notable attempts have been made recently to develop

Prepared for this volume.

specific theoretical models for the ecology of public administration. However, one disturbing feature, which is shared by most models, is that they are based solely upon intuitive and *a priori* assumptions concerning the relationship of bureaucracy to other societal systems. Consequently, although these models may make important contributions in terms of descriptive analysis and imaginative classificatory schema, their development towards explanatory theory is hampered by a serious lack of empirical background.

At this early stage in the development of the field, it might be useful to give some consideration to the problem of finding types of analysis which are best suited to the task of developing an adequate empirical basis for ecological models given the limited quantity and quality of available data. This problem has been largely neglected in the construction of existing models, but it is of some importance for the development of a body of explanatory theory in ecological study.

An empirical foundation for ecological studies

In any new field of investigation, the preliminary data which are gathered tend to be somewhat general and subject to a high degree of error. Concepts are imprecise and lacking in operational definition, the measuring instruments are crude and still to be refined and strong stable relationships between variables are difficult to establish. What is needed at this stage is a method of analysis which is capable of producing some degree of order to the seemingly disordered collection of observations. One particular set of methods which has been successfully applied to this task in other fields is correlational analysis. Correlational techniques, such as factor analysis, can be used to determine an initial patterning among a large number of different variables. It is this pattern of relationships which may serve as an empirical foundation for theory construction and model-building.

Perhaps the utility of correlational analysis for the present stage of development in ecological studies will become more evident if the expected outcomes of such an analysis are considered. The following points may serve also as an outline for the analysis to be presented in this study.

A. The Initial Selection of Variables: All theoretical models require an initial selection of variables for consideration from a large number of possible choices. Whereas this selection process is largely implicit or intuitive in current ecological model-building, correlational analysis provides a procedure which is both explicit and empirical. By correlating a large number of variables with any criterion variable of interest, it is possible to order all variables in terms of the relative strength of their association with the criterion variable. On the basis of this empirical ordering, variables may be selected or ignored according to whether they show a high or low degree of relationship with the criterion variable. In the construction of ecological models, selection of variables could be accomplished by using some measure of bureaucracy as the criterion variable.

B. The Empirical Determination of Factors: On intuitive grounds, a factor refers to an abstract category of classification which unites and gives meaning to any particular set of variables. In existing models, several factors are set up initially and then variables are assigned to these factors. Correlational or factor analysis reverses this procedure.

An empirical factor is defined as a set of variables which correlate more highly with each other than with all other variables outside the set. By constructing a complete intercorrelation matrix, certain factoring techniques can be applied in order to determine what empirical factors best order the data under consideration. In this manner, factors are defined on the basis of the empirical patterning of the variables, rather than on the basis of pre-conceived assumptions concerning ecological classification.

C. The Specification of Ecological Variables: Once the factors or underlying dimensions have been extracted, variables can be given various factor weightings which represent the relative contribution they make to several different factors. As a hypothetical example, we might expect that an advanced degree of urbanization would have a high factor loading on the economic factor, but we might also find that it contributes substantially to the socio-cultural and communications factors.

The significance of this procedure for model-building is twofold. Firstly, it provides an empirical specification of the relationships between variables and factors and secondly, it allows us to give a more precise empirical meaning to any given ecological variable.

Finally, the pattern of relationships which emerges from the analysis may suggest a number of hypotheses for further testing. It may be found, for example, that literacy rate is not directly related to the extent of bureaucratic development, but that the relationship is mediated indirectly through several other variables, such as economic development, educational attainment or newspaper circulation. It should be noted that correlational analysis demonstrates an association between two variables and not a causal sequence. However, it does provide an empirical basis for the formulation of causal hypotheses for further investigation by other methods.

Before proceeding to the analysis outlined above, some discussion of available data is necessary.

Notes on available data and methodology

In their book, *World Handbook of Political and Social Indicators* (1964), Russett *et. al.* have used extant statistical records to rank-order a large number of countries on a selected set of system variables. The correlational analysis at the end of the book is similar in many respects to the type of analysis suggested here. Unfortunately, this set of data is not appropriate for the present study, since it does not contain any measures of bureaucracy and its exclusive dependence on statistical records precludes the measurement of many variables of interest for studies in comparative public administration.

A second set of data, Banks and Textor's computer printout, *A Cross Polity Survey,* is more appropriate for this study, since it does contain one measure of bureaucracy as well as a number of ecological variables of direct relevance for comparative studies in administration (Banks and Textor, 1963). Although a full discussion of the Banks and Textor data will not be presented here, the following points are of some importance for the development of an empirical framework for ecological studies.

A. An Empirical Framework for Ecological Models: The Banks and Textor data covers what is claimed to be an exhaustive sampling of world polities and so the measures generated represent highly generalized trends across all world polities. It is for this and the following reasons that I have chosen to speak of developing an empirical framework, rather than an ecological model, on the basis of this data.

The main guidelines for the ecological study of comparative administration were first presented by Robert Dahl almost two decades ago (1947). In this seminal paper, Dahl particularly stressed the need to limit the scope of ecological studies to the unique patterning of system variables within one society only. This approach has been followed by Riggs in his monograph, *The Ecology of Public Administration* (1961), in which he has selected three countries and limited his analysis to each of these countries respectively.

While recognizing the validity of this approach for the development of specific ecological models, there may still be some value in developing a universal and generalizable framework for comparative studies. Before we can specify what is unique to the ecological pattern of a single country, it will be necessary to know what constitutes the general features of the pattern.

B. A Measure of Bureaucracy: The measure of bureaucracy used in this study is the one included in Banks and Textor's set of variables. Although this measure is subject to an unknown degree of error in that it is based on the subjective ratings of experts in the field and despite its ambiguous definition, it is the only measure available. Each polity in their sample has been classified into one of the following categories:

Modern — generally effective and responsible civil service, performing in a functionally specific, non-ascriptive social context;

Semi-modern	largely rationalized bureaucratic structure of limited efficiency because of shortage of skilled personnel, inadequate recruitment criteria, excessive intrusion of non-administrative organs, or partially non-congruent social institutions;
Transitional	largely rationalized ex-colonial bureaucratic structure in the process of personnel nationalization and adaptation to the servicing or restructuring of autochthonous social institutions;
Traditional	largely non-rationalized bureaucratic structure performing in the context of ascriptive or deferential stratification system.

(Banks and Textor, p. 112–11)

Banks and Textor present a printout for all the significant cross-breaks using the 'Modern' and 'Semi-modern' versus 'Transitional' and 'Traditional' split on the bureaucratic measure. Statistically, the Chi-square and Fisher-exact statistics are used to give an indication of the relative strength of a relationship between any two variables. However, since the value of Chi-square varies with different sample sizes and the Fisher-exact values are often so close to zero that only .000 is reported, these statistics are unsuitable for the purposes of ordering the variables in terms of the degree of their association with the bureaucratic measure. To overcome these difficulties, all Chi-square values at or beyond the .05 level of significance were converted to coefficients of contingency, which corrects for sample size and may be read like the usual correlation coefficient.

This procedures made it possible to rank order all selected variables in terms of the strength of their relation to the measure of bureaucracy. The result may be seen in Table 1. In this table, it is seen that the variable, "Historically or Significantly Westernized" best differentiates the polities with either Modern or Semi-modern bureaucracies from those with either Transitional or Traditional bureaucracies (Rank 1, c.c. = .582). On the other hand, the variable ranked as number 25, "System Style Is More Mobilizational" is least related to the measure of bureaucracy (c.c. = .176). For convenience, in this study reference will be made to the rank number of the variable and the Banks and Textor variable number is included for reference use by the reader only.

Table I

CROSS-BREAKS FOR BANKS AND TEXTOR'S MEASURE OF BUREAUCRACY, (NO. 180); MODERN AND SEMI-MODERN VS. TRANSITIONAL AND TRADITIONAL.

(VARIABLES RANK-ORDERED BY DEGREE OF CORRELATION)

RANK NO.	B&T V. NO.	C.C. VALUE	VARIABLE DESCRIPTION AND CROSS-BREAK SPLIT
1	75	.582	Historically or Significantly Westernized (vs. Opposite)
2	29	.559	High Urbanization (vs. Low)
3	117	.531	Interest Articulation by Associational Groups Is Significant. Moderate or Limited (vs. Negligible)
4	45	.518	Literacy Rate Is Above 50% (vs. below 50%)
5	43	.515	Economic Development Status Is Very High, High or Low (vs. Very Low)
6	30	.506	Agricultural Population Is Very Low, Low or Medium (vs. High)
7	85	.490	Political Modernization Is Advanced (vs. Transitional)
8	164	.453	Leadership Charisma Is Negligible (vs. Significant)
9	36	.450	C.N.P. Per Capita Is High or Medium (vs. Low or Very Low)
10	89	.430	Ideological Orientation Is Conventional (vs. Other)
11	54	.424	Newspaper Circulation Is 100 or more per 1,000 persons (vs. Less)
12	107	.389	Autonomous Groups Fully Tolerated in Politics (vs. Not)
13	105	.387	Electoral System Is Competitive (vs. Partly or Not)
14	101	.381	Representative Character of the Regime Is Polyarchic (vs. Not)
15	175	.379	Legislature Is Fully or Partially Effective (vs. Opposite)

TABLE I (Continued)

RANK NO.	B&T V. NO.	C.C. VALUE	VARIABLE DESCRIPTION AND CROSS-BREAK SPLIT
16	99	.372	Government Stability present from World War II (vs. Opposite)
17	125	.366	Interest Articulation by Anomic Groups Is Infrequent (vs. Opp.)
18	68	.349	Linguistically Homogeneous (vs. Heterogeneous)
19	34	.349	Gross G.N.P. is Very High, High, Medium or Low (vs. Very Low)
20	153	.338	Party System Is Stable (vs. Moderately or Unstable)
21	26	.319	Population Density Is High, Medium (vs. Low)
22	114	.261	Sectionalism Is Negligible (vs. Extreme or Moderate)
23	111	.225	Political Enculturation Is High or Medium (vs. Less)
24	66	.193	Religiously Homogeneous (vs. Heterogeneous)
25	92	.176	System Style Is Mobilizational (vs. Less)

A CORRELATIONAL ANALYSIS

BUREAUCRACY AND THE RELATIVE IMPORTANCE OF ECOLOGICAL VARIABLES. Existing ecological models include a number of different system variables, political, socio-cultural or economic. However, since they lack the necessary empirical basis, the problem of assessing the relative importance for different systems to the development and maintenance of bureaucracy must remain at the level of intuition. At this level, some degree of bias due to these implicit or explicit assumptions is inevitable. For example, although Riggs includes at least five different systems in his "Sala Model," he appears to give a predominantly socio-cultural emphasis to his interpretations of the roles which salas, clects and nepotism play in the bureaucratic structures of prismatic societies. On the other hand, a model like Dorsey's "Information-Energy Model" places a great deal of weight on economic and technological factors, but gives little consideration to social and political factors (Riggs, 1962; Dorsey, 1962).

If the variables in Table 1 are examined in terms of the relative degree of their associations with the bureaucratic measure, many interesting features may be observed which may, or may not, support existing assumptions concerning the relative importance of various ecological variables for the existence of an advanced bureaucracy. A few of these features are discussed below.

A. Bureaucracy and economic variables: In general, the economic indices in Table 1 are ranked high on the list. These are, "Economic Development Status" (rank 5, c.c. = .515) and "G.N.P. Per Capita" (rank 9, c.c. = .450). If the ratio of agricultural to non-agricultural population is interpreted as an indicator of industrial development, this measure also ranks with the main economic indices (rank 6, c.c. = .506). It is possible that the degree of westernization, (rank 1) and urbanization (rank 2) reflect, among other things, a relatively advanced state of economic development.

These observations serve to supplement the results of an analysis by Russett and his colleagues, in that they found that economic factors play a vital role in the development of almost all the major institutions in a society (Russett, 1964). Although Russett did not include a measure of bureaucracy in his analysis, these results show that it is no exception to this finding.

B. Bureaucracy and communication variables: There are few variables which are direct indicators of the communication system in this data, but those which do appear are closely related to the measure of bureaucracy. "Literacy Rate" (rank 4, c.c. = .518) and "Newspaper Circulation" (rank 11, c.c. = .424) are probably the most explicit indices of communication capacity, with the degree of westernization and urbanization again serving as indirect measures. In view of the importance of a developed system of communications for effective bureaucratic performance, it is surprising that, with one or two notable exceptions, communication variables have been largely neglected in current ecological model-building.

C. Bureaucracy and socio-cultural variables: The features of interest here are not so much the relationships which did occur, but some expected relationships which failed to show up strongly. For example, one might expect that homogeneity of language would be a socio-cultural measure which would correlate highly with effective bureaucracy, since it may represent a more basic homogeneity of values and it would certainly reduce the communication barriers inherent in a polylingual society. However, this variable is seen as relatively unimportant in the list (rank 18, c.c. = .349). A related variable, religious homogeneity, is also low on the list (rank 24, c.c. = .193). Again, one might expect that the degree of sectionalism which exists would be more closely related to the measure of bureaucracy than it is (rank 22, c.c. = .261).

D. Bureaucracy and political variables: Some people have proposed that a stable and representative political system is a necessary precondition for the development and maintenance of effective bureaucracy (cf. Friedrich, 1950). However, in Table 1 the measure of governmental stability used by Banks and Textor appears well down the list (rank 16, c.c. = .372), as do many of the indicators of representative government (cf. variables ranked 13, 14, 15 and 20).

The political indices most closely related to the bureaucratic measure are "Interest Articulation by Associational Groups" (rank 3, c.c. = .531), "Ideological Orientation Is Conventional" (rank 10, c.c. = .430) and "Leadership Charisma Is Negligible" (rank 8, c.c. = .453), all of which represent factors other than the purely political. Eisenstadt (1959) and Riggs (1961) have both placed some importance on the necessity of associationalism, as opposed to ascriptivism, as a socio-political basis for effective bureaucracy. Interest articulation by associational groups is a compromisable process which can be mediated through the bureaucratic structure, whereas the uncompromising demands of closed and conflicting ascriptive groups present what are often insuperable difficulties for effective bureaucratic performance.

In general, the data appear to support the assumption that it is effective bureaucracy which is the pre-condition for representative and stable government, rather than *vice versa*. Effective bureaucracy is seen to be highly dependent on a relatively advanced level of economic development, literacy, urbanization and communication capacity, all of which appear higher on the list in Table 1 than many of the direct indices of representative government.

THE EMPIRICAL DETERMINATION OF ECOLOGICAL FACTORS. By utilizing other parts of the Banks and Textor printout data, it would be possible to construct a complete intercorrelation matrix which included all the variables in Table 1. In order to determine what factors account for the greatest amount of the variance in such a matrix, several different factoring techniques could be applied. One method which is suitable for our purpose is the technique of "unfolding the matrix," developed by Coombs (1964). However, the services of a large computer would be required to factor a matrix of the size contemplated here, and since the necessary time and money were not available at the time of writing, a full-scale analysis of the data was not possible. Instead, for the purposes of illustration, a smaller matrix consisting of twelve representative variables has been constructed and unfolded by hand. (see Table 2 for the matrix).

The unfolding of the smaller matrix produced four fairly distinct factors and one residual factor. These factors are represented in tabular form for discussion in the next section. It should be noted that, although the factors have been given descriptive labels, such as political and economic, that these labels are somewhat arbitrary and open to various interpretations. What is actually represented by these factors are the empirically determined underlying dimensions which best order the data in Table 2.

INTERRELATIONSHIPS AMONG FACTORS AND ECOLOGICAL VARIABLES. In the discussion of the factors which follows, attention is directed to the following considerations.

In accordance with the rules for correlational analysis presented earlier, each factor can be examined in terms of whether the core variables intercorrelate more highly with each other than with variables outside the set, and also, whether the core variables order all other variables in a similar manner.

Since factors may be thought of as mediating the relationships between different ecological variables and bureaucracy, it will be of interest to observe how closely each factor relates to the bureaucratic measure.

By observing the position of any given variable in the overall pattern of relationships, it is possible to trace not only its direct relationship with the bureaucratic measure, but also how this relationship is mediated indirectly through other factors and associated variables. This aspect of the analysis is a source for hypothesis formulation concerning the specific relationships between different variables.

Finally, by considering the relative contribution which any given variable makes to several different factors, it is possible to give a more determinative empirical meaning to the variable in question.

These considerations serve as a framework for the discussion of the factors which are presented below.

A. The economic factor: The following table shows the lists of intercorrelations for the two core economic variables, "Economic Development Status"[1] and "Per Capita Gross National Product."[2] If a more complete specification of any variable is desired, reference may be made to the variable description in Table 1 by means of the rank numbers preceding the variables listed below.

It is observed that the two key economic variables correlate highly (.602) and that they order their respective lists of intercorrelates similarly, thus forming the core of the economic factor.

Although the relative rank of the bureaucratic measure is low on both lists, when it is compared with the other factors in terms of the values of the contingency coefficients, its relationship with the economic factor is one of the highest. An examination of the variables which correlate highly with the core economic variables suggest a number of hypotheses of interest.

The high ranking of Literacy Rate on both lists may

[1] In terms of the Banks and Textor definition and the specific crossbreak used here, those polities which are rated high on "Economic Development Status" are those with "self-sustaining" or "sustained" economic growth, or those which have a reasonable prospect of achieving this status by the mid-1970's (see Banks and Textor, p. 65).

[2] Polities rated as "High" on "Per Capita Gross National Product" by Banks and Textor, are those with $600 G.N.P. Per Capita or more (see Banks and Textor, p. 63).

TABLE

INTERCORRELATION MATRIX OF 12

	BUREAUCRACY MODERN OR SEMI-MODERN	WESTERNIZED (1)	ASSOCIATIONAL GRPS (3)	LITERACY (4)
Bureaucracy Modern or Semi-Modern	—			
Westernized (1)	.582	—		
Associational Grps (3)	.531	.588	—	
Literacy (4)	.518	.555	.442	—
Economic Develop. (5)	.515	.572	.490	.542
G.N.P. Per Cap. (9)	.450	.534	.446	.559
Ideology Conventional (10)	.430	.564	.546	.471
Newspapers, 100+ (11)	.424	.496	.367	.560
Autonomous Grps Tolerated (12)	.389	.510	Not Given	.418
Linguistically Homogeneous (18)	.349	.318	.256	.338
Political Enculturation (23)	.010	.245	Not Given	.291
Urbanization (2)	.559	.554	.542	.511

II

Selected Variables from Table I.

ECONOMIC DEVEL. (5)	G.N.P. PER CAP. (9)	IDEOLOGY CONVENTIONAL (10)	NEWSPAPERS 100+ (11)	AUTONOMOUS GRPS TOLERATED (12)	LINGUIST. HOMOG. (18)	POLITICAL ENCULTURAT. (23)	URBANIZATION (2)
—							
.602	—						
.540	.485	—					
.514	.610	.488	—				
.465	.470	.600	.423	—			
.233	.258	.350	.312	.254	—		
.246	.238	.286	.287	Given	.256	—	
.603	.537	.505	.498	.407	.383	.179	—

ECONOMIC DEVELOPMENT STATUS

	(2)	Urbanization	.603
*	(9)	G.N.P. Per Capita	.602
	(1)	Westernization	.572
	(4)	Literacy Rate	.542
	(10)	Ideology Is Conventional	.540
**	(–)	Bureaucracy Modern/Semi.	.515
	(11)	Newspaper Circulation	.514
	(3)	Associational Groups	.490
	(12)	Autonomous Groups Tol.	.465
	(23)	Political Enculturation	.246
	(18)	Linguistic Homogeneity	.233

PER CAPITA G.N.P.

	(11)	Newspaper Circulation	.610
*	(5)	Economic Development	.602
	(4)	Literacy Rate	.559
	(2)	Urbanization	.537
	(1)	Westernization	.534
	(10)	Ideology Conventional	.485
	(12)	Autonomous Groups Tol.	.470
	(3)	Associational Groups	.463
**	(–)	Bureaucracy Modern/Semi.	.450
	(18)	Linguistic Homogeneity	.285
	(23)	Political Enculturation	.238

* Core variable correlation
** Bureaucratic measure

indicate the necessity of an advanced degree of economic development for the operation and maintenance of a wide-scale educational system. All relationships are circular to some extent, but the relatively high literacy rate, together with some degree of consumer power, (G.N.P. Per Capita) might explain why Newspaper Circulation is so closely related to the economic factor. It is not surprising to see that Urbanization is ranked high on both lists, since it points to the possibility that there exists some degree of industrialization, or at least some centralization of commercial activities in a society. The moderate relationship of Westernization to the economic factor is probably redundant in that it contributes only those aspects of Westernization which are reflected already in the variables above.

In view of the high value of many of the intercorrelations

in this table, it may be concluded that the economic factor, together with those variables it mediates most strongly, is of considerable importance for the development and maintenance of effective bureaucracy.

B. The communication factor: The two core variables for the communication factor are, "Literacy Rate"[3] and "Newspaper Circulation."[4]

The communication factor is so similar to the economic factor that there is little reason to separate them on empirical grounds. Both factors order the variables in much the same

LITERACY RATE

*	(11)	Newspaper Circulation	.560
	(9)	G.N.P. Per Capita	.559
	(1)	Westernization	.555
	(5)	Economic Development	.524
**	(–)	Bureaucracy Modern/Semi.	.518
	(2)	Urbanization	.511
	(10)	Ideology Conventional	.471
	(3)	Associational Groups	.442
	(12)	Autonomous Groups Tol.	.418
	(18)	Linguistic Homogeneity	.338
	(23)	Political Enculturation	.291

NEWSPAPER CIRCULATION

	(9)	G.N.P. Per Capita	.610
*	(4)	Literacy Rate	.560
	(5)	Economic Development	.514
	(2)	Urbanization	.498
	(1)	Westernization	.496
	(10)	Ideology Conventional	.488
**	(–)	Bureaucracy Modern/Semi.	.424
	(12)	Autonomous Groups Tol.	.423
	(3)	Associational Groups	.367
	(18)	Linguistic Homogeneity	.312
	(23)	Political Enculturation	.287

* Core variable Correlation
** Bureaucratic measure

3 In terms of Banks and Textor's classification and the specific cross-break used, polities with a literacy rate of 50% or better are rated as high (see Banks and Textor, p. 66)

4 Polities rated as high in "Newspaper Circulation" by Banks and Textor are those with a circulation of 100 or more per 1,000 persons (see Banks and Textor, p. 69).

manner and are similarly related to the bureaucratic measure. However, since many of the variables used in this study are of such a general nature as to permit multiple interpretations, it is convenient to treat them as separate factors for the purpose of discussion.

It has already been hypothesized that the strong set of relationships between Literacy Rate, Newspaper Circulation and G.N.P. Per Capita has significance for effective bureaucratic performance insofar as it is mediated by the economic factor. However, the same set of relationships has significance for bureaucracy in the degree to which they reflect upon the capacities of a society's communications system. The necessity for having effective means of mass communication and a public which is capable of receiving and transmitting written communications has generally been overlooked in ecological studies which seek to specify the prerequisites for effective public administration. The variable Urbanization may also have a somewhat different meaning for the communication factor than it had for the economic factor in that it reflects the communication advantages which are inherent in the social and geographical propinquity to be found in centers of high population concentration.

Even though these hypothesized relationships are heavily dependent upon economic variables, it is apparent that the communication factor does have an independent contribution of some importance to make to the effective performance of administrative systems.

C. The political factor: The following are the two core variables and their intercorrelations for what has been labelled the "political factor." The core variables are "Ideological Orientation Is Conventional"[5] and "Autonomous Groups Are Tolerated in Politics."[6]

[5] By Banks and Textor's definition, polities are "conventional," rather than "doctrinal," "developmental," "situational" or "traditional," in ideological orientation if, "there exist conventionalized procedures for the achieving and legitimization of new or changed power relationships, even though access to the conventions in question is effectively denied a majority of the population" (see Banks and Textor, p. 80).

[6] Banks and Textor rate polities highly on the variable, "Freedom of Group Opposition" if, ". . . autonomous groups [are] free to enter politics and able to oppose the government." (see Banks and Textor, p. 87).

IDEOLOGICAL ORIENTATION
IS CONVENTIONAL

*	(12)	Autonomous Groups Tol.	.600
	(1)	Westernization	.564
	(3)	Associational Groups	.546
	(5)	Economic Development	.540
	(2)	Urbanization	.505
	(11)	Newspaper Circulation	.488
	(9)	G.N.P. Per Capita	.485
	(4)	Literacy Rate	.471
**	(–)	Bureaucracy Modern/Semi.	.430
	(18)	Linguistic Homogeneity	.350

AUTONOMOUS GROUPS ARE
TOLERATED IN POLITICS

*	(10)	Ideology Conventional	.600
	(1)	Westernization	.510
	(9)	G.N.P. Per Capita	.470
	(5)	Economic Development	.465
	(11)	Newspaper Circulation	.423
	(4)	Literacy Rate	.418
	(2)	Urbanization	.407
**	(–)	Bureaucreacy Modern/Semi.	.389
	(18)	Linguistic Homogeneity	.254
		(Data missing: Assoc. Grps)	

* Core variable correlation
** Bureaucratic measure

The two core variables correlate highly and order all other variables in a similar way. However, of all the factors presented, the political factor is the least related to the bureaucratic measure which appears at the bottom of both lists. Since this relationship is relatively weak in its more direct form, it is all the more important that the more indirect relationships be examined. A few hypotheses concerning indirect relations between bureaucracy and the political factor are presented below.

The variable, "Associational Groups," is closely related to the core political variable, "Ideology Is Conventional." Although Banks and Textor do not present a printout table for it, it is also possible that the degree of interest articulation by associational groups and the degree to which autonomous groups are tolerated in politics is also highly related. If this is so, the following relationships are hypothesized.

The political significance of associationalism is that it provides a compromisable basis for interest articulation which, when linked with an advanced degree of economic development, is likely to be related to the reduction of sharp differences in ideological orientation within a society. This set of conditions would help to provide a political environment in which autonomous groups are more likely to be tolerated. The significance of this for public bureaucracy is ambiguous since, while it may create a more complex set of authority and responsibility relationships, it is also clear that a stabilized and routinized political situation is a more congenial environment for the effective functioning of bureaucracy.

D. A socio-political factor: The two key variables which constitute the core of the fourth empirical factor are "Historically or Significantly Westernized"[7] and "Interest Articulation by Associational Groups."[8] Although it is not clear what descriptive label is most appropriate for this factor, for the purposes of discussion, it is tentatively labelled as a socio-political factor. The intercorrelates of the two key variables are presented below.

The requirements that the two core variables intercorrelate highly and that they order other variables similarly are adequately met. It is also observed that the bureaucratic measure shows a fairly high degree of correlation on both core variables, particularly the variable Westernization. However, due to its rather general and ambiguous definition, it is unclear what the socio-political significance of westernization is for the development and maintenance of advanced public bureaucracy. However, the strong relationship between Westernization and Inter-

[7] For Banks and Textor, the label "historically western" refers to those polities which are located within the limits of the old Ottoman Empire with the addition of Greece. "Significantly westernized" presumably refers to polities outside this area which are either derivative, or have been profoundly influenced by historically western polities (see Banks and Textor, p. 75).

[8] The main characteristics of associational groups are, ". . . explicit representation of the interests of a particular group, orderly procedures for the formulation of interests and demands and the transmission of these demands to other political structures, such as political parties, legislatures, bureaucracies" (see Banks and Textor, p. 89).

WESTERNIZATION

* (3)	Associational Groups	.588
** (–)	Bureaucracy Modern/Semi.	.582
(5)	Economic Development	.572
(10)	Ideology Conventional	.564
(4)	Literacy Rate	.555
(2)	Urbanization	.554
(9)	G.N.P. Per Capita	.534
(11)	Newspaper Circulation	.496
(18)	Linguistic Homogeneity	.318

INTEREST ARTICULATION BY ASSOCIATIONAL GROUPS

* (1)	Westernization	.588
(10)	Ideology Conventional	.546
(2)	Urbanization	.542
** (–)	Bureaucracy Modern/Semi.	.531
(5)	Economic Development	.490
(9)	G.N.P. Per Capita	.463
(4)	Literacy Rate	.422
(11)	Newspaper Circulation	.367
(18)	Linguistic Homogeneity	.256

* Core variable correlation
** Bureaucratic measure

est Articulation by Associational Groups may give some clues for hypothesis formulation.

Interest articulation through associational groups is primarily a political process, but the basis for the existence of associational groups is mainly socio-cultural. The possible contributions which westernization makes to this basis may consist of the advanced degree of economic development and urbanization which is related to westernization. Increased industrial urbanization may indicate the rise of secularization in a society following the break-down of geographically dispersed and localized ascriptive groupings and this is possibly an important pre-condition for the development of associational groups. In turn, the significance of associational groups for effective bureaucratic performance has been mentioned earlier in that it provides a compromisable basis for the demands made by different groups upon bureaucracy, whereas the exclusive and conflicting demands of ascriptive groups present great difficulties for public administration. Westernization also makes other indirect contributions to the bureaucratic measure through its high association with literacy rate and the existence of a conventional ideological orientation, both of which have been discussed earlier.

Conclusion

The correlational analysis presented in this study is admittedly a very limited sample of what might have been accomplished if a full-scale analysis had been possible. However, it may have served to illustrate some potential contributions which a full-scale empirical framework would have to make to the development of specific models of the ecology of public administration. In conclusion, some of these contributions are summarized.

One of the first tasks of model-building is the selection of variables for inclusion in the model. The present study has demonstrated that, by means of correlational techniques, a selection from a large number of variables can be made on objective grounds rather than on *ad hoc* and intuitive bases.

Another preliminary task in the construction of models is the definition of analytic terms and categories which are to be used in the formulation of basic assumptions and propositions. In models of the ecology of public administration, these terms will include the definition of basic institutional structures in society, such as the economic, political and socio-cultural systems. In this study, these systems have been defined empirically through the use of factor analysis. In factor analysis, the empirical factors which represent institutional systems are based on the pattern of relationships which emerges from the intercorrelations among a large set of variables. This procedure has many advantages over the usual method of first defining the systems intuitively and then assigning variables to the systems in terms of the intuitive definitions.

Many of the ecological variables used in current models are of such a general nature that a precise definition of them is difficult and their significance for bureaucracy is unclear. In factor analysis, it is possible to give a more complete specification to any variable by observing its relationship with other factors and associated variables. In the analysis presented here, for example, the degree of urbanization is seen to contribute substantially to several different factors. This suggests that the usual definition of urbanization in terms of population density is a highly general one which could probably be broken down into more specific components. Different terms could be given to different aspects of urbanization, insofar as it has economic, political or socio-cultural significance for bureaucracy. Another example is that the variable "Interest Articulation by Associational Groups" was found to have socio-cultural significance for bureaucracy in addition to the political meaning which is normally attributed to it.

Once the selection of variables and the formulation of basic assumptions and propositions have been achieved in model-building, the long process of hypothesis derivation and testing can begin. The present study has shown that correlational analysis may make an important contribution to this aspect of model-building also. Some examples of hypotheses which were suggested by the patterning of the variables emerging from the sample analysis in this study are to be found in the discussion sections dealing with the four main factors which were extracted.

Finally, the task of developing specific models for the unique patterning of ecological variables within one particular society is facilitated by knowing what are the features which are general to all societies. This universal patterning of ecological relationships would be provided by the empirical framework which has been suggested and illustrated in this study.

References

Banks, A. S. and Textor, R. B., *A Cross-Polity Survey* (Cambridge: M.I.T. Press), 1963.

Coombs, C. H., *A Theory of Data* (New York: Wiley), 1964.

Dahl, Robert A., "The Science of Public Administration: Three Problems," *Public Administration Review*, Vol. 7 (1947), pp. 1–11.

Dorsey, J. T., Jr., "An Information-Energy Model," in Ferrel Heady and Sybil L. Stokes (eds.) *Papers in Comparative Administration* (Ann Arbor: Institute of Public Administration), 1962.

EISENSTADT, S. N., "Bureaucracy, Bureaucratization and Debureaucratization," in this volume.

FRIEDRICH, CARL J., *Constitutional Government and Democracy* (Boston: Ginn and Company), 1949.

RIGGS, FRED W., "An Ecological Approach: The 'Sala' Model," in this volume.

———, *The Ecology of Public Administration* (New Delhi: Asia Publishing House), 1961.

RUSSETT, B. M., ALKER, H. R., DEUTCH, K. W. and LASSWELL, H. D., *World Handbook of Political and Social Indicators* (New Haven: Yale University Press), 1964.

Selected Bibliography

The organization of the bibliography follows the organization of the book. An additional "miscellaneous" section includes items of general interest, with particular emphasis on comparative local government.

By and large the bibliography does not include items found in Heady and Stokes, *Comparative Public Administration: A Selective Annotated Bibliography* (1960), which remains the most comprehensive work in the field. Neither does it include, generally, bibliographical items which appear in the introduction to the book or in the various selections.

Abbreviations of Journals Cited

ABS	American Behavioral Scientist
AJES	American Journal of Economics and Sociology
AJS	American Journal of Sociology
AMJ	Advanced Management Journal
APSR	American Political Science Review
AS	Asian Survey
ASQ	Administrative Science Quarterly
ASR	American Sociological Review
CJA	Chinese Journal of Administration (Taiwan)
CPA	Canadian Public Administration
CQ	China Quarterly
CS	Current Sociology
CSSH	Comparative Studies in Society and History
EDCC	Economic Development and Cultural Change
HO	Human Organization
ICLQ	The International and Comparative Law Quarterly
IDR	International Development Review
IJPA	Indian Journal of Public Administration
ILR	International Labour Review
IO	International Organizations
IRAS	International Review of Administrative Sciences
ISSB	International Social Science Bulletin (changed to International Social Science Journal)
JAS	Journal of Asian Studies
JIA	Journal of International Affairs

JLAO	Journal of Local Administration Overseas
JMAS	Journal of Modern African Studies
JP	Journal of Politics
MJPS	Midwest Journal of Political Science
NTJ	National Tax Journal
NZJPA	New Zealand Journal of Public Administration
PA (L)	Public Administration (London)
PA (S)	Public Administration (Sydney)
PAIA	Public Administration in Israel and Abroad (Annual)
PAR	Public Administration Review
PF/FP	Public Finance/Finance Publique
PJPA	Philippine Journal of Public Administration
POQ	Public Opinion Quarterly
PPR	Public Personnel Review
PS	Political Studies
PSQ	Political Science Quarterly
RA	La Revue Administrative (Paris)
RP	Res Publica (Brussels)
SAQ	South Atlantic Quarterly
SF	Social Forces
SLG	Soviet Law and Government
SQ	Sociological Quarterly
SR	Social Research
SS	Soviet Studies
SSR	Sociology and Social Research
UAQ	Urban Affairs Quarterly
WP	World Politics
WPQ	Western Political Quarterly

General bibliographies

"Bibliography on Administrative Law (1940–1957)," *IRAS,* Vol. 23, No. 2 (1957), 257–261.

"Bibliography on Court Control of Public Authorities," *IRAS,* Vol. 23, No. 4 (1957), 544–550.

"Bibliography on International and Supernational Civil Service," *IRAS,* Vol. 23, No. 3 (1957), 406–408.

Bicker, William, David Brown, Herbert Malakoff, and William J. Gore, *Comparative Urban Development: An Annotated Bibliography.* Papers in Comparative Public Administration, Special Series: No. 5, Comparative Administration Group, American Society for Public Administration, 1965.

Boston University, African Studies Program, Development Research Center, *Selected Bibliography of French Language Works on*

Governmental and Administrative Problems (With Special Attention to Africa). Boston: 1963.

Boston University, African Studies Program, Development Research Center, *A Selective Bibliography of Books, Articles, and Documents on the Subject of African Administrative Problems.* Boston: 1964.

Carleton University, School of Public Administration, *Library Selected List of Current Materials on Canadian Public Administration: Cumulative Issues of No. 1–17 (September 1954–December 1962)*. Ottawa, Ontario: n.d.

École Nationale d'Administration, "Liste bibliographique (1946–1963)," *RA,* No. 104 (1965), 139–146.

EISENSTADT, S. N., "Bureaucracy and Bureaucratization, a Trend Report and Bibliography," *CS,* Vol. 7, No. 1 (1958), 99–164.

HEADY, FERREL, "Recent Literature on Comparative Public Administration," *ASQ,* Vol. 5, No. 1 (1960), 134–154.

HEADY, FERREL, and SYBIL L. STOKES, *Comparative Public Administration; A Selective Annotated Bibliography.* Ann Arbor: The University of Michigan, Institute of Public Administration, 1960.

JONES, GARTH N., and ROBERT N. GIORDANO, *Planned Organizational Change: A Working Bibliography.* CAG Occasional Papers, 1964.

LENGYEL, PETER, "The International Civil Service: A Short Survey of Literature," *IJPA,* Vol. 7, No. 4 (1961), 543–546.

Public Administration: A Select List of Books and Periodicals. London: Longmans, Green & Co., for the British Council, 1964.

RAPHAELI, NIMROD, "Selected Articles and Documents on Comparative Public Administration," *APSR* (March 1963, and subsequent issues).

RIGGS, FRED W., "Notes on Literature Available for the Study of Comparative Public Administration," *APSR,* Vol. 47, No. 2 (1954), 515–537.

SAVAGE, PETER R., "Public Administration in Literature: A Bibliographical Essay," *PJPA,* Vol. 9, No. 1 (1965), 60–70.

SPITZ, ALAN A., and EDWARD W. WEIDNER, *Development Administration: An Annotated Bibliography.* Honolulu: East-West Center Press, 1963.

TICKNER, FRED J., "A Survey and Evaluation of Comparative Research," *PAR,* Vol. 19, No. 1 (1959), 19–25.

United Nations, *Remedies Against the Abuse of Administrative Authority: Selected Studies* (mimeo). ST/TAO/HR/19. New York: United Nations, 1964.

U.S. Department of State, Agency for International Development, *Development Administration and Assistance; An Annotated Bibli-*

ography. PA Prints and Reprints No. 45. Washington, D.C.: July, 1963.

———, *Political Development: A Bibliography*. External Research Paper 159. Washington, D.C.: August, 1964.

Bureaucratic systems: 'ideographic' approach

A. Historic

Barker, Sir Ernest, *The Development of Public Services in Western Europe, 1660–1930*. New York: Oxford University Press, 1944.

Beyer, William C., "The Civil Service of the Ancient World," *PAR*, Vol. 19, No. 4 (1959), 243–249.

Durand, Charles, *Quelques aspects de l'administration préfectorale sous la Consulat et l'Empire*. Aix-en-Provence: La Pansée universitaire, 1962.

Eisenstadt, S. N., "Internal Contradictions in Bureaucratic Polities," *CSSH*, Vol. 1, No. 1 (1958), 58–75.

d'Eszlary, Charles, "Les administrations camérales de Brandebourg et de la monarchie des Habsbourg et leurs effets sur les administrations modernes," *IRAS*, Vol. 30, No. 2 (1964), 171–178.

Fesler, James W., "French Field Administration: The Beginnings," *CSSH*, Vol. 5, No. 1 (1962), 76–111.

Greel, H. G., "Beginnings of Bureaucracy in China: The Origin of Hsien," *JAS*, Vol. 23, No. 2 (1964), 155–184.

Herson, Lawrence J. R., "China's Imperial Bureaucracy: Its Direction and Control," *PAR*, Vol. 17, No. 1 (1957), 44–53.

Hsu, Cho-Yun, "The Changing Relationship Between Local Society and the Central Political Power in Former Han: 206 B.C.–8 A.D.," *CSSH*, Vol. 7, No. 4 (1965), 358–370.

Jiang, Joseph P. L., "The Mo Liao System in Ch'ing Administration," *PJPA*, Vol. 7, No. 4 (1963), 258–267.

Kim, Paul S., "Dynamics of the Japanese Imperial Civil Service under the Meiji Constitution, 1889–1945," *PPR*, Vol. 26, No. 2 (1965), 122–127.

Kracke Jr., E. A., *Civil Service in Sung China*. Cambridge: Harvard University Press, 1953.

Lindsay of Birker, Lord, "The Public Service in China," *PA (S)*, Vol. 14, No. 4 (1955), 214–228.

Marsh, Robert M., "Bureaucratic Constraints on Nepotism in the Ch'ing Period," *JAS*, Vol. 19, No. 2 (1960), 117–133.

MENZEL, JOHANNA M. (ed.), *The Chinese Civil Service—Career Open to Talent?* Boston: D. C. Heath and Co., 1963.

DES ROTOURS, ROBERT, *Traité des Fonctionnaires et Traité de l'Armée.* Leydon: E. J. Brill, 1947–48.

SHAW, STANFORD J., *The Financial and Administrative Organization and Development of Ottoman Egypt, 1517–1798.* Princeton: Princeton University Press, 1962.

SPITZER, ALAN B., "The Bureaucrat as Proconsul: The Restoration Prefect and the *police generale,*" *CSSH,* Vol. 7, No. 4 (1965), 371–392.

B. WESTERN

Articles on Austrian Public Administration, *IRAS,* Vol. 28, No. 2 (1962).

BEXELIUS, ALFRED, "The Swedish Institution of the Justiticombudsman," *IRAS,* Vol. 27, No. 3 (1961), 243–256.

BONNAUD-DELAMARE, ROGER, "Le préfet dans la cadre de la Constitution française de 1958," *IRAS,* Vol. 27, No. 1 (1961), 5–15.

LORD BRIDGES, "The Relationship Between Ministers and the Permanent Departmental Head," *CPA,* Vol. 7, No. 3 (1964), 269–281.

BROWN, R. G. S., "Organization Theory and Civil Service Reform," *PA (L)*, Vol. 43 (1965), 313–330.

CAIDEN, NAOMI, "An Ombudsman for Australia?" *PA (S)*, Vol. 23, No. 2 (1964), 97–115.

CHAPEL, YVES, "Conditions of Employment of the Staffs of Government Departments in Western Europe," *ILR,* Vol. 87, No. 4 (1963), 328–360.

CHESTER, D. N., "The British Treasury and Economic Planning," *IJPA,* Vol. 10, No. 2 (1964), 159–171.

CRABBE, V., "Les problèmes de la décentralisation en Belgique," *RP,* Vol. 6, No. 4 (1964), 372–381.

DELAMOTHE, A. DUTHEILLET, "Ministerial Cabinets in France," *PA (L)*, Vol. 43 (1965), 365–382.

DIAMANT, ALFRED, "Bureaucracy in Western Europe," *PAR,* Vol. 19, No. 3 (1959), 198–203.

Fabian Society, *The Administrators—The Reform of the Civil Service.* London: Fabian Society, 1964.

FISCHBACH, OSKAR GEORG, *Bundesbeamtengesetz.* Cologne: Carl Heymanns, 1964.

France, Articles on Public Administration, *IRAS,* Vol. 31, No. 1 (1965).

FRANKEL, CHARLES, "Bureaucracy and Democracy in the New Europe," *Daedalus,* Vol. 93, No. 1 (1964), 471–492.

GRAHAM, L. M., "Do Politicians Rely on Administrators to Ease Their Burden of Work?" *NZJPA,* Vol. 27, No. 1 (1965), 37–43.

GRÉGOIRE, ROGER, *The French Civil Service.* Brussels: International Institute of Administrative Sciences, 1964.

Hochschule für Verwaltungswissenschaften Speyer, *Wandlungen der rechtstaatlichen Verwaltung.* Berlin: Duncken & Humblot, 1962.

HODGETTS, J. E., "Challenge and Response: A Retrospective View of the Public Service of Canada," *CPA,* Vol. 7, No. 4 (1964), 409–421.

HURWITZ, STEPHAN, "Le controleur general de l'administration civil et militaire au Danemark," *IRAS,* Vol. 22, No. 3 (1956), 181–190.

Istituto per il progresso dell'amministrazione publica, *Atti del primo convegno nazionale dei cultori di scienza e tecnica dell'amministrazione publica.* Milan: Giuffré, 1964.

JACOB, HERBERT, *German Administration Since Bismark.* New Haven: Yale University Press, 1963.

KASTARI, PAAVO, "The Parliamentary Ombudsman: His Functions, Position, and Relation to the Chancellor of Justice in Finland," *IRAS,* Vol. 28, No. 4 (1962), 391–405.

KEELING, C. D. E., "Treasury Centre for Administrative Studies," *PA* (*L*), Vol. 43 (1965), 191–198.

LANGROD, GEORGES, "L'experience allemande du 'ombudsman' militaire," *RA,* No. 97 (1964), 72–75.

———, "Le nouveau status des fonctionnaires en Espagne," *IRAS,* Vol. 30, No. 3 (1964), 263–271.

MAGNET, JACQUES, *La Cour des Comptes.* Paris: Berger-Levrault, 1965.

MALLABY, SIR GEORGE, "The Civil Service Commission: Its Place in the Machinery of Government," *PA* (*L*), Vol. 42 (1964), 1–10.

MCDOWELL, R. B., *The Irish Administration, 1801–1914.* London: Routledge & Kegan Paul, 1964.

MEGHEN, P. J., "Central-Local Relationships in Ireland," *Administration,* Vol. 13, No. 3 (1965), 107–122.

NAIRNE, P. D., "Management and the Administrative Class," *PA* (*L*), Vol. 42 (1964), 113–122.

NUALLAIN, C. O., "Education and Training for Administration in Some European Countries," *Administration,* Vol. 11, No. 1 (1963), 54–61.

PAPASTATHOPOULOS, CATHERINE D., "Civil Service Reforms in Greece: 1950–1964," *IRAS,* Vol. 30, No. 4 (1964), 373–384.

PARRIS, HENRY, "Twenty Years of L'Ecole Nationale d'Administration," *PA* (*L*), Vol. 43 (1965), 395–412.

PINNEY, EDWARD L., "Latent and Manifest Bureaucracy in the West German Parliament: The Case of the Bundesrat," *MJPS,* Vol. 6, No. 2 (1962), 149–164.

RIDLEY, F., and J. BLONDEL, *Public Administration in France*. London: Routledge & Kegan Paul, 1964.

ROBERTSON, JOHN F., "The Royal Commission on State Services in New Zealand," *PA (L)*, Vol. 43 (1965), 1–14.

ROSENTHAL, ALBERT, "The Ombudsman—Swedish 'Grievance Man,'" *PAR*, Vol. 24, No. 4 (1964), 226–230.

ROWAT, D. C., "The Study of Public Administration in Canada," *PA (L)*, Vol. 40 (1962), 319–323.

———, "Finland Defenders of the Law," *CPA*, Vol. 4, Nos. 3 & 4 (1961), 316–325, 412–415.

SCHAFFER, B. B., "Decision-Making and the Civil-Military Experience," *PA (S)*, Vol. 23, No. 4 (1964), 328–342.

SWEETMAN, L. T., "Prefects and Planning: France's New Regionalism," *PA (L)*, Vol. 43 (1965), 15–30.

TAMMELIN, PAUL, "Rationalization in Swedish Public Administration," *IRAS*, Vol. 28, No. 4 (1962), 415–418.

UOTILA, JAAKKO, "Improving Public Administration in Finland," *IRAS*, Vol. 27, No. 1 (1961), 65–70.

C. COMMUNIST

CHANG, Y. N., "Industrial Administration in Communist China," *WPQ*, Vol. 9, No. 4 (1956), 850–872.

FISHER, JACK, "City Planning and Housing Administration in Yugoslavia," *UAQ*, Vol. 1, No. 2 (1965), 59–71.

GINSBURG, G., and A. STAHNKE, "The Genesis of the People's Procuratorate in Communist China; 1949–1951," *CQ*, Vol. 20, No. 4 (1964), 1–37.

GUIBERT, JEAN-LOUIS, "La réforme de l'énterprise sovietique: mythes et réalités," *Promotions*, No. 73 (1965), 33–58.

KAMINS, ROBERT M., "'Democratic Centralism': Local Finance in the Soviet Union," *NTJ*, Vol. 15, No. 4 (1962), 358–367.

LANGROD, GEORGES, "La renaissance de la science administrative en URSS et dan les démocraties populaires," *IRAS*, Vol. 29, No. 1 (1963), 22–29.

———, "Quelques récentes tendances administratives en régime communiste," *IRAS*, Vol. 28, No. 1 (1962), 16–30.

LUZHIN, A. V., "Improving the Administrative-Territorial Structure of the Soviet State," *SLG*, Vol. 1, No. 4 (1963), 15–22.

MARTONYI, JEAN, "La jurisdiction au service de la légalité de l'administration hongroise," *IRAS*, Vol. 28, No. 3 (1962), 269–281.

MORGAN, GLENN G., "The Soviet Procuracy's 'General Supervision' Function," *SS*, XI, No. 2 (1959), 142–172.

PRONINA, V. S., "On the Nature of State Committees in the USSR," *SLG,* Vol. 3, No. 1 (1964), 14–22.

SZAMEL, J., "Les tâches de la science administrative dans les pays socialistes," *IRAS,* Vol. 30, No. 3 (1964), 297–303.

SZAWLOWSKI, RICHARD, "Le contrôle étatique en Union Sovietique," *IRAS,* Vol. 28, No. 3 (1962), 325–335.

TICHOMIROV, IU. A., "The Production-Territorial Principle in the Organization and Functioning of the Administrative Apparatus," *SLG,* Vol. 3, No. 1 (1964), 3–13.

———, "Representative Organs of Government and the Development of Government Administration During the Period of the Building of Communism," *SLG,* Vol. 1, No. 2 (1962), 12–22.

TICKNER, F. J., "Public Administration in Yugoslavia," *IJPA,* Vol. 5, No. 3 (1959), 293–301.

DEVELOPMENT ADMINISTRATION

ADU, A. L., *The Civil Service in New African States.* London: George Allen & Unwin Ltd., 1965.

AHMAD, MUNEER, *The Civil Servant in Pakistan.* Karachi: Oxford University Press, 1964.

ASHAGRIE, KEBEBEW, "Some Problems of the Public Service in Ethiopia," *CPA,* Vol. 8, No. 3 (1965), 293–300.

ASHFORD, DOUGLAS F., *Morocco-Tunisia: Politics and Planning.* Syracuse: University of Syracuse Press, 1965.

ATTIR, A., "Administration and Development," *IRAS,* Vol. 30, No. 4 (1964), 335–344.

BOUTEILLE, PAUL, "La fonction publique et le développement économique," *IRAS,* Vol. 31, No. 2 (1965), 91–103.

BRADY, JAMES R., "Notes on Leadership Problems and Public Administration in Indonesia," *PJPA,* Vol. 7, No. 1 (1963), 27–35.

BROWN, DAVID S., "The Key to Self-Help: Improving the Administrative Capabilities of Aid-Receiving Countries," *PAR,* Vol. 24, No. 2 (1964), 67–77.

BURKE, FRED R., *Tanganyika: Pre-Planning.* Syracuse: Syracuse University Press, 1965.

CLIFFORD-VAUGHAN, FREDERIC, "La structure administrative d'un état africain: L'Ethiopie," *RA,* No. 98 (1964), 186–188.

CONK, A. C., and N. K. SAVUN, *Turkish Public Administration: A Report on the Rationalization of State Organization.* Bloomington: Indiana Universty, 1963.

CROW, RALPH E., and ADNAN ISKANDAR, "Administrative Reform in Lebanon, 1958–1959," *IRAS,* Vol. 27, No. 3 (1961), 293–307.

DALAND, ROBERT (ed.), *Perspectives of Brazilian Public Administration.* Volume I of the Comparative Series in Brazilian Public Administration. Los Angeles: University of Southern California, 1963.

DANG, NGHIEM, "Toward a Philosophy of Public Administration in Vietnam," *PJPA,* Vol. 7, No. 2 (1963), 67–90.

DROR, YEHEZKEL, "Nine Characteristics of Governmental Administration in Israel," *PAIA,* No. 5 (1965), 6–17.

EISENSTADT, S. N., "Initial Institutional Patterns of Political Modernization," *Civilisations,* Vol. 12, No. 4 (1962), 461–472, and Vol. 13, No. 1 (1963), 15–26.

———, "Breakdowns of Modernization," *EDCC,* Vol. 12, No. 4 (1964), 345–367.

FORTINI, NAPOLÉON, "L'Administration au Sénégal," *RA,* No. 102 (1964), 644–650.

FRIEDMANN, JOHN, *Venezuela: From Doctrine to Dialogue.* Syracuse: Syracuse University Press, 1965.

FULLER, C., and R. CHAMBERS, "Training for the Administration of Development in Kenya," *JLAO,* Vol. 4, No. 2 (1965), 109–117.

GABLE, RICHARD W., and WILLIAM B. STORM, "Problems of Institution Building in a Developing Country: An Iranian Experience," *CJA,* No. 5 (1965), 17–21.

GALBRAITH, JOHN K., "Public Administration and the Public Corporation," *IJPA,* Vol. 7, No. 4 (1961), 438–446.

GARDNER, WALLACE W., "Management in a Developing Nation," *CJA,* No. 2 (1964), 15–21.

GAZIER, M., *et al.,* "La modernisation des administrations centrales," *Promotions,* No. 68 (1964), 103–110.

GLYNN, F. J., "Africanization and Job Analysis in Tanganyika," *JLAO,* Vol. 2, No. 3 (1963), 140–148.

GOODNOW, HENRY R., *The Civil Service of Pakistan; Bureaucracy in a New Nation.* New Haven: Yale University Press, 1964.

GRANT, C. H., "The District Commissioner System in British Guiana," *JLAO,* Vol. 4, No. 4 (1965), 244–259.

GRASSMUCK, GEORGE, *Polity, Bureaucracy, and Interest Groups in the Near East and North Africa.* CAG Occasional Papers (June 1965).

GRASSMUCK, GEORGE, and KAMAL SALIBI, *Reformed Administration in Lebanon.* Ann Arbor: Center for the Near Eastern and North African Studies, The University of Michigan, 1964.

GROSS, BERTRAM M., "National Planning: Findings and Fallacies," *PAR,* Vol. 25, No. 4 (1965), 263–273.

GUNTHER, J. T., "The Public Service and Political Development in Papau and New Guinea," *PA (S)*, Vol. 24, No. 3 (1965), 249–262.

GUPTA, L. C., "Decentralized Implementation: Some Administrative Problems," *IJPA,* XI, No. 2 (1965), 251–273.

HARRIS, RICHARD L., "The Role of the Civil Servant in West Africa," *PAR,* Vol. 25, No. 4 (1965), 314–328.

HEAPHEY, JAMES, "The Organization of Egypt: Inadequacies of a Non-political Model for Nation-Building," *WP,* Vol. 18, No. 2 (1966), 177–193.

HEISLER, HELMUTH, "Continuity and Change in Zambian Administration," *JLAO,* Vol. 4, No. 3 (1965), 183–193.

HENDERSON, KEITH M., "Sensitivity Training in a Middle East Culture," *PPR,* Vol. 26, No. 3 (1965), 141–146.

HENTGEN, E. F., "La formation des cadres administratifs des pays en voie de développement: Programmes et mannière d'enseigner," *IRAS,* Vol. 30, No. 3 (1964), 277–284.

HSUEH, S. S. (ed.), *Public Administration in Southeast Asia.* Brussels: International Institute of Administrative Sciences, 1962.

JOINER, C. A., and R. JUMPER, "Organizing Bureaucrats: South Viet Nam's National Revolutionary Civil Servants' League," *AS,* Vol. 3, No. 2 (1963), 203–215.

KILSON, MARTIN, "African Political Change and the Modernisation Process," *JMAS,* Vol. 1, No. 4 (1963), 425–440.

KOCHAV, DAVID, "Administrative Aspects of Development Planning in Israel," *PAIA,* No. 5 (1965), 23–32.

KRIESBERG, MARTIN (ed.), *Public Administration in Developing Countries.* Washington, D.C.: Brookings, 1965.

KURUVILLA, P. K., "Problems of Public Administration in Developing Countries With Special Reference to India," *CPA,* Vol. 8, No. 1 (1965), 66–107.

LAPALOMBARA, JOSEPH, *Alternative Strategies for Developing Administrative Capabilities in Emerging Nations.* CAG Occasional Papers (1965).

LARSEN, WILLIAM F., "Government Administration in the Republic of Korea," *IRAS,* Vol. 27, No. 3 (1961), 311–316.

LEVY, MARION J., "Some Aspects of 'Individualism' and the Problem of Modernization in China and Japan," *EDCC,* Vol. 10, No. 3 (1962), 225–240.

LINDBLOM, CHARLES E., "Economics and the Administration of National Planning," *PAR,* Vol. 25, No. 4 (1965), 274–283.

LUCHAIRE, F., "The Political and Administrative System of the Territories of the Comores," *JLAO,* Vol. 4, No. 2 (1965), 88–98.

MALHOTRA, RAM CHAND, "Public Administration in Nepal," *IJPA,* Vol. 4, No. 4 (1958), 451–464.

MICAUD, CHARLES A., *et al., Tunisia: The Politics of Modernization.* London: Pall Mall Press, 1964.

NGUYEN, HUU CHAU, *Structures, institutions et développement économique dans les pays sous-développés.* Paris: Librairie générale de droit et de jurisprudence, 1964.

PARANJAPE, H. K., "Political and Administrative Problems of Implementing the Indian Plan," *IJPA,* Vol. 9, No. 4 (1963), 608–648.

PENNOCK, J. ROLAND (ed.), *Self-Government in Modernizing Nations.* Englewood Cliffs, N.J.: Prentice-Hall, Inc., 1964.

PORTNER, S., "Racionalizacion de la administracion en la Organizacion Pan-Americana de la Salud," *IRAS,* Vol. 29, No. 4 (1963), 357–370.

RAMOS, CARLOS P., "Problems of Evaluating Technical Assistance in Developing Countries," *PJPA,* Vol. 8, No. 4 (1964), 303–307.

RAPHAELI, NIMROD, "Agrarian Reform in Iraq: Some Political and Administrative Problems," *Journal of Administration Overseas,* Vol. 5, No. 2 (1966), 102–111.

RATIER, JACQUES, "La lutte contre le sous-devéloppement administratif," *Promotions,* No. 63 (1962), 121–142.

RICHARD, SANDRA, "Development of Managerial Resources for Industrializing Countries," *AMJ,* Vol. 30, No. 3 (1965), 70–73.

RICHARDSON, SAM, *Decolonization and the District Officer.* CAG Occasional Papers, 1963.

RIGGS, FRED W., *Census and Notes on Clientele Groups in Thai Politics and Administration.* Bangkok: Thammasat University; and Bloomington: Indiana University, 1963.

———, *Modernization and Development Administration.* CAG Occasional Papers (January 1966).

RIVKIN, ARNOLD, "The Politics of Nation-Building: Problems and Preconditions," *JIA,* Vol. 16, No. 2 (1962), 131–143.

RIZOS, EVANGELOS JOHN, "Technical Assistance Project Administration," *IRAS,* Vol. 31, No. 1 (1965), 35–44.

ROBBINS, LORD LIONEL CHARLES, "The Role of Management in Economic Development," *AMJ,* Vol. 30, No. 3 (1965), 24–33.

ROUGEVIN-BAVILLE, MICHEL, "The Organization and Content of Training for Public Administration in Africa," *JLAO,* Vol. 2, No. 3 (1963), 123–136.

ROUSSEAU, J., "Sur le rôle de la fonction publique dans des pays en voie de devéloppement," *RA,* No. 95 (1965), 438–441.

Roxas, Sixto K., "The Problems of Public Administration for Economic Development," *PJPA,* Vol. 9, No. 1 (1965), 3–9.

Sayre, Wallace S., "Some Problems of Public Administration in a Developing Economy," *IJPA,* Vol. 8, No. 2 (1962), 1–16.

Shuster, James R., "Bureaucratic Transition in Morocco," *HO,* Vol. 24, No. 1 (1965), 53–58.

Siegel, Gilbert B., "Administration, Values, and the Merit System in Brazil," *PPR,* Vol. 24, No. 3 (1963), 163–167.

Silberman, Bernard S., "The Bureaucracy and Economic Development in Japan," *AS,* Vol. 5, No. 11 (1965), 529–537.

Silva, Benedicto (ed.), *A Reforma Administrative Brasileira.* Rio de Janeiro: Impresna Nacional, 1963.

Silvera, Victor, "Le Droit de la fonction publique des anciens ressortissants d'etats ou territoires décolonisés," *RA,* No. 102 (1964), 604–609.

Smith, T. R., "International Administration in the South Pacific," *NZJPA,* Vol. 25, No. 2 (1963), 41–58.

Snowiss, Leo M., "The Education and Role of the Superior Civil Service in India," *IJPA,* Vol. 7, No. 1 (1961), 6–25.

Sutton, Joseph L., *Problems of Politics and Administration in Thailand.* Bloomington: Indiana University, 1963.

Swerdlow, Irving (ed.), *Development Administration Concepts and Problems.* Syracuse: Syracuse University Press, 1963.

Tanner, R. E. S., "The Belgian and British Administrations in Ruanda-Urundi," *JLAO,* Vol. 4, No. 3 (1965), 202–211.

Thomas, Ladd M., "Centralism in the Philippines: Past and Present Causes," *SR,* Vol. 30, No. 2 (1963), 203–219.

———, "Thai Administration," *NZJPA,* Vol. 25, No. 1 (1962), 3–33.

Thompson, Victor A., "Administrative Objectives for Development Administration," *ASQ,* Vol. 9, No. 1 (1964), 91–108.

———, "Bureaucracy and Innovation," *ASQ,* Vol. 10, No. 1 (1965), 1–20.

Thurber, Clarence E., "Training Administrators for Developing Countries," *IDR,* Vol. 3, No. 2 (1961), 34–38.

Tilman, Robert O., *Bureaucratic Transition in Malaya.* Durham: Duke University Press, 1964.

Tordoff, William, "Regional Administration in Tanzania," *JLAO,* Vol. 3, No. 1 (1965), 63–90.

United Nations, Department of Economic and Social Affairs, *A Handbook of Public Administration; Current Concepts and Practice with Special Reference to Developing Countries.* New York: United Nations No. 61.II.H.2, 1961.

VENKATARAMAN, K., "Local Finance in Developing Countries," *JLAO,* Vol. 4, No. 3 (1965), 194–201.

VEPA, RAM K., "Safeguards in Panchayati Raj Administration," *IJPA,* Vol. 10, No. 2 (1964), 257–277.

WARRELL-BOWRING, W. J., "The Reorganization of the Administration in Kenya," *JLAO,* Vol. 2, No. 4 (1963), 188–194.

WEIDNER, EDWARD W., *Technical Assistance in Public Administration Overseas: The Case for Development Administration.* Chicago: Public Administration Service, 1964.

WEINSTEIN, BRIAN, "Guinea's School of Public Administration," *JLAO,* Vol. 4, No. 4 (1965), 239–243.

WENGERT, EGBERT S., "Approach to the Study of Technical Assistance," *PJPA,* Vol. 5, No. 3 (1961), 185–193.

WHITE, BYRON, "Puerto Rico—A Partial Developmental Model," *AJES,* Vol. 22, No. 4 (1963), 539–542.

WICKWAR, W. HARDY, *Modernization of Administration in the Near East.* Beirut: Khayat, 1963.

THEORIES, MODELS, AND CONCEPTUAL SCHEMES

ADAM, H. T., *Les organismes internationaux spécialisés—Contribution à la théorie générale des établissement publics internationaux.* Paris: Librairie générale de droit et de jurisprudence, 1965. 2 Vols.

APPLEBY, PAUL H., "Comparative Public Administration," *IJPA,* Vol. 1, No. 1 (1955), 3–7.

APTER, DAVID E., "A Comparative Method for the Study of Politics," *AJS,* Vol. 64, No. 2 (1958), 221–237.

———, *Political Kingdom of Uganda: A Study in Bureaucratic Nationalism.* Princeton: Princeton University Press, 1961.

———, *The Politics of Modernization.* Chicago: University of Chicago Press, 1965.

BENDIX, REINHARD, "Concepts and Generalizations in Comparative Sociological Studies," *ASR,* Vol. 28, No. 4 (1963), 532–539.

BRAIBANTI, RALPH, "The Civil Service of Pakistan: A Theoretical Analysis," *SAQ,* Vol. 63, No. 2 (1959), 258–304.

———, "Reflections on Bureaucratic Corruption," *PA* (*L*), 40 (1962), 357–374.

BURKHEAD, JESSE, "Toward a Study of Comparative Public Finance," *PAR,* Vol. 11, No. 4 (1951), 205–212.

CAHNMAN, WERNER J., "Ideal Type Theory: Max Weber's Concept and Some of Its Derivations," *SQ,* Vol. 6, No. 3 (1965), 268–280.

CROZIER, MICHEL, "Power Relationships in Modern Bureaucracies," *IJPA*, Vol. 7, No. 1 (1961), 32–38.

———, *The Bureaucratic Phenomenon*. London: Tavistock Publications, 1964.

DEUTCH, KARL W., "On Communications Models in the Social Sciences," *POQ*, Vol. 16, No. 3 (1952), 356–380.

DROR, YEHEZKEL, "The Planning Process: A Facet Design," *IRAS*, Vol. 29, No. 1 (1963), 46–59.

ESMAN, MILTON J., "Japanese Administration—A Comparative View," *PAR*, Vol. 7, No. 2 (1947), 100–112.

ETZIONI, AMITAI, *A Comparative Analysis of Complex Organizations*. The Free Press of Glencoe, Inc., 1961.

FALLERS, LLOYD, *Bantu Bureaucracy*. Cambridge University Press, n.d.

FESLER, JAMES W., "Approaches to the Understanding of Decentralization," *JP*, Vol. 27, No. 3 (1965), 536–566.

FRIEDMANN, JOHN, *The Social Context of National Planning Decisions: A Comparative Approach*. CAG Occasional Papers (1965).

HAAS, MICHAEL, "Comparative Analysis," *WPQ*, Vol. 15, No. 2 (1962), 294–303.

HALL, RICHARD H., "The Concept of Bureaucracy: An Empirical Assessment," *AJS*, Vol. 69, No. 1 (1963), 32–40.

———, "Bureaucracy and Small Organizations," *SSR*, Vol. 48, No. 1 (1963), 39–46.

HARRIS, RICHARD L., and ROBERT M. KEARNEY, "A Comparative Analysis of the Administrative Systems of Canada and Ceylon," *ASQ*, Vol. 8, No. 3 (1963), 339–360.

HEADY, FERREL, *Public Administration: A Comparative Perspective*. Englewood Cliffs, N.J.: Prentice-Hall, Inc., 1966.

Data in Comparative Research, Special Issue of *International Social Science Journal*, Vol. 16, No. 1 (1964).

JANOWITZ, MORRIS, *The Military in the Political Development of New Nations: An Essay in Comparative Analysis*. Chicago: Chicago University Press, 1964.

JOHNSON, HUBERT C., "Concept of Bureaucracy in Cameralism," *PSQ*, Vol. 79, No. 3 (1964), 378–402.

KATZ, SAUL M., *A Systems Approach to Development Administration*. Papers in Comparative Public Administration. Special Series No. 6. Comparative Administration Group, American Society for Public Administration, 1965.

KHAN, MOHAMMED HUMAYUN, *Authority Behavior: An Empirical Approach to Comparative Public Administration*. Ph.D. Dissertation. University of Southern California, 1965.

KHOSLA, R. P., "Bureaucrats—The Loss of Vision," *IJPA,* Vol. 11, No. 1 (1965), 35–41.

LERNER, DANIEL, *The Passing of the Traditional Society*. Glencoe, Illinois: The Free Press of Glencoe, 1958.

LITCHFIELD, EDWARD H., "Notes on a General Theory of Administration," *ASQ,* Vol. 1, No. 1 (1956), 3–29.

LUHMANN, NIKLAS, *Funktionen und Folgen formales Organisation.* Berlin: Duncker & Humblot, 1964.

MACRIDIS, ROY C., "The Area Concept," *ABS,* Vol. 5, No. 10 (1962), 3–4.

MEYER, POUL, *Administrative Organization: A Comparative Study of the Organization of Public Administration.* London: Stevens & Sons, 1957.

MILNE, R. S., "Comparisons and Models in Public Administration," *PS,* Vol. 10, No. 1 (1962), 1–14.

MONTGOMERY, JOHN, and WILLIAM SIFFIN (eds.), *Politics, Administration and Change: Approaches to Development.* New York: McGraw Hill, 1966.

PRESTHUN, ROBERT V., "Social Bases of Bureaucratic Organization," *SF,* Vol. 38, No. 2 (1959), 103–109.

———, "Weberian vs. Welfare Bureaucracy in Traditional Society," *ASQ,* Vol. 6, No. 1 (1961), 1–24.

——— (with Sevda Erem), *Statistical Analysis in Comparative Administration: The Turkish Conseil d'etat.* Ithaca: Cornell University Press, 1958.

REZAZADEH, REZA, "The Concept of Centralization and Decentralization: An Analysis and Evaluation," *IRAS,* Vol. 27, No. 4 (1961), 425–430.

RIGGS, FRED W., *Administration in Developing Countries; The Theory of Prismatic Society.* Boston: Houghton Mifflin Company, 1964.

———, *The Ecology of Public Administration.* New Delhi: Asia Publishing House, 1961.

———, "The Use of Models for Administrative Analysis: Confusion or Clarity?" *IJPA,* Vol. 6, No. 3 (1960), 225–242.

RUSSETT, BRUCE M., *et al., World Handbook of Political and Social Indicators.* New Haven: Yale University Press, 1964.

SHILS, EDWARD, *Political Development in New States.* S'Gravenhage, Holland: Mouton, 1962.

SISSON, C. H., *The Spirit of British Administration and Some European Comparisons.* London: Faber & Faber, 1959.

SUBRAMANIAN, V., "Graduates in the Public Services: A Comparative Study of Attitudes," *PA (L)*, 35 (1957), 373–393.

———, "Middle Range Models in Comparative Administrative Studies," *IJPA,* Vol. 10, No. 4 (1964), 625–630.

THOMPSON, VICTOR A., "Bureaucracy and Innovation," *ASQ,* Vol. 10, No. 1 (1965), 1–20.

TUCKER, ROBERT C., "Towards a Comparative Politics of Movement Regimes," *APSR,* Vol. 60, No. 2 (1961), 281–289.

WALKER, H., "Theory and Methods in Comparative Public Administration," *ISSB,* Vol. 7, No. 3 (1955), 606–615.

WILLIAMS, VIRGIL, "Bureaucratic Proliferation: A Theoretical Approach," *AJES,* Vol. 22, No. 3 (1963), 337–345.

MISCELLANEOUS

AKEHURST, M. B., "Renewal of Fixed-Term Contracts of Employment in International Organizations," *IRAS,* Vol. 31, No. 2 (1965), 83–90.

ALDERFER, HAROLD F., *Local Government in Developing Countries.* New York: McGraw Hill Book Company, 1964.

BAUMAN, ZYGMUNT, *The Limitations of "Perfect Planning."* CAG Occasional Papers (July, 1964).

BLOCH, ROGER, and JAQUELINE LEFÉVRE, *La fonction publique internationale et Européene.* Paris: Librairie générale de droit et de jurisprudence, 1963.

BOCK, EDWIN (ed.), *Essays on the Case Method in Public Administration.* Brussels: International Institute of Administrative Sciences, 1962.

BRAIBANTI, RALPH, and JOSEPH J. SPENGLER (eds.), *Administration and Economic Development.* Durham: Duke University Press, 1963.

BYRT, W. J., "The Two Cultures in Administration," *PA (S)*, Vol. 24, No. 3 (1965), 214–223.

CALDWELL, G. H., "Unity of Command: A Comparison of the Top Level Organization Structures of the Government of Canada and Large Scale Private Enterprises," *CPA,* Vol. 7, No. 4 (1964), 510–545.

CALDWELL, LYNTON K., *Planned Control of the Biophysical Environment.* CAG Occasional Papers (June 1964).

DROR, Y., "Administrative Agencies and Courts: Some Patterns of Inter-organizational Relations," *IRAS,* Vol. 30, No. 3 (1964), 285–296.

EVANS, ROGER-WARREN, "French and German Administrative Law: With some English Comparisons," *ICLQ,* Vol. 14, No. 4 (1965), 1104–1123.

HARTFIEL, GÜNTER, LUTZ SEDATIS, and DICTER CLAESENS, *Beamte und Angestellte in der Verwaltungspyramide—Organisationssoziologische über das Entscheidungshandeln in des Kommunalverwaltung.* Berlin: Duncker & Humblot, 1964.

HEXNER, ERVIN P., "The Executive Board of the International Monetary Fund: A Decision-Making Instrument," *IO,* Vol. 18, No. 1 (1964), 74–96.

HOSEH, LOUIS E., "Public Administration on the International Frontier," *PPR,* Vol. 25, No. 3 (1964), 165–170.

Indian Institute of Public Administration, *Cases in Indian Administration.* New Delhi: 1963.

ITO, HANYA, "Self-Government, Local Finance, and Democracy," *PF/FP,* Vol. 20, No. 1–2 (1965), 118–136.

KINCH, M. B., "Qualified Administrative Staff in the Local Government Service," *PA (L)*, 43 (1965), 173–190.

LANGROD, GEORGES, *The International Civil Service.* Leyden: A. W. Sythoff; and Dobbs Ferry, New York: Oceana Publications, Inc., 1963.

MACCABE, JOSEPH W., "OPEX—The United Nations programme for the provision of operational executive and administrative personnel: Its origin and its subsequent developments," *IRAS,* Vol. 31, No. 2 (1965), 127–132.

MARTIN, ROSCOE C. (ed.), *Public Administration and Democracy* (essays in honor of Paul H. Appleby). Syracuse: Syracuse University Press, 1965.

MILNE, R. S., "Administrators, Experts and Training in the Civil Service," *PJPA,* Vol. 6, No. 4 (1962), 272–278.

MOLITOR, ANDRÉ, "Public Administration Towards the Future," *IRAS,* Vol. 27, No. 4 (1961), 375–384.

PIPER, DON C., and T. COLE (eds.), *Post-Primary Education and Political and Economic Development.* Durham: Duke University Press, 1964.

PYE, LUCIEN W., and SYDNEY VERBA, *Political Culture and Political Development.* Princeton: Princeton University Press, 1965.

REINING, HENRY, *The Fourth Dimension: The Administration of Development and the University's Role.* CAG Special Series No. 3 (1964).

ROWAT, DONALD C., *The Ombudsman.* Toronto: Toronto University Press, 1965.

SAWER, G., *Ombudsman.* Melbourne: Melbourne University Press, 1964.

SCHECHTER, ALAN H., *Interpretation of Ambiguous Documents by International Administrative Tribunals.* London: Stevens, 1964.

SOEMARDJAN, S., "Bureaucratic Organization in a Time of Revolution," *ASQ*, Vol. 2, No. 2 (1957), 182–199.

STEINER, KURT, *Local Government in Japan*. Stanford: Stanford University Press, 1965.

STONE, DONALD C. (ed.), *Education in Public Administration* (A Symposium on Teaching Methods and Materials). Brussels: International Institute of Administrative Sciences, 1963.

SUSKI, JULIAN G., "The Structure of Municipal Government in Canada and in Europe," *CPA*, Vol. 8, No. 3 (1965), 307–324.

TORRE, MOTTRAM (ed.), *The Selection of Personnel for International Service*. Geneva: World Federation for Mental Health, 1963.

TREVES, G., *Government Organization for Economic Development*. Brussels: International Institute of Administrative Sciences, 1963.

WARD, ROBERT E., and DANKWART RUSTOW, *Political Modernization in Japan and Turkey*. Princeton: Princeton University Press, 1964.

WRAITH, RONALD, *Local Government in West Africa*. London: George Allen & Unwin, 1964.